Management Across Cultures:
Insights from Fiction and Practice

For Douglas and Carol

Management Across Cultures:
Insights from Fiction and Practice

Sheila M. Puffer
Northeastern University

Foreword by Alfred Zeien, Chairman and CEO, The Gillette Company

First published 1996

Blackwell Publishers, Inc.
238 Main Street
Cambridge, Massachusetts 02142

Blackwell Publishers Ltd.
108 Cowley Road
Oxford OX4 1JF
UK

Library of Congress Cataloging-in-Publication Data

Sheila M. Puffer
  Management across cultures: insights from fiction and practice / Sheila M. Puffer.
    p. cm.
  Includes bibliographical references.
  ISBN 1-55786-673-2 (pbk.)
    1. Management—Cross-cultural studies. 2. International business enterprises—Management—Social aspects. 3. Intercultural communication. I. Title.
  HD38.P83 1996
  658.4—dc20   95-51328
                                                                    CIP

British Library Cataloguing in Publication Data

A CIP catalogue record for this book is available from the British Library.

Typeset by AM Marketing

Cover photograph by Katherine Giuffre

Printed in the United States of America

This book is printed on acid-free paper

◇

Table of Contents

◆

◇

Foreword

◆

The communications technology revolution and falling world trade barriers have created international growth opportunities for companies worldwide. As they pursue these opportunities, executives face the daunting challenges of doing business and living outside their own culture.

In any business, the key to success is finding and training the best managerial talent. In a global business, managers with multi-country experience are invaluable. At The Gillette Company, these managers know the difference between male grooming habits in Argentina and the United States, between labor relations in France and China. It is not the differences that matter so much, as the manager's skill in adapting to them, a skill gained through international experience.

A successful multi-country business also requires a strong corporate culture to provide uniform standards for business conduct anywhere in the world. A strong corporate culture, which can be codified in a formal Mission and Values statement, instills in all managers the same perspective, the same ground rules to apply in decision-making.

In this book, Sheila Puffer uses fact and fiction to communicate lessons in global management. The fiction selections speak from the heart and mind about the problems individuals and families confront while working and living outside their home country. The managerial writings provide real-life examples and practical advice for dealing with these issues.

From both a corporate and individual perspective, "Management Across Cultures: Insights from Fiction and Practice" offers valuable counsel on succeeding in the global marketplace.

Alfred M. Zeien
Chairman and Chief Executive Officer
The Gillette Company

◇

Preface

◆

Dramatic advances in communications, technology, and transportation bring the world into our homes and workplaces like never before. Such developments also provide unprecedented opportunities for traveling and working abroad, as well as for interacting with people from abroad in one's own country. Doing business internationally requires a broad set of managerial skills and a clear understanding of other cultures.

Business journals and articles are excellent sources of information on managerial skills, and fiction can offer deep insights into other cultures by crystallizing experience. This volume combines these two complementary literatures to help managers working in international contexts learn valuable skills in an enjoyable and entertaining way. When using this approach in *Managerial Insights From Literature* (PWS-Kent, 1991), I focused on managerial readings and short stories primarily in an American context. Rapid developments in international business have made it appealing to expand this concept to a global context. The book is intended for managers and professionals engaged in or planning to engage in international business. They might read the book independently, with international colleagues, or as part of a management development program. The book is also designed for students in business schools, other social sciences, international studies, and courses in literature across the curriculum.

Consistent with the scope of the book, an international cast has assisted in its preparation. I am indebted to my colleagues who expertly reviewed the book proposal and critiqued the selections: Dr Ariane Berthoin Antal, director of the Ashridge International

Institute for Organizational Change in Archamps, France; Dr John Clemens, director of the Hartwick Institute for Humanities and Leadership at Hartwick College in Oneonta, New York; and Dr David Ricks, vice-president for Academic Affairs at the American Graduate School of International Management in Glendale, Arizona.

MBA students at Northeastern University collected and commented on dozens of selections, only a fraction of which appear in the book because of space limitations. I am extremely grateful to all of them for their hard work and willingness to share their cultural backgrounds: Tatiana Kozlova from Russia, Vesna Nastova from Macedonia in the former Yugoslavia, and Jennifer Sherwin, an American fluent in Spanish who has worked in Central America. Thanks are also due to Northeastern University College of Business Administration Dean Ira Weiss, Senior Associate Dean Roger Atherton, and Professor Brendan Bannister for providing research assistants and release time to complete the book.

The staff at Blackwell Publishers were also very helpful. I thank Rolf Janke for his continued support and encouragement and Mary Riso, Dana Silliman, Jan Leahy, and Megan Zuckerman for their excellent editorial and technical assistance. I would also like to thank the authors and publishers of the selections for granting permission to reprint their work. As always, I am indebted to my family for their patience, understanding, and encouragement, and for their avid interest in other cultures.

Sheila Puffer
Boston, 1996

◇

Introduction

◆

Consider a typical day of a customer service representative in a computer software company located in a rural town two hours west of Boston. Her voice mail recorded a 7 a.m. call from the Dusseldorf rep who needs help assisting a customer in Stockholm with a difficult software installation. The Massachusetts rep e-mails the software developer in Los Angeles to find out where the product is currently being beta tested. First thing that morning, the developer provides the name of a Tokyo client conducting beta tests on hardware similar to the Swedish firm's. The Massachusetts rep obtains the necessary details in a call to her Japanese counterpart and has him relay them to the German rep. The latter then calls the Swedish customer, walks him through the installation, and faxes the information to the Massachusetts rep for future reference. Within a day, the company has drawn on resources from around the world to solve a customer's complex and highly specific problem.

Such global transactions are rapidly becoming the norm in business. More and more companies, large and small, are conducting business worldwide, entering new markets and finding reliable and cost-effective new suppliers. Competitive pressures for high quality and low prices, and ever shorter product life cycles, virtually compel a great many companies to actively participate in the global marketplace for survival and growth. As a result, growing numbers of people are finding that their work involves contact with individuals in other countries. Some people travel abroad occasionally on brief business trips, some live in another country for several years, and countless others correspond with business associates around the world without ever leaving home.

Unfortunately, the diversity of cultures and business practices throughout the world can pose serious obstacles to business success, if it is not well understood. But in today's fast-paced business environment, how can anyone possibly find the time to learn how to do business in other countries, let alone gain an appreciation of other cultures? To serve these two objectives, this book offers a collection of business articles and short stories. While perhaps seeming an unlikely combination, the two writing styles actually complement each other: the business articles provide practical guidelines and concrete examples in straightforward prose, while the stories convey cultural subtleties and shades of meaning in rich literary language. The business articles can be used to analyze issues and suggest solutions for problems raised in the stories. Selections have been chosen to represent a variety of countries and business situations as well as humorous and serious topics. Authors from around the world provide cultural and managerial insights from an insider's perspective.

The volume is organized into three parts, each with short stories followed by managerial articles arranged by topic. Part One, *Making Sense of the Cross-Cultural Experience,* illustrates the stages of adjustment typically experienced during exposure to other cultures. The opening story in *Initial Confusion* depicts a natural reaction to unfamiliar circumstances: feelings of helplessness often cause frustration and resentment toward the new country and its people. Adjustment usually occurs within four to six months, and satisfaction with the new culture increases. Much of the cultural confusion can be reduced by taking language lessons, but stories in *Learning the Language* show that language acquisition has its own frustrations as well as joys. *Family Adjustment to a New Culture* addresses a key issue in international assignments: children's education and spouses' careers are the major obstacles to relocating abroad. *Re-Entry* highlights some of the difficulties often experienced on repatriation: people feel out of touch with the business unit to which they are returning, sense their international experience is not appreciated, and have difficulty socializing with friends and family members who lack their expanded cultural awareness. The managerial readings concluding Part One discuss cultural and organizational causes of misunderstandings, international variations of business English, the balance between expatriates' loyalty to parent and local operations, and a training program for joint venture managers.

Part Two, *Managing Within Different Cultures,* illustrates a variety of workplace issues in different countries. The selections in *The Meaning of Work and Personal Values* serve as a reminder that, in addition to providing economic necessities, work fulfills social and achievement needs. *Power and Authority* includes examples of superiors exercising authority over subordinates, as well as subordinates devising ways to influence or retaliate against superiors. *Status and Hierarchy* explores these themes further, underscoring organizational members' implicit understanding of the roles and status attached to various hierarchical levels. The managerial readings in Part Two explore business practices and managerial styles in three Chinese-speaking countries, more than a dozen western European countries, an African country, Mexico, and Russia.

Part Three, *Managing Globally Across Cultures,* begins with *Ethics.* Managers must first understand the ethical value system of their counterparts from other cultures by discussing similarities and differences, to come to an agreement about mutually acceptable business practices. Two stories illustrate how unethical behavior destroys trust and undermines business success. *Cultures in Contact, Cultures in Change* shows how people from other cultures influence one another through exposure to different ways of thinking and acting while working together. Most of the stories have a negative tone. However, the managerial readings offer valuable suggestions for successful cross-cultural interactions, including strategies for resolving ethical conflict and negotiating effectively, in addition to organizational practices and procedures for developing transnational managers and creating international teams.

Developing cultural sensitivity and global managerial skills is a continuous process. The stories and managerial readings in this volume can help make the process enjoyable and enlightening, rather than onerous and intimidating.

Part I:

◇

Making Sense of the Cross-Cultural Experience

◆

Section 1: Initial Confusion

Travel to other countries can be exciting and enriching, but initial confusion on arrival is difficult to avoid, even with the best preparation. In **Name Six Famous Belgians,** a well-intentioned Philadelphia couple vacation in Europe in search of "a certain degree of insulation from the abrasions of life." They encounter instead a series of bewildering and irritating situations. Compounding their confusion and distaste are unpleasant past experiences that keep them from seeing other cultures in a positive light.

Section 2: Learning the Language

Language is the key to understanding and functioning in a culture. **English as a Second Language** is a testimony to the fortitude and determination of immigrants to America to seize the opportunity for a new life. For them, learning English is a matter of survival. Written by an English instructor, the story profiles immigrants who practice their new language skills by recounting incidents from their lives of extreme hardship and violent conditions in the developing world.

The Awful German Language is the light-hearted account of a famous frustrated "language student." Attempting to learn German more than a century ago, American humorist Mark Twain drolly complains, "Surely there is not another language that is so slipshod and systemless, and so slippery and elusive to the grasp." Rather

1

than master its complexities, he declares that the German language needs reforming and offers eight suggestions to simplify it.

Section 3: Family Adjustment to a New Culture

Living abroad is often a family affair, with adjustment to the new culture difficult for both accompanying family members and the employed person. In **Saree of the Gods**, an Indian couple try to adapt to life in New York by inviting two American couples for dinner. The husband's objective is to build closer relationships with his work colleagues, but his newly arrived wife is unable to accept the cultural differences. An accident that damages her dress incites her to resent the guests and blame her husband for "lavishing food and liquor that they could scarcely afford on the people that were yet to be called friends."

A Japanese wife harbors similar feelings of unease in **From Paris**. Unhappy living for ten years in France and wanting their son to be educated in Japan, she presses her husband to get a transfer back to Tokyo. Tired of "tightrope walking" as a customer escort in a Japanese trading company, he agrees. But the firm denies his request and instead uses him as a scapegoat in a bad business deal. Eventually, the wife and son return to Japan, while the husband is transferred to Tanzania.

Family members can feel more at ease in a new culture by keeping ties with their homeland. Schools offering classes in the home culture are one such link. In **Ethnic School**, a Hungarian immigrant to Australia takes great pride in running a school where parents and children learn the culture and geography of the "Old Country." However, he fears the school's days are numbered.

Section 4: Re-Entry

Returning to one's native country can be a disorienting, if not shocking, experience. Exposure to another culture alters a person's perspective and prompts questions about one's own culture. After thirteen years in New York, the Irish-American in **Home Sickness** returns to his native village in Ireland to regain his health. Finding Ireland "too bleak a life," he returns to his bartending job in the United States. Years later, in retirement, he reflects on the pastoral beauty of Ireland that is his "unchanging silent life." Feelings of homesickness overcome him in both countries.

In **Yard Sale**, the culture of Polynesia "clearly got into the bones" of a young Peace Corps volunteer in Samoa. Returning to Cape Cod after a two-year assignment, he nearly drives his aunt to distraction with incessant stories about how life in Samoa is better than it is in the United States. Greater sensitivity to his aunt's point of view would have helped smooth the young man's re-entry and made her more receptive to his experiences.

Section 5: Managerial Insights

As these stories illustrate, making sense of cross-cultural experiences can be an onerous and confusing experience. Yet, cultural differences may not be as big a problem in international business as is usually thought. **Do Cultural Differences Make a Business Difference?** concludes that contextual factors also play a great role in business success. Results of a study of eight U.S. firms acquired by foreign partners suggest that organizational and technical compatibility are more important success factors, although they are sometimes mislabeled as cultural characteristics.

Learning a foreign language is a formidable task, as is evident in the stories in **Learning the Language.** Although they would be well advised to do so, native English-speaking people are often spared this task because international business partners frequently speak English. **"Englishes" in Cross-Cultural Business Communication** cautions, however, that miscommunication can still occur because of differences in English usage and misunderstanding of cultural meanings. Tips to reduce the incidence of bypassing in cross-cultural communication are provided.

Maintaining loyalty to both the home office and operations abroad is a delicate balance for managers in international assignments. The stories in **Family Adjustment to a New Culture** and **Re-Entry** show how people can feel pulled in one direction or the other. **Serving Two Masters: A Study in Expatriate Allegiance** reports that, while such loyalty is critical for business success, only one-fourth of U.S. expatriates are highly committed to both offices. Firms can help develop dual commitment by clarifying roles, reducing role conflict, and giving discretion in decision making.

Managers of joint ventures are especially vulnerable to pressures from parent firms that have conflicting motives, policies, and cultures. **Self-Management Training for Joint Venture General Managers** provides a six-step program to enable such managers to direct their behavior toward priority activities and set a course for the venture's operations that meets the partners' objectives. Grounded in social cognitive theory, the training program consists of self-assessment, goal setting, self-monitoring, self-evaluation, written contracts, and maintenance through skill practice.

Section 1: Initial Confusion

◇

1.1 Name Six Famous Belgians

◆

David R. Slavitt

What they give you when you check into the Villa Igiea is a little card to carry with you – but not in your wallet, presumably – to certify that you are a guest in the hotel and that you are insured. The pamphlet that comes with the card explains the insurance policy the hotel carries that covers you in case your pocket is picked, your wallet stolen, your purse snatched, or even worse. If you have a mind to, you can read through the impressive document until you get to the clause about how, if you are hospitalized, your next of kin will be brought to Palermo from anywhere in the world. Or about how, if you are killed, your body will be shipped home at no charge to your estate.

Bad as it is back in Philadelphia, it has not yet come to this. But then Palermo has had a couple of millennia headstart.

With a straight face, Harry thanked the desk clerk, but when they got up to their room, he and Joan made nervous jokes about it. Out through the double doors of their balcony they could see the glassy Mediterranean, more pacific than the Pacific. They simply couldn't believe it – not that there could be such lawlessness as the

Source: David R. Slavitt, "Name Six Famous Belgians," *Short Stories Are Not Real Life*, David R. Slavitt, 1991, pp. 43–57. Reprinted by permission of Louisiana State University Press. Copyright © 1987, 1988, 1990, 1991 by David R. Slavitt.

insurance company's document implied, but that it could be so taken for granted. Harry supposed it was remotely possible that this could be a gesture the management made to give the tourists a pleasant frisson of fear, to suggest without seriously inconveniencing anyone the depredations either of the Mafia or merely of the desperately poor. It would be going too far to subject their guests to the disagreeable business of an actual mugging.

Far from the center of town, the Villa Igiea is secluded in its own gardened enclave. From the balcony of their room, Harry and Joan could look left to the open sea. A little to the right, they could see a couple of giant cranes of the port. The city itself, though, was out of sight, even farther to the right and behind them. Harry's idea had been that a certain degree of insulation from the abrasions of life in a strange and poor city would be a good thing, especially on the first days of their visit when they were still acclimating themselves not only to local customs but also to the water and the time of day. Recovering from jet lag, they wanted at least the possibility of respite from assaults by Sicilian exuberance.

And it looked as though it would work out just as they'd hoped. The only trouble was that, being a little way out of town, they had to drive to do any sight-seeing or to eat anywhere except in the hotel dining room, and the map Avis had given them was almost useless. It did not show one-way streets, which was essential in a place like Palermo. Navigation was further complicated by the absence of any systematic posting of street signs. It was one thing to find a street on a map, but quite another to find it out in the real world. This was Joan's job, and she complained a lot. Harry complained, too, about the stick shift of the underpowered and overgeared Fiat Uno they'd been given and the erratic driving habits of the Sicilians, who slowed down for red lights but did not feel obligated to come to anything as deferential as a full stop. And people on motor scooters wove through the traffic in a demonstration of a death wish, the fulfillment of which was occasionally celebrated by a blare of sirens from ambulances and police cars, which in their haste contributed to the excitement and general sense of peril.

It was in an attempt to circumvent the busy center of town and save themselves a little time and stress that they got lost on the morning of their second day. And perhaps they were a little crabby with each other, too. Joan kept insisting that Harry pull over and stop so that she could find where they were on the wretched Avis map. Eventually he did so, but gracelessly. He stared through the windshield, making no effort to hide his impatience with her. Hers was an easier job, after all, and if he could do the driving, then she ought to be able to keep track of where they were and where they wanted to go. He waited while she pored over the tiny print of the map on her lap, and then quite suddenly she screamed. Harry turned toward her, not yet thinking anything, but shocked, this being an excessive display of her frustration with the map and with him. He was startled and puzzled, and not quite certain that he'd seen what he thought he'd seen – the blur of a disappearing hand.

"He tried to grab my purse," Joan said. Her voice was high, not shrill but unnaturally thin.

Harry's head turned further. Through the back window, he could see – no question now – the would-be purse snatcher, straddling a bicycle perhaps six feet behind the car, and ready to flee if they should try to pursue him. He might have been thirteen or so. He looked even younger, maybe eleven, but then Sicilians are small, and the diet of the poorest of them must be very meager indeed.

"Drive!" Joan commanded through clenched teeth, her voice still strained. "Let's get out of here."

He drove. They rolled the windows up until they were almost closed and checked the door locks. They kept going until they found an unfrightening part of town and a place where they could park and go into a bar for a coffee. It had been an invasion, of course, a terrible intrusion, and what had kept the boy from getting the purse was the seatbelt that had covered the shoulder strap of Joan's purse, securing it. They'd left their passports and most of their traveler's checks back at the hotel. And for the first time they had been wearing their moneybelts, light navy-blue nylon articles that they had strapped on that morning after breakfast, feeling a little silly. And, Harry reminded Joan, there was that insurance policy the hotel carried!

She laughed, a single sardonic snort. No harm had been done. Still, the idea of the thing was nasty, the disesteem it implied that one human being should have for another. That the thief had been only a child made it worse, if anything. Youngsters are supposed to be innocent and only later to fall from grace as they are called by the necessities of survival to compromise their original principles of fairness and decency. (This was the fiction to which they pre-tended to subscribe most of the time, if only because the alternative was so uncomfortable: what kind of a world would it be in which such risks and violences are normal?)

The carping about the driving and the map reading stopped, now that something more serious had intruded upon them. With a studied determination – so as not to admit to themselves or each other that they had been defeated or even much affected by this small, nasty incident – they pushed on with their search for the road to Monreale, found it, made their pilgrimage, and even managed to enjoy the extraordinary cathedral with its dazzling mosaics and the cloister next door with that wonderfully various colonnade.

By that evening the incident had been all but forgotten. Neither of them at any rate made mention of it. It is possible, of course, that one or the other of them might have found this omission just a bit peculiar, might have wondered at the other's diffidence, but for her part she might have been reluctant to probe at what was perhaps a tender place. And he might have attributed to her silence a solicitude that was at once welcome and intolerable – because he hated to be condescended to or treated as other than healthy and sane. The closest they'd come to that kind of therapeutic attention had been her asking him, back home in the dark, when neither had to look at the other's facial expression or body language, if he was sure he wanted to go to Italy.

"It's Magna Graecia we're going to see," he had said, "Greek ruins and a few Norman churches and some Bourbon buildings."

"I know," she had said, "but still . . ."

"It's okay," he'd told her.

How far beyond that could she have pushed?

And here he was, and even after what had happened, he seemed to be okay.

For the next few days, it was okay. He was, or it was. Nobody else in Palermo tried to rob them or mug them or kill them. And they drove out, heading east toward Cefalù, with memories of good food and fine buildings and some memorable statuary in the archaeological museum. And most of the good stuff was still to come: Taormina, the mosaics in the remains of the Imperial Villa at Piazza Armerina, and the avenue of temples in Agrigento. And their mood was okay – good enough at least so that at the worst each was, for the sake of the other, putting up a good front. But as each of them knew, to be able still to do that is to be in reasonable shape.

They both had the feeling that they deserved a good time. For one thing they hadn't taken a vacation in almost two years. For another, they'd spent all those evenings planning this trip, working out the sights they wanted to see, and the distances, and the hotels where it would be fun to stay. One of the high points was going to be Agrigento, which was perhaps grounds for a certain skepticism. To have excessive expectations is to be vulnerable to disappointment. Still, there was a picture of the Temple of Concord on the cover of their *Blue Guide* showing between the inner and outer colonnades a narrow swath of sky, and one could see the rough texture of the caramel-colored marble stucco of the columns, which had been baking in the Sicilian sun for a couple of millennia. That the editors had put this on the cover meant it had to be good, didn't it? That was an accolade even greater than its three stars in the text and its bold print in the index.

They were wary, but it was impossible for them never to let their hopes off the leash. And as it turned out, they were astonished, absolutely delighted when the Villa Athena porter, having shown them to their room, drew back the curtains, opened the shutters of the French windows that gave onto their patio, and stood back to reveal, just outside and up a little rise, the avenue of the temples. Directly in front of them was the Temple of Concord, in such a remarkable state of preservation that it looked theatrical. It was odd, certainly, so that Harry laughed, not at the temple or even at himself and his wariness, but just because a thing like that could be in the world, could be real, let alone so close. It was like an exotic bird that had lit on a branch right outside their window, an unlooked-for grace. Joan reacted in much the same way but didn't laugh, because she didn't want to scare it away.

There was no point in going anywhere or doing anything. They didn't have to discuss it. They decided just to stay where they were, drink things from the Frigo-bar, and look at the temple. Later they'd go out, climb up to it, and walk around it, but that could keep a while, until the cool of the afternoon. For now, it was more than enough that they could just stare at it, try to grasp it, try to let it soak in. Joan put on her bathing suit and went out to the terrace with a book so that she could sun herself, reading a sentence or two but then looking up every now and again for another confirmation that, yes, it was still there, presiding over its quarter of the sky. Inside, Harry lay down on the bed and watched television, not because he was interested in dubbed American soap operas but for the contrast between the familiarly tacky program and what was there outside the room, unfamiliar and untacky, and available to him without his even having to turn his head. All he had to do was adjust his eyeballs ever so slightly and there it was, not a figment of his imagination, but real, actual, substantial. The program changed to something called "Dada-Oompah," just as dumb but Italian. The building did not go away.

"Okay?" he called out.

"Terrific!" she answered. And then, after a beat, she ventured to ask, "Happy?"

"Oh, yeah!"

The terrace, it turned out, was not theirs alone but was shared with the room across the hall, which was why there was a row of planters down the middle. Late that afternoon, Harry and Joan walked over to inspect the Temple of Herakles, the Temple of Hera, the Temple of Zeus, and their own – they actually thought of it that way now – Temple of Concord. When they got back to their room, they found that their neighbors had established themselves on the terrace, as of course it was their right to do. They were a slightly younger couple, in their early forties maybe, English as it turned out. He was an investment banker. She was in publishing. She was Dotty. He was Paul.

It wasn't as bad as it might have been. In fact, there was a kind of advantage to small talk with the English couple much like the benefit of having the television set turned on. One could talk about ordinary things, exchange trivial information – that *nespolle*, for instance, those unimpressive little fruits they had been seeing on restaurant dessert carts, were the medlars Giovanni Verga mentioned in his title, or that Luigi Pirandello had been born down there, between the new city and the sea. And then one could glance again at the ridge and see the Temple of Concord, still there, still gorgeous, or perhaps even slightly more gorgeous, those earth-brown tones having deepened now as the sun sank toward the horizon.

The two couples sat there on either side of their planter-divider, drinking Campari and soda from their Frigo-bars and keeping watch on the temple. Paul said that the great event at the hotel was sitting in the outdoor dining pavilion and watching the temple disappear into the darkness and then reemerge abruptly when they turned the arc lights on. It was a good idea to plan to eat around eight in order to catch this. Harry thanked him. There was a delicate moment in which each considered making the suggestion that the four of them dine together, but nobody said anything. Perhaps each had been waiting for one of the others to make the overture that never came. At any rate, the moment passed. They finished their drinks and wished one another a good evening.

But when Harry and Joan went down to dinner, they saw that almost all the tables were occupied. A bus had deposited a crowd of tourists, Germans mostly, who weren't staying at the hotel but were eating there, perhaps for that dramatic moment of the illumination Paul had talked about. Harry and Joan had already resigned themselves to waiting, but the head waiter came back to ask if they would like to share the far table with the couple there who had suggested that they join them. They looked to see Paul and Dotty waving encouragingly.

"Shall we?" Harry asked.

"We can't not," Joan said.

They followed the head waiter to Paul and Dotty's table, thanked them, and sat down. The English couple had arrived just a few moments earlier and had not yet ordered. Harry suggested champagne as the only appropriate way to toast that temple off to the south. Or the closest local equivalent, which was Asti Spumanti.

It was a pleasant dinner, and, yes, there was a moment when the lights switched on and the temple, a dimmed shape, sprang back into a sudden and almost garish clarity. After their meal, they went into the bar for coffee and exchanged itineraries and stories. At one point, Paul mentioned an odd custom Dotty had heard of when she'd gone to the Frankfurt Book Fair. Some of the London publishers take the ferry across to Ostend and then drive to Frankfurt because it's cheaper that way, he said. And as they make their way through Belgium, the game is to name six famous Belgians before they get to the German border. "And the wonderful thing," he said, "is that it can't be done."

"Can't it?" Harry asked, though not combatively. "Leopold and Beaudoin, for starters. And Paul-Henri Spaak."

"Yes, but then it gets tough," Paul said, grinning.

"I guess it does. Glière, maybe. His people were Belgian, anyway."

"Doubtful, but okay."

"Hercule Poirot?" Joan asked.

"He's fictional. He doesn't count, I'm afraid," Dotty said, shaking her head. "People always try him when they get desperate enough."

"Okay, okay," Joan agreed.

"Maybe that's a good thing, though," Harry said. "I mean, that it's so tough. I like the idea of ordinary people leading ordinary lives."

"And eating good food. The food in Brussels is wonderful," Paul said.

"Famous people," Harry said, "are frequently villains."

There was a moment, but the conversation resumed, and there were suggestions about their all getting together again one day, in New York, maybe, or in London. They actually exchanged addresses before they went up to their hallway to separate and retire for the night.

"Nice people," Joan said, once the door was closed.

"Yes, they were," Harry said.

"Well, they still are, aren't they?"

"I suppose so, yes," he admitted. And then, as an afterthought, "Funny about the Belgians. I can't think of any more."

"Neither can I."

They did get swindled once. They discovered it only when they were back in Palermo waiting for the ferry to take them up to Naples. They went into a little place on the Via Cavour for iced coffee, and at the cashier's desk, Harry peeled off what he thought was the right amount of Italian money, only to be told that one of the bills he'd offered, a five-hundred-lire note, was no good. These had been recalled more than a year ago. There was a coin now for that denomination – which was worth at the time maybe thirty-three cents. Harry shook his head, realizing that he'd been taken, that only tourists would be ignorant enough to be victimized this way, and put the worthless note back into his wallet. But he didn't seem really upset. Joan observed all this and was encouraged. And she began to relax, now that Sicily was mostly behind them.

They took the Tirrenia, which got them to Naples at six in the morning. Their plans were to spend a few days in Naples, going down to Pompeii and Herculaneum, and then to take a *rapido* up to Rome to do some shopping and be entertained by some of

Harry's old friends. The trip, Joan thought, had gone well enough. They'd not only not had a bad time, but they'd enjoyed an affirmatively good one. And when they got to Naples, Harry again seemed no more than wryly amused by the petty thievery of the cab driver who had charged so exorbitantly for a ride of only a few blocks from the dock to their hotel on the Via Partenope, claiming surcharges because it was Sunday morning, because it was not yet seven so the night rates were still in effect, and because they had baggage and he'd been obliged to open the trunk. Harry groused that he'd thought he was hiring the entire cab, trunk included, but he paid and he even smiled.

So Joan thought she could relax. She took only the precautions any prudent American tourist tries to remember to take, always walking so that Harry was on the street side and taking care that her bag was clutched tightly under her arm. And in Naples they never came any closer to getting robbed than they had on that second day in Palermo. Their net loss to crime on the whole trip was that thirty-three cents, the value of that recalled note.

The assault – if it was an assault – came from a different and altogether unexpected quarter, from the soccer madness that gripped the nation and especially caught up the Neapolitans. The World Cup matches were going on in Mexico, and all over Naples there were Italian flags hanging out of apartment windows, the official red-white-and-green tricolor or homemade banners with "Forza Italia" lettered in those colors. Sometimes they stretched across streets from one building to another, on lines that were ordinarily used to hang laundry.

Harry and Joan went out to dinner one night at a little pizzeria they'd found a few blocks from the hotel. It had looked lively enough when they'd first spotted it, crowded and inviting, but this evening it was almost deserted. And the waiter spent most of his time in the back room, watching the Italian team struggle with the South Koreans in an effort not to get eliminated. Evidently, all of Naples was engaged in this effort half a world away, for whenever the Italian team did something good, there would be an encouraging blast of automobile horns from the cars outside. It was all right if they wanted to enjoy themselves that way, but the waiter's inattention was irksome. Harry had to get up and find him to ask for the bill.

"Didn't you want coffee?" Joan asked.

"Yes, but not there. Let's go someplace else. Someplace nice – where they care about the customers. This is nuts."

"It's sports. You like sports."

"This is worse than that. It's nationalism. It's madness. What the hell difference will it make to anybody in Naples if the Italian team beats the South Koreans?"

"It takes their minds off their troubles," she suggested, not wanting to argue.

"What minds? It lets them reveal their true character. That's what it really does. And that's ugly."

Joan could have answered him in a number of ways. He'd been the one who had insisted on Italy, for God's sake! And she'd once asked him, point-blank, "Are you sure you want to do this?" But he'd looked at her and nodded, as if to say that he wasn't going to be deprived of Italy, too.

As if to say that it was not significant that the thug who had broken into his mother's house to burglarize it, whom his mother had confronted, and who had bludgeoned her to death happened to be Italian. Two years later, Harry had been talking about Italy, about Sicily in particular, and how he'd never been there. It made perfect sense, but Joan was shrewd enough to distrust sense. She'd seen Harry piece himself back together, a crude patching job like that of a child mending a sugar bowl he had dropped, gluing the shards together as well as he could.

She'd asked him that, but only once. Because when he reacted, it was unpredictable whether he would lash out or just collapse inwardly. And in neither event was it good to be close by.

They walked from the pizzeria back past their hotel and on toward the Piazza del Martiri, the district of chic shops where they had noticed a flossy coffee bar and gelateria with outside tables. There were plenty of empty tables now, and there were a couple of waiters standing ready to bring ice cream or coffee. They weren't inside, huddled around some television set. Harry seemed satisfied, and he and Joan sat down and ordered – coffee ice cream for her and *zuppa inglese* ice cream for him. The waiter brought their order right away.

And then, in Mexico City, the Italians came from behind to beat the South Koreans, and in Naples, everybody went wild. They bolted from their apartments, jumped into their cars or onto their motorcycles or scooters, unfurled their enormous flags and banners, and raced through the streets yelling and blowing their horns. The street, which had been quiet a moment before, was alive with people now, swarming with traffic, loud, blaring, grating, triumphant, frenzied, insisting on the wonderfulness of their being Italians, their national pride and ebullience bubbling up and spewing forth.

She watched Harry retreating into himself, watched his color drain, the muscles along his jaw twitch, the tears well up in his eyes and spill down his cheeks. What they were insisting upon was exactly what he could not bear, what he hated: the barbarousness that was the verso of their culture, their potentiality for cruelty and violence, the thuggish nastiness they could assume when they assembled into crowds for a Mussolini to harangue, passionate oafs ready to be seduced by villains and clowns.

"You want to go?" she asked.

He couldn't speak. He only nodded.

He threw a few thousand lire onto the table. He hesitated. Then he threw that worthless five-hundred-lire note onto the pile with it.

They started back toward the hotel, a matter of five blocks or so, but they were a long five blocks, and there were wide streets to cross, dangerous in the Mezzogiorno at the best of times and utterly intimidating now. There was a couple on a Vespa, a young man with a young woman behind him, and they had a dog running along beside them on a leash, and the dog was struggling to keep up. Joan saw it and saw that Harry saw it, noting his grimace of pain and rage . . . and she could do nothing.

Back at the hotel, their bed had been turned down. The shutters were closed and the heavy draperies pulled closed, but they could still hear the blare of horns, that mindless mechanical braying as tireless as it was inescapable. The best they could do was to undress and go to bed. Harry took a long pull of brandy from the bottle they carried with them, got into bed, and put his head under a pillow that could not possibly have blocked out the noise but maybe muffled it a little.

Joan turned on the television set, found a channel that was broadcasting something other than the gloating interviews about the soccer victory – an old "Mission Impossible" episode, actually – and turned up the volume. There was no response from Harry, but at least he didn't object. Eventually, she supposed, he'd fall asleep. And eventually he did.

In the morning they were subdued, like people with hangovers, but they did what they'd planned to do. They went over to Capri for the day, didn't like it, came back, packed, and took the train to Rome early the next morning.

Rome was all right. "River City," one of their American friends who lived there called it. They were there for three days, during which Joan kept looking surreptitiously at her watch, counting the hours until they could make their way through Da Vinci's impressive array of guards and inspectors and board the plane heading home.

For those first few weeks after their return, friends in Philadelphia asked them about their vacation and where they'd gone. The first time it happened, Harry surprised Joan, lying badly and outrageously. "Belgium," he said, absolutely straight-faced.

"Oh? And how was it?" they asked, politely.

Harry let Joan tell them. It was, at last, something she could do, something he could let her do for him.

"Wonderful," she said. "Very peaceful. A wonderful country."

"The whole time? In Belgium?"

"Oh, yes," Harry said, glancing at her in a quick look of acknowledgment that was like an embrace. "It's a fine place. The food in Brussels is wonderful."

Section 2: Learning the Language

◇

2.1 English as a Second Language

◆

Lucy Honig

Inside Room 824, Maria parked the vacuum cleaner, fastened all the locks and the safety chain and kicked off her shoes. Carefully she lay a stack of fluffy towels on the bathroom vanity. She turned the air conditioning up high and the lights down low. Then she hoisted up the skirt of her uniform and settled all the way back on the king-sized bed with her legs straight out in front of her. Her feet and ankles were swollen. She wriggled her toes. She threw her arms out in each direction and still her hands did not come near the edges of the bed. From here she could see, out the picture window, the puffs of green treetops in Central Park, the tiny people circling along the paths below. She tore open a small foil bag of cocktail peanuts and ate them very slowly, turning each one over separately with her tongue until the salt dissolved. She snapped on the TV with the remote control and flipped channels.

The big mouth game show host was kissing and hugging a woman playing on the left-hand team. Her husband and children were right there with her, and *still* he encircled her with his arms. Then he sidled up to the daughter, a girl younger than her own Giuliette, and *hugged* her and kept *holding* her, asking questions. None of his business, if this girl had a boyfriend back in Saginaw!

Source: Lucy Honig, "English as a Second Language," *The Witness*, 1990, pp. 60–74, Vol. IV, No. 1. Reprinted by permission of Lucy Honig.

"Mama, you just don't understand." That's what Jorge always said when she watched TV at home. He and his teenaged friends would sit around in their torn bluejeans dropping potato chips between the cushions of her couch and laughing, writhing with laughter while she sat like a stone.

Now the team on the right were hugging each other, squealing, jumping up and down. They'd just won a whole new kitchen – refrigerator, dishwasher, clothes washer, microwave, *everything!* Maria could win a whole new kitchen too, someday. You just spun a wheel, picked some words. She could do that.

She saw herself on TV with Carmen and Giuliette and Jorge. Her handsome children were so quick to press the buzzers the other team never had a chance to answer first. And they got every single answer right. Her children shrieked and clapped and jumped up and down each time the board lit up. They kissed and hugged that man whenever they won a prize. That man put his hands on her beautiful young daughters. That man pinched and kissed *her,* an old woman, in front of the whole world! Imagine seeing *this* back home! Maria frowned, chewing on the foil wrapper. There was nobody left at home in Guatemala, nobody to care if a strange man squeezed her wrinkled flesh on the TV.

"Forget it, Mama. They don't let poor people on these programs," Jorge said one day.

"But poor people need the money, they can win it here!"

Jorge sighed impatiently. "They don't give it away because you *need* it!"

It was true, she had never seen a woman with her kids say on a show: My husband's dead. Jorge knew. They made sure before they invited you that you were the right kind of people and you said the right things. Where would she put a new kitchen in her cramped apartment anyway? No hookups for a washer, no space for a two-door refrigerator . . .

She slid sideways off the bed, carefully smoothed out the quilted spread, and squeezed her feet into her shoes. Back out in the hall she counted the bath towels in her cart to see if there were enough for the next wing. Then she wheeled the cart down the long corridor, silent on the deep blue rug.

Maria pulled the new pink dress on over her head, eased her arms into the sleeves, then let the skirt slide into place. In the mirror she saw a small dark protrusion from a large pink flower. She struggled to zip up in back, then she fixed the neck, attaching the white collar she had crocheted. She pinned the rhinestone brooch on next. Shaking the pantyhose out of the package, she remembered the phrase: the cow before the horse, wasn't that it? She should have put these on first. Well, so what. She rolled down the left leg of the nylons, stuck her big toe in, and drew the sheer fabric around her foot, unrolling it up past her knee. Then she did the right foot, careful not to catch the hose on the small flap of scar.

The right foot bled badly when she ran over the broken glass, over what had been the only window of the house. It had shattered from gunshots across the dirt yard. The chickens dashed around frantically, squawking, trying to fly, spraying brown feathers into the air. When she had seen Pedro's head turn to blood and the two oldest boys dragged away, she swallowed every word, every cry, and ran with the two girls. The fragments of glass stayed in her foot for all the days of hiding. They ran and ran and ran and somehow Jorge caught up and they were found by their own side and smuggled out. And still she was silent, until the nurse at the border went after the glass and drained the mess inside her foot. Then she sobbed and screamed, "Aaiiiee!"

"Mama, stop thinking and get ready," said Carmen.

"It is too short, your skirt," Maria said in Spanish. "What will they say?"

Carmen laughed. "It's what they all wear, except for you old ladies."

"Not to work! Not to school!"

"Yes, to work, to school! And Mama, you are going for an award for your English, for all you've learned, so please speak English!"

Maria squeezed into the pink high heels and held each foot out, one by one, so she could admire the beautiful slim arch of her own instep, like the feet of the American ladies on Fifth Avenue. Carmen laughed when she saw her mother take the first faltering steps, and Maria laughed too. How much she had already practiced in secret, and still it was so hard! She teetered on them back and forth from the kitchen to the bedroom, trying to feel steady, until Carmen finally sighed and said, "Mama, quick now or you'll be late!"

She didn't know if it was a good omen or a bad one, the two Indian women on the subway. They could have been sitting on the dusty ground at the market selling corn or clay pots, with the bright-colored striped shawls and full skirts, the black hair pulled into two braids down each back, the deeply furrowed square faces set in those impassive expressions, seeing everything, seeing nothing. They were exactly as they must have been back home, but she was seeing them *here,* on the downtown IRT from the Bronx, surrounded by businessmen in suits, kids with big radio boxes, girls in skin-tight jeans and dark purple lipstick. Above them, advertisements for family planning and TWA. They were like stone-age men sitting on the train in loincloths made from animal skins, so out of place, out of time. Yet timeless. Maria thought, they are timeless guardian spirits, here to accompany me to my honors. Did anyone else see them? As strange as they were, nobody looked. Maria's heart pounded faster. The boys with the radios were standing right over them and never saw them. They were invisible to everyone but her: Maria was utterly convinced of it. The spirit world had come back to life, here on the number 4 train! It was a miracle!

"Mama, look, you see the grandmothers?" said Carmen.

"Of course I see them," Maria replied, trying to hide the disappointment in her voice. So Carmen saw them too. They were not invisible. Carmen rolled her eyes and smirked derisively as she nodded in their direction, but before she could put her derision into words, Maria became stern. "Have respect," she said. "They are the same as your father's people." Carmen's face sobered at once.

She panicked when they got to the big school by the river. "Like the United Nations," she said, seeing so much glass and brick, an endless esplanade of concrete.

"It's only a college, Mama. People learn English here, too. And more, like nursing, electronics. This is where Anna's brother came for computers."

"Las Naciones Unidas," Maria repeated, and when the guard stopped them to ask where they were going, she answered in Spanish: to the literacy award ceremony.

"*English,* Mama!" whispered Carmen.

But the guard also spoke in Spanish: take the escalator to the third floor.

"See, he knows," Maria retorted.

"That's not the point," murmured Carmen, taking her mother by the hand.

Every inch of the enormous room was packed with people. She clung to Carmen and stood by the door paralyzed until Cheryl, her teacher, pushed her way to them and greeted Maria with a kiss. Then she led Maria back through the press of people to the small group of award winners from other programs. Maria smiled shakily and nodded hello.

"They're all here now!" Cheryl called out. A photographer rushed over and began to move the students closer together for a picture.

"Hey Bernie, wait for the Mayor!" someone shouted to him. He spun around, called out some words Maria did not understand, and without even turning back to them, he disappeared. But they stayed there, huddled close, not knowing if they could move. The Chinese man kept smiling, the tall black man stayed slightly crouched, the Vietnamese woman squinted, confused, her glasses still hidden in her fist. Maria saw all the cameras along the sides of the crowd, and the lights, and the people from television with video machines, and more lights. Her stomach began to jump up and down. Would she be on television, in the newspapers? Still smiling, holding his pose, the Chinese man next to her asked, "Are you nervous?"

"Oh yes," she said. She tried to remember the expression Cheryl had taught them. "I have worms in my stomach," she said.

He was a much bigger man than she had imagined from seeing him on TV. His face was bright red as they ushered him into the room and quickly through the crowd, just as it was his turn to take the podium. He said hello to the other speakers and called them by their first names. The crowd drew closer to the little stage, the people standing farthest in the back pushed in. Maria tried hard to listen to the Mayor's words. "Great occasion . . . pride of our city . . . ever since I created the program . . . people who have worked so hard . . . overcoming hardship . . . come so far." Was that them? Was he talking about them already? Why were the people out there all starting to laugh? She strained to understand, but still caught only fragments of his words. "My mother used to say . . . and I said, Look, Mama . . ." He was talking about *his* mother now; he called her Mama, just like Maria's kids called *her*. But everyone laughed so hard. At his mother? She forced herself to smile; up front, near the podium, everyone could see her. She should seem to pay attention and understand. Looking out into the crowd she felt dizzy. She tried to find Carmen among all the pretty young women with big eyes and dark hair. There she was! Carmen's eyes met Maria's; Carmen waved. Maria beamed out at her. For a moment she felt like she belonged there, in this crowd. Everyone was smiling, everyone was so happy while the Mayor of New York stood at the podium telling jokes. How happy Maria felt too!

"Maria Perez grew up in the countryside of Guatemala, the oldest daughter in a family of 19 children," read the Mayor as Maria stood quaking by his side. She noticed he made a slight wheezing noise when he breathed between words. She saw the hairs in his nostrils, black and white and wiry. He paused. "Nineteen children!" he exclaimed, looking at the audience. A small gasp was passed along through the crowd. Then the Mayor looked back at the sheet of paper before him. "Maria never had a chance to learn to read and write, and she was already the mother of five children of her own when she fled Guatemala in 1980 and made her way to New York for a new start."

It was her own story, but Maria had a hard time following. She had to stand next to him while he read it, and her feet had started to hurt, crammed into the new shoes. She shifted her weight from one foot to the other.

"At the age of 45, while working as a chambermaid and sending her children through school, Maria herself started school for the first time. In night courses she learned to read and write in her native Spanish. Later, as she was pursuing her G.E.D. in Spanish, she began studying English as a Second Language. This meant Maria was going to school five nights a week! Still she worked as many as 60 hours cleaning rooms at the Plaza Hotel.

"Maria's ESL teacher, Cheryl Sands, says – and I quote – 'Maria works harder than any student I have ever had. She is an inspiration to her classmates. Not only has she learned to read and write in her new language, but she initiated an oral history project in which she taped and transcribed interviews with other students, who have told their stories from around the world.' Maria was also one of the first in New York to apply for amnesty under the 1986 Immigration Act. Meanwhile, she has passed her enthusiasm for education to her children: her son is now a junior in high school, her youngest daughter attends the State University, and her oldest daughter, who we are proud to have with us today, is in her second year of law school on a scholarship.''

Two older sons were dragged through the dirt, chickens squawking in mad confusion, feathers flying. She heard more gunshots in the distance, screams, chickens squawking. She heard, she ran. Maria looked down at her bleeding feet. Wedged tightly into the pink high heels, they throbbed.

The Mayor turned toward her. "Maria, I think it's wonderful that you have taken the trouble to preserve the folklore of students from so many countries." He paused. Was she supposed to say something? Her heart stopped beating. What was folklore? What was preserved? She smiled up at him, hoping that was all she needed to do.

"Maria, tell us now, if you can, what was one of the stories you collected in your project?"

This was definitely a question, meant to be answered. Maria tried to smile again. She strained on tiptoes to reach the microphone, pinching her toes even more tightly in her shoes. "Okay," she said, setting off a high-pitched ringing from the microphone.

The Mayor said, "Stand back," and tugged at her collar. She quickly stepped away from the microphone.

"Okay," she said again, and this time there was no shrill sound. "One of my stories, from Guatemala. You want to hear?"

The Mayor put his arm around her shoulder and squeezed hard. Her first impulse was to wriggle away, but he held tight. "Isn't she wonderful?" he asked the audience. There was a low ripple of applause. "Yes, we want to hear!"

She turned and looked up at his face. Perspiration was shining on his forehead and she could see by the bright red bulge of his neck that his collar was too tight. "In my village in Guatemala," she began, "the mayor did not go along – get along – with the government so good."

"Hey, Maria," said the Mayor, "I know exactly how he felt!" The people in the audience laughed. Maria waited until they were quiet again.

"One day our mayor met with the people in the village. Like you meet people here. A big crowd in the square."

"The people liked him, your mayor?"

"Oh, yes," said Maria. "Very much. He was very good. He tried for more roads, more doctors, new farms. He cared very much about his people."

The Mayor shook his head up and down. "Of course," he said, and again the audience laughed.

Maria said, "The next day after the meeting, the meeting in the square with all the people, soldiers come and shoot him dead."

For a second there was total silence. Maria realized she had not used the past tense and felt a deep, horrible stab of shame for herself, shame for her teacher. She was a disgrace! But she did not have more than a second of this horror before the whole audience began to laugh. What was happening? They couldn't be laughing at her bad verbs? They couldn't be laughing at her dead mayor! They laughed louder and louder and suddenly flashbulbs were going off around her, the TV cameras swung in close, too close, and the Mayor was grabbing her by the shoulders again, holding her tight, posing for one camera after another as the audience burst into wild applause. But she hadn't even finished! Why were they laughing?

"What timing, huh?" said the Mayor over the uproar. "What d'ya think, the Republicans put her here, or maybe the Board of Estimate?" Everyone laughed even louder and he still clung to her and cameras still moved in close, lights kept going off in her face and she could see nothing but the sharp white poof! of light over and over again. She looked for Carmen and Cheryl, but the white poof! poof! poof! blinded her. She closed her eyes and listened to the uproar, now beginning to subside, and in her mind's eye saw chickens trying to fly, chickens fluttering around the yard littered with broken glass.

He squeezed her shoulders again and leaned into the microphone. "There are ways to get rid of mayors, and ways to get rid of mayors, huh Maria?"

The surge of laughter rose once more, reached a crescendo, and then began to subside again. "But wait," said the Mayor. The cameramen stepped back a bit, poising themselves for something new.

"I want to know just one more thing, Maria," said the Mayor, turning to face her directly again. The crowd quieted. He waited a few seconds more, then asked his question. "It says here 19 children. What was it like growing up in a house with 19 children? How many *bathrooms* did you have?"

Her stomach dropped and twisted as the Mayor put his hand firmly on the back of her neck and pushed her toward the microphone again. It was absolutely quiet now in the huge room. Everyone was waiting for her to speak. She cleared her throat and made the microphone do the shrill hum. Startled, she jumped back. Then there was silence. She took a big, trembling breath.

"We had no bathrooms there, Mister Mayor," she said. "Only the outdoors."

The clapping started immediately, then the flashbulbs burning up in her face. The Mayor turned to her, put a hand on each of her shoulders, bent lower and kissed her! Kissed her on the cheek!

"Isn't she terrific?" he asked the audience, his hand on the back of her neck again, drawing her closer to him. The audience clapped louder, faster. "Isn't she just the greatest?"

She tried to smile and open her eyes, but the lights were still going off – poof! poof! – and the noise was deafening.

"Mama, look, your eyes were closed *there*, too," chided Jorge, sitting on the floor in front of the television set.

Maria had watched the camera move from the announcer at the studio desk to her own stout form in bright pink, standing by the Mayor.

"In my village in Guatemala," she heard herself say, and the camera showed her wrinkled face close up, eyes open now but looking nowhere. Then the mayor's face filled the screen, his forehead glistening, and then suddenly all the people in the audience, looking ahead, enrapt, took his place. Then there was her wrinkled face again, talking without a smile. ". . . soldiers come and shoot him dead." Maria winced, hearing the wrong tense of her verbs. The camera shifted from her face to the Mayor. In the brief moment of shamed silence after she'd uttered those words, the Mayor drew his finger like a knife across his throat. And the audience began to laugh.

"Turn it off!" she yelled to Jorge. "Off! This minute!"

Late that night she sat alone in the unlighted room, soaking her feet in Epsom salts. The glow of the television threw shadows across the wall, but the sound was off. The man called Johnny was on the screen, talking. The people in the audience and the men in the band and the movie stars sitting on the couch all had their mouths wide open in what she knew were screams of laughter while Johnny wagged his tongue. Maria heard nothing except brakes squealing below on the street and the lonely clanging of garbage cans in the alley.

She thought about her English class and remembered the pretty woman, Ling, who often fell asleep in the middle of a lesson. The other Chinese students all teased her. Everyone knew that she sewed coats in a sweatshop all day. After the night class she took the subway to the Staten Island Ferry, and after the ferry crossing she had to take a bus home. Her parents were old and sick and she did all their cooking and cleaning late at night. She struggled to keep awake in class; it seemed to take all her energy simply to smile and listen. She said very little and the teacher never forced her, but she fell further and further behind. They called her the Quiet One.

One day just before the course came to an end the Quiet One asked to speak. There was no reason, no provocation – they'd been talking informally about their summer plans – but Ling spoke with a sudden urgency. Her English was very slow. Seeing what a terrible effort it was for her, the classmates all tried to help when she searched for words.

"In my China village there was a teacher," Ling began. "Man teacher." She paused. "All children love him. He teach mathematic. He very –" She stopped and looked up toward the ceiling. Then she gestured with her fingers around her face.

"Handsome!" said Charlene, the oldest of the three Haitian sisters in the class.

Ling smiled broadly. "Handsome! Yes, he very handsome. Family very rich before. He have sister go to Hong Kong who have many, many money."

"*Much* money," said Maria.

"Much, much money," repeated Ling thoughtfully. "Teacher live in big house."

"In China? Near you?"

"Yes. Big house with much old picture." She stopped and furrowed her forehead, as if to gather words inside of it.

"Art? Paint? Pictures like that?' asked Xavier.

Ling nodded eagerly. "Yes. In big house. Most big house in village."

"But big house, money, rich like that, bad in China," said Fu Wu. "Those year, Government bad to you. How they let him do?"

In *my* country," said Carlos, "government bad to you if you got *small* house, *no* money."

"Me too," said Maria.

"Me too," said Charlene.

The Chinese students laughed.

Ling shrugged and shook her head. "Don't know. He have big house. Money gone, but keep big house. Then I am little girl." She held her hand low to the floor.

"I *was* a little girl," Charlene said gently.

"I *was*," said Ling. "Was, was." She giggled for a moment, then seemed to spend some time in thought. "We love him. All children love – all children did loved him. He giving tea in house. He was – was – so handsome!" She giggled. All the women in the class giggled. "He very nice. He learn music, he go . . . he went to school far away."

"America?"

Ling shook her head. "Oh no, no. You know, another . . . west."

"Europa!" exclaimed Maria proudly. "Espain!"

"No, no, another."

"France!" said Patricia, Charlene's sister. "He went to school in France?"

"Yes, France," said Ling. Then she stopped again, this time for a whole minute. The others waited patiently. No one said a word. Finally she continued. "But big boys in more old school not like him. He too handsome."

"Oooh!" sang out a chorus of women. "Too handsome!"

"The boys were jealous," said Carlos.

Ling seized the word. "Jealous! Jealous! They very jealous. He handsome, he study France, he very nice to children, he give tea and cake in big house, he show picture on wall." Her torrent of words came to an end and she began to think again, visibly, her brow furrowing. "Big school boys, they . . ." She stopped.

"Jealous!" sang out the others.

"Yes," she said, shaking her head "no." "But more. More bad. Hate. They hate him."

"That's bad," said Patricia.

"Yes, very bad." Ling paused, looking at the floor. "And they heat."

"Hate."

"No, they heat."

All the class looked puzzled. Heat? Heat? They turned to Cheryl.

The teacher spoke for the first time. "Hit? Ling, do you mean hit? They hit him?" Cheryl slapped the air with her hand.

Ling nodded, her face somehow serious and smiling at the same time. "Hit many time. And also so." She scooted her feet back and forth along the floor.

"Oooh," exclaimed Charlene, frowning. "They kicked him with the feet."

"Yes," said Ling. "They kicked him with the feet and hit him with the hands, many many time they hit, they kick."

"Where this happened?" asked Xavier.

"In the school. In classroom like . . ." She gestured to mean their room.

"In the school?" asked Xavier. "But other people were they there? They say stop, no?"

"No. Little children in room. They cry, they . . ." She covered her eyes with her hand, then uncovered them. "Big boys kick and hit. No one stop. No one help."

Everyone in class fell silent. Maria remembered: they could not look at one another then. They could not look at their teacher.

Ling continued. "They break him, very hurt much place." She stopped. They all fixed their stares on Ling, they could bear looking only at her. "Many place," she said. Her face had not changed, it was still half smiling. But now there were drops coming from her eyes, a single tear down each side of her nose. Maria would never forget it. Ling's face did not move or wrinkle or frown. Her body was absolutely still. Her shoulders did not quake. Nothing in the shape or motion of her eyes or mouth changed. None of the things that Maria had always known happen when you cry happened when Ling shed tears. Just two drops rolled slowly down her two pale cheeks as she smiled.

"He very hurt. He *was* very hurt. He blood many place. Boys go away. Children cry. Teacher break and hurt. Later he in hospital. I go there visit him." She stopped, looking thoughtful. "I went there." One continuous line of wetness glistened down each cheek. "My mother, my father say don't go, but I see him. I say, 'You be better?' But he hurt. Doctors no did helped. He alone. No doctor. No nurse. No medicine. No family." She stopped. They all stared in silence for several moments.

Finally Carlos said, "Did he went home?"

Ling shook her head. "He go home but no walk." She stopped. Maria could not help watching those single lines of tears moving down the pale round face. "A year, more, no walk. Then go."

"Go where?"

"End."

Again there was a deep silence. Ling looked down, away from them, her head bent low.

"Oh, no," murmured Charlene. "He died."

Maria felt the catch in her throat, the sudden wetness of tears on her own two cheeks, and when she looked up she saw that all the other students, men and women both, were crying too.

Maria wiped her eyes. Suddenly all her limbs ached, her bones felt stiff and old. She took her feet from the basin and dried them with a towel. Then she turned off the television and went to bed.

◇

2.2 The Awful German Language

◆

Mark Twain

A little learning makes the whole world kin.

– Proverbs xxxii, 7

I went often to look at the collection of curiosities in Heidelberg Castle, and one day I surprised the keeper of it with my German. I spoke entirely in that language. He was greatly interested; and after I had talked awhile he said my German was very rare, possibly a "unique;" and wanted to add it to his museum.

If he had known what it had cost me to acquire my art, he would also have known that it would break any collector to buy it. Harris and I had been hard at work on our German during several weeks at that time, and although we had made good progress, it had been accomplished under great difficulty and annoyance, for three of our teachers had died in the meantime. A person who has not studied German can form no idea of what a perplexing language it is.

Surely there is not another language that is so slipshod and systemless, and so slippery and elusive to the grasp. One is washed about in it, hither and hither, in the most helpless way; and when at last he thinks he has captured a rule which offers firm ground to take a rest on amid the general rage and turmoil of the ten parts of speech, he turns over the page and reads, "Let the pupil make careful note of the following *exceptions*." He runs his eye down and

Source: Mark Twain, "The Awful German Language," *A Tramp Abroad*, 1972, pp. 290–307, Vol. II.

finds that there are more exceptions to the rule than instances of it. So overboard he goes again, to hunt for another Ararat and find another quicksand. Such has been, and continues to be, my experience. Every time I think I have got one of these four confusing "cases" where I am master of it, a seemingly insignificant preposition intrudes itself into my sentence, clothed with an awful and unsuspected power, and crumbles the ground from under me. For instance, my book inquires after a certain bird – (it is always inquiring after things which are of no sort of consequence to anybody): "Where is the bird?" Now the answer to this question, – according to the book, – is that the bird is waiting in the blacksmith shop on account of the rain. Of course no bird would do that, but then you must stick to the book. Very well, I begin to cipher out the German for that answer. I begin at the wrong end, necessarily, for that is the German idea. I say to myself, "*Regen* (rain) is masculine – or maybe it is feminine – or possibly neuter – it is too much trouble to look now. Therefore, it is either *der* (the) Regen, or *die* (the) Regen, or *das* (the) Regen, according to which gender it may turn out to be when I look. In the interest of science, I will cipher it out on the hypothesis that it is masculine. Very well – then *the* rain is *der* Regen, if it is simply in the quiescent state of being *mentioned*, without enlargement or discussion – Nominative case; but if this rain is lying around, in a kind of a general way on the ground, it is then definitely located, it is *doing something* – that is, *resting* (which is one of the German grammar's ideas of doing something), and this throws the rain into the Dative case, and makes it *dem* Regen. However, this rain is not resting, but is doing something *actively*, – it is falling, – to interfere with the bird, likely, – and this indicates *movement*, which has the effect of sliding it into the Accusative case and changing *dem* Regen into *den* Regen." Having completed the grammatical horoscope of this matter, I answer up confidently and state in German that the bird is staying in the blacksmith shop "wegen (on account of) *den* Regen." Then the teacher lets me softly down with the remark that whenever the word "wegen" drops into a sentence, it *always* throws that subject into the *Genitive* case, regardless of consequences – and that therefore this bird staid in the blacksmith shop "wegen *des* Regens."

N. B. I was informed, later, by a higher authority, that there was an "exception" which permits one to say "wegen *den* Regen" in certain peculiar and complex circumstances, but that this exception is not extended to anything *but* rain.

There are ten parts of speech, and they are all troublesome. An average sentence, in a German newspaper, is a sublime and impressive curiosity; it occupies a quarter of a column; it contains all the ten parts of speech – not in regular order, but mixed; it is built mainly of compound words constructed by the writer on the spot, and not to be found in any dictionary – six or seven words compacted into one, without joint or seam – that is, without hyphens; it treats of fourteen or fifteen different subjects, each enclosed in a parenthesis of its own, with here and there extra parentheses which re-enclose three or four of the minor parentheses, making pens within pens: finally, all the parentheses and reparentheses are massed together between a couple of king-parentheses, one of which is placed in the first line of the majestic sentence and the other in the middle of the last line of it – *after which comes the* VERB, and you find out for the first time what the man has been talking about; and after the verb – merely by way of ornament, as far as I can make out, – the writer shovels in "*haben sind gewesen gehabt haben geworden sein,*" or words to that effect, and the monument is finished. I suppose that this closing hurrah is in the nature of the flourish to a man's signature – not necessary, but pretty. German books are easy enough to read when you hold them before the looking-glass or stand on your head, – so as to reverse the construction, – but I think that to learn to read and understand a German newspaper is a thing which must always remain an impossibility to a foreigner.

Yet even the German books are not entirely free from attacks of the Parenthesis distemper – though they are usually so mild as to cover only a few lines, and therefore when you at last get down to the verb it carries some meaning to your mind because you are able to remember a good deal of what has gone before.

Now here is a sentence from a popular and excellent German novel, – with a slight parenthesis in it. I will make a perfectly literal translation, and throw in the parenthesis-marks and some hyphens for the assistance of the reader, – though in the original there are no parenthesis-marks or hyphens, and the reader is left to flounder through to the remote verb the best way he can:

"But when he, upon the street, the (in-satin-and-silk-covered-now-very-unconstrainedly-after-the-newest-fashion-dressed) government counsellor's wife *met,*" etc., etc.[1]

That is from "The Old Mamselle's Secret," by Mrs. Marlitt. And that sentence is constructed upon the most approved German model. You observe how far that verb is from the reader's base of operations; well, in a German newspaper they put their verb away over on the next page; and I have heard that sometimes after stringing along on exciting preliminaries and parentheses for a column or two, they get in a hurry and have to go to press without getting to the verb at all. Of course, then, the reader is left in a very exhausted and ignorant state.

We have the Parenthesis disease in our literature, too; and one may see cases of it every day in our books and newspapers: but with us it is the mark and sign of an unpracticed writer or a cloudy intellect, whereas with the Germans it is doubtless the mark and sign of a practiced pen and of the presence of that sort of luminous intellectual fog which stands for clearness among these people. For surely it is *not* clearness, – it necessarily can't be clearness. Even a jury would have penetration enough to discover that. A writer's ideas must be a good deal confused, a good deal out of line and sequence, when he starts out to say that a man met a counsellor's wife in the street, and then right in the midst of this so simple undertaking halts these approaching people and makes them stand still until he jots down an inventory of the woman's dress. That is manifestly absurd. It reminds a person of those dentists who secure your instant and breathless interest in a tooth by taking a grip on it with the forceps, and then stand there and drawl through a tedious anecdote before they give the dreaded jerk. Parentheses in literature and dentistry are in bad taste.

The Germans have another kind of parenthesis, which they make by splitting a verb in two and putting half of it at the beginning of an exciting chapter and the *other half* at the end of it. Can any one conceive of anything more confusing than that? These things are called "separable verbs." The German grammar is blistered all over with separable verbs; and the wider the two portions of one of them are spread apart, the better the author of the crime is pleased with his performance. A favorite one is *reiste ab*, – which means *departed*. Here is an example which I culled from a novel and reduced to English:

"The trunks being now ready, he DE- after kissing his mother and sisters, and once more pressing to his bosom his adored Gretchen, who, dressed in simple white muslin, with a single tuberose in the ample folds of her rich brown hair, had tottered feebly down the stairs, still pale from the terror and excitement of the past evening, but longing to lay her poor aching head yet once again upon the breast of him whom she loved more dearly than life itself, PARTED."

However, it is not well to dwell too much on the separable verbs. One is sure to lose his temper early; and if he sticks to the subject, and will not be warned, it will at last either soften his brain or petrify it. Personal pronouns and adjectives are a fruitful nuisance in this language, and should have been left out. For instance, the same sound, *sie,* means *you,* and it means *she,* and it means *her,* and it means *it,* and it means *they,* and it means *them.* Think of the ragged poverty of a language which has to make one word do the work of six, – and a poor little weak thing of only three letters at that. But mainly, think of the exasperation of never knowing which of these meanings the speaker is trying to convey. This explains why, whenever a person says *sie* to me, I generally try to kill him, if a stranger.

Now observe the Adjective. Here was a case where simplicity would have been an advantage; therefore, for no other reason, the inventor of this language complicated it all he could. When we wish to speak of our "good friend or friends," in our enlightened tongue, we stick to the one form and have no trouble or hard feeling about it; but with the German tongue it is different. When a German gets his hands on an adjective, he declines it, and keeps on declining it until the common sense is all declined out of it. It is as bad as Latin. He says, for instance:

SINGULAR.

Nominative – Mein gut*er* Freund, my good friend.
Genitive – Mein*es* gut*en* Freund*es,* of my good friend.
Dative – Mein*em* gut*en* Freund, to my good friend.
Accusative – Mein*en* gut*en* Freund, my good friend.

PLURAL.

N. – Mein*e* gut*en* Freund*e,* my good friends.
G. – Mein*er* gut*en* Freund*e,* of my good friends.
D. – Mein*en* gut*en* Freund*en,* to my good friends.
A. – Mein*e* gut*en* Freund*e,* my good friends.

Now let the candidate for the asylum try to memorize those variations, and see how soon he will be elected. One might better go without friends in Germany than take all this trouble about them. I have shown what a bother it is to decline a good (male) friend; well this is only a third of the work, for there is a variety of new distortions of the adjective to be learned when the object is feminine, and still another when the object is neuter. Now there are more adjectives in this language than there are black cats in Switzerland, and they must all be as elaborately declined as the examples above suggested. Difficult? – troublesome? – these words cannot describe it. I heard a Californian student in Heidelberg say, in one of his calmest moods, that he would rather decline two drinks than one German adjective.

The inventor of the language seems to have taken pleasure in complicating it in every way he could think of. For instance, if one is casually referring to a house, *Haus,* or a horse, *Pferd,* or a dog, *Hund,* he spells these words as I have indicated; but if he is referring to them in the Dative case, he sticks on a foolish and unnecessary *e* and spells them Hause, Pferde, Hunde. So, as an added *e* often signifies the plural, as the *s* does with us, the new student is likely to go on for a month making twins out of a Dative dog before he discovers his mistake; and on the other hand, many a new student who could ill afford loss, has bought and paid for two dogs and only got one of them, because he ignorantly bought that dog in the Dative singular when he really supposed he was talking plural, – which left the law on the seller's side, of course, by the strict rules of grammar, and therefore a suit for recovery could not lie.

In German, all the Nouns begin with a capital letter. Now that is a good idea; and a good idea, in this language, is necessarily conspicuous from its lonesomeness. I consider this capitalizing of nouns a good idea, because by reason of it you are almost always able to tell a noun the minute you see it. You fall into error occasionally, because you mistake the name of a person for the name of a thing, and waste a good deal of time trying to dig a meaning out of it. German names almost always do mean something, and this helps to deceive the student. I translated a passage one day, which said that "the infuriated tigress broke loose and utterly ate up the unfortunate fir-forest" (*Tannenwald*). When I was girding up my loins to doubt this, I found out that Tannenwald in this instance, was a man's name.

Every noun has a gender, and there is no sense or system in the distribution; so the gender of each must be learned separately and by heart. There is no other way. To do this one has to have a memory like a memorandum book. In German, a young lady has no sex, while a turnip has. Think what overwrought reverence that shows for the turnip, and what callous disrespect for the girl. See how it looks in print – I translate this from a conversation in one of the best of the German Sunday-school books:

"*Gretchen*. Wilhelm, where is the turnip?

"*Wilhelm*. She has gone to the kitchen.

"*Gretchen*. Where is the accomplished and beautiful English maiden?

"*Wilhelm*. It has gone to the opera."

To continue with the German genders: a tree is male, its buds are female, its leaves are neuter; horses are sexless, dogs are male, cats are female, – Tom-cats included, of course; a person's mouth, neck, bosom, elbows, fingers, nails, feet, and body, are of the male sex, and his head is male or neuter according to the word selected to signify it, and *not* according to the sex of the individual who wears it, – for in Germany all the women wear either male heads or sexless ones; a person's nose, lips, shoulders, breast, hands, hips, and toes are of the female sex; and his hair, ears, eyes, chin, legs, knees, heart, and conscience, haven't any sex at all. The inventor of the language probably got what he knew about a conscience from hearsay.

Now, by the above dissection, the reader will see that in Germany a man may *think* he is a man, but when he comes to look into the matter closely, he is bound to have his doubts; he finds that in sober truth he is a most ridiculous mixture; and if he ends by trying to comfort himself with the thought that he can at least depend on a third of this mess as being manly and masculine, the humiliating second thought will quickly remind him that in this respect he is no better off than any woman or cow in the land.

In the German it is true that by some oversight of the inventor of the language, a Woman is a female; but a Wife (*Weib*) is not, – which is unfortunate. A Wife, here, has no sex; she is neuter; so, according to the grammar, a fish is *he*, his scales are *she*, but a fishwife is neither. To describe a wife as sexless may be called under-description; that is bad enough, but over-description is surely worse. A German speaks of an Englishman as the *Engländer*; to change the sex, he adds *inn*, and that stands for Englishwoman, – *Engländerinn*. That seems descriptive enough, but still it is not exact enough for a German; so he precedes the word with that article which indicates that the creature to follow is feminine, and writes it down thus:

"*die* Engländer*inn*," – which means "the *she-Englishwoman*." I consider that that person is over-described.

Well, after the student has learned the sex of a great number of nouns, he is still in a difficulty, because he finds it impossible to persuade his tongue to refer to things as "*he*" and "*she*," and "*him*" and "*her*," which it has been always accustomed to refer to as "*it*." When he even frames a German sentence in his mind, with the hims and hers in the right places, and then works up his courage to the utterance-point, it is no use, – the moment he begins to speak his tongue flies the track and all those labored males and females come out as "*its*.". . .

I suppose that in all languages the similarities of look and sound between words which have no similarity in meaning are a fruitful source of perplexity to the foreigner. It is so in our tongue, and it is notably the case in the German. Now there is that troublesome word *vermählt:* to me it has so close a resemblance, – either real or fancied, – to three or four other words, that I never know whether it means despised, painted, suspected, or married; until I look in the dictionary, and then I find it means the latter. There are lots of such words and they are a great torment. To increase the difficulty there are words which *seem* to resemble each other, and yet do not; but they make just as much trouble as if they did. For instance, there is the word *vermiethen* (to let, to lease, to hire); and the word *verheirathen* (another way of saying to *marry*). I heard of an Englishman who knocked at a man's door in Heidelberg and proposed, in the best German he could command, to "verheirathen" that house. Then there are some words which mean one thing when you emphasize the first syllable, but mean something very different if you throw the emphasis on the last syllable. For instance, there is a word which means a runaway, or the act of glancing through a book, according to the placing of the emphasis; and another word which signifies to *associate* with a man, or to *avoid* him, according to where you put the emphasis, – and you can generally depend on putting it in the wrong place and getting into trouble.

There are some exceedingly useful words in this language. *Schlag,* for example; and *Zug*. There are three-quarters of a column of Schlags in the dictionary, and a column and a half of Zugs. The word Schlag means Blow, Stroke, Dash, Hit, Shock, Clap, Slap, Time, Bar, Coin, Stamp, Kind, Sort, Manner, Way, Apoplexy, Wood-Cutting, Enclosure, Field, Forest-Clearing. This is its simple and *exact* meaning, – that is to say, its restricted, its fettered meaning; but there are ways by which you can set it free, so that it can soar away, as on the wings of the morning, and never be at rest. You can hang any word you please to its tail, and make it mean anything you want to. You can begin with *Schlag-ader*, which means artery, and you can hang on the whole dictionary, word by word, clear through the alphabet to *Schlag-wasser*, which means bilge-water, – and including *Schlag-mutter*, which means mother-in-law.

Just the same with *Zug*. Strictly speaking, Zug means Pull, Tug, Draught, Procession, March, Progress, Flight, Direction, Expedition, Train, Caravan, Passage, Stroke, Touch, Line, Flourish, Trait of Character, Feature, Lineament, Chess-move, Organ-stop, Team, Whiff, Bias, Drawer, Propensity, Inhalation, Disposition: but that thing which it does *not* mean, – when all its legitimate pendants have been hung on, has not been discovered yet.

One cannot over-estimate the usefulness of Schlag and Zug. Armed just with these two, and the word *Also*, what cannot the foreigner on German soil accomplish? The German word *Also* is the equivalent of the English phrase "You know," and does not mean anything at all, – in *talk*, though it sometimes does in print. Every time a German opens his mouth an *Also* falls out; and every time he shuts it he bites one in two that was trying to *get* out.

Now, the foreigner, equipped with these three noble words, is master of the situation. Let him talk right along, fearlessly; let him pour his indifferent German forth, and when he lacks for a word, let him heave a *Schlag* into the vacuum; all the chances are that it fits it like a plug, but if it doesn't let him promptly heave a *Zug* after it; the two together can hardly fail to bung the hole; but if, by a miracle, they *should* fail, let him simply say *Also!* and this will give him a moment's chance to think of the needful word. In Germany, when you load your conversational gun it is always best to throw in a *Schlag* or two and a *Zug* or two, because it doesn't make any difference how much the rest of the charge may scatter, you are bound to bag something with *them*. Then you blandly say *Also*, and load up again. Nothing gives such an air of grace and elegance and unconstraint to a German or an English conversation as to scatter it full of "Also's" or "You-knows."

In my note-book I find this entry:

July I. – In the hospital yesterday, a word of thirteen syllables was successfully removed from a patient, – a North-German from near Hamburg; but as most unfortunately the surgeons had opened him in the wrong place, under the impression that he contained a panorama, he died. The sad event has cast a gloom over the whole community.

That paragraph furnishes a text for a few remarks about one of the most curious and notable features of my subject, — the length of German words. Some German words are so long that they have a perspective. Observe these examples:

Freundschaftsbezeigungen.

Dilettantenaufdringlichkeiten.

Stadtverordnetenversammlungen.

These things are not words, they are alphabetical processions. And they are not rare; one can open a German newspaper any time and see them marching majestically across the page, – and if he has any imagination he can see the banners and hear the music, too. They impart a martial thrill to the meekest subject. I take a great interest in these curiosities. Whenever I come across a good one, I stuff it and put it in my museum. In this way I have made quite a valuable collection. When I get duplicates, I exchange with other collectors, and thus increase the variety of my stock. Here are some specimens which I lately bought at an auction sale of the effects of a bankrupt bric-a-brac hunter:

GENERALSTAATSVERORDNETENVERSAMMLUNGEN.

ALTERTHUMSWISSENSCHAFTEN.

KINDERBEWAHRUNGSANSTALTEN.

UNABHAENGIGKEITSERKLAERUNGEN.

WIEDERERSTELLUNGSBESTREBUNGEN.

WAFFENSTILLSTANDSUNTERHANDLUNGEN.

Of course when one of these grand mountain ranges goes stretching across the printed page, it adorns and ennobles that literary landscape, – but at the same time it is a great distress to the new student, for it blocks up his way; he cannot crawl under it, or climb over it, or tunnel through it. So he resorts to the dictionary for help, but there is no help there. The dictionary must draw the line somewhere, – so it leaves this sort of words out. And it is right, because these long things are hardly legitimate words, but are rather combinations of words, and the inventor of them ought to have been killed. They are compound words with the hyphens left out. The various words used in building them are in the dictionary, but in a very scattered condition; so you can hunt the materials out, one by one, and get at the meaning at last, but it is a tedious and harassing business. I have tried this process upon some of the above examples. "Freundschaftsbezeigungen" seems to be "Friendship demonstrations," which is only a foolish and clumsy way of saying "demonstrations of friendship." "Unabhaengigkeitserklaerungen" seems to be "Independencedeclarations," which is no improvement upon "Declarations of Independence," so far as I can see. "General-staatsverordnetenversammlungen" seems to be "Generalstates-representativesmeetings," as nearly as I can get at it, – a mere rhythmical, gushy euphemism for "meetings of the legislature," I judge. We used to have a good deal of this sort of crime in our literature, but it has gone out now. We used to speak of a thing as a "never-to-be-forgotten" circumstance, instead of cramping it into the simple and sufficient word "memorable" and then going calmly about our business as if nothing had happened. In those days we were not content to embalm the thing and bury it decently, we wanted to build a monument over it.

But in our newspapers the compounding-disease lingers a little to the present day, but with the hyphens left out, in the German fashion. This is the shape it takes: instead of saying "Mr. Simmons, clerk of the county and district courts, was in town yesterday," the new form puts it thus: "Clerk of the County and District Court Simmons was in town yesterday." This saves neither time nor ink, and has an awkward sound besides. One often sees a remark like this in our papers: "*Mrs.* Assistant District Attorney Johnson returned to her city residence yesterday for the season." That is a case of really unjustifiable compounding; because it not only saves no time or trouble, but confers a title on Mrs. Johnson which she has no right to. But these little instances are trifles indeed, contrasted with the ponderous and dismal German system of piling jumbled compounds together. I wish to submit the following local item, from a Mannheim journal, by way of illustration:

"In the daybeforeyesterdayshortlyaftereleveno'clock Night, the inthistownstandingtavern called 'The Wagoner' was downburnt. When the fire to the onthedownburninghouseresting Stork's Nest reached, flew the parent Storks away. But when the bytheraging, firesurrounded Nest *itself* caught Fire, straightway plunged the quickreturning Mother Stork into the Flames and died, her Wings over her young ones outspread."

Even the cumbersome German construction is not able to take the pathos out of that picture, – indeed, it somehow seems to strengthen it. This item is dated away back yonder months ago. I could have used it sooner, but I was waiting to hear from the Father-Stork. I am still waiting.

"*Also!*" If I have not shown that the German is a difficult language, I have at least intended to do it. I have heard of an American student who was asked how he was getting along with his German, and who answered promptly: "I am not getting along at all. I have worked at it hard for three level months, and all I have got to show for it is one solitary German phrase, – '*Zwei glas,*' " (two glasses of beer). He paused a moment, reflectively; then added with feeling: "But I've got that *solid!*"

And if I have not also shown that German is a harassing and infuriating study, my execution has been at fault, and not my intent. I heard lately of a worn and sorely-tried American student who used to fly to a certain German word for relief when he could bear up under his aggravations no longer, – the only word in the whole language whose sound was sweet and precious to his ear and healing to his lacerated spirit. This was the word *Damit*. It was only the *sound* that helped him, not the meaning;[2] and so, at last, when he learned that the emphasis was not on the first syllable, his only stay and support was gone, and he faded away and died.

I think that a description of any loud, stirring, tumultuous episode must be tamer in German than in English. Our descriptive words of this character have such a deep, strong, resonant sound, while their German equivalents do seem so thin and mild and energyless. Boom, burst, crash, roar, storm, bellow, blow, thunder, explosion; howl, cry, shout, yell, groan; battle, hell. These are magnificent words; they have a force and magnitude of sound befitting the things which they describe. But their German equivalents would be ever so nice to sing the children to sleep with, or else my awe-inspiring ears were made for display and not for superior usefulness in analyzing sounds. Would any man want to die in a battle which was called by so tame a term as a *Schlacht*? Or would not a consumptive feel too much bundled up, who was about to go out, in a shirt collar and a seal ring, into a storm which the bird-song word *Gewitter* was employed to describe? And observe the strongest of the several German equivalents for explosion, – *Ausbruch*. Our word Toothbrush is more powerful than that. It seems to me that the Germans

could do worse than import it into their language to describe particularly tremendous explosions with. The German word for hell, –
Hölle, – sounds more like *helly* than anything else; therefore, how
necessarily chipper, frivolous, and unimpressive it is. If a man were
told in German to go there, could he really rise to the dignity of
feeling insulted?

Having now pointed out, in detail, the several vices of this language, I now come to the brief and pleasant task of pointing out
its virtues. The capitalizing of the nouns I have already mentioned.
But far before this virtue stands another, – that of spelling a word
according to the sound of it. After one short lesson in the alphabet,
the student can tell how any German word is pronounced without
having to ask; whereas in our language if a student should inquire
of us, "What does B, O, W, spell?" we should be obliged to reply,
"Nobody can tell what it spells when you set if off by itself; you
can only tell by referring to the context and finding out what it
signifies, – whether it is a thing to shoot arrows with, or a nod of
one's head, or the forward end of a boat."

There are some German words which are singularly and power-
fully effective. For instance, those which describe lowly, peaceful,
and affectionate home life; those which deal with love, in any and
all forms, from mere kindly feeling and honest good will toward
the passing stranger, clear up to courtship; those which deal with
outdoor Nature, in its softest and loveliest aspects, – with meadows
and forests, and birds and flowers, the fragrance and sunshine of
summer, and the moonlight of peaceful winter nights; in a word,
those which deal with any and all forms of rest, repose, and peace;
those also which deal with the creatures and marvels of fairyland;
and lastly and chiefly, in those words which express pathos, is the
language surpassingly rich and effective. There are German songs
which can make a stranger to the language cry. That shows that
the *sound* of the words is correct, – it interprets the meanings with
truth and with exactness; and so the ear is informed, and through
the ear, the heart.

The Germans do not seem to be afraid to repeat a word when
it is the right one. They repeat it several times, if they choose. That
is wise. But in English, when we have used a word a couple of times
in a paragraph, we imagine we are growing tautological, and so we
are weak enough to exchange it for some other word which only

approximates exactness, to escape what we wrongly fancy is a greater blemish. Repetition may be bad, but surely inexactness is worse.

There are people in the world who will take a great deal of trouble to point out the faults in a religion or a language, and then go blandly about their business without suggesting any remedy. I am not that kind of a person. I have shown that the German language needs reforming. Very well, I am ready to reform it. At least I am ready to make the proper suggestions. Such a course as this might be immodest in another; but I have devoted upwards of nine full weeks, first and last, to a careful and critical study of this tongue, and thus have acquired a confidence in my ability to reform it which no mere superficial culture could have conferred upon me.

In the first place, I would leave out the Dative Case. It confuses the plurals; and, besides, nobody ever knows when he is in the Dative Case, except he discover it by accident, – and then he does not know when or where it was that he got into it, or how long he has been in it, or how he is ever going to get out of it again. The Dative Case is but an ornamental folly, – it is better to discard it.

In the next place, I would move the Verb further up to the front. You may load up with ever so good a Verb, but I notice that you never really bring down a subject with it at the present German range, – you only cripple it. So I insist that this important part of speech should be brought forward to a position where it may be easily seen with the naked eye.

Thirdly, I would import some strong words from the English tongue, – to swear with, and also to use in describing all sorts of vigorous things in a vigorous way.[3]

Fourthly, I would reorganize the sexes, and distribute them according to the will of the Creator. This as a tribute of respect, if nothing else.

Fifthly, I would do away with those great long compounded words; or require the speaker to deliver them in sections, with intermissions for refreshments. To wholly do away with them would be best, for ideas are more easily received and digested when they come one at a time than when they come in bulk. Intellectual food is like any other; it is pleasanter and more beneficial to take it with a spoon than with a shovel.

Sixthly, I would require a speaker to stop when he is done, and not hang a string of those useless "haben sind gewesen gehabt haben geworden seins" to the end of his oration. This sort of gew-gaws undignify a speech, instead of adding a grace. They are, therefore, an offense, and should be discarded.

Seventhly, I would discard the Parenthesis. Also the re-parenthesis, the re-re-parenthesis, and the re-re-re-re-re-re-parentheses, and likewise the final wide-reaching all-enclosing King-parenthesis. I would require every individual, be he high or low, to unfold a plain straightforward tale, or else coil it and sit on it and hold his peace. Infractions of this law should be punishable with death.

And eighthly and last, I would retain *Zug* and *Schlag,* with their pendants, and discard the rest of the vocabulary. This would simplify the language.

I have now named what I regard as the most necessary and important changes. These are perhaps all I could be expected to name for nothing; but there are other suggestions which I can and will make in case my proposed application shall result in my being formally employed by the government in the work of reforming the language.

My philological studies have satisfied me that a gifted person ought to learn English (barring spelling and pronouncing) in thirty hours, French in thirty days, and German in thirty years. It seems manifest, then, that the latter tongue ought to be trimmed down and repaired. If it is to remain as it is, it ought to be gently and reverently set aside among the dead languages, for only the dead have time to learn it. . . .

Endnotes

1. "Wenn er aber auf der Strasse der in Sammt und Seide gehüllten jetz sehr ungenirt nach der neusten mode gekleideten Regierungsrathin begegnet."

2. It merely means, in its general sense, "*herewith.*"

3. "*Verdammt,*" and its variations and enlargements, are words which have plenty of meaning, but the *sounds* are so mild and ineffectual that German ladies can use them without sin. German ladies who could not be induced to commit a sin by any persuasion or compulsion, promptly rip out one of these harmless little words when they tear their dresses or don't like the soup. It sounds about as wicked as our "My gracious." German ladies are constantly saying, "Ach! Gott!"

"Mein Gott!" "Gott in Himmel!" "Herr Gott!" "Der Herr Jesus!" etc. They think our ladies have the same custom, perhaps; for I once heard a gentle and lovely old German lady say to a sweet young American girl: "The two languages are so alike – how pleasant that is; we say 'Ach! Gott!' you say '*Goddam.*'"

Section 3: Family Adjustment to a New Culture

◇

3.1 Saree of the Gods

◆

G. S. Sharat Chandra

One of the things that Prapulla had insisted was to have a place waiting for them in New York where other Indian immigrants lived. She had worried a great deal over this sudden change in her life. First, there was her fear of flying over Mount Everest, a certain intrusion over Lord Shiva's territory which he did not approve of for any believing Hindu. Then the abrupt severance of a generation of relationships and life in a joint family. She had spent many a restless night. In daylight, she'd dismiss her nightmares as mere confusions of a troubled mind and set herself to conquer her problems as she faced them, like the educated and practical woman that she was. If anything happened to the transgressing jet, she would clutch her husband and child to her breasts and plummet with at least a partial sense of wholeness, to whatever ocean the wrath of the god would cast her. She would go down like those brave, legendary sea captains in the history books and movies. But moving over to the West, where you lived half the year like a monk in a cave because of the weather, was something she was unable to

Source: G. S. Sharat Chandra, "Saree of the Gods," *Short Story International*, 1981, pp. 43–50.

visualize. Besides, how was she going to manage her household without the maid-servant and her stalwart mother-in-law? To be left alone in a strange apartment all day while Shekar went to work was a recurring fear. She had heard that in New York City, even married women wore mini-skirts or leather slacks and thought nothing of being drunk or footloose, not to mention their sexual escapades in summer in parks or parked automobiles. But cousin Manjula who had returned from the States was most reassuring:

"All that is nonsense! Women there are just like women here! Only they have habits and customs quite different from ours. There are hundreds of Indian families in New York. Once you've acclimatized yourself to the country, you'll find it hard to sit and brood. You may run into families from Bangalore in the same apartment house, who knows!"

Prapulla liked the apartment house as soon as she saw some sareed women in the lobby. It was Shekar who looked distraught at the Indian faces. In the time it took for them to arrive from the airport to the apartment, he had seen many of his brown brethren on the city streets, looking strange and out of place. Now he dreaded being surrounded by his kind, ending up like them building little Indias in the obscure corners of New York. He wasn't certain what Prapulla thought about it. She was always quiet on such subjects. Back in India, she was a recluse when it came to socializing and on the few occasions they had entertained foreigners at the firm, she would seek the nearest sofa as a refuge and drop her seven yards of brocade at anchor. She left the impression of being a proper Hindu wife, shy, courteous and traditional.

En route to New York on the jumbo, Shekar had discreetly opened up the conversation about what she'd wear once they were in America. At the mention of skirts she had flared up so defiantly he had to leave the seat. For Prapulla, it was not convenience but convention that made the difference. She had always prized her sarees, especially the occasions she wore her wedding saree with its blue handspun silk and its silver border of gods. There were times she had walked into a crowded room where others were dressed differently and had relished the sudden flush of embarrassment on their faces at her exquisite choice of wear.

The first day of their new life went quite smoothly. When Shekar returned from the office, she was relieved to hear that all had gone well and he had made friends with two of his American colleagues.

Shekar described them. Don Dellow was in the firm for fifteen years and was extremely pleasant and helpful. Jim Dorsen and his wife Shirley had always wanted to visit India and shared great interest in the country and its culture.

"I bought them lunch at the corner deli, you know, and you should've seen their faces when I asked for corned beef on rye!" Shekar chuckled. It was during that weekend that Shekar suggested they ought to invite the Dellows and the Dorsens for dinner so she could meet and get to know the wives. Prapulla shrugged her shoulders. It was so soon. She was still unaccustomed to walking into the sterilized supermarkets where you shopped like a robot with a pushcart, led on to the products by where they lay waiting like cheese in a trap, rather than having them beseech you like the vendors and merchants in the bazaars and markets in her country. Besides, everything had a fixed price tag. The frozen vegetables, the canned fruits and spices, the chicken chopped into shapes that were not its own but of the plastic, all bothered her. But Shekar had not complained about her cooking yet. He was so busy gabbing and gulping, she wasn't even sure he knew what was on the plate. Then Shekar walked in from the office Thursday and announced he had invited his friends for dinner on Saturday.

"They both accepted with great delight. It's rather important I develop a strong bond with them."

Prapulla pulled out a pad and started making the shopping list. Shekar was about to ask her what she'd wear but changed his mind.

The Dorsens arrived first. Shirley Dorsen introduced herself and immediately took a liking to Prapulla. The Dellows, caught in traffic, came late. Judy Dellow was a lean Spanish woman in her late twenties. She wore a velvet dress with lace cuffs and asked for bourbon. The living room filled with the aroma of spices. In the background, Subbalakshmi recited on the stereo.

"What sort of music is this?" Jim asked, looking somewhat sullen. He had just finished his drink. Shirley was on her fourth.

"Karnatak music," explained Prapulla. "Subbalakshmi is the soprano of South Indian music. She sings mostly devotional songs and lyrics."

"Sounds rather strange and off key to me," said Jim nodding his head in dismay. He sang for the church choir on Sundays.

Shekar announced dinner. He had set the wine glasses next to the handloomed napkins like he had seen in *Good Housekeeping*. As soon as everyone was seated, he abruptly got up. "Gee! I forgot to pour the wine!" he despaired. When he returned, he held an opaque bottle with a long German name.

"What kind of wine is it?" asked Jim.

"The best German riesling there is!" replied Shekar with authority.

"My, you do know your liquor!" said Shirley, impressed.

"Like a book!" quipped Prapulla.

"It's a misconception," Shekar continued hastily, "that French wines are the best. Germans actually mastered the art of wine making long before the French. Besides, you can't beat a German riesling to go with Indian food."

"Excellent!" said Jim. Shekar filled the glasses apologizing again for not having filled them beforehand. "You see, good wine has to be chilled right," he added avoiding Prapulla's unflinching stare. They began to eat. Shirley attacked everything, mumbling superlatives between mouthfuls. Shekar kept a benevolent eye on the plates and filled them as soon as they were empty. Prapulla sat beaming an appropriate smile. When everyone had their fill, Prapulla got up for dessert.

"Is it going to be one of the exotic Indian sweets?" Shirley asked.

"Of course," butted Shekar.

Prapulla returned from the kitchen with Pepperidge Farm turnovers. "Sorry, I had an accident with the jamoons," she said meekly.

"Don't worry dear. Turnovers do perfectly well," said Shirley, giving her an understanding look.

Shekar had placed a box of cigars on the coffee table. As they all sat, he offered it to his guests who waved it away in preference to their own crumpled packages of Salem. Don and Jim talked about a contract the firm had lost. A junior engineer from Bombay who used to work for the firm had bungled it. They asked Shekar if he knew the man. Shekar had already stiffened in the chair but he pressed for details. But they veered the conversation away from the topic to compliment him on his choice of brandy.

Prapulla entered with a tray of coffee mixed with cream and sugar, just like back home. Subbalakshmi coughed, cleared her throat and strummed the veena in prayer.

Judy raved about Prapulla's saree. Prapulla, momentarily saved from embarrassment over the coffee, began to explain the ritual importance of the wedding saree. She pulled the upper part from her shoulder and spread it on the table. The silver border with the embroidered legend of the creation of the universe, the different avatars of Lord Shiva and the demons he killed while on earthly mission gleamed under the light. Her favorite one depicted Shiva drinking the poison emitted by the sea serpent with which the universe was churned from the ocean. The craftsman had even put a knot of gold at Shiva's neck to indicate the poison the god had held in his throat. A sheer triumph of skill.

"With the exception of Shiva as the begging ascetic, the saree-maker has woven all the other avatars. This blank space on the border perhaps is the space left to challenge our imagination!" mused Prapulla. Shirley, with a snifterful of brandy leaned from her chair for a closer look. The brandy tipped. "Oh no!" screamed everyone. Judy ran into the kitchen for a towel but the alcohol hissed like a magical serpent over the saree spreading its poisonous hood. The silver corroded fast and the avatars, disfigured or muti-lated, almost merged. Prapulla sat dazed, just staring at her saree. The silence was unbearable. Jim puffed on his pipe like a condemned man. Judy, after trying valiantly to wipe the brandy, bent her head over her hand. Shirley looked red, like she was either going to scream or giggle. Shekar came to the rescue:

"Don't worry. I know a way I can lift the smudges. It's nothing!"

No one believed him. Prapulla abruptly got up and excused her-self.

"I guess we should better be leaving," said Don looking at his watch. "I've to drive the babysitter home and she lives three traffic jams away!"

Shekar hurried to the closet for their coats. "I hope you enjoyed the dinner!" he said meekly, piling up the coats over his shoulder. Prapulla appeared at the door in a different saree. She seemed to have recollected herself and felt bad about everyone leaving so soon. "You know, my husband is right. I've already dipped the saree border in the lotion. It'll be as good as new by morning," she said. They shook hands and Shirley hugged Prapulla and rocked her. "I'll call you dear, let me know how it comes off!" she whispered drunkenly and backed into her coat like an animal perfectly trained.

Prapulla stood at the door with one hand on her stomach, and as the guests disappeared down the elevator, she banged the door shut and ran into the bedroom. She remembered the day she had shopped for the saree. It was a week before her wedding. The entire family had gone to the silk bazaar and spent the day looking for the perfect one. They had at last found it in the only hand-spun saree shop in the market. The merchant had explained that the weaver who had knitted the god into its border had died soon after, taking his craft with him. This was his last saree, his parting gift to some lucky bride. "You modern young people may not believe in old wives tales, but I know that he was a devotee of Shiva. People say the Lord used to appear for him!" the merchant had said.

She sobbed into her shoulders. Where was she going to find a replacement? How was she ever going to explain the tragedy to her family? A wedding saree, selected by the bride became her second self, the sail of her destiny, the roof that protected her and her offspring from evil. She rushed to Ratri's room to make sure that no mythical serpent or scorpion had already appeared over her daughter's head.

She could hear Shekar washing the dishes in the kitchen and turning the sinkerator that gurgled like a demon with its gulletful of leftovers. She found the impulse to make sure that Shekar had not fallen into it. It was not really Shirley's fault. It was the brandy that her "Americanized" husband kept pouring into her glass. He was so imitative and flippant, lavishing food and liquor that they could scarcely afford on people that were yet to be called friends. He had drunk more than he should have as if to prove that he held his liquor well enough to win points for promotion! Who really discovered brandy? Shekar had brackishly turned the picture of Napoleon on the bottle toward his guests, but surely it must have been a demon who despised her or was sent to convey the god's displeasure at her mixed company, her expatriatism.

She grew tired of her mind's hauntings. There was no way to change the events or turn back now. When Ratri grew up, she would cut the saree and make a dress for her. She'd write to her mother-in-law and send money for a special puja at the temple.

In her dream, it was her funeral. Four priests carried her on bamboo. The family walked behind. Shekar, dressed in traditional dhoti walked ahead with the clay vessel of hot coals with which he'd kindle the first spark of fire. The procession moved briskly to the crematory grounds. A pyre was built and her corpse decked with her favorite flowers was laid on top. Someone tied the border of the saree firmly to a log. The bereaved went around chanting the necessary hymns and the priests sprinkled holy water over her.

Suddenly she was ablaze. She felt nothing but an intense heat around her. The flames did not seem to touch her. She pinched herself. She was not on the pyre but was standing with her family. It was her wedding saree wrapped around a giant bottle of brandy that was burning! Inside the bottle a demon danced, spitting fire. The avatars slowly uncurled from the silver border like an inflated raft and ascended the smoke. They were all in miniature, fragile in their postures and luminous. The brandy in the bottle foamed and swirled like an ocean. The demon raved in its ring of fire. Prapulla screamed. One of the uncles gently touched her on the arm and said:

"Do not be alarmed. The demon points its tongue upwards. The gods have flown to their proper heaven."

When she woke herself from the nightmare, Shekar was soundly snoring on the bedside. The sky outside hung in a spent, listless grayness. She could see a haze of light back of a skyscraper. Dawn would soon brim the horizon of her new world with neither birds nor the song of priests in the air. She sat in the dark of the living room with the saree on her lap, caressing its border absentmindedly. A brittled piece broke and fell.

◇

3.2 From Paris

◆

Ryō Takasugi

I

Matsuoka sat relaxed, with his feet propped up on his desk and the soles of his shoes facing Komiya. "I just got a telex from our Tokyo Main Office. It says that the Queen is coming to Paris later next week. Luckily she'll only be here for three days this time. It won't be too bad. I hope you can handle it. She's supposed to go to London from here. She has two others with her."

"No problem. Three days will be manageable. Last time was rough; she stayed for a week and a half!" Komiya's Westerner-like face cracked into a smile from relief rather than joy.

"She's fond of you. The crank may be coming to Europe mostly to see you." Matsuoka looked up at Komiya, flashing a grin.

"Please! You don't have to rub it in!"

"Settle down. You can't be all that unhappy having a VIP chase you. I guess women fall apart at the sight of a good-looking man no matter how old they are. Or is it your *Français* that's gotten her hooked?"

"That's enough! This is no spring chicken we're talking about.[1] The woman must be sixty, a granny. She makes me sick." Komiya scowled in disgust. In fact, the memory of the overperfumed, heavily made-up woman could make him cry. Komiya was embarrassed to

---

Source: Ryō Takasugi, "From Paris," *Made in Japan and Other Japanese Business Novels*, edited and translated by C. Prindle, 1989, pp. 91–110. Reprinted by permission of M. E. Sharpe, Inc., Armonk, NY 10504.

be seen in her company, although there was no denying that someone else might call her adorable. Everything was a matter of preference. It wasn't as if she didn't have her cute side. She even had
something rather childish about her.

"Say what you want, she's very important to us. Be sure to do
everything you can. Her company buys half its raw material from
us. As far as I know we're their number one trader."

"I know, I know. Why else am I breaking my back without a
word of complaint?" Komiya laughed, remembering that he had
just finished complaining.

"Good! That's the spirit," said Matsuoka, pulling his feet off his
desk. "The Queen is a superwoman and ruler of her husband, the
company president. There's a saying in Tōa Chemicals that you're
a goner if she ever turns on you. Just be sure to get on her good
side. Here's her three-day itinerary." Matsuoka handed over a piece
of paper. The "itinerary" was very simple, just her flight schedule
and a timetable of her visit to a chemical company.

"Other than the afternoon of the second day when she goes to
P-Company, her schedule is wide open. Think up something good
for her. And reserve rooms at the Ritz as soon as possible. She
seems to like that hotel."

"All right, I'll get on it."

Komiya left the manager's office, stopped at the restroom, and
then went back to his desk. One of the major tasks of the trading
company employees living abroad was to escort the company's business customers and their relations, as well as any officials from the
main office. This was particularly true of Komiya, who practically
made a full-time job of the practice. He knew painfully well how
critically his relationship to his clients affected business negotiations
with his company.

Three levels of hospitality were offered by the company. The
levels were set by the main office or branch offices overseas. Rank
C, the lowest, generally meant just treating a casual visitor to a
meal. Rank B included meals and trips to the airport. Rank A was
further divided into A-1, A-2, and A-3. In the A-3 rank, the company
paid expenses in full for the entire period of the guests' stay, and
a staff with a good command of the country's language accompanied
them night and day.

Noriko Hasegawa naturally rated A-3. Plus, being as she was,
everything had to be first-rate. The cost to the company was enor-

mous. But on the other hand, Noriko's extravagance was insignificant compared to the several billion yen business that T-Trading
Company did with her company.

Ryōhei Komiya was the manager's attaché at the Paris branch
office of T-Trading Company, a trading conglomerate. He worked
in the General Business Department. Thirteen years after graduating
from a university, his rank was only one step short of section chief,
but this was already his tenth year in Paris. During the first three
years with the T-Trading Company, he had worked at the Chemical
Product Division in the main office in Tokyo. During his first two
years in Paris, he was in charge of the three-nation trade of chemical
products. What got him started as the manager's attaché was a tour
through Europe by President and Mrs. Hasegawa of Tōa Chemicals.
The couple was very pleased with Komiya's services.

Komiya was a public relations specialist of sorts. Although he
jokingly referred to himself as "Mr. Tour-Guide," the rest of the
office never trifled his role. Everyone knew that his fluent English
and French had tempted Mr. and Mrs. Hasegawa to ask the president
of T-Trading Company to make him a tour-guide.

Because Paris is a popular sightseeing spot for the Japanese, visitors
streamed in incessantly throughout the year. Komiya was completely
tied up. Others envied his opportunities to drink, eat, and have fun,
yet still get paid for it by the company, but to Komiya, there was
nothing fun about it. He had already lost his taste for fancy food.
He wished he could make a clean break with the same old business
and get into real work. But the company would not consider letting
go of this handyman, the attaché to the manager. His wife's pleading
to go back to Japan and his parents' pressing for his return via
telephone and letters from Tokyo had been getting on his nerves.
He had come to the point where he sincerely wished for a new
posting. He was genuinely homesick.

Ten years was too long, no matter how he tried to justify it. The
managers had changed three times since he'd been there. Ordinarily,
promising staff were promoted to other offices every three years or
so. Only so-called local employees stayed at a single post longer.
Cases like Komiya's were unheard of in the reputable T-Trading
Company, which employed nearly ten thousand people.

A longing to return to Japan had grown within him. He had
pressed the manager on this point numerous times. He had once
written a long petition to the Personnel Office and the Chemical

Product Headquarters in Tokyo, but to no avail. He felt more desperate after reading Marco Polo's *Record of the East,* spending three months with the help of a dictionary.

II

Back at his desk, Komiya's next-door neighbor, deputy department chief of the General Business Office, a homely-faced Satomi, talked to him in a low voice. Satomi was two years Komiya's senior.

"Is it a VIP visit this time?"

"It's Mrs. Hasegawa."

"Oh no! Her again! Wasn't she here just last month?"

"Amen. Don't you know it. I guess these big shots have to travel a lot."

"It's great that you got picked out. She sure knows who can best show her around and introduce her to the bigwigs of Paris. I've got to respect you for that."

"I just got harassed about it by the manager. The nerve of him. I wish you could take my place. My job is a bigger strain than you think."

"I don't know, you may be right. But it's all yours since nobody else can do it. I guess that's how it goes. When it comes to speaking French fashionably, my kind just can't cut it, even if we stand on our heads." Satomi shrugged his shoulders, his palms facing upward.

Komiya was chafed by Satomi's manner, but said nothing.

"Well, permit me to go back to checking through vouchers, something my kind can do." Satomi spoke in a theatrically slovenly way, and went back to his desk.

The chain of events this morning led Komiya to decide that he would definitely have to go back to Tokyo this year. The decision jelled his frustration and took him straight back to the manager's office.

"Now what?" asked Matsuoka, looking up at Komiya who stood in front of his desk glaring at him. Matsuoka lit a cigarette.

"Manager, would you see to it that I go back to the main office at the June personnel rotation? I don't remember how many times I've asked you this before, but I mean it this time. In the first place, do you realize that I've worked here for ten years? And I've been doing the same work all that time."

"Ah, is it ten years already?" said Matsuoka as if it had nothing to do with him, and blew out some cigarette smoke. "If I were you, I would be delighted to stay in Paris."

"But I'm not. I have to think about my child's education. My wife is going out of her mind these days. If you keep me here much longer, it'll become a morale problem for you."

"Goodness! You seem determined. You know that you're vitally important here, and even the personnel department in Tokyo can't move you as it wishes. It's really not my decision."

"Seriously. I might have to leave the company if you don't act on this."

"So, now you're threatening me, huh?" Matsuoka finally scowled.

"Well, I'm not asking for anything so outrageous, am I?"

"Why all of a sudden, though?"

"This isn't sudden at all. This is my second request since you came here."

"I never thought you'd come down on me quite so hard." Matsuoka had been smoking languidly, but abruptly crushed the butt in an ashtray, got up, and told Komiya to have a seat. "Komiya-kun, haven't you heard anything from the Queen?"

"What am I supposed to hear?"

"When my predecessor tried to take you out of our Paris office, the personnel office in Tokyo called it off. It was because Mrs. Hasegawa didn't want that to happen. She wanted you here. You see, it's very convenient for her to have you here. I hear that she calls you Ryōhei and treats you like her own son. Apparently, she has threatened either our president or manager that she would drop her business with us if we transferred you." Matsuoka narrated in a stern expression. "What I'm trying to get at is that you have to get the Queen's permission if you really want to move out of this office. Why don't you make use of her visit this time, and talk to her when you catch her in a good mood?"

"Are you kidding me? Do you really mean this crap?" Komiya stared at Matsuoka, flabbergasted.

"What do you mean? Of course I'm serious."

"This is the most ridiculous story I've ever heard. I know how important Tōa is to us, but it's beyond me that our company lets her step into our personnel problems. If you mean that our company is dancing to Mrs. Hasegawa's tune, it doesn't make sense." Komiya almost laughed.

But Matsuoka shook his head, still keeping a hard expression, "That's what you think. You think it's a joke. But think about this: Mrs. Hasegawa comes to Europe a dozen times every year. Especially these days, she's all over Paris, for opera, ballet, Japanese dance, you name it. She's drowning in art. She's deep into cultural exchanges, too. She needs you here. You're too valuable and useful. Her talk about cancelling orders may be an exaggeration, but she has plenty of reason to keep you here."

Komiya didn't know what to say.

"Why else would our company keep you in Paris for more than ten years?"

Komiya's face tensed and his heart sank.

"I should say that the best thing for you to do is to talk to the Queen directly. You are better acquainted with her than anyone else."

"I will, but what a mess! How unbelievable! This is really bizarre."

"Let's face it: life is full of strange things. But, personally, I would appreciate it if you kept still for a while. You are the Ace of our Paris office, and indispensable. I don't want to lose you. I've been here for less than a year. I need your help, and in fact, I wouldn't know what to do without you."

"You are kind to put it that way, but I can't end my life in Paris. And I'm dying to get out of the escort business – it's been ten years."

"Believe me, I feel for you." Matsuoka took a cigarette out of a case with a sulky expression on his face, and kept tapping the table with the filtered end.

III

Noriko Hasegawa arrived at the Charles de Gaulle Airport with her two secretaries in late April. Trees in Paris were just beginning to bud. Although Noriko had traveled for about seventeen hours via the North Pole, she showed no sign of fatigue. Komiya couldn't help but be impressed by her energy. In contrast, her companions, an elderly man and a secretary-like man, were bleary-eyed and obviously exhausted.

As soon as she saw him, Noriko walked briskly over to Komiya and gave him a hug and kiss. Komiya was ready for this, but because of what Matsuoka had said, he couldn't respond to her as easily as usual.

"This time, I came only for business. I'm taking the place of my husband."

"I'm glad to see you looking so well. And how is your husband?"

"He's going strong. Too much so in fact. He's got so many meetings he can't manage to leave Tokyo."

"Well, I'll get the full report later. You probably want to go to the hotel first. I reserved you a suite at the Ritz."

"Thank you. I'm lucky to have my Ryōhei in Paris."

"Glad to be of service."

"My husband appreciates you, too. He keeps telling me that nobody in Tōa compares to you when it comes to the ways of the world. He wants you to quit the T-Trading Company and come to ours, but we want you in Paris too, so . . ."

"I'm flattered." Komiya bowed lightly, but the memories of Matsuoka's earlier comments made him very uneasy.

Komiya took the three guests by Mercedes Benz to their hotel, went back to his office, and returned to the Ritz at six o'clock to pick them up. The Mercedes was the manager's vehicle. There was a chauffeur, a local employee, but Komiya had decided to drive himself, making more room for the three guests. He had chartered a taxi for the evening trip, however, because Matsuoka was with him this time.

Matsuoka and Komiya found Noriko in her luxurious hotel suite, all prepared to go out with them in a dark evening dress. She summoned her two companions by telephone and introduced them to Matsuoka and Komiya for the first time. The elderly man's name was Okiyama, the director and head of the president's office. The younger introduced himself as Arai, a member of the secretarial office.

They had a duck dish at the Restaurant Tour D'Argent in Bandome Square, as they viewed the Notre Dame Cathedral on the other side of the river. Afterward, Komiya accompanied Noriko to a nightclub until midnight, and then went home with a promise to meet for lunch the next day in the Ritz dining room. Matsuoka had left after the dinner, making apologies, "Maybe it's best if a hybrid like me gave the floor over to you." Komiya couldn't tell if Matsuoka was trying to please Noriko or to keep a respectful distance from her by leaving her with Komiya.

Komiya found an opportunity to appeal to Noriko on the evening of her second day in Paris. Okiyama and Arai had gone off on their own somewhere. He sat face to face with Noriko in a room of the Japanese restaurant Miki on the Champs Elysées. Nicely waited on by a Japanese waitress in a navy-blue kimono, they exchanged sake cups. Noriko was petite, but when it came to drinking, she was a giant. She had had an incredible number of drinks. She was chirpy, but her bloodshot eyes were already halfway closed.

"My husband will be jealous to hear that you and I drank sake all by ourselves."

Komiya decided that this was the once-and-for-all chance.

"Mrs. Hasegawa, I've been in Paris for ten years now. Would you please consider releasing me from my Paris assignment?" What he was trying to say sounded odd to him, but at least he spoke earnestly. He felt the effect of the sake instantly wear off, and realized that he had just thrown a wet blanket over the little private party. "The manager told me that he couldn't transfer me without your permission." Komiya scratched his head to indicate embarrassment. At the same time, he felt bad about posing a sorry figure in front of Noriko. He simply couldn't bite at her the way he did with Matsuoka.

"What are you talking about, Ryōhei? What do I have to do with it?"

"You must know how much influence you and your husband have on our company. I need your help. My wife is going crazy and I feel powerless." This time Komiya managed to make it sound humorous.

"I know your wife. She seems like the type to like it here. Talking about your wife, why didn't you bring her with you tonight?"

"Oh, I'm sorry. I forgot to give you her best regards. She has a slight cold, and couldn't come."

"Oh, poor Ryōhei! It must be hard for you if your wife has a cold and is going crazy at the same time." Noriko's tone was ambivalent. She gulped another cupful.

"Our child will be in school next year. My wife is an only child, and her parents are very anxious to have her back. It worries me."

"For Heaven's sake, I thought you were more of a male chauvinist."

"I'm sorry."

"Don't worry. I'll have my husband talk to Okamoto. But really, we aren't the ones to decide your future, you know." Perhaps out of sorts to some degree, Noriko arched her eyebrows sharply. The deepened wrinkles on the corners of her eyes exposed her age. The man she called "Okamoto" happened to be the president of the T-Trading Company. Her appellation without a title made plain her power over the T-Trading Company. Komiya felt insulted, but said nothing.

"Don't trading company employees enjoy working abroad? I had imagined that London and Paris are the best of all possibilities. What's so great about going back to Tokyo?"

Komiya didn't answer.

"An alternative is that you leave your T-Trading company and come to ours." Noriko made her vocal cords ring high, and banged the table with her palms. "That's it! What a great idea! A trading company isn't a place to stay forever. Nothing is waiting for you at the end of it all. On the other hand, you'll be a smashing success in Tōa. I'm sure my husband will extend a hearty welcome. I'll talk with him as soon as I get back. That's it. That's what you should do!" Noriko was excited about her own idea.

As her nickname Amazon indicated, Noriko had an insider's wisdom about the nature of trading companies. Komiya was impressed.

The development of the Japanese economy was impossible without trading companies. No small number of "trading company men"[2] go so far as to embrace an evangelic passion to serve their country. As a result, a new expression "civildom"[3] was created to pair up with the existing "officialdom." It referred mostly to the "topflight trading company men,"[4] and suggested that the private sectors abroad contributed to Japan in the same capacity as the diplomatic corps. Actually, only a very limited number of internationally minded, globe-trotting and able trading company men remained in civildom. A majority dropped out or were casually thrown out of the competitive arena like a used dishcloth.

Even among leading industries, the attrition rate of trading company men was high. Many young people had glowing ideas of trading companies, but the reality was dismal. In fact, international commerce was one of the most hazardous of enterprises. It was a world of clear meritocracy. Getting along without committing a major offense was not enough. Komiya shuddered when he tried to estimate how many of his peers would survive to retirement age.

The whole process was like tightrope walking. How many trading company men in their thirties and forties had resigned and gone into manufacturing and other foreign investment enterprises?

Komiya was one of those who had once entertained some of the civildom consciousness. But the escort business had cremated such idealism. His memory was littered with tragic examples, like the person who killed himself after incurring a great deficit in the Chicago wheat trade, or the one who passed away from an endemic disease in Africa. Noriko's words, "it isn't a place to stay forever," weighed heavily on him. Nevertheless, he couldn't imagine himself leaving the T-Trading Company just yet. It was also upsetting to realize that he hadn't done any work of significance as yet. He had put a great store on future possibilities.

Not knowing how resolute Noriko was, Komiya could only simper. He would modestly judge her remarks to be a drunkard's mischief, but couldn't get it out of his head when Noriko cast an excited glance at him and kept on saying, "Ryōhei, let's do that. My company needs someone like you so badly we can taste it."

"I'm flattered. But I should at least go back to Tokyo, do some work, and recover from culture shock before trying to work for a first-rate company like yours," Komiya pussyfooted with a noncommittal answer.

"What culture shock? How can a henpecked husband like you feel it?"

Noriko was starting to slur her words. But her final clear words – which were delivered with her back pulled up straight – truly showed her size. "I'll take care of your transfer to Tokyo. But make sure that you follow proper procedure. You write a request to your personnel office. And don't mention my husband and me. We aren't supposed to be more than bystanders."

"Thank you very much." Komiya bowed deeply, and happily mused that it might not be a bad idea to move to Tōa Chemicals sometime in the future.

IV

It was after the long holidays in May that Makiguchi, personnel department chief of the T-Trading Company, was summoned by President Okamoto through the latter's secretary. Makiguchi tightened his necktie, braced himself, and knocked on the president's door.

"Have a seat." Okamoto lifted his eyes from the paper he was reading, removed his gold-framed glasses, and strolled over to the sofa Makiguchi was on.

"I met President Hasegawa of Tōa Chemicals at a party yesterday, and heard something funny. He wants us to bring Komiya back from our Paris office. I thought that Komiya was Mrs. Hasegawa's pet. Has he done something wrong? He guided me around Paris more than once. He did a great job."

"Now that you've mentioned him, it comes back to my mind that Komiya has sent me a transfer request. Do you suppose it's a coincidence that the president's request and Komiya's letter arrived at the same time?"

"Hmm, that's interesting. The president's exact words were, 'I hear that Komiya has been in Paris for ten years now. Why don't you let him go somewhere else?' You know that it was President Hasegawa himself who had stopped our former president from replacing Komiya. I don't know whether to believe him or not."

"Mrs. Hasegawa just returned from Paris. I'm sure Komiya showed her around. Have you heard anything about it?"

"No, nothing beyond what President Hasegawa has told me. He said that Komiya had helped him and his wife a great deal, so he wants to give him a big welcoming party when he comes back. It didn't seem like he held anything against Komiya-kun, and he hopes that we find someone at least halfway as good. I told him not to worry because our company has plenty of qualified people."

"Does that mean that we should bring Komiya back?"

"I suppose so. I don't know what happened in Paris, but it couldn't be too bad. I'll let you pick his post over here. For the one in Paris, try someone more fluent in English and French than Komiya. I want Tōa to see how resourceful we are."

"I'll try." Makiguchi nodded and left. Back in his office, he asked the section chief to compile a fast list of several good-looking men in their thirties who were fluent in English and French.

One week later, Komiya received the order to return to the Tokyo office. He was impressed with Noriko's influence in Tōa Chemicals. Invited to lunch by Makiguchi immediately on his return to Tokyo, he was unknowingly interviewed about the details of his conversation with Noriko in Paris.

"If it's the Hasegawa couple's wish, it would be difficult to say 'No' wouldn't it?" Makiguchi glanced at Komiya as he lackadaisically fished for information.

"I don't think so. I didn't make any promises. Personally, I would like to work here for another ten or twenty years, that is, if I'm allowed to."

"But her request to free you from your Paris job is based on her plan to scout you for her company. If she thinks that you're going with them, you can't refuse. In other words, you've got to say 'Yes' to her."

"You aren't talking sense, Manager." Komiya raised his voice, coloring.

"As you know," said Makiguchi, picking his teeth with a toothpick, "the relationship between the T-Trading Company and Tōa Chemicals is very close. I don't think our president can refuse if President Hasegawa asked for you. Especially if this transfer is prefaced by Mrs. Hasegawa's talk with you in Paris, I'm sure the Hasegawas assume that you're coming."

"What about my plans, though?"

"You don't think this offer is exactly bad for you, do you?" Makiguchi went on smiling loosely. "One way or the other, you make out."

"Not necessarily. I know I'm only a two-bit salary man but I still don't like Tōa's way of doing things. I'm going to turn them down."

"Aren't you brave. Take it easy."

"I suppose I should take their offer, but I've always seen myself as a trading company man. Please don't give up on me yet. Besides, even if Tōa makes an official offer, don't I get a choice?" Komiya smiled bitterly. He felt that there was something wrong about the whole situation.

"The world we live in is not logical."

"Mrs. Hasegawa could have been leading me on in Paris. It seems unlikely that they would actually ask for me. You may find out that you've misread the situation."

"As far as I'm concerned, it's just too bad to lose a talent like you. Our company is just beginning to get a payoff for your training. But if Tōa asks, we'll just have to smile and let you go. That would probably be best for everyone."

"Sentiment has lost its popularity. It's a cutthroat world. No point in worrying until it happens," Komiya laughed, wondering who was advising whom.

V

Makiguchi outlined the essentials of his talk for President Okamoto and the Managing Director of Personnel, Yokouchi, and appended his own view that Komiya would most certainly move to Tōa. The two seniors did no more than make halfhearted "Hmm, hmm" sounds, but they appeared to have resigned themselves to the possible outcome.

Komiya was the only one from his age group to be promoted to the section chief level at the time of the June 1 personnel rotation. And Makiguchi's decision to give Komiya the post of the head of the Chemical Product Synthetic Resins First Section was based on a deal he had made with Miyagawa, chief of the Chemical Product Division.

The former section chief of the Chemical Product Division, Kihara, Komiya's senior by three years, was an upstart star among his age group, and had sped quickly up the "elitist highway." While he did high caliber work, his connection to the company as a distant relative of the president had helped pave a rosy way for him. Komiya couldn't help but be excited about taking over Kihara's post. What Komiya didn't realize, unfortunately, was that he had been chosen for a devious reason. Komiya did notice at the time of his transfer that his predecessor looked beaten. It bothered him at first, but he was too taken up by his new assignments to be concerned. Kihara left for the New York Branch Office too soon. There was no time for Komiya to learn that he was to be Kihara's scapegoat, set up to cover his predecessor's errors and to save face.

The story went like this: At the end of the year before, the oil-producing countries raised the price of crude. As a result, the cost of raw materials for a great variety of commodities rose. Fears of a price hike resulted in an early placement of purchase orders and a subsequent shortage of vinyl chloride resins. Precisely when the shortage was at its peak, R-Country in Eastern Europe made soundings through the Japanese embassy to see if Japanese trading companies might be interested in purchasing its surplus vinyl chloride resins. The products of this country were inferior to Japan's, but this happened to be the time when companies could not afford to argue over quality. Various trading companies jumped into the purchasing competition. It was a seller's market even for a low-quality product.

Nevertheless, the manufacturers identified the low-quality products as substandard. They would not buy them. Some trading companies quickly caught on to this new development and discontinued importing, but the T-Trading Company missed the chance to pull out. It accumulated a 5,000-ton stockpile. This was entirely Kihara's fault.

Just then, the price of vinyl chloride resins started to drop precipitously, as a repercussion of the surplus stocks and a general recession. From the peak price 190 yen per kilogram, the price was down to 150 yen in March, and the future market looked weaker yet. Because the import price from R-Country was 170 yen per kilogram upon unloading, there was a loss of 20 yen per kilogram and 100 million yen for 5,000 tons. A 100 or 200 million yen loss was nothing to be startled by; it occurred every now and then. But the problem was that the 5,000-ton stock had no buyers. The loss for the 5,000 tons was 850 million yen, not counting storage costs and interest. Kihara had struggled to recapitalize but nothing worked. Adding up the costs of storage, interest, and others, the loss easily exceeded one billion yen. Komiya returned from Paris just when his company was struggling with this problem.

Komiya's face had flashed across Makiguchi's mind when he was informed about Kihara by the Synthetic Resins Division head, Yoshioka. He saw no harm in putting the blame onto someone who would be leaving the company soon. In the highly competitive trading company, a one billion yen loss would be blamed on the staff in charge, the supervisor division head, and in some serious cases, even the department head. But in Makiguchi's plan, Komiya would shoulder the burden alone. And by freeing up the Chemical Products Division head and the Synthetic Resins Division head, Makiguchi could make them feel indebted to him. He could even gain the gratitude of the president. And most important, he could save the company's "Prince" Kihara. Were Komiya not under the spell of culture shock, and had he familiarized himself earlier with the everyday transactions, he would have questioned the abnormal quantity of vinyl chloride resins imported from R-Country. But his mind was not quite all there.

VI

It was a hot late July day. Makiguchi invited Komiya out to lunch at a neighborhood restaurant.

"Haven't you heard from President Hasegawa, yet?"

"No. It must have been a joke after all. It had to be a joke."

"No news to our president, either. What if you reminded Mrs. Hasegawa?"

Komiya looked at Makiguchi terror-stricken. First he thought that Makiguchi was teasing him, but it didn't take long to figure out that he was dead serious.

"To be frank, you'll have a better future there. Our executives think so, too," Makiguchi continued.

"What do you mean? Does T-Trading Company want me out?" Komiya stared at Makiguchi.

"It's not that we don't need you. It's just that we have planned things on the premise that you would be recruited by Tōa. I want you to understand that it was a special arrangement that got you appointed section chief."

"Aren't you basically telling me to quit the T-Trading Company? Did I slip up? Is there some reason why I should be leaving?"

"Nothing like that." Makiguchi hastened to wave his hand across his face in response to Komiya's impassioned voice. "You haven't done anything wrong. But I think you should talk to the Hasegawa couple. How shall I say it . . . a man of your capacity will do well no matter where you go. If you are going there anyway, I think that the higher echelons of our company would rather have you move right now and make Tōa feel indebted to us."

"Please don't make excuses. It's hard for me to resign until I'm convinced that the T-Trading Company doesn't want me. Do you understand my point? It's been less than two months since I got my new post."

"You don't have to raise your voice; I'm right here. Just finish your meal."

"I can't. How can I?" Komiya put down his silverware and took a long look at Makiguchi.

Knowing the Hasegawas' strong personalities, and particularly of Mrs. Hasegawa, Makiguchi had thought that they would be coming for Komiya posthaste. The realization that they hadn't done so nearly three months after Komiya's return started grating on him. If Komiya had no place to go, Makiguchi had to come up with a way to get rid of him. He may have miscalculated.

Makiguchi contracted a business newswriter and obtained a report on the inside affairs of Tōa. The report said that Tōa's bullish facility investment had backfired, and that the company was presently in a financial crisis. In panic, it had cut back production, but this alone was not enough to make up for the slow growth. The interest payment for the new sodium hydroxide production facility, which had been installed on misadvice from the government, magnified the crisis. Tōa's economy floundered so badly that its main banks were compelled to suggest a major layoff.

"I'm afraid I didn't find out anything beyond what everyone at the T-Trading Company already knows." The financial reporter hung up the telephone after this sarcastic remark.

Makiguchi was totally unprepared to learn about Tōa's disaster. He absentmindedly stared into space for a while. *So, this was why the Hasegawa couple didn't send for Komiya. Tōa must be in a poor way if it is laying people off.*

If the Chemical Products Headquarters was to get rid of the bad quality vinyl stock by the mid-September account-closing day, not much time was left. After some serious thinking, Makiguchi called in the head of the Synthetic Resins Division, Yoshioka.

"I think that Taiwanese factories will be buying up the chloride resins. The price is going to be less than half of what we paid, but it's better than nothing," said Yoshioka. "Komiya worked hard for this. Our actual loss will be around 600 million yen, but you know, we should consider ourselves lucky if we can make up for even a small portion of our loss. Since the overall synthetic resins trade is in the black, we really didn't have to send Kihara to New York in such a hurry, in a way." Yoshioka spoke unconcernedly as he picked his nose. His greasy and shiny face was well suntanned from playing golf, and he had about him the air of an active and able trading company man.

"But we can't let this slide. Somebody has to take responsibility for the loss sooner or later," Makiguchi answered.

"If you are thinking of Komiya, you can't send him to Tōa. They're having problems right now."

"Yes, apparently. But a group of people including our president have made an arrangement about Komiya. I'm stuck. Or, perhaps I can slip him in Yamada's slot. Yamada will be finishing up his three-year term in Tanzania soon."

"Oh brother! From 'gay Paris' to Tanzania is a big step down! I'm not sure I can put him through that."

"I'm with you, but what else can we do? Our excuse will be that we want to see whether Komiya will sink or swim."

"When can you send him out there?"

"On September first, I hope."

"You should at least wait until October first. That will give him just about four months in Tokyo."

"All the same, he'll wonder what this is all about. I wonder if he will connect this transfer to the chloride resin problem." Makiguchi felt a pang of conscience and grimaced.

"Of course he's going to wonder, but I doubt he'll figure it out. I hear he didn't even suspect the problem when he picked up the new assignment. It was Kihara who bought the chloride resins from R-Country. There's no changing that. But we can say that Komiya miscalculated the time for selling the stock. That way, it figures that I as his senior would receive an official reprimand," Yoshioka said.

"We've made poor Komiya pay to keep Kihara clean. But we did it because of Mrs. Hasegawa's offer."

"Ha, you're turning everything on Mrs. Hasegawa." Yoshioka lowered his voice and stuck out the tip of his tongue.

VII

Komiya interpreted the transfer order as Makiguchi's expression of annoyance about how he had behaved. Perhaps Makiguchi thought he was too uppity with the senior staff in general and particularly with Makiguchi. The best he could do now was to leave his wife and child in Tokyo and go to Tanzania by himself. At the same time, the possibility of leaving the company also piqued his curiosity. Really, he couldn't help being rankled by the way things were going. Why did the aspiring star of his age group have to be exiled to Africa after a mere four months' service in Tokyo? The worst was that people had begun to wonder. They suspected that Komiya had gotten into an unidentified scandal and was not allowed to stay in Tokyo. This transfer simply did not make sense.

Komiya visited President Hasegawa of Tōa one afternoon towards the end of September, shortly before his trip to Tanzania. The purpose was to say goodbye. He had made an appointment through a secretary, but when he walked in to the president's office, Mrs. Hasegawa was there.

"I hear that you are being sent to a very distant country. Did they find the skeletons in your closet?" Noriko wagged her slanderous tongue at Komiya, giving him quite a turn.

"Not at all. I'm all square. I can't figure this out myself, but as the saying goes, 'the life of a government official is not an enviable one.' There's nothing I can do about it."

"Paris is where you belong. You would look out of place in Tanzania. What if you went back to Paris?"

"Things aren't that simple."

"Your successor, what's his name . . . ?"

"You mean Orihara?"

"Yes, I suppose his name was Orihara. His French is good, but he's a little dense. If you want, I can push for your return."

"Come on, that's enough. You're ruining my reputation. How can I ask them to send Komiya back to Paris?" interjected President Hasegawa, pulling a cigar out of his mouth.

"I'll ask Okamoto." Noriko was not daunted.

"Thank you for your concern, but I've had enough of Paris. Tanzania is more interesting." Komiya put on a bold front, doing his best to appear satisfied. In the end, Mrs. Hasegawa made no mention of his moving to Tōa. Komiya couldn't lie to himself; he would have liked a job offer. He wasn't sure if he would have accepted it, but he wished that she had at least offered.

Had Noriko forgotten everything she had said in Paris? Or was she just keeping it to herself? Perhaps the labor union wouldn't let the president hire someone new when the company was about to practice a mass layoff.

After two months in Tanzania, Komiya received a letter from his colleague, Ohta. The letter explained in full about the vinyl chloride incident. It said that Ohta heard it from an old colleague who now worked in the Synthetic Resins Department. Komiya got cold shudders at this discovery, but there was nothing he could do.

◇

3.3 Ethnic School

◆

András Dezsery

Mihály had a big shock this morning. When he walked outside, right on top of his huge shelter, as he called it, hovered the steel arm of a multi-storey crane, its chain almost touching the rusty iron roof. It was moving very slowly, like a pendulum, in the windless hot air.

"There is no question about this," he thought timidly. "This crane will destroy my school and me. Today is the day they foreshadowed."

"What is going on?" he asked.

He knew the answer anyhow. Most of the small old cottages in the neighborhood were already demolished and the gardens changed into a huge hole. More and more workers, doing all sorts of jobs, dressed in shorts, their chests gleaming with sweat, all looking alike, wearing helmets.

To investigate further, Mihály moved out through the huge door into the narrow lane called Holland Place. The only sound was the monotonous noise from panelbeaters at the rear of a factory.

Mihály straightened his sign: Ethnic School. The second line read, Friday nights. By Appointment, in smaller letters.

"I will not be able to open the school tonight, any more. They warned me . . ." But, stubborn as I am, I wanted to stay," he murmured to himself, "for the sake of the school."

Source: András Dezsery, "Ethnic School," *Neighbors: Multicultural Writing of the 1980's,* edited by R. H. Holt, 1991, pp. 49–52. Reprinted by permission of András Dezsery.

The hard-wearing jarrah floor, stained by him to a glossy velvet-brown sheen, would have done any community hall proud. Sometimes he let some migrants use his ex-factory "hall" for wedding receptions.

On his lonely evenings he carved a few folkcraft imitations: shelves, bookends, and such.

Everywhere one looked there were mementos from the Old Country placed lovingly on any flat surface, high and low. There were vases, candleholders, prints of old masters, his military belt, hand-woven rugs, embroidered tablecloths, and many more small items.

Along one wall hung a large map of Europe. He had pasted it on to some cardboard for support. That was the teaching aid for his geography lessons. On the map he had neatly marked all important rivers, mountains, lakes and towns. Around the edges of this map he had pinned postcards from his land of birth.

Many of the pieces in his school had been donated by the parents of his pupils. Anyone entering could very well imagine being in a folk museum. Magazines, in his native language, were bound into volumes, with some bundles tied with ribbons showing his national colours instead of plain string.

And, towering above all, that dreadful crane.

Inside his domain the heat was stifling. There were no windows to open up, only air-vents – as was usual in old factories such as this.

His friend, a stonemason, frustrated with his work as a hospital orderly, had built him a beautiful flower container out of different stones found in South Australia. It was a piece of art, and the stonemason, true to his profession, had carved his name into the right-hand corner of his creation. Mihály had been well pleased with the work and had at once planted different ferns and climbers in it. He was glad that he had agreed to have the box built on a movable base, though he had never thought that he would shift. Now it looked very much like this would be the case.

Mihály had planted all the vegetables he needed; and, climbing above his vegetable patch, was a vine, heavy with grapes. In his imagination, he had long ago decided that it was the famous wine from Badacsony, the Barossa Valley back home. He had also planted all the favourite flowers of his youth – tulips, geraniums, violets and poppies.

Above the gate he had, with the help of one of his countrymen, erected a roof on four posts, typical of the country houses in Hungary, his homeland. The roof was designed and built by a former architect who, because he could not get his diploma recognized, had become a long-distance truckdriver. This man worked for selected friends on his days off to overcome his frustrations and unhappiness.

Then there was Orzsi, the stray cat with a pronounced limp on the left hind leg, caused no doubt by some accident. He had tamed her by talking to her quietly over quite a long period. The name of the cat was Hungarian, like most things around him.

Near the fence stood a small building, like a cubicle, which was actually his shower and toilet. The little building was almost totally hidden away beneath the ivory creeper and the shadow of the big fig tree. Somewhere behind or underneath, he really did not know, lived his sleepy lizard. He called him János.

Mihály, the ethnic, Orzsi the cat and János the lizard had formed themselves into a family of three, hidden away from outsiders, mostly not eager to make contacts with new people.

Picking up a millet broom, he swept once more outside the Holland Place entrance. The building was not in the right place to use as a school, he suddenly realized. Looking up at the blue sky he once again saw the crane. "I will lose my school anyhow," he sighed.

The Inspector is also late, Mihály thought. The letter from the Education Department had said 3 o'clock, and it was getting nearer to four. Just then the Inspector arrived, full of smiles. Mihály's jaw dropped in amazement, which obviously showed plainly on his face. The Inspector was a young woman, dressed in a sarong, black eyes sparkling and even, white teeth. What a lovely face, Mihály thought, stepping back in surprise, and what a figure. Embarrassed by his own reaction, he did not know what to do and finally uttered some form of greeting.

She tried to put him at his ease, "It was very difficult to find you," she smiled. "I parked my car in front of the Brecknock Hotel, in King William Street." Mihály's thoughts were racing like windmills in his head. She would have totally misunderstood my reaction, he worried, but before he could start to talk to her the children arrived.

The twins, Adam and Timothy, were first, followed closely by Piroska and her friend, Pavel, each carrying a single flower.

What more could a man really want? Mihály, changeable in his moods as in his jobs, was quite stubborn when it came to teaching – not at all the given thing for an educator; but Mihály never gave in to reality. Now the time is here, he thought, when I shall have to give in.

The two dangers were very clear in his mind. The bite of the crane and the outcome of the first inspection, set up for today.

The kids are late and no parents have arrived yet, thought Mihály, nervous and overreacting. They will not turn up because of the inspection. I should not have told them about it at all.

Slowly he started wiping the blackboard with a damp sponge, watching the cat washing itself, sprawled out on his favorite self-carved chair.

Mihály guided the children to their places with his eyes. Piroska and Pavel sat down next to Adam, Timothy sat on the other side of the aisle. The three cousins, Ali, Laci and Pisti, arrived with their parents, filling up the second row, sitting down on the small folding chairs.

Ms T., the Inspector, looked around the makeshift school and her heart sank. It was heartbreaking for her to see. One could feel the spirit behind it, self-made from volunteer help and goodwill.

But all this was as collapsible as the chairs and the card table which doubled as the teacher's desk.

Mihály knew that his performance was wanting. He had a disturbing feeling, realizing that his speech was not understood by the Inspector at all, and that the rest of the audience held trouble following him, too. He acted clumsily, not finding things lying right under his nose. Finally, in desperation, he started to play some music he had pre-recorded on a tape for part of his lessons. The children and all adults, with the exception of one of the fathers and Mihály, started forming a circle for the dance. Mihály had to stand by to switch the old, worn-out tape-recorder off, when the tattered tape got stuck. Ms T., who had placed herself on the edge of the circle, wanted to join in, but eventually just watched the group of small children and overdressed adults hopping around with cries of pleasure. They obviously enjoyed the fast dance, and she, to her amazement, found herself clapping her hands to the rhythm. Surprised, she realized that the small group consisted of different language groups.

On parting they shook hands. This personal touch sealed a successful visit. On the way out he handed her some flowers that he had cut earlier. She accepted them with a smile.

After her departure Mihály walked back into the school area of his place. Dejected, he played a tune on his *furulya*. He could not bring himself to go outside into the garden, with its well-known walls. He was not really thinking of any grant he might be able to get.

He knew that he had failed; but what about her? Ms T., an Indian lady, a newcomer like Mihály, who had come from Budapest, could not have missed the surprised look on his face when they met.

He did not shut the huge sliding doors, even though it was quite late. Foolishly, he kept hoping that someone would come but, deep inside, he knew that this was but a dream that would not come true. He knew that he had failed: not with his school, not with his method of teaching.

The crane dangled over his place, moving slowly – to and fro. Mihály finally shut the doors.

Like the sunshine making a bright spot in the middle of the shadows as it shines through the branches of a tree, he lay between the neighboring buildings, on his campbed, sleepless. He knew that he had failed.

Section 4: Re-Entry

◇

4.1 Home Sickness

◆

George Moore

He told the doctor he was due in the barroom at eight o'clock in the morning; the barroom was in a slum in the Bowery; and he had only been able to keep himself in health by getting up at five o'clock and going for long walks in the Central Park.

"A sea voyage is what you want," said the doctor. "Why not go to Ireland for two or three months? You will come back a new man."

"I'd like to see Ireland again."

And he began to wonder how the people at home were getting on. The doctor was right. He thanked him, and three weeks after he landed in Cork.

As he sat in the railway carriage he recalled his native village, built among the rocks of the large headland stretching out into the winding lake. He could see the houses and the streets, and the fields of the tenants, and the Georgian mansion and the owners of it; he and they had been boys together before he went to America. He remembered the villagers going every morning to the big house to work in the stables, in the garden, in the fields – mowing, reaping, digging, and Michael Malia building a wall; it was all as clear as if it were yesterday, yet he had been thirteen years in America; and when the train stopped at the station the first thing he did was to look round for any changes that might have come into it. It was the same blue limestone station as it was thirteen years ago, with

---

Source: George Moore, "Home Sickness," *Short Stories from the Irish Renaissance*, edited by Gonzalez, Whitstone, 1993, pp. 65–70.

the same five long miles between it and Duncannon. He had once walked these miles gaily, in little over an hour, carrying a heavy bundle on a stick, but he did not feel strong enough for the walk today, though the evening tempted him to try it. A car was waiting at the station, and the boy, discerning from his accent and his dress that Bryden had come from America, plied him with questions, which Bryden answered rapidly, for he wanted to hear who were still living in the village, and if there was a house in which he could get a clean lodging. The best house in the village, he was told, was Mike Scully's, who had been away in a situation for many years, as a coachman in the King's County, but had come back and built a fine house with a concrete floor. The boy could recommend the loft, he had slept in it himself, and Mike would be glad to take in a lodger, he had no doubt. Bryden remembered that Mike had been in a situation at the big house. He had intended to be a jockey, but had suddenly shot up into a fine tall man, and had become a coachman instead; and Bryden tried to recall his face, but could only remember a straight nose and a somewhat dusky complexion.

So Mike had come back from King's County, and had built himself a house, had married – there were children for sure running about; while he, Bryden, had gone to America, but he had come back; perhaps he, too, would build a house in Duncannon, and – his reverie was suddenly interrupted by the carman.

"There's Mike Scully," he said, pointing with his whip, and Bryden saw a tall, finely built, middle-aged man coming through the gates, who looked astonished when he was accosted, for he had forgotten Bryden even more completely than Bryden had forgotten him; and many aunts and uncles were mentioned before he began to understand.

"You've grown into a fine man, James," he said, looking at Bryden's great width of chest. "But you're thin in the cheeks, and you're very sallow in the cheeks, too."

"I haven't been very well lately – that is one of the reasons I've come back; but I want to see you all again."

"And thousand welcome you are."

Bryden paid the carman, and wished him Godspeed. They divided the luggage, Mike carrying the bag and Bryden the bundle, and they walked round the lake, for the townland was at the back of the domain; and while walking he remembered the woods thick and well forested; now they were wind worn, the drains were choked, and the bridge leading across the lake inlet was falling away. Their way led between long fields where herds of cattle were grazing, the road was broken – Bryden wondered how the villagers drove their carts over it, and Mike told him that the landlord could not keep it in repair, and he would not allow it to be kept in repair out of the rates, for then it would be a public road, and he did not think there should be a public road through his property.

At the end of many fields they came to the village, and it looked a desolate place, even on this fine evening, and Bryden remarked that the country did not seem to be as much lived in as it used to be. It was at once strange and familiar to see the chickens in the kitchen; and, wishing to reknit himself to the old customs, he begged of Mrs. Scully not to drive them out, saying they reminded him of old times.

"And why wouldn't they?" Mike answered, "he being one of ourselves bred and born in Duncannon, and his father before him."

"Now, is it truth ye are telling me?" and she gave him her hand, after wiping it on her apron, saying he was heartily welcome, only she was afraid he wouldn't care to sleep in a loft.

"Why wouldn't I sleep in a loft, a dry loft! You're thinking a good deal of America over here," he said, "but I reckon it isn't all you think it. Here you work when you like and you sit down when you like; but when you've had a touch of bloodpoisoning as I had, and when you have seen young people walking with a stick, you think that there is something to be said for old Ireland."

"You'll take a sup of milk, won't you? You must be dry," said Mrs. Scully.

And when he had drunk the milk Mike asked him if he would like to go inside or if he would like to go for a walk.

"Maybe resting you'd like to be."

And they went into the cabin and started to talk about the wages a man could get in America, and the long hours of work.

And after Bryden had told Mike everything about America that he thought of interest, he asked Mike about Ireland. But Mike did not seem to be able to tell him much. They were all very poor – poorer, perhaps, than when he left them.

"I don't think anyone except myself has a five-pound note to his name."

Bryden hoped he felt sufficiently sorry for Mike. But after all Mike's life and prospects mattered little to him. He had come back in search of health, and he felt better already; the milk had done him good, and the bacon and the cabbage in the pot sent forth a savory odor. The Scullys were very kind, they pressed him to make a good meal; a few weeks of country air and food, they said, would give him back the health he had lost in the Bowery; and when Bryden said he was longing for a smoke, Mike said there was no better sign than that. During his long illness he had never wanted to smoke, and he was a confirmed smoker.

It was comfortable to sit by the mild peat fire watching the smoke of their pipes drifting up the chimney, and all Bryden wanted was to be left alone; he did not want to hear anyone's misfortunes, but about nine o'clock a number of villagers came in, and Bryden remembered one or two of them – he used to know them very well when he was a boy; their talk was as depressing as their appearance, and he could feel no interest whatever in them. He was not moved when he heard that Higgins the stonemason was dead; he was not affected when he heard that Mary Kelly, who used to go to do the laundry at the Big House, had married; he was only interested when he heard she had gone to America. No, he had not met her there; America is a big place. Then one of the peasants asked him if he remembered Patsy Carabine, who used to do the gardening at the Big House. Yes, he remembered Patsy well. He had not been able to do any work on account of his arm; his house had fallen in; he had given up his holding and gone into the poorhouse. All this was very sad, and to avoid hearing any further unpleasantness, Bryden began to tell them about America. And they sat round listening to him; but all the talking was on his side; he wearied of it; and looking round the group he recognized a ragged hunchback with grey hair; twenty years ago he was a young hunchback and, turning to him, Bryden asked him if he were doing well with his five acres.

"Ah, not much. This has been a poor season. The potatoes failed; they were watery – there is no diet in them."

These peasants were all agreed that they could make nothing out of their farms. Their regret was that they had not gone to America when they were young; and after striving to take an interest in the fact that O'Connor had lost a mare and a foal worth forty pounds, Bryden began to wish himself back in the slum. And when they left the house he wondered if every evening would be like the present one. Mike piled fresh sods on the fire, and he hoped it would show enough light in the loft for Bryden to undress himself by.

The cackling of some geese in the street kept him awake, and he seemed to realize suddenly how lonely the country was, and he foresaw mile after mile of scanty fields stretching all round the lake with one little town in the far corner. A dog howled in the distance, and the fields and the boreens between him and the dog appeared as in a crystal. He could hear Michael breathing by his wife's side in the kitchen, and he could barely resist the impulse to run out of the house, and he might have yielded to it, but he wasn't sure that he mightn't awaken Mike as he came down the ladder. His terror increased, and he drew the blanket over his head. He fell asleep and awoke and fell asleep again, and lying on his back he dreamed of the men he had seen sitting round the fireside that evening, like specters they seemed to him in his dream. He seemed to have been asleep only a few minutes when he heard Mike calling him. He had come halfway up the ladder, and was telling him that breakfast was ready.

"What kind of a breakfast will he give me?" Bryden asked himself as he pulled on his clothes. There were tea and hot griddle cakes for breakfast, and there were fresh eggs; there was sunlight in the kitchen, and he liked to hear Mike tell of the work he was going to be at in the farm – one of about fifteen acres, at least ten of it was grass; he grew an acre of potatoes, and some corn, and some turnips for his sheep. He had a nice bit of meadow, and he took down his scythe, and as he put the whetstone in his belt Bryden noticed a second scythe, and he asked Mike if he should go down with him and help him to finish the field.

"It's a long time since you've done any mowing, and it's heavier work than you think for. You'd better go for a walk by the lake." Seeing that Bryden looked a little disappointed he added, "if you like you can come up in the afternoon and help me to turn the grass over." Bryden said he would, and the morning passed pleasantly by the lakeshore – a delicious breeze rested in the trees, and the reeds were talking together, and the ducks were talking in the reeds; a cloud blotted out the sunlight, and the cloud passed and the sun shone, and the reed cast its shadow again in the still water; there was a lapping always about the shingle; the magic of returning health was sufficient distraction for the convalescent; he lay with his eyes fixed upon the castles, dreaming of the men that had manned the battlements; whenever a peasant driving a cart or an ass or an old woman with a bundle of sticks on her back went by, Bryden kept them in chat, and he soon knew the village by heart. One day the landlord from the Georgian mansion set on the pleasant green hill came along, his retriever at his heels, and stopped surprised at finding somebody whom he didn't know on his property. "What, James Bryden!" he said. And the story was told again how ill health had overtaken him at last, and he had come home to Duncannon to recover. The two walked as far as the pinewood, talking of the county, what it had been, the ruin it was slipping into, and as they parted Bryden asked for the loan of a boat.

"Of course, of course!" the landlord answered, and Bryden rowed about the islands every morning; and resting upon his oars looked at the old castles, remembering the prehistoric raiders that the landlord had told him about. He came across the stones to which the lake dwellers had tied their boats, and these signs of ancient Ireland were pleasing to Bryden in his present mood.

As well as the great lake there was a smaller lake in the bog where the villagers cut their turf. This lake was famous for its pike, and the landlord allowed Bryden to fish there, and one evening when he was looking for a frog with which to bait his line he met Margaret Dirken driving home the cows for the milking. Margaret was the herdsman's daughter, and lived in a cottage near the Big House; but she came up to the village whenever there was a dance, and Bryden had found himself opposite to her in the reels. But until this evening he had had little opportunity of speaking to her, and he was glad to speak to someone, for the evening was lonely, and they stood talking together.

"You're getting your health again," she said, "and will be leaving us soon."

"I'm in no hurry."

"You're grand people over there; I hear a man is paid four dollars a day for his work."

"And how much," said James, "has he to pay for his food and for his clothes?"

Her cheeks were bright and her teeth small, white, and beautifully even; and a woman's soul looked at Bryden out of her soft Irish eyes. He was troubled and turned aside, and catching sight of a frog looking at him out of a tuft of grass, he said:

"I have been looking for a frog to put upon my pike line."

The frog jumped right and left, and nearly escaped in some bushes, but he caught it and returned with it in his hand.

"It is just the kind of frog a pike will like," he said. "Look at its great white belly and its bright yellow back."

And without more ado he pushed the wire to which the hook was fastened through the frog's fresh body, and dragging it through the mouth he passed the hooks through the hind legs and tied the line to the end of the wire.

"I think," said Margaret, "I must be looking after my cows; it's time I got them home."

"Won't you come down to the lake while I set my line?"

She thought for a moment and said:

"No, I'll see you from here."

He went down to the reedy tarn, and at his approach several snipe got up, and they flew above his head uttering sharp cries. His fishing rod was a long hazel stick, and he threw the frog as far as he could in the lake. In doing this he roused some wild ducks; a mallard and two ducks got up, and they flew towards the larger lake in a line with an old castle; and they had not disappeared from view when Bryden came towards her, and he and she drove the cows home together that evening.

They had not met very often when she said: "James, you had better not come here so often calling to me."

"Don't you wish me to come?"

"Yes, I wish you to come well enough, but keeping company isn't the custom of the country, and I don't want to be talked about."

"Are you afraid the priest would speak against us from the altar?"

"He has spoken against keeping company, but it is not so much what the priest says, for there is no harm in talking."

"But if you're going to be married there is no harm in walking out together."

"Well, not so much, but marriages are made differently in these parts; there isn't much courting here."

And next day it was known in the village that James was going to marry Margaret Dirken.

His desire to excel the boys in dancing had caused a stir of gaiety in the parish, and for some time past there had been dancing in every house where there was a floor fit to dance upon; and if the cottager had no money to pay for a barrel of beer, James Bryden, who had money, sent him a barrel, so that Margaret might get her dance. She told him that they sometimes crossed over into another

parish where the priest was not so averse to dancing, and James
wondered. And next morning at Mass he wondered at their simple
fervor. Some of them held their hands above their head as they
prayed, and all this was very new and very old to James Bryden.
But the obedience of these people to their priest surprised him.
When he was a lad they had not been so obedient, or he had
forgotten their obedience; and he listened in mixed anger and won-
derment to the priest, who was scolding his parishioners, speaking
to them by name, saying that he had heard there was dancing going
on in their homes. Worse than that, he said he had seen boys and
girls loitering about the road, and the talk that went on was of one
kind – love. He said that newspapers containing love stories were
finding their way into the people's houses, stories about love, in
which there was nothing elevating or ennobling. The people listened, accepting the priest's opinion without question. And their
pathetic submission was the submission of a primitive people clinging to religious authority, and Bryden contrasted the weakness and
incompetence of the people about him with the modern restlessness
and cold energy of the people he left behind him.

One evening, as they were dancing, a knock came to the door,
and the piper stopped playing, and the dancers whispered:

"Someone has told on us; it is the priest."

And the awestricken villagers crowded round the cottage fire,
afraid to open the door. But the priest said that if they didn't open
the door he would put his shoulder to it and force it open. Bryden
went towards the door, saying he would allow no one to threaten
him, priest or no priest, but Margaret caught his arm and told him
that if he said anything to the priest, the priest would speak against
them from the altar, and they would be shunned by the neighbors.

"I've heard of your goings-on," he said – "of your beer drinking
and dancing. I'll not have it in my parish. If you want that sort of
thing you had better go to America."

"If that is intended for me, sir, I'll go back tomorrow. Margaret
can follow."

"It isn't the dancing, it's the drinking I'm opposed to," said the
priest, turning to Bryden.

"Well, no one has drunk too much, sir," said Bryden.

"But you'll sit here drinking all night," and the priest's eyes went
to the corner where the women had gathered, and Bryden felt that

the priest looked on the women as more dangerous than the porter. "It's after midnight," he said, taking out his watch.

By Bryden's watch it was only half past eleven, and while they were arguing about the time, Mrs. Scully offered Bryden's umbrella to the priest, for in his hurry to stop the dancing the priest had gone out without his; and, as if to show Bryden that he bore him no ill will, the priest accepted the loan of the umbrella, for he was thinking of the big marriage fee that Bryden would pay him.

"I shall be badly off for the umbrella tomorrow," Bryden said, as soon as the priest was out of the house. He was going with his father-in-law to the fair. His father-in-law was learning him how to buy and sell cattle. The country was mending, and a man might become rich in Ireland if he only had a little capital. Margaret had an uncle on the other side of the lake who would give twenty pounds, and her father would give another twenty pounds. Bryden had saved two hundred pounds. Never in the village of Duncannon had a young couple begun life with so much prospect of success, and some time after Christmas was spoken of as the best time for the marriage; James Bryden said that he would not be able to get his money out of America before the spring. The delay seemed to vex him, and he seemed anxious to be married, until one day he received a letter from America, from a man who had served in the bar with him. This friend wrote to ask Bryden if he were coming back. The letter was no more than a passing wish to see Bryden again. Yet Bryden stood looking at it, and everyone wondered what could be in the letter. It seemed momentous, and they hardly believed him when he said it was from a friend who wanted to know if his health were better. He tried to forget the letter, and he looked at the worn fields, divided by walls of loose stones, and a great longing came upon him.

The smell of the Bowery slum had come across the Atlantic, and had found him out in his western headland; and one night he awoke from a dream in which he was hurling some drunken customer through the open doors into the darkness. He had seen his friend in his white duck jacket throwing drink from glass to glass amid the din of voices and strange accents; he had heard the clang of money as it was swept into the till, and his sense sickened for the barroom. But how should he tell Margaret Dirken that he could not marry her? She had built her life upon this marriage. He could not tell her that he would not marry her . . . yet he must go. He felt as if he were being hunted; the thought that he must tell Margaret that he could not marry her hunted him day after day as a weasel hunts a rabbit. Again and again he went to meet her with the intention of telling her that he did not love her, that their lives were not for one another, that it had all been a mistake soon enough. But Margaret, as if she guessed what he was about to speak of, threw her arms about him and begged him to say he loved her, and that they would be married at once. He agreed that he loved her, and that they would be married at once. But he had not left her many minutes before the feeling came upon him that he could not marry her – that he must go away. The smell of the barroom hunted him down. Was it for the sake of the money that he might make there that he wished to go back? No, it was not the money. What then? His eyes fell on the bleak country, on the little fields divided by bleak walls; he remembered the pathetic ignorance of the people, and it was these things that he could not endure. It was the priest who came to forbid the dancing. Yes, it was the priest. As he stood looking at the line of the hills the barroom seemed by him. He heard the politicians, and the excitement of politics was in his blood again. He must go away from this place – he must get back to the barroom. Looking up, he saw the scanty orchard, and he hated the spare road that led to the village, and he hated the little hill at the top of which the village began, and he hated more than all other places the house where he was to live with Margaret Dirken – if he married her. He could see it from where he stood – by the edge of the lake, with twenty acres of pasture land about it, for the landlord had given up part of his demesne land to them.

He caught sight of Margaret, and he called her to come through the stile.

"I have just had a letter from America."

"About the money?"

"Yes, about the money. But I shall have to go over there."

He stood looking at her, wondering what to say; and she guessed that he would tell her that he must go to America before they were married.

"Do you mean, James, you will have to go at once?"

"Yes," he said, "at once. But I shall come back in time to be married in August. It will only mean delaying our marriage a month."

They walked on a little way talking, and every step he took James felt that he was a step nearer the Bowery slum. And when they came to the gate Bryden said:

"I must walk on or I shall miss the train."

"But," she said, "you are not going now – you are not going today?"

"Yes," he said, "I am coming back."

"If you are coming back, James, why don't you let met go with you?"

"You couldn't walk fast enough. We should miss the train."

"One moment, James. Don't make me suffer; tell me the truth. You are not coming back. Your clothes – where shall I send them?"

He hurried away, hoping he would come back. He tried to think that he liked the country he was leaving, that it would be better to have a farmhouse and live there with Margaret Dirken than to serve drinks behind a counter in the Bowery. He did not think he was telling her a lie when he said he was coming back. Her offer to forward his clothes touched his heart, and at the end of the road he stood and asked himself if he should go back to her. He would miss the train if he waited another minute, and he ran on. And he would have missed the train if he had not met a car. Once he was on the car he felt himself safe – the country was already behind him. The train and the boat at Cork were mere formulae; he was already in America.

And when the tall skyscraper stuck up beyond the harbor he felt the thrill of home that he had not found in his native village and wondered how it was that the smell of the bar seemed more natural than the smell of fields, and the roar of crowds more welcome than the silence of the lake's edge. He entered into negotiations for the purchase of the barroom. He took a wife, she bore him sons and daughters, the barroom prospered, property came and went; he grew old, his wife died, he retired from business, and reached the age when a man begins to feel there are not many years in front of him, and that all he has had to do in life has been done. His children married, lonesomeness began to creep about him in the evening, and when he looked into the firelight, a vague tender reverie floated up, and Margaret's soft eyes and name vivified the dusk. His wife and children passed out of mind, and it seemed to him that a memory was the only real thing he possessed, and the desire to see Margaret again grew intense. But she was an old woman, she had married, maybe she was dead. Well, he would like to be buried in the village where he was born.

There is an unchanging, silent life within every man that none knows but himself, and his unchanging silent life was his memory of Margaret Dirken. The barroom was forgotten and all that concerned it, and the things he saw most clearly were the green hillside, and the bog lake and the rushes about it, and the greater lake in the distance, and behind it the blue line of wandering hills.

◇

4.2 Yard Sale

◆

Paul Theroux

As things turned out, Floyd had no choice but to spend the summer with me in East Sandwich. To return home to find his parents divorced was awkward; but to learn that they had already held their yard sale was distinctly shaming. I had been there and seen my sister's ghastly jollity as she disposed of her old Hoover and shower curtains and the chair she had abandoned caning; Floyd senior, with a kind of hostile generosity, turned the whole affair into a potlatch ceremony by bestowing his power tools on his next-door neighbor and clowning among his junk with the word "free-bie." "Aunt Freddy can have my life jacket," he crowed. "I'm not your aunt," I said, but I thanked him for it and sent it via the local church to Bangladesh, where I hoped it would arrive before the monsoon hit Chittagong. After the yard sale, they made themselves scarce – Floyd senior to his Boston apartment and his flight attendant, my sister to the verge of a nervous breakdown in Cuttyhunk. I was glad to be deputized to look after little Floyd, and I knew how relieved he would be, after two years in the Peace Corps in Western Samoa, to have some home cooking and the sympathetic ear of his favorite aunt. He, too, would be burdened and looking for buyers.

At Hyannis Airport, I expected a waif, an orphan of sorts, with a battered suitcase and a heavy heart. But Floyd was all smiles as

Source: Paul Theroux, "Yard Sale," *World's End and Other Stories,* Paul Theroux, 1979, pp. 39–49. Copyright © 1979 by Paul Theroux, used with permission of Wylie, Aitken & Stone, Inc.

he peered out of the fuselage, and when the steps were lowered and he was on them, the little plane actually rocked to and fro: Floyd had gained seventy-five pounds. A Henry Moore moppet of raw certainty, he was dark, with hair like varnished kapok and teeth gleaming like Chiclets. He wore an enormous shirt printed with bloated poppies, and the skirtlike sarong that Margaret Mead tells us is called a *lava-lava*. On his feet were single-thong flip-flops, which, when he kicked them off – as he did in the car, to sit cross-legged on the bucket seat – showed his toes to be growing in separate directions.

"Wuppertal," he said, or words to that effect. There was about him a powerful aroma of coconut oil and a rankness of dead leaves and old blossoms.

"Greetings," I said.

"That's what I just said."

"And welcome home."

"It doesn't seem like home anymore."

We passed the colonial-style (rough-hewn logs, split-rail fence, mullion windows) Puritan Funeral Home, Kopper Krafts, the pizza joints, and it occurred to me that this part of Route 132 had changed out of all recognition. I thought: Poor kid.

The foreknowledge that I would be led disloyally into loose talk about his father's flight attendant kept me silent about his parents' divorce. I asked him about Samoa; I was sure he was aching to be quizzed. This brought from him a snore of approval and a native word. I mentioned his sandals.

He said, "My mother never wears sandals. She's always barefoot!"

I determined upon delicacy. "It's been a hard year."

"She says the craziest things sometimes."

"Nerves."

Here was the Hyannis Drive-In Movie. I was going to point out to him that while he had been away, they had started holding drive-in church services on Sunday mornings – an odd contrast to Burt Reynolds in the evenings, the sacred and profane in the same amphitheater. But Floyd was talking about his father.

"He's amazing, and what a sailor! I've known him to go out in a force-nine gale. He's completely reckless."

Aren't the young downright? I thought. I did not say anything about the life jacket his old man had given me; I was sure he had done it out of malice, knowing full well that what I really coveted was the dry pinewood sink lost in the potlatch.

"Floyd," I said, with a shrill note of urgency in my voice – I was frantic to drag him off the topic I knew would lead him to his parents' fractured marriage – "what about Samoa?"

"Sah-moa," he said, moving his mouth like a chorister as he corrected my pronunciation. So we have an emphatic stammer on the first syllable, do we? I can take any amount of well-intentioned pedantry, but I draw the line at condescension from someone I have laboriously diapered. It was so difficult for me to mimic this unsayable word that I countered with "And yet, I wonder how many of them would get Haverhill right?"

Floyd did not move from his Buddah posture. "Actually, he's wicked right-wing, and very moralistic about things. I mean, deep down. He hates change of any kind."

"You're speaking of – ?"

"My father."

Your psychiatrists say grief is a great occasion for rationalizing. Still, the Floyd senior I knew was indiscernible through this coat of whitewash. He was the fiery engine of change. Though my sentence was fully framed, I didn't say to his distracted son, That is a side of your father I have not been privileged to observe.

"Mother's different."

"How so?"

"Confident. Full of beans. Lots of savvy."

And beside herself in Cuttyhunk. Perhaps we do invent the friends and even the parents we require and yet I was not quite prepared for what Floyd said next.

"My sister's pretty incredible, too. I've always thought of myself as kind of athletic, but she can climb trees twice as fast as me."

This was desperate: he had no sister. Floyd was an only child. I had an overwhelming desire to slap his face, as the hero does in B movies to bring the flannel-mouthed fool to his senses.

But he had become effusive. "My sister . . . my brother . . . my grandmother" – inventing a fictitious family to make up for the one that had collapsed in his absence.

I said, "Floyd dear, you're going to think your old auntie is horribly literal-minded, but I don't recognize your family from anything you've said. Oh, sure, I suppose your father *is* conservative – the roué is so often a puritan underneath it all. And vice versa.

Joseph Smith? The Mormon prophet? What was it, fifty wives? 'When I see a pretty girl, I have to pray,' he said. His prayers were answered! But listen, your mother's had a dreadful time. And, um, you don't actually have any brothers or sisters. Relax. I know we're under a little strain, and absolutely bursting with Samoa, but – "

"In Samoa," he said, mocking me with the half sneeze of its correct pronunciation, "it's the custom to join a local family. You live with them. You're one of them."

"Much as one would join the Elks around here?"

"It's wicked complicated."

"More Masonic – is that it?"

"More Samoan. You get absorbed kind of. They prefer it that way. And they're very easygoing. I mean there's no word for bastard in Samoan."

"With so little traffic on the roads, there's probably no need for it. Sorry. I see your point. But isn't that taking the extended family a bit far? What about your parents?"

"He thatches roofs and she keeps chickens."

"Edith and Floyd senior?"

"Oh, them" was all he said.

"But you've come home!"

"I don't know. Maybe I just want to find my feet."

Was it his turn of phrase? I dropped my eyes and saw a spider clinging to his ankle. I said, "Floyd, don't move – there's a creature on your foot."

He pinched it lovingly. "It's only a tattoo."

That seemed worse than a live spider, which had the merit of being able to dance away. I told him this, adding, "Am I being fastidious?"

"No, ethnocentric," he said. "My mother has a mango on her knee."

"Not a banjo?" When I saw him wince, I said, "Forgive me Floyd. Do go on – I want to hear everything."

"There's too much to tell."

"I know the feeling."

"I wouldn't mind a hamburger," he said suddenly. "I'm starving."

Instead of telling him I had a cassoulet waiting for him in East Sandwich, I slowed down. It is the fat, not the thin, who are always famished; and he had not had a hamburger in two years. But the

sight of fast food woke a memory in him. As he watched the disc
of meat slide down a chute to be bunned, gift-wrapped, and clamped
into a small Styrofoam valise, he treated me to a meticulous description of the method of cooking in Samoa. First, stones were heated,
he said, then the hot stones buried in a hole. The uncooked food
was wrapped in leaves and placed on the stones. More hot stones
were piled on top. Before he got to the part where the food, stones,
and leaves were disinterred, I said, "I understand that's called labor
intensive, but it doesn't sound terribly effective."

He gave me an odd look and excused himself, taking his little
valise of salad to the drinking fountain to wash it.

"We always wash our food before we eat."

I said, "Raccoons do that!"

It was meant as encouragement, but I could see I was not doing
at all well.

Back at the house, Floyd took a present out of his bag. You sat
on it, this fiber mat. "One of your miracle fibers?" I said. "Tell me
more!" But he fell silent. He demurred when I mentioned tennis,
and at my suggestion of an afternoon of recreational shopping he
grunted. He said, "We normally sleep in the afternoon." Again I
was a bit startled by the plural pronoun and glanced around, half
expecting to see another dusky islander. But no – Floyd's was the
brotherly folk "we" of the native, affirming the cultural freemasonry
of all Polynesia. And it had clearly got into his bones. He had
acquired an almost catlike capacity for slumber. He lay for hours
in the lawn hammock, swinging like a side of beef, and at sundown
entered the house yawning and complaining of the cold. It was my
turn to laugh: the thermometer on the deck showed eighty-one
degrees.

"I'll bet you wish you were at Trader Vic's," I said over the
cassoulet, trying to avert my ethnocentric gaze as Floyd nibbled the
beans he seized with his fingers. He turned my Provençal cuisine
into a sort of astronaut's pellet meal.

He belched hugely, and guessing that this was a ritual rumble of
Samoan gratitude, I thanked him.

"Ironic, isn't it?" I said. "You seem to have managed marvelously
out there in the Pacific, taking life pretty much as you found it.
And I can't help thinking of Robert Louis Stevenson, who went to
Samoa with his sofas, his tartans, his ottoman, and every bagpipe
and ormolu clock from Edinburgh in his luggage."

"How do you know that?" he asked.

"Vassar," I said. "There wasn't any need for Stevenson to join a Samoan family. Besides his wife and his stepson, there were his stepdaughter and her husband. His wife was a divorcée, but she was from California, which explains everything. Oh, he brought his aged mother out, too. She never stopped starching her bonnets, so they say."

"Tusitala," said Floyd.

"Come again?"

"That was his title. 'Teller of tales.' He read his stories to the Samoans."

"I'd love to know what they made of 'Weir of Hermiston.'" It was clear from Floyd's expression that he had never heard of the novel.

He said gamely, "I didn't finish it."

"That's not surprising – neither did Stevenson. Do much reading, Floyd?"

"Not a lot. We don't have electricity, and reading by candlelight is really tough."

" 'Hermiston' was written by candlelight. In Samoa, it would be an act of the greatest homage to the author to read it that way."

"I figured it was pointless to read about Samoa if you live there."

"All the more reason to read it, since it's set in eighteenth-century Scotland."

"And he was a *palagi*."

"Don't be obscure, Floyd."

"A white man."

Only in the sense that Pushkin was an octoroon and Othello a soul brother, I thought, but I resisted challenging Floyd. Indeed, his saturation in the culture had made him indifferent to the bizarre. I discovered this when I drew him out. What was the food like after it was shoveled from beneath the hot stones? On Floyd's report it was uninspired: roots, leaves, and meat, sweated together in this subterranean sauna. What kind of meat? Oh, all kinds; and with the greatest casualness he let it drop that just a week before, he had eaten a flying fox.

"On the wing?" I asked.

"They're actually bats," he said. "But they call them – "

"Do you mean to tell me that you have eaten a bat?"

"You act as if it's an endangered species," he said.

"I should think that Samoans are if that's part of their diet."

"They're not bad. But they cook them whole, so they always have a strange expression on their faces when they're served."

"Doesn't surprise me a bit. Turn up their noses, do they?"

"Sort of. You can see all their teeth. I mean, the bats'."

"What a stitch!"

He smiled. "You think that's interesting?"

"Floyd, it's matchless."

Encouraged, he said, "Get this – we use fish as fertilizer. Fish!"

"That's predictable enough," I said, unimpressed. "Not far from where you are now, simple folk put fresh fish on their vegetable gardens as fertilizer. Misguided? Maybe. Wasteful? Who knows? Such was the nature of subsistence farming on the Cape three hundred years ago. One thing, though – they knew how to preach a sermon. Your agriculturalist is so often a God-fearing man."

This cued Floyd into an excursion on Samoan Christianity, which sounded to me thoroughly homespun and basic, full of good-natured hypocrisy that took the place of tolerance.

I said, "That would make them – what? Unitarians?"

Floyd belched again. I thanked him. He wiped his fingers on his shirtfront and said it was time for bed. He was not used to electric light: the glare was making him belch. "Besides, we always go to bed at nine."

The hammering some minutes later was Floyd rigging up the hammock in the spare room, where there was a perfectly serviceable double bed.

"We never do," I called.

Floyd looked so dejected at breakfast, toying with his scrambled egg and sausage, that I asked him if it had gone cold. He shrugged. Everything was hunky-dory, he said in Samoan, and then translated it.

"What do you normally have for breakfast?"

"Taro."

"Is it frightfully good for you?"

"It's a root," he said.

"Imagine finding your roots in Samoa!" Seeing him darken, I added, "Carry on, Floyd. I find it all fascinating. You're my window on the world."

But Floyd shut his mouth and lapsed into silence. Later in the morning, seeing him sitting cross-legged in the parlor, I was put in mind of one of those big lugubrious animals that look so homesick behind the bars of American zoos. I knew I had to get him out of the house.

It was a mistake to take him to the supermarket, but this is hindsight; I had no way of anticipating his new fear of traffic, his horror of crowds, or the chilblains he claimed he got from air conditioning. The acres of packaged foods depressed him, and his reaction to the fresh-fruit department was extraordinary.

"One fifty-nine!" he jeered. "In Samoa, you can get a dozen bananas for a penny. And look at that," he said, handling a whiskery coconut. "They want a buck for it!"

"They're not exactly in season here on the Cape, Floyd."

"I wouldn't pay a dollar for one of those."

"I had no intention of doing so."

"They're dangerous, coconuts," he mused. "They drop on your head. People have been known to be killed by them."

"Not in Barnstable County," I said, which was a pity, because I felt like aiming one at his head and calling it an act of God.

He hunched over a pyramid of oranges, examining them with distaste and saying that you could buy the whole lot for a quarter in a village market he knew somewhere in remote Savai'i. A tray of mangoes, each fruit the rich color of old meerschaum, had Floyd gasping with contempt: the label stuck to their skins said they were two dollars apiece, and he had never paid more than a nickel for one.

"These cost two cents," he said, bruising a grapefruit with his thumb, "and they literally give these away," he went on, flinging a pineapple back onto its pile. But his disbelief was nothing compared to the disbelief of shoppers, who gawped at his *lava-lava*. Yet his indignation at the prices won these people over, and amid the crashing of carts I heard the odd shout of "Right on!"

Eventually I hauled him away, and past the canned lychees ("They grow on trees in China, Floyd!") I became competitive. "What about split peas?" I said, leading him down the aisles. "Scallops? Indian pudding? Dreft? Clorox? What do you pay for dog biscuits? Look, be reasonable. What you gain on mangoes, you lose on maple syrup!"

We left empty-handed. Driving back, I noticed that Floyd became even gloomier. Perhaps he realized that it was going to be a long summer. I certainly did.

"Anything wrong, Floyd?"

He groaned. He put his head in his hands. "Aunt Freddy, I think I've got culture shock."

"Isn't that something you get at the other end? I mean, when the phones don't work in Nigeria or you find ants in the marmalade or the grass hut leaks?"

"Our huts never leak."

"Of course not," I said. "And look, this is only a *palagi* talking, but I have the unmistakable feeling that you would be much happier among your own family, Floyd."

We both knew which family. Mercifully, he was gone the next day, leaving nothing behind but the faint aroma of coconut oil in the hammock. He never asked where I got the price of the Hyannis-Apia airfare. He accepted it with a sort of extortionate Third World-er's wink, saying, "That's very Samoan of you, Aunt Freddy." But I'll get it back. Fortunately, there are ways of raising money at short notice around here.

Section 5: Managerial Insights

◇

5.1 Do Cultural Differences Make a Business Difference?

◆

Rosabeth Moss Kanter
Richard Ian Corn

In search of cultural differences

As economies globalize and organizations increasingly form cross-border relationships, there is a resurgence of interest in the management problems caused by national cultural differences – in values, ideologies, organizational assumptions, work practices, and behavioral styles – spawning research reminiscent of national character studies following the Second World War.

Such findings are often consistent with stereotypes evoked by managers to explain others and themselves. Cultural generalizations roll easily off the tongues of people in our studies. For example: several Europeans predicted problems Volvo and Renault could have in combining Volvo's Swedish egalitarianism with Renault's French hierarchy. A German executive working in a French-American alliance commented that Germans and Americans had more

Source: Rosabeth Moss Kanter and Richard Ian Corn, "Do Cultural Differences Make a Business Difference?," excerpted from *Journal of Management Development*, 1994, pp. 5–23, Vol. 13. Reprinted by permission of Rosabeth Moss Kanter.

values in common than either did with the French, invoking this as an explanation for why an American sent to London to lead the integration team was viewed as incompetent by the French partner for failing to make authoritative decisions [1].

Furthermore, people often assume cultural heterogeneity creates tensions for organizations. Managers, even within a single country, often prefer homogeneity to heterogeneity, because shared experiences and culture are a basis for trust [1].

Yet, while national cultural differences clearly exist at some level of generality, it is more difficult to specify how the presence of such differences affects organizational and managerial effectiveness.

The foreign acquisitions study

To learn more about managerial issues provoked by cultural differences, we looked for situations in which cross-cultural interactions might produce organizational tensions.

We looked for a test in the realm of foreign acquisitions, in which cultural differences would perhaps play a greater role. Foreign acquisitions of US companies increased over the last decade. In 1990, 446 such deals, valued at $46.2 billion, were completed, compared with only 126 deals valued at $4.6 billion in 1982. Foreign acquisitions of US companies accounted for 28.1 per cent of the total value of merger and acquisition activity involving at least one company in 1990, compared with only 7.6 per cent in 1982 [2]. This acquisition situation, we proposed, would heighten American managers' awareness of their own culture and its contrast to the acquirer's culture, as they merged operations or shifted control over decisions. Since American companies were more accustomed to acquiring foreign operations than being acquired, the "reversal of roles" experienced when being acquired would perhaps exaggerate tensions enough to bring cultural issues to the surface. Therefore, we developed a pilot project with eight companies.

The companies

Approximately 75 interviews with senior and middle managers were conducted by Harvard Business School teams in 1992 and 1993 at eight mid-sized New England-based American companies which had been acquired by foreign companies in the period between mid-1987 and 1990 (with one exception acquired in 1984). All companies had enough experience with the foreign parent to provide time for cross-cultural contact to occur and any problems to surface; but the acquisition was also recent enough for managers to have fresh memories.

The circumstances surrounding the acquisitions differed in some respects. One was a strictly arm's-length financial investment in which a well-known sporting goods manufacturer was acquired by a Venezuelan financial group as its only US holding in a leveraged buyout from investors who had acquired it two years earlier; as long as profits were high, there was minimal contact with the parent. In two other cases, there was a history of relationships between the foreign parent and the acquired company prior to the acquisition: a family-owned retailer had developed a business partnership with a larger but also family-owned British chain four years before the acquisition as part of a succession plan; and a metals manufacturer had formed a number of joint ventures with a Japanese conglomerate beginning seven years before the acquisition, turning to its Japanese partner as a defensive tactic against a hostile takeover threat. Other acquisitions also stemmed from financial distress: an armaments manufacturer was bought by a British conglomerate after the US company faltered under a sequence of four different American owners; an abrasives manufacturer was bought by a French company as a "white knight" in a takeover battle with a British company; and a US retailer was sold to a Japanese retailer when it no longer fit its US manufacturing company parent's strategy. In many of the cases, then, foreign acquirers were sought by the US companies to solve a problem.

Two of the companies, given the pseudonyms Metalfab and Hydrotech, were observed by the second author in particular depth. Both were engineering-oriented manufacturing companies with operations primarily in the US and annual sales between $100 and $200 million. Both were previously owned by financially-troubled US parents whose core business was in a different industry, and both were bought by well-respected, internationally-experienced companies in the same industry. Corn conducted 30 interviews at Metalfab, a manufacturer of fabricated metal products acquired about five years earlier by Fabritek, pseudonym for a Swedish manufacturer in the same business. He also conducted 21 interviews at Hydrotech, a designer and manufacturer of hydraulic systems acquired about three years earlier by Gruetzi, pseudonym for a German-Swiss manufacturer of industrial energy systems. But while Metalfab was acquired by a company of similar size and was operating at a pre-tax profit, Hydrotech's new parent was much larger and more diversified geographically and technologically, and Hydrotech was accumulating significant losses [3].

Overview of the findings

The interviews at all eight companies focused on the history of the companies' relationships, their business situations and business strategies, the amount and kind of cross-cultural contact between managers, difficulties and how they had been resolved, and any organizational changes which had come about as a result of the merger. We expected cultural differences to play a prominent role in the dynamics of the integration, especially because so many questions probed these issues specifically – from asking for characterizations of "typical" American and parent country managers to comparing managerial styles in concrete situations. (The study was thus "biased" towards finding cultural differences and tensions because of them.) We expected many difficulties to arise, necessitating many organizational changes, and we expected American companies to resist learning from their foreign company parents. We also expected some combinations to be more volatile than others, such as the Japanese-American interactions, either because of prejudice or because of values and style differences.

We found, instead, that nationality-based culture was one of the less significant variables affecting the integration of the companies and their organizational effectiveness. We found that relatively few issues or problems arose which could be labelled "cultural," even though managers were able to identify style differences easily that fit common cultural patterns. We also found that very few measures were taken to facilitate cultural integration. Only a moderate number of difficulties were encountered or organizational changes necessitated, and US companies learned from their foreign parents. Furthermore, there was no discernible pattern of cultural compatibility; all nationalities worked well with their American acquisitions.

In general, mergers and acquisitions create significant stress on organizational members, as separate organizational cultures and strategies are blended, even within one country [4]. Differences in national cultures are assumed to add another layer of complexity to the merger process. But our findings suggest that contextual factors play the dominant role in determining the smoothness of the integration, the success of the relationship, and whether or not cultural differences become problematic. These findings lead us to conclude that the significance of cultural differences between employees or managers of different nationalities has been overstated. Cultural values or national differences are used as a convenient explanation for other problems, both interpersonal and organizational, such as a failure to respect people, group power and politics, resentment at subordination, poor strategic fit, limited organizational communication, or the absence of problem-solving forums. Such differences are invoked as explanations for the uncomfortable behavior of others when people have limited contact or knowledge of the context behind the behavior.

Culture versus context as an explanatory factor

Most interviewees were able to identify a number of ways in which they differed "culturally" from their foreign colleagues in values, interpersonal style, and organizational approach. Many of these "fit" the position of countries on dimensions Hofstede [5] identified, especially power distance and individualism/collectivism.

The first difference issue mentioned, however, was an objective one: Language problems. A majority of Americans found the difficulty in overcoming language differences with all but the British acquirers to be the biggest "negative" surprise of their respective mergers. One American at Metalfab stated that "during initial meetings, we assumed that when we spoke English to the Swedes and they nodded their heads, they understood what we were saying. Now we realize the nods only meant that they heard the words." Employees at Metalfab and Hydrotech also recalled meetings in which their foreign colleagues would agree to adopt some new procedure, "only to go right back to doing things the same old way as soon as they left the meeting."

American employees noted cultural differences in decision-making styles. Many argued that their foreign parents' management team took a longer-term view. Americans at Hydrotech and Metalfab routinely expressed frustration with the unwillingness of German-Swiss and Swedish managers to make decisions without a great deal of analysis. Europeans noted the American reputation for fast, less thoughtful decisions. A British manager involved in the armaments company acquisition said, "Unlike American companies which manage by quarterly numbers, we at UK headquarters base our strategy and business policies on long-term positioning."

American interviewees also identified a number of differences in interpersonal style between themselves and their foreign colleagues which they attributed to national culture. The Swiss were described as "very orderly and efficient," the Swedes were universally described as being very serious. British managers were described as less emotional, less community-oriented, more deliberate, and much less likely to "shoot from the hip" than Americans. Europeans were described by nearly all American employees as being more formal, less open and outgoing, and slower to form friendships than are Americans. Japanese managers were described as very courteous and polite.

Several Metalfab employees stated that the Swedes were much more likely to argue with each other publicly than were Americans. One American official recalled that in the early days of the merger, he and an American colleague would stare at each other in board meetings while the Swedes argued among themselves. The American manager claimed that his American colleagues would have been much more likely to discuss such differences privately. The Swedes were also described as having less respect for authority and greater willingness to confront their superiors publicly than are Americans – signs of low power distance in Hofstede's terms. Other employees stated that Swedish managers are not as "results-oriented" as Americans when it comes to running meetings, ending meetings without a resolution or an understanding of the next steps. Swedes were described by several American employees as very critical, both of themselves and others. One American manager stated that "Americans are taught that it is more constructive to give pats on the back than to focus entirely on shortcomings as the Swedes are inclined to do."

In short, most of those interviewed found differences between themselves and their foreign colleagues to be clearly identifiable and immediately noticeable following their respective mergers. Employees attributed a majority of these differences to national culture.

But a closer analysis of these responses reveals a tendency for employees to attribute to culture differences which are more situationally-driven. For example, several employees stated the Swedes were unwilling or incapable of adjusting their planning and forecasting assumptions in light of changes in the environment, that the Swedes were more determined than are Americans, to meet old budget targets. This may reflect the fact that as parent, the Swedes and German-Swiss have the ultimate responsibility for financial results. Similarly, slower decision making may reflect the fact that the Swedish parent involves more people in the decision-making process than does its American subsidiary. Of course, the use of greater participation may itself reflect differences in values between Americans and Swedes, but it may also reflect differences in parent and subsidiary or in country-specific industry practices.

Senior managers generally had more direct contact with the foreign parent and thus more contextual information. They were much more likely to identify differences in business context that explained apparent differences in "cultural values." Senior executives at the American retailer acquired by a British company attributed differences in management practices to differences in business environments in the US and UK. For example, the British company appeared to be less interested in people and more interested in facilities. But this was because its operating expenses tended to be weighted more towards rent than to labour, because British supermarkets were typically located in expensive urban areas, whereas in the US supermarkets were generally found outside the commercial core of the city, and US chains had unions which drove up labor costs.

There was also a tendency for American employees to attribute interpersonal difficulties with foreign colleagues to cultural differences without recognizing that Americans act in much the same way. There are recent public examples of American board meetings interrupted by public bickering. The popularity of the view that committees rarely accomplish anything similarly attests to the fact that Europeans are not the only ones who have difficulty establishing clear agendas in their meetings. Finally, in the US, American employees frequently complain about superiors who rarely hand out constructive criticism. In sum, Americans were routinely able to identify a number of differences between themselves and their foreign colleagues, but the attribution of these differences to nationality often seemed to be misdirected. Additionally, in many cases, these differences are more suggestive of perception than of reality.

Perhaps it was more convenient to attribute differences to culture than to context because of the popularity of national character stereotypes. The role of national sterotypes was made clear in contrasting what American managers said about their own foreign acquirers (whom they knew well) compared with other nationalities (which they knew less well). An American senior executive at the sporting goods manufacturer had highly positive things to say about his Venezuelan parent, calling Venezuelans "lovable, amiable, showing a high degree of concern for people." In contrast, he said, "The companies you do not want to have take you over are the Germans and the Japanese. They feel they know how to do it better and just come in and take over." But the companies in our study acquired by Japanese and German-Swiss parents reported just the opposite – that the Japanese, for example, were eager to learn from the American companies they acquired. In short, the greater the experience with managers from another country, the less reliance on negative stereotypes.

Furthermore, while many interviewees were able to identify behavioral style differences between American managers and their foreign parents, they also spoke of cultural compatibilities in values, business strategies, and organizational approach. Such similarities overrode style differences. Both retailers in the pilot study, for example, spoke of the common concerns and philosophies they shared with their foreign parent – one Japanese, one British.

Finally, just because people could point to differences, that did not mean that the differences had operational consequences. Interviewees were asked to assess the extent to which cross-cultural differences created difficulties in the relationship between parent and subsidiary. Interestingly, many employees felt that although differences exist between their cultures, such differences did not create significant problems for employees. This finding cuts to the heart of this study's central question: if cultural differences between a parent and subsidiary do not necessarily lead to significant interorganizational conflict, what factors moderate the relationship between cutural heterogeneity and organizational conflict? Why do American employees of foreign companies feel that cultural differences between their own firm and their foreign parent have not been particularly problematic? Here, our findings suggest that a number of contextual factors act as mediators in determining whether or not these differences will be problematic.

Contextual factors as key determinants of cross-cultural relationship success

Six factors emerged in the pilot study that accounted for the ease with which the merger was implemented and the relatively few difficulties attributed to national cultural differences:

1. the desirability of the relationship, especially in contrast to recent experiences of the acquired companies;
2. business compatibility between the two companies, especially in terms of industry and organization;
3. the willingness of the acquirer to invest in the continued performance of the acquiree and to allow operational autonomy while performance improved;
4. mutual respect and communication based on that respect;
5. business success; and
6. the passage of time.

Relationship desirability

The first issue sets the stage for whether the relationship begins with a positive orientation. When people are in distress, poorly-treated in previous relationships, have had positive experiences with their foreign rescuer, and play a role in initiating relationship discussions, they are much more likely to view the relationship as desirable and work hard to accommodate to any differences in cultural style so that the relationship succeeds.

First, almost all of the companies in the pilot study were acquired by foreigners after a period of financial distress. A Hydrotech employee said, "Everyone here was aware of the firm's financial problems at the time of the acquisition. News of the purchase was viewed favourably. Gruetzi kept our doors from being padlocked. Everyone recognized that without Gruetzi, Hydrotech might not have made it." While Metalfab did not have Hydrotech's financial problems at the time of its acquisition, its employees took comfort from Fabritek's strong financial condition at the time of the takeover. The abrasives company was rescued by its French acquirer as a "white knight in a takeover battle." In all these cases, people were thus more likely to view their acquirers as saviors than villains. Cultural problems were therefore not problematic.

When asked to describe their initial reaction to the acquisitions, interviewees in several companies began with a description of how difficult life had been under its former parent. Several foreign parents in our study therefore compared favorably with each subsidiary's former US parents. Hydrotech and Metalfab's former parents had neither understood the business of its subsidiary nor shown any desire to invest in their subsidiary's long-term growth. The armaments company had four recent owners, several of whom stripped corporate assets and art collections, an experience one manager referred to as being "raped." Under new owners who cared about them, employees were therefore more inclined to tolerate and adapt to cultural differences.

In other cases, national differences were not a problem because the US and non-US companies had spent several years getting to know each other through joint ventures. The British retailer and the Japanese conglomerate had long worked closely with the American companies they eventually bought. Nearly every respondent at Matalfab and Hydrotech spoke with high regard for their parent's technical expertise, manufacturing skill, knowledge of the international marketplace, and reputation for quality. As one employee commented, "Our concerns about the takeover were quickly put to rest. After all, Gruetzi was not an unknown quantity. They were an industry leader and we had worked with them on several projects in the past." In contrast, respondents who were less familiar with the operations of their acquirer appear to have been the most concerned and apprehensive about the news of the merger when it was first announced. As one employee recalled, "At first I was sickened by the announcement, but when I saw Fabritek's product line and the obvious potential for synergy, I became extremely excited." Several respondents also mentioned that if the acquirer had a reputation for dismantling its acquisitions, they would have been far less sanguine about the takeover and the possibilities for success.

Reputation was based not only on past direct experience but also on assumptions about how "companies like that" behaved. One Metalfab employee claimed that compared with other countries, "the Swedes are just like us." The conventional wisdom at Metalfab was that Scandinavian firms had a history of keeping their acquisitions intact.

Finally, the ability to choose made a difference. In several cases, the companies themselves initiated the search for a foreign partner. The element of surprise that creates anxiety and uncertainty was missing. A Hydrotech employee stated: "We wanted to be sold; I viewed the announcement as a real positive – someone wanted to buy us!"

Business compatibility

Organizational similarities were more important to most companies than national cultural differences. At the time of their respective mergers, employees of Metalfab, Hydrotech, and both retailers in the study took immediate comfort from the fact that their new acquirers were in the same industry as they, especially the retailer sold by an American manufacturer to a Japanese retailer. As one Hydrotech employee stated: "Our former parent showed no commitment to, or interest in, our business. Now, there is a much better fit." Another employee stated: "Everyone was initially apprehensive about the takeover but at least we were bought by a company which understands and cares about our business. This turned our initial apprehension into excitement." Along similar lines, Metalfab employees reacted very favorably to the news that "a metal company was purchasing a metal company."

Organizational similarity meant that employees could feel that they play important roles in carrying out their parent's strategy and believe that their parent values their contribution. As one Hydrotech employee stated: "Despite the fact that Gruetzi is a much larger company than our former parent was, it is easier to see how we fit into their plans." Thus, at both Hydrotech and Metalfab, the benefits of the merger were transparent to employees. As one manager stated, "This was an easy announcement to make; the merger spoke for itself."

Employees at Hydrotech and Metalfab felt that sharing a common technical orientation with their parent allowed both organizations to more easily overcome national differences. Several employees emphasized what a pleasure it was to work with a parent organization that understands the business they are in. As one engineer stated, "our two firms are like twins that were separated at birth." Employ-

ees at both Hydrotech and Metalfab also feel that their parents'
expertise and credibility in the industry has made it easier to accept
them in the role of acquirer. One Metalfab employee's comment
captured the attitude of the firm's employees towards foreign ownership when he claimed: "It doesn't bother me in the least that our
parent is a foreign company because we speak the same language,
Metal!" A majority of those interviewed concluded that they would
now prefer being taken over by a foreign company in the same
business than by an American firm in a different industry.

Investment without interference

Of all the actions taken by a foreign partner, none seems to have
a more positive impact on morale and on attitudes towards foreigners
than a foreign owner's decision to invest capital in its subsidiaries.
Fabritek spent $11 to 12 million upgrading the production facilities
of its US subsidiary during each of the first two years following the
acquisition and has invested an additional $6 to 8 million annually
ever since. Gruetzi has similarly invested in new equipment for
Hydrotech's Ohio production facility. To most American employees, such investment demonstrated that its new parent was committed to the company's long-term health.

When investment was accompanied by operational autonomy,
the relationship was viewed very favorably and cross-cultural tensions
minimized. In three cases – sporting goods manufacturer acquired
by a Venezuelan company and both the retailer and the manufacturer
acquired by Japanese companies – feeling lack of cultural tensions
was a function of the minimal interference of the foreign company
in its new US operations. "They let us do what we are good at," said
an executive at the sporting goods firm, "which is make money."

Employees at Hydrotech and Metalfab were surprised by the
extent to which their parents allowed them to manage their own
operations. As one Hydrotech employee stated: "Things have
turned out much better than I originally expected. Gruetzi has not
overmanaged us, they kept our management team intact, and we
have not been forced to spend a lot of our time defending ourselves."
Metalfab employees were similarly pleased that their parent has
allowed the firm to retain day-to-day control: "While our parent
provides us with suggestions, they have allowed us to run the show
here." We argue that American employees are less likely to view

cultural heterogeneity as a problem when foreign management allows such autonomy along with adding resources.

It should be pointed out that complete autonomy was not welcomed by all employees; a minority of employees (those dissatisfied with their firm's policies) mentioned that they would be happier if the parent took a more active role in managing its subsidiary. At least one Hydrotech engineer wished that Gruetzi would force the company to standardize its designs and acquire better tools for its engineers to work with. At Metalfab, several employees expressed disappointment that its parent had not prevented the company from moving operations to Mexico. Furthermore, that high degrees of autonomy have possibly slowed down the speed with which the merged organizations develop a common culture. Several Metalfab employees reported that it has been difficult to "pull our two families together and get the message out to customers that we are *one* firm." Still, for the Americans autonomy generally meant that they did not feel foreigners were imposing "foreign ways" on them, which made them more tolerant of differences rather than resistant to them.

Open communication and mutual respect

Nearly all interviewees agreed that open communication and showing mutual respect are critical to developing trust and ensuring a successful partnership. One retailer, for example, felt that its new Japanese parent wanted to learn from American practice, which made them feel valued and made rapport with the Japanese easy to develop. Tensions occurred, in contrast, when foreign colleagues did not show respect for American technology and expertise. At Fabritek, Swedish engineers and marketing personnel initially viewed Metalfab's traditional, composite products as inferior to their own, all-metal product, which required tighter engineering and manufacturing tolerances in order to ensure a perfect seal. As a result, Americans said that the Swedes saw themselves as "the real engineers" in the company. (But note here that the tensions were caused by *technical* differences, not cultural ones.) Similarly, Hydrotech engineers described their German-Swiss colleagues as very arrogant and protective about Gruetzi's products; there was a feeling that Hydrotech engineers should not "tamper" with their parent's designs.

Employee sensitivity to possible cultural differences played a significant role in reducing outbreaks of cross-cultural tension. One Hydrotech employee reasoned that cultural clashes had been avoided mainly because employees had been so concerned that such tensions could occur that they put more effort into trying to understand one another. Similar concerns led executives at Fabritek and Metalfab to schedule frequent meetings with each other soon after the merger; these meetings improved understanding and lessened tension between the two firms. Ironically, one senior American official recalled that he had rarely met with executives from the firm's former US parent "even though they were located right down the road from the company." Though formal cross-cultural training programs were rare, open communication helped build relationships. Sensitivity to cultural differences and willingness to deal with problems directly minimized organizational tension.

Business success

Nothing succeeds like success. People are willing to overlook cultural differences in relationships which bring clear benefits. But unsuccessful ventures produce squabbling even among people who are culturally similar.

Creating opportunities for joint success between parent and subsidiary promotes acceptance of cross-cultural differences and creates support for the relationship. Several months before Hydrotech's acquisition by Gruetzi, a company project had "gone sour" due to a technical malfunction. After the merger, Hydrotech used Gruetzi's technology to solve the problem. For the many employees who had suffered through the project's difficulties, this single act sold the virtue of the partnership. Another Hydrotech employee stated: "We had not realized how quickly Gruetzi's technology could be put to use. In only one year, our department was able to bid on two projects and win a $45 million contract." Nothing could possibly send a more positive message about the benefits of partnership than winning business because of it.

Ongoing financial performance affects the quality and nature of communications between parent and subsidiary, and thus plays a role in determining whether or not cultural differences are viewed as problematic. If success reduces tensions, deteriorating performance increases them. Employees noted that travel budgets came under increasing pressure during periods of poor performance, and thus, fewer meetings take place between American and foreign employees. In difficult times, communication between parent and subsidiary may deteriorate as employees in each organization focus on their own problems. Finally, poor performance leads to frustration, finger-pointing, and reduced trust. One Hydrotech manager noticed that as Gruetzi has encountered more financial difficulties, they became increasingly demanding of Hydrotech and focused more on the company's short-term operating results than in the past.

The passage of time

Does time heal all wounds? Time, at least, reduces anxieties and replaces stereotypes with a more varied view of other people. The levels of cross-cultural tension vary as a function of the stage in the relationship-building process. Anxieties at Hydrotech and Metalfab were highest during the days immediately following the announce-ment of each takeover. This initial anxiety declined as the merger entered a transition phase in which management showed reluctance to create conflict. Employees of both subsidiaries also reacted posi-tively to foreign management's willingness to discuss issues and listen to their concerns at that time. According to one employee, "these meetings made us feel good about the changes and made us realize how alike our philosophies were." But during the transition phase, employees also underestimated the degree of cultural hetero-geneity and the potential for conflict to erupt. As management began to focus on more substantive issues and the amount of com-munications between American and foreign employees grew, a new realization set in that the cultural differences between the two firms were greater than initially realized, which required more awareness and sensitivity to avoid conflict. It appears likely then, that employee perceptions of cross-cultural tension are affected by the passage of time and by the merger process itself. One might also expect that employee attitudes towards cultural heterogeneity will change as Americans and foreign employees work together and become more familiar with each others' customs and values.

Mistrust is always more likely at early stages of relationships. People at Hydrotech and Metalfab felt their new foreign parents were particularly guarded in discussing their technology during the first months together. As one employee mentioned: "It was like playing poker during the first year. You always got an answer to your question but the question was answered as narrowly as possible – even when, by withholding information, the answer was misleading." But another engineer recognized the significance of sharing technology noting that "when our parent provides us with technology, they are giving us their life's work."

The negative side of cross-cultural interaction: threat and prejudice

Positive views of the relationship between US company and foreign parent predominated, but they were not universal in the companies studied. Top management and those with the greatest day-to-day contact were most likely to be favorable. Those at lower ranks anxious about the implications for their careers were more likely to express negative views, including prejudice and resentment, reacting the most nationalistically to the news of a foreign takeover. One American reported how "sick" he was over the fact that "this country is gradually being sold off to foreigners."

Some higher level managers commented that they would have been more comfortable if their acquirer had been American, but this preference did not seem to affect the relationship. A manager at the armaments company reported: "We would rather have been bought by a US company. There is an element of national pride, especially in our industry. We are very patriotic. There is no one in the company that would say we are a British firm. We all wear and buy 'made in USA' products." Still, nationalist sentiments did not prevent this manager from declaring the relationship a success and identifying very few cross-cultural problems.

The most significant factor in determining employee reactions to acquisition was self-interest: how the change would affect their own standing in the firm. Virtually all interviewees reacted to news of the acquisition with the same question: "How will this impact on my career in this organization?" Those employees who were most likely to suffer a loss of prestige or power, or who had reason to feel threatened by the mergers were most likely to react unfavorably to it.

However, the fact that the vast majority of employees in both companies did not react in this way attests to just how apparent the benefits of these mergers were to most employees. Therefore threat could work both ways; if the foreign company improved performance, jobs would be saved. A manager at the armaments company observed, "The community and employees understand there are differences between us and the British. But for them, having good jobs is more valuable. When corporate survival is at stake, people cannot afford to have culture become an issue."

Attitudes were shaped by symbolic acts taken by the foreign parents as much as by more substantive actions. One Metalfab employee recalled the day that Fabritek's president arranged to have group photographs taken of all employees in the US so that they could be shown to people back in Sweden. "Fabritek immediately impressed me as a very people-oriented company."

The attribution of organizational problems to national culture

Our findings suggest, then, that contextual factors act to either fan the flames of intergroup conflict and cross-cultural polarization or encourage organizational members to accept these differences. In the pilot study, organizational and technical compatibilities overwhelm cultural differences. Cultural differences thus seem to be a residual category to which people attribute problems in the absence of a supportive context. Cultural differences do not automatically cause tensions. But when tensions do arise – often due to situational factors such as lack of communication or poor performance – people blame many of the organizational difficulties they encounter on cultural heterogeneity – on the presence of others who seem different – rather than to the context within which these problems took place. This view is consistent with Chris Argyris's perspective on defensive routines in organizations [6].

Why do people blame culture for problems and ascribe differences between their own behavior and that of their foreign colleagues to dispositional factors (the kind of people they are) rather than to situational factors (the organizational context)?

First, cultural heterogeneity presents a conspicuous target for employees to point at when looking for an explanation for their problems. Such differences are readily apparent in early stages of contact between people who differ in a visible way, such as race, gender, or language, especially when there are only a few "tokens" such as expatriate managers among many "locals" [2]. Preconceived notions and prejudices which employees bring into the evaluative process increase the likelihood that people will attribute behavior to nationality.

In-group favoritism is evoked in situations of cross-cultural contact. Research has shown that people want to favor members of their own group (the in-group) over others. Motivational theorists hold that self-esteem is enhanced if people value their own group and devalue other groups [7, 8]. Such favoritism leads to a set of cognitive biases which reinforce the distinction between in-group and out-group members. People expect in-group members to display more desirable and fewer undesirable behaviors than out-group members [9]. As a result, people are more likely to infer negative dispositions from undesirable and out-group behaviors than from undesirable in-group behaviors, and are less likely to infer positive dispositions from desirable out-group behaviors than from desirable in-group behaviors [10–13]. Furthermore, people tend to remember behavior which is congruent with their expectations over behavior which is inconsistent with their views [14, 15]. Thus, memories reinforce in-group favoritism as well. In-group biases are especially likely to form when individuals identify strongly with their group and when in-group members view other groups as a threat [7].

During an acquisition process, employees who work for, and identify with their company for many years suddenly find that another firm, with its own culture visions, values, and ways of doing things is responsible for their future. Cross-border mergers offer a particularly favorable environment for such biases to develop because group membership is clearly defined by national as well as organizational boundaries. At both Hydrotech and Metalfab, in-group favoritism and cognitive biases may have been the driving forces behind the tendency among Americans to attribute wrongfully "bad news" to their foreign parent (i.e. out-group members). In one case, Hydrotech management had frozen salaries and extended the required working week from 40 to 44 hours after the merger in an effort to "impress Gruetzi by showing a willingness to make a few difficult decisions." Many Hydrotech junior employees attributed this unpopular policy to Gruetzi's management. Ironically, according to one middle-level manager, when Gruetzi found out about these changes, they gave Hydrotech's president one month to reverse the policy.

In another example, soon after Metalfab announced plans to transfer some of its manufacturing operations to Mexico, rumors began circulating on the factory floor that the Swedes were behind the decision. When senior management in the US found out about the rumors, the company's president called a meeting with all employees and took full responsibility for the decision. But many blue-collar workers continued to blame the Swedes for this unpopular move. They also attributed the decision to downsize the American workforce to the company's foreign parent.

A second explanation for why cultural differences are inappropriately invoked is called the "fundamental attribution error" [16] – a tendency to attribute one's own behavior to the situation but others' behavior to their "character." People attribute negative behavior of foreign colleagues to their nationality or culture (dispositional factors) rather than to situational or contextual factors which are operating behind the scenes [17]. For example, Metalfab interviewees initially viewed their Swedish colleagues as fractious (i.e. "the Swedes are a stubborn people") before it occurred to them that language problems had caused many early misunderstandings. They attributed the fact that their Swedish colleagues were more engineering oriented and less marketing oriented to national biases ("Swedes design bulldozers for the kind of work a garden shovel could do") rather than to differences in product features and to the requirements of the European market. For example, rigid engineering standards for Fabritek's all-metal products required engineers in Sweden to play a more central role in the parent's operations, whereas the competitiveness of the US market demanded that marketing personnel play a more critical role in US decision making. But those who had more direct contact with the foreign parent, such as senior managers, also had more contextual information and were less likely to make the "fundamental attribution error."

If in-group biases and the fundamental attribution error are behind the tendency to view cultural heterogeneity as problematic, what steps might management take to promote inter-organizational co-operation in cross-border mergers? Our findings suggest that actions which make the relationship desirable, reduce uncertainty, show respect for the other group, create communication channels, and ensure business success will encourage employees to identify with their foreign colleagues and view the company as one organization. Creating an atmosphere of mutual respect, promoting open communication, investing in the future, maximizing opportunities to experience joint success, and taking steps to familiarize employees with their counterpart's products and markets reduce the likelihood that cultural differences will be viewed as a source of organizational tension.

Conclusion

These pilot study findings are only suggestive, of course. We have a small number of cases from one region. While none of them can yet be called a long-term success, they have survived a period of integration during which other companies which perhaps did experience debilitating cultural problems could have called off the marriage. We could be looking only at the "winners" that managed cultural differences well. Indeed, those companies experiencing problems were more likely to turn down our request to participate in the pilot study. But if tilted towards successes, then this research points to some of the circumstances that contribute to successful cross-cultural relationships. And since we "biased" the interviews towards identification of cultural differences and cultural tensions, the relative absence of tension gives additional weight to our argument that contextual and situational factors, such as technical fit, business performance, and abundant communication, are more significant determinants of relationship effectiveness.

Employees at each of the companies studied were able to identify a number of cultural differences between their own organization and that of their parent. Nevertheless, few employees viewed cultural heterogeneity as a significant source of tension in their firm. Such findings lend support to the notion that national cultural differences do not necessarily increase the amount of tension between organizations or make partnerships among companies from different countries untenable.

This article proposes that there are a number of factors which help to determine how employees react to foreign ownership. It calls into question the assumption that the larger the social distance or cultural gap between the national cultures of two merged organizations, the greater will be the potential for strain in the relationship between employees. The findings from our pilot study suggest contextual factors are extremely important mediators in cross-cultural relationships. These factors influence how cultural differences are interpreted and whether they are viewed by employees as problematic. Indeed, they may even determine whether "cultural differences" are identified at all.

References

1. Kanter, R.M., *Men and Women of the Corporation,* Basic Books, New York, NY, 1977.

2. *M&A Almanac,* Vol. 26 No. 6, 1992, p. 54.

3. Kanter, R.M., Applbaum, K. and Yatsko, P., *FCB and Publicis (A): Forming the Alliance,* Harvard Business School Case Records, Boston, MA, 1993.

4. Kanter, R.M., *When Giants Learn to Dance: Mastering the Challenges of Strategy, Management, and Careers in the 1990s,* Simon and Schuster, New York, NY, 1989.

5. Hofstede, G., *Cultures and Organization,* McGraw-Hill, New York, NY, 1991.

6. Argyris, C., *Overcoming Organizational Defenses: Facilitating Organizational Learning,* Allyn & Bacon, Boston, MA, 1990.

7. Tajfel, H. and Turner, J.C., "An Integrative Theory of Intergroup Conflict," in Austin, W.S. and Worchel, S. (Eds), *The Social Psychology of Intergroup Relations,* Brooks/Cole, Monterey, CA, 1979, pp. 33–47.

8. Turner, J.C., *Rediscovering the Social Group: A Self-categorization Theory,* Blackwell, Oxford, 1987.

9. Howard, J.W. and Rothbart, M., "Social Categorization and Memory for In-group and Out-group Behavior," *Journal of Personality and Social Psychology,* Vol. 38 No. 2, 1980, pp. 301–10.

10. Taylor, D.M. and Jaggi, V., "Ethnocentrism and Causal Attribution in a South Indian Context," *Journal of Cross Cultural Psychology,* Vol. 5 No. 2, 1974, pp. 162–71.

11. Allen, V.L. and Wilder, D.A., "Categorization, Belief Similarity, and Intergroup Discrimination," *Journal of Personality and Social Psychology,* Vol. 32 No. 6, 1975, pp. 971–7.

12. Allen, V.L. and Wilder, D.A., "Group Categorization and Attribution of Belief Similarity," *Small Group Behavior,* Vol. 10 No. 1, 1979, pp. 73–80.

13. Pettigrew, T.F., "The Ultimate Attribution Error: Extending Allport's Cognitive Analysis of Prejudice," *Personality and Social Psychology Bulletin,* Vol. 5 No. 4, 1979, pp. 461–76.

14. Hastie, R. and Kumar, P.A., "Person Memory: Personality Traits as Organizing Principles in Memory for Behavior," *Journal of Personality and Social Psychology,* Vol. 37 No. 1, 1979, pp. 25–38.

15. Srull, T.D., Lichtenstein, M. and Rothbart, M., "Associative Storage and Retrieval Processes in Person Memory," *Journal of Experimental Psychology: Learning, Memory and Cognition,* Vol. 11 No. 2, 1985, pp. 316–45.

16. Ross, L., "The Intuitive Psychologist and His Shortcomings: Distortions in the Attribution Process," in Berkowitz, L. (Ed.), *Advances in Experimental Social Psychology,* Vol. 10, Academic Press, New York, NY, 1977, pp. 173–220.

17. Jones, E.E. and Nisbett, R.E., "The Actor and the Observer: Divergent Perceptions of the Causes of Behavior," in Jones, E.E., Kanouse, D.E., Kelley, H.H., Nisbett, R.E., Valins, S. and Weiner, B. (Eds), *Perceiving the Causes of Behavior,* General Learning Press, Morristown, NJ, 1971, pp. 79–94.

◇

5.2 "Englishes" in Cross-Cultural Business Communication

◆

Naoki Kameda

"Send us your message again in English!" This was a stern telex reply from the headquarters of a multinational firm in the Hague to their subsidiary in Paris. The Paris secretary had sent a telex in her mother tongue, French. The headquarter's reply must surely have hurt the pride of the French workers, who are known for loving their own language. This one example, a true story, heard from the Tokyo subsidiary, illustrates two interesting facts:

1. English is prescribed as a common language within many multinational firms for their internal communications. In some multinational firms, there is an unwritten law that each subsidiary must use English for its communications with other subsidiaries and with headquarters.
2. In one known multinational firm, neither the Netherlands where it has its headquarters nor France where it has a subsidiary has English as its mother tongue. However, English is the international language used.

In the business world today non-native speakers use English primarily to communicate with other non-native users – for example, Japanese with Koreans, Koreans with Taiwanese, Taiwanese with Indonesian, Indonesian with Greek, Greek with Portuguese, etc. The president of a Swiss company, who is German, visits the Far East twice a year with an executive director of his French subsidiary, who is French, for purchasing products from Asia. The problem is

Source: Naoki Kameda, " 'Englishes' in Cross-Cultural Communication," *The Bulletin*, March 1992, pp. 3–8.

neither can speak his counterpart's lanaguage. Each must use English all the time to communicate with each other. Their business language when doing business with their Asian suppliers is of course English.

Chinese business people, often called overseas Chinese, must resort to English to communicate with other Chinese people when the two parties are from different places because each one's own Chinese is mutually unintelligible when spoken, due to the influence of dialect.

It is said English has emerged over the last 40 years as the world's premier international language. It is even said English has in essence become a world language, the common property of all cultures. But, is it really so?

Tables 5.2.1–5 give some interesting insights about English as an international language.

The number of people around the world who speak the English language is considerable. Over 300 million people speak it as a mother tongue or first language, another 300 million use it as a second language, and between 100 million and 300 million speak it as a foreign language. In total, between 700 million and 1 billion people speak English. The latter figure represents one fifth of the world's population.

Table 5.2.1   The world's major mother tongues

	Speakers (in millions)	% of world population
Chinese (Han)	1,031.3	20.6
English	309.9	6.2
Spanish	246.0	4.9
Hindi	219.0	4.4
Bengali	166.8	3.3
Russian	166.0	3.3
Arabic	160.2	3.2
Portuguese	149.3	3.0
Japanese	122.5	2.4
French	84.7	1.7
Total	2,655.7	53.0

Table 5.2.2   Countries with the largest number of English mother tongue users

	English first language speakers (in millions)	Total population (in millions)	% of English first language speakers
USA	216.18	243.77	88.7
UK	53.00	56.87	93.3
Canada	15.84	25.85	61.3
Australia	13.80	16.18	85.3
Irish Republic	3.38	3.56	94.9
New Zealand	3.12	3.34	93.4
South Africa	1.85	34.97	5.3
Zimbabwe	0.69	8.64	8.0
Jamaica	0.64	2.37	27.0
Liberia	0.35	2.35	15.0
Others	12.88		
Total	321.81		

Source: *Britannica World Data Book, 1988.*
"Others" includes English Creole and English bilingual speakers.

Table 5.2.3   Geographic locations where English is both the official and the majority first language used

Location	% of population using English as first language	Location	% of population using English as first language
Anguilla	100.0	Isle of Man	100.0
Antigua & Barbados	95.8	Monserrat	100.0
Australia	85.3	Jersey	100.0
Bermuda	93.0	New Zealand	93.4
British Virgin Isles	91.6	Norfolk Isles	100.0
Canada	61.3	St Helena	100.0
Cayman Isles	100.0	Turks & Caicos Isles	100.0
Falkland Isles	100.0	UK	93.3
Grenada	96.0	USA	88.7
Guam	35.0	US Virgin Isles	81.0
Guernsey	100.0	Western Samoa	52.0
Irish Republic	94.9		

Source: *Britannica World Data Book, 1988.*

Table 5.2.4 Estimated population of countries where English is used as an official or second language (in millions)

Total population of countries where English is an official language	222.0
Other Commonwealth countries	14.2
Pakistan	10.6
Total	246.8

Sources: *Britannica World Data Book, 1988,* and *English: A World Commodity* (London: The Economist Intelligence Unit Limited, 1989).

Table 5.2.5 Estimated number of ESL speakers (in millions)

Population of countries where English is spoken as a first or second language	246
Mother tongue speakers	32
Non-mother tongue speakers	214
Estimated ESL speakers	30
Non-English speakers	184

Source: *English: A World Commodity,* EIU, *1989.*

Widespread use of English: reasons

Some factors have been already introduced by scholars to explain the spread of English – such as English usage in science and technology, English usage by developing countries, the structure of the language, etc.

Whatever the reasons may be, it is an indisputable fact that the number of countries where people speak English as their mother tongue or official language and the number of people who speak it far exceed those of other languages.

The actual structure of the language itself is also contributing to the spread of English as a world language. English is relatively easy to pronounce. The basic syntax is fairly straightforward, as is the fact that English has dispensed with gender systems and has less inflection and declension than most other languages such as French and German possess.

Because of this easy structure and accessibility, English has gained the position of the first foreign language for those who can't make themselves understood in their mother tongue when communicating with foreigners.

As the name suggests, the operations of a multinational firm are spread over many countries. The mother tongues of the senders and the receivers of the firm's internal communications are all different. If, therefore, they were to be allowed to use their own languages, the whole operations system of the firm might collapse; time and money involved with translation work would be enormous and cause considerable loss to the firm.

One of the big ten trading companies in Japan has been using English for their telex communications with their Warsaw office. The reasons given were as follows:

1. To meet the requirements of the Polish Import and Export Agency, which officially prescribes that the language to be used for negotiations with them must be either Polish or English.
2. To make the local employees feel like "first string" members of the firm. They may lose their interest and will to work if the day's telex messages are not understandable to them.
3. To avoid misunderstanding instructions from the headquarters in Tokyo and details of negotiations with the Agency or details of negotiations forwarded from the Warsaw office to the head office in Tokyo.
4. To eliminate the need for translation, thus keeping at a minimum the work load of the Japanese representatives at the Warsaw office.

In the special report *English: A World Commodity*, Brian McCallen writes, "Many linguists are beginning to reject the notion of a blanket unaccountable noun 'English' with its suggestion of a relatively homogeneous language and suggest instead the term 'Englishes.' The key issue here is that each country which speaks the language can inject aspects of its own culture into the usage. Though differences in grammar, syntax, and pronunciation may result, the language still remains comprehensive to speakers of the 'standard' variety." This remark implies that English has become not just a national language used internationally, but rather a true international language.

Nonstandard "Englishes" usage: samples

To identify Nonstandard "Englishes," one must first have knowledge of Standard English. In their *International English: A Guide to Varieties of Standard English*, Peter Trudgill and Jean Hannah define Standard English as one of the different variants of modern

English written and spoken by educated native speakers. It naturally includes different varieties of English known as "English as a Foreign Language," or EFL, and "English as a Second Language," or ESL, both being taught to the students of English at schools in foreign countries. They take two major varieties of English as Standard English: British English written and spoken by educated native speakers in England, Wales, Scotland, North Ireland, the Republic of Ireland, Australia, New Zealand, and South Africa; and North American English which educated people in the States and Canada use for writing and speaking. These varieties can be categorized as United States English and Canadian English respectively.

All other varieties of English can be defined as Nonstandard English. Some examples of Nonstandard English collated from Nigeria, India, Singapore, and the Philippines, countries using English as their official or joint official language, are as follows:

1. Ramesh said he will be coming here soon, isn't it?
2. Patricia has left the company, is it?
3. We are here since yesterday.
4. When you will receive our L/C, please advise us.
5. I wonder where is he.
6. I can't got it, too.
7. He is not around.
8. He suggested me to meet with you in Bombay.
9. She hasn't had no idea, also.
10. Hasn't he come back yet?
    Yes = he hasn't come back yet.
    No = he has come back already.
11. Don't you mind my smoking?
    Yes = Please go ahead. I don't mind at all.

These are just a few of the patterns and expressions often seen and heard when communicating with non-natives. Listed are only those whose usage is accepted in a given local speech community – not a single person's misuse.

These expressions would be marked by a teacher of English as incorrect usage or mistakes. But, with these expressions in actual use, non-native speakers are doing business with their foreign counterparts. It is interesting to note that number 10 is one from Nigeria and number 11 is from the Philippines. "Yes, no" mistakes are not a birthmark nor a patent of Japanese.

Bypassing in cross-cultural business communication

Many businessmen from countries other than the ten whose mother tongue is Standard English are doing business with the Englishes cited. In their business communication, however, such minor grammatical errors, or what could perhaps be called divergent forms of Standard English, hardly cause misunderstanding. The actual misunderstanding in their business communication takes place outside the scope of the style of Englishes.

It is the misunderstanding caused by bypassing. As Haney (1979) observes, "Bypassing is the name for the miscommunication pattern which occurs when the *sender* (speaker, writer, and so on) and the *receiver* (listener, reader, and so forth) *miss each other with their meanings*" (p. 285).

The following examples obtained from business experience illustrate bypassing. The first is an exchange of telexes between the Import Manager of a German company in Munich and a Tokyo office. (R stands for "Received" and S stands for "Sent.")

(R) RE OUR CONTAINER: PLS ADVISE BY RTN TLX TIME OF DEPARTURE, E.T.A. AND VESSEL USED.

(S) M.S. CHEVALIER PAUL IS TO LEAVE TOKYO ON FEB 12 AND ARRIVE AT HAMBURG ON MARCH 12.

(R) PLS ADVISE TIME OF DEPARTURE, E.T.A. AND VESSEL.

(S) RCVD UR TLX N WISH TO ADVISE U ALL INFO WAS ALREADY GIVEN TO U ON JAN 26. MS CHEVALIER PAUL IS LEAVING ON FEB 12 N ARRIVING AT HAMBURG ON MARCH 12.

(R) WHERE IS OUR CONTAINER???

(R) MR. CHEVALIER PAUL WILL HE VISIT US IN MUNICH? IF SO, PLS ADVISE SO I CAN MEET HIM. PLS ALSO EXPLAIN WHAT HIS POSITION IS.

(S) UR CONTAINER CHEVALIER PAUL IS SOMEWHERE ON THE HIGH SEA OF THE INDIAN OCEAN N EXPECTED TO ARRIVE AT HAMBURG ON OR ABOUT MARCH 12. M.S. STANDS FOR MOTOR SHIP NOT FOR MONSIEUR IN FRENCH.

(R) EVERYTHING IS CLEAR REGARDING MR-MS CHEVALIER PAUL. WE ALL HAD A GOOD LAUGH HERE. WILL PLACE A NEW ORDER ABOUT 14-21 DAYS AFTER RECEIPT OF CONTAINER.

This example precisely illustrates bypassing. The words of issue are M-S and M-R. It was thought that the import manager who had used the trade terms ETA (Estimated Time of Arrival) was familiar with the abbreviation MS for Motor Ship as used in export and import practice.

A second example occurred recently when products were shipped to Portugal under the requested payment terms C.A.D. Experience of shipment under this payment condition to a Greek customer had been previously mutually accepted to be the same as D/P (Documents against Payment) at sight because it is Cash Against Documents. In the usual case, D/P is always with an at sight condition. If the terms are wanted with usance, it should be changed to D/A (Documents against Acceptance). Goods were shipped and the bill and shipping documents were negotiated at the bank for cash. A month passed and the bank advised that the payment was not yet settled and wanted the buyer coerced for payment. The representative in Lisbon responded that payment would definitely be made when the goods were ready for custom clearance, but as yet the goods had not arrived.

The reason for the misunderstanding was the simple letter "D." The buyer, from the beginning, meant this "D" as "Delivery," that is, local delivery of the goods, as Cash Against Delivery. The seller took "D" to mean "Documents," the interpretation of C.A.D. based on the standard usage of the payment terms prevailing in Europe.

The word "Delivery" used in the international trade practice is interchangeable with "Shipment" unless otherwise specified such as "Deliver to (place of delivery) in Sydney by 30 September 1989." The Sale of Goods Act, 1893, Section 32, gives such a definition as – (1) Delivery to carrier. – Where, in pursuance of a contract of sale, the seller is authorized or required to send the goods to the buyer, delivery of the goods to a carrier, whether named by the buyer or not, for the purpose of transmission to the buyer, is *prima facie* deemed to be a delivery of the goods to the buyer.

Not everyone who does international business knows this definition. A known American buyer in Los Angeles has his own definitions on several trade terms that often appeared in correspondence. To him "Delivery" meant delivery to his store in the States. "September" delivery meant that he expects products to be delivered to his store in September.

Causes of bypassing

The causes of these three bypassing cases can be classified roughly into the following three factors:

1. The absence of general agreement
2. Egocentric interpretation
3. Self-conceited conception

If there were general agreements between the two parties in each case on the words such as M.S., C.A.D., and Delivery, they could have easily avoided such a miscommunication. However, individuals are selfish and apt to think that they know what they know because they know what they know. It is often forgotten that people have different cultures, customs, values, etc. and understandably give different meanings to words.

People give their own meanings to words they perceive. Words do not "mean" at all. Only people "mean." And, people give entirely different meanings to words, meanings which they have acquired through experience which is completely different from that of others. In Athens a few years ago, a local businessman took an international visitor to a hilltop near his office for lunch. The visitor saw an old building that looked like a monastery in the distance. He said, "Look! That's a nice OLD monastery down there." The amazed businessman replied, "Old? You said it's an old building? It's still a new construction, built in 16th century." For the Greek people a monastery built in 16th century is still a new building. Meanings are really in people not in words.

When a Japanese traveller was in India some 20 years ago, there was a turmoil in Bombay; a large group of local Indian people started rioting against Chinese people living there. Many Chinese people were threatened. The local Japanese society held a committee meeting and were discussing how their members and their families could be free from the Indians' possible attack on them. They were about to decide each family should put a large Hinomaru rising-sun mark on the door of each house to tell Indian people "We are Japanese not Chinese." Only the Japanese traveller objected to the idea. He said that there was no guarantee that Indian people knew that the sign of a round red mark on a white background signified Japan's national flag. "Instead, simply write down 'Not Chinese' because Indian people can read English," he said.

This anecdote condenses the causes of bypassing or the three factors mentioned: the absence of general agreement, egocentric interpretation, and self-conceited conception.

The Hinomaru or a rising-sun flag is nothing but just a piece of cloth or paper if there isn't national and governmental general agreement that it signifies the national flag and the symbol of Japan. It must be realized, however, that the span of the scope in which the general agreement works is not limitless. There is a limit beyond which it doesn't work at all. Had the Japan Society's committee members been more astute, they would have realized that not everyone can identify the Japanese flag.

Another example is one easily overlooked. Many authors of English literature, or even those of business English textbooks, suggest students should not write, "He is tall," which is only a subjective opinion. "He stands six feet four" allows no misconception, but another problem arises. Suppose the reader is not American, not familiar with measurement in feet and inches, and does not know the average height of American men. Can such a reader give a judgement, accurate or vague, whichever it may be? Can the reader tell, with this bit of information, that the man in question is tall? Unfortunately he can't.

To follow what the authors suggest, one must write "He's got 165 square meters of land in Ginza" instead of "He is rich." But, the number of people who can associate the land with the man's richness is limited. For those who have no knowledge of the Ginza's extraordinary land prices, the sentence only means a man's possession of relatively small land in a place called Ginza.

This may be one of the most difficult aspects of cross-cultural communication. In order to convey a message across the boundary of a cultural sphere to the receiver, some additional information must be given to complete the message. "He stands six feet four and is tall in our society," or "He has a land of 165 square meters in Ginza. One tsubo (3.3 m2) costs roughly US$500,000 down there."

Yamamoto Takashi of Tokyo University says in *Language and Communication*, "In order to make the transmission of an idea by language or communication possible, it is not enough that the sender (speaker, writer) and the receiver (listener, reader) share the knowledge of the language used. To make such an utterance as 'Challenger has exploded' transmitted, the sender and the receiver must be able to share their empirical knowledge that 'Challenger' refers to a spaceship.

If the receiver has no such knowledge, the sender must explain to the receiver, 'You know, Challenger is an American space shuttle.' The reason why communication between races or ethnic groups and between different generations doesn't go smoothly is that the sender and the receiver share fewer ways of thinking, such as customs, systems, traditions, cultures – the criteria necessary for verbal communication."

The message is the message received

Much failure to communicate is due to lack of imagination, a failure to put oneself into the position of the other person, a lack of empathy. We must not assume that our readers know as much about the topic in our message as we do. Be considerate of readers and put yourself in their places and in their situations, and most of the communication problems will be solved.

Once there was a good passage full of empathy to readers of an English newspaper in Japan. It went like this ". . . the high school textbooks are scheduled to go into use next April, *when the school year begins.*" The writer of the article put himself in the shoes of his readers from other countries in which the school year does not always start in April, even though it would sound redundant to Japanese readers. Additional information or expansion of your message is thus important.

When communicating across societies and cultures in Englishes, attention should be paid to the following:

1. Assume the receiver of your message may not interpret the words you used in the same way as you intended.
2. Do not assume the receiver knows as much about the topic or the new words in the message as yourself.
3. Assume, when you are the receiver, the sender of the message you have received might have given another meaning to the words which may be quite different from yours.

Some suggestions to help make communication more comprehensive are:

1. Have your secretary, colleagues, superiors, or any other third party read what you have written before you pass it on to a typist or telex/fax operator.

2. Expand your message by adding as much information as possible so that the receiver may not receive too little information. Ask yourself what he needs to know in order to comprehend the message, and give him what you think he should know, thereby making what you know what he knows.

3. Do not try to interpret the message you receive by giving your own meaning to it when you find it difficult to understand the message. Ask the sender immediately to restate it in other words.

"Be considerate of others and put yourself into the position of the other person." This is the teaching of *You-Consideration* advocated by late Professor Ozaki and the key to successful human-centered communication in Englishes across business and cultures.

References

Adam, J. H. (1982). *Longman Dictionary of Business English*. London: Longman Group Limited.

Haney, W. V. (1979). *Communication and Interpersonal Relations*. New York: Richard Irwin.

Itoh, K. (1987). *This Is Plain English*. Tokyo: Babel Press.

Kameda, N. (1977). Empathy in International Business Communication. *The ABCA Bulletin, 40*(4), 25–27.

McCallen, B. (1989). English: A World Commodity, The International Market for Training in English As a Foreign Language, Special Report No. 1166, *The Economist Intelligence Unit* (pp. 1–25). London: The Economist Intelligence Unit Limited.

Ozaki, S. (1975). Business English from a Human Point of View. *The Journal of Business Communication, 12*(2).

Torao, S. (1966). *Principles of International Sale of Goods*. Tokyo: Ikubunsha.

Trudgill, P., & Hannah, J. (1985). *International English: A Guide to Varieties of Standard English*. London: Arnold Publishers Ltd.

Yamamoto, T. (1988). *Language and Communication*. Tokyo: Tokyo University Press.

5.3 Serving Two Masters: A Study in Expatriate Allegiance

◆

Stewart Black and Hal Gregersen

To succeed in today's competitive world market, expatriate managers need to be committed to both the parent firm and the local operation. They must also be able to integrate the objectives of both organizations. Research suggests, however, that expatriate managers with this dual allegiance are rare. When serving two masters, most overseas employees tend to lean too far toward one, creating extra costs and unfortunate consequences for themselves and their organizations.

Expatriate managers generally fit into one of four simplified patterns of allegiance: They may be overly committed to the parent firm, or to the local operation. Or they may be highly committed to both organizations, or to neither. In the following pages, the causes and consequences associated with each pattern are explained through actual case studies. The information was accumulated through numerous interviews and surveys (in which most managers asked that their names and the names of their employers be disguised).[1] An analysis of what firms are actually doing follows, as do guidelines for effectively developing expatriates with dual allegiance.

Source: Stewart Black and Hal Gregersen, "Serving Two Masters: A Study in Expatriate Allegiance," excerpted from *Innovations in International Compensation*, 1992, pp. 3–11. Reprinted by permission from *Innovations in International Compensation*, Copyright © 1992 by Organization Resources Counselors, Inc.

The consequences of split allegiance

Expatriate managers who are partial to the local office tend to understand the host culture and economy. Unfortunately, however, their priorities have been known to interfere with the execution of company plans at the global level. One of Honda's senior executives reports that the manufacturer incurred many "nontrivial" costs during the coordination of a global marketing strategy for the new Honda Accord. Some expatriate managers in Europe refused to fully support the new Accord, which had been restyled for a global market, because they felt it was much too conservative for their local markets.

Meanwhile, expatriates who are overly committed to the parent company often impede company progress in the host location; since this type of expatriate usually does not understand the local culture, he or she tends to have difficulty implementing policies and procedures issued by the home office. The director of the medical equipment division of a large U.S. multinational firm recently failed in his attempt to establish home-office financial reporting and accounting procedures, which were inappropriate for the company's newly acquired French subsidiary.

When the dual allegiance of expatriates is not managed effectively, a downward cycle of events typically takes place. The stages of this decline are:

1. Unbalanced dual allegiance among expatriates leads to a variety of failures during and after international assignments.
2. As managers hear about these failures, companies have difficulty attracting top international candidates.
3. Increasingly inferior candidates are sent overseas, resulting in worse organizational results and an increasing number of failed careers.
4. The pool of willing and qualified candidates becomes even smaller.
5. Over time, a company loses its competitive position overseas and fails to develop leadership with the international understanding needed for organizational success.

How does a company avoid this cyclical trap? The first step is to understand the makeup of the various types and patterns of expatriate allegiance (see exhibit to follow).

Expatriates who see themselves as free agents

Paul Jackson is a vice president and general manager for the Japanese subsidiary of a large West Coast bank. In the ten years since he

Matrix of Expatriate Allegiance

| | | Allegiance to the Local Operation | |
		Low	High
Allegiance to the Parent Firm	Low	Expatriates Who See Themselves as Free Agents	Expatriates Who Go Native
	High	Expatriates Who Leave Their Hearts at Home	Expatriates Who See Themselves as Dual Citizens

graduated with a master's degree, he has held four positions in four different companies. An Asian studies undergraduate major, Paul spoke and wrote advanced intermediate Chinese at the time of graduation. During his undergraduate studies, he spent two years in Japan, at which time his knowledge of Japanese was close to the professional level.

Paul was sent on a three-year assignment to Hong Kong after having worked for two years at the headquarters of his first company, a major East Coast bank. Although the expatriate package he received was extremely generous, Paul felt little loyalty to his parent firm or to its local Hong Kong operation. First and foremost, Paul was committed to his career. The bank invested a substantial amount of time and money in his language and technical training. He worked hard, but was always on the alert for better jobs and pay. Two years into his Hong Kong assignment he found a better position in another firm and took it. Four years into that assignment he took a job with a different U.S. bank in its Taiwan operation. Four years later he took the job in Japan with the West Coast bank.

In an interview in which Paul related his work history, he said, "I can't really relate to your question about which organization I feel allegiance to. I do my job, and I do it well. I play for whatever team needs me and wants me. I'm like a free agent in baseball or a hired gun in the old West. If the pay and job are good enough, I'm off. You might say, 'Have international expertise, will travel.'"

Paul is part of a network of "hired-gun free agents" in the Pacific Rim comprising ten or so American managers hired as expatriates (not as local hires). The members of this group are either bi- or trilingual and have spent over half of their professional careers in the Far East. They help one another maintain their free-agent status by exchanging information about various Far East operations that need experienced expatriate managers.

Hired-gun free agents.   Generally, hired guns are happy with their free-agent careers overseas and believe they would have difficulty moving up the headquarters hierarchy of any company back home. Their reasons are several. First, they feel their children are better off abroad than at home, from a general perspective and from an educational standpoint. (Expatriate children genally attend private international schools at company expense.) Second, they want to retain the extra benefits in their expatriate packages. Third, they believe that the position they would get on returning home would not offer them the status, freedom, and power they enjoy overseas.

Companies tend to view such employees with ambivalence. On the positive side, these expatriates are experienced overseas residents; they have proven they can succeed on assignment and are slightly less expensive to support than expatriates from home. In addition, most of them have acquired important skills, such as speaking a foreign language, which are rarely found among a company's internal executive ranks. In short, they will not be among the 15 to 20 percent of American expatriates who fail on overseas assignment because of serious problems adjusting to foreign cultures.[2]

On the negative side, hired guns are known for putting their own goals before the company's. They often leave with little warning, so replacing them is costly and difficult, and their knowledge about the company subsidiary and host location can seldom be applied to the company's global strategy, since they rarely repatriate to the home office.

Plateaued-career free agents.   Another type of expatriate with little commitment to either the parent or local operation embarks on assignment as a home-country employee, not as an international expert. These expatriates' careers "plateaued" at headquarters, so they feel little commitment to the home office. Unfortunately, starting an expatriate assignment with low commitment to the parent firm often results in low commitment to the local operation.

Generally, plateaued free agents accept overseas assignments to improve their chances for growth in the company, or to acquire a generous expatriate package. One plateaued free agent explained, "I figured I was stalled in my job [back in North Carolina], so why not take a shot at an overseas assignment, especially given what I'd heard about the high standard of living even mid-level managers enjoyed overseas?"

Plateaued free agents often become expatriates in companies that encourage candidates to select themselves for overseas assignments. Chances are particularly good for them when a company places a low value on international operations and encourages a self-selection process. High-potential managers are unlikely to volunteer for overseas work when the place to get ahead is at home.

Lack of predeparture cross-cultural training reinforces low levels of commitment to the parent firm and local operation. "If the company does not care about me, why should I care about the company?" expatriates tend to ask. Meanwhile, a lack of understanding for the local culture and people often prevents a commitment to the local operation from developing. Roughly 70 percent of all American expatriates receive no predeparture cross-cultural training.

Unlike hired-gun free agents, many plateaued-career free agents are unhappy in their overseas assignments. Because of their low level of commitment, they usually put little effort into adjusting to the local operation and culture. They may suffer a failed assignment as a result, which interferes with career advancement and may severely affect their sense of identity and self-confidence.

The company pays a price too. It spends approximately $100,000 to $250,000 to bring an expatriate home and send out a replacement. In addition, poor expatriate performances often damage company relationships with clients and suppliers. Then again, the "leadership gap" that often occurs during the replacement process can further damage the local operation's internal and external relationships. Back at headquarters, meanwhile, rumors might spread that international posts are the "kiss of death," discouraging good candidates from applying for overseas work.

Even when plateaued free agents do not fail in their assignments, their lack of commitment can be costly. The experience of a certain expatriate who lives in Taiwan and works for a major U.S. aircraft manufacturer is typical:

Bob Brown is a plateaued manager who transferred overseas three years ago. He does not enjoy living in Taiwan and neither does his family. When his wife and daughter have asked repeatedly to go home, Bob has argued that he has no job to return to. His daughter has become so depressed that she has started to do poorly in school. Her distress and other pressures have put a severe strain on Bob's marriage. As a result of his assignment, Bob's home life is in a shambles and work merely means a paycheck, albeit a fat one (compensation and benefits total $210,000 per year). Given Bob's attitude about work and his general lack of commitment, it is unlikely he is giving his company its money's worth.

Expatriates who go native

Generally, expatriates who "go native" are highly committed to the local operation and feel little commitment to the parent firm. Consider Gary Ogden, who has been overseas for half of his 15 years with a large computer company. Currently, he is on his third international assignment, in Paris, where he is the country manager for his company's instrument division in France.

As seasoned expatriates, Gary, his wife, and their three daughters (ages 6, 9, and 11) quickly adjusted to life in France. Gary's French is not perfect, but decent. His daughters' language skills are amazing, however. They are attending local schools and have become fluent in French. The Ogdens frequently take trips to museums, nearby cities, and other points of interest. Having been in France for 18 months, Gary has requested an extension; his contract requires him to stay only another six months. Regarding commitment, he said, "My first commitment is to the unit here. In fact, half the time I feel like corporate [the parent firm] is a competitor I must fight rather than a benevolent parent I can look to for support."

People like Gary who have lived overseas for years and are skilled at adjusting to foreign cultures tend to identify strongly with the local operation at the expense of the parent firm. Managers who spend many years away from home seldom link their sense of identity with the parent firm. Literally and psychologically, headquarters becomes a distant organization compared with the local operation.

The going native syndrome occurs often in companies that have cadres of "career internationalists." It also crops up when headquarters does not establish strong ties with its subsidiaries through such mechanisms as expatriate sponsors (individuals assigned to keep expatriates abreast of events at headquarters).

What are the consequences of having an expatriate whose allegiance is local? Let's consider Gary Ogden again. Gary feels that he often has to fight the parent company – that it is a competitor. His fighting techniques have to be subtle because he knows that his international assignment is temporary and that his fortunes ultimately depend on headquarters' evaluations.

"Sometimes I simply ignore their directives if I do not think they are appropriate or relevant to our operations," Gary explained. "If it's really important, eventually someone from regional or corporate will hassle me and I have to respond. If it is not important or if they think I implemented what they wanted, they just leave me alone. As long as the general results are good, it does not seem like there are big costs to this approach."

On occasion, Gary has fought corporate overtly, an approach that hurt him at headquarters, but helped him gain the trust and loyalty of his local-national employees. Their loyalty increased his effectiveness in the country, which ultimately brought him brownie points and leniency at headquarters.

Gary nearly left his firm when he repatriated after his two previous international assignments. He complained that he did not have the responsibility in the United States that he enjoyed overseas and that the company did not take his international experience seriously. (Our research found that most repatriated expatriates – regardless of commitment pattern – feel that their companies do not tap them for enough information when making global decisions. Ninety-one percent of U.S. expatriates felt this way, 97 percent of Japanese expatriates, and 89 percent of Finnish expatriates.) Gary's low commitment to the parent firm heightened the salience of these factors as justification for quitting. Both times, however, his requests for overseas assignments were granted, so he did not leave the company.

Expatriates who go native frequently implement only those home-office policies that they consider fit for the host location. In doing so, they sometimes go against the grain of a company's global strategy, disrupting its worldwide coordination. The result can be extremely costly to the company. In addition, such expatriates are unlikely to stay long enough after repatriation to pass on their knowledge of international business.

Nevertheless, many corporate executives recognize that expatriates who go native are not all bad. Their high level of allegiance to the local operation, which generally leads to an understanding of local culture, often results in two positives: (1) the development or adaptation of products and services that are well targeted to the local market and (2) managerial approaches that improve productivity among local-national employees.

The importance of modifying a managerial style to suit local-national employees must not be overlooked. Americans, especially, tend to select their expatriates primarily according to domestic track records. They assume that anyone who manages well in New York will do fine in Tokyo or Hong Kong. The evidence suggests this is not necessarily true.[3]

Expatriate managers who go native can be especially effective in firms at the multidomestic stage of globalization that are made up of independent overseas units, each of which is trying to succeed in a specific national or regional market. In this situation, the premium is on understanding the local market and the local-national people and culture, and the primary information flow is within the local operation, rather than between it and the parent firm.

Expatriates who leave their hearts at home

The third type of expatriate manager has a high level of allegiance to the parent firm, but little allegiance to the foreign operation. Earl Markus is such an expatriate. He is on his first overseas assignment in Belgium as the managing director of the European headquarters of a large building-supplies company's "do-it-yourself" retail division. In his 22 years with the company Earl moved up from store manager to Southwest regional manager to vice president of finance. Since Earl's two children are in college, they did not move overseas with their parents.

When Earl was sent overseas, the European operations were fairly new. Earl's mission for the next three years was to increase the number of retail outlets from the nine that existed in Belgium to 50 throughout Western Europe. The president and CEO of the American parent firm assigned the COO, Frank Johnson, to sponsor Earl and work closely with him during his three-year assignment.

One year into the assignment Earl is on schedule and has opened 15 new outlets in three countries, but he is frustrated. He seriously considered returning home more than once last year. He finds the Europeans lazy and slow to respond to directives. His allegiance is to the home office, and he looks forward to returning home when his assignment is over.

To explain his frustration, Earl discussed what happened when he implemented a new inventory system. Eight months into the assignment Frank Johnson suggested that Earl implement the new computerized inventory system that had just been phased into all the American outlets. Frank was excited about the cost-saving potential that the new system offered, as well as the reduction in shrinkage, or theft, that it promised. It was working well back home, so why not in Europe?

The system required that designated employees make a daily sales record and take a weekly random inventory of specific items. Within 48 hours, these reports had to be sent to the central office, where evaluations concerning the sales and inventory of each store and the company as a whole could be generated. Forms and procedural manuals were printed and a two-day seminar was conducted for all the European store managers, the director of operations, and relevant members of his staff. Two months later, when Earl inquired about how the system was operating, he discovered it was not. He said the European managers could give only "lame excuses" about why the system would not work, especially in Belgium.

This case is typical of expatriates whose allegiance is strongly tilted in favor of the parent firm. Like Earl, such expatriates usually spent many years working in the home office, and their sense of identity is linked with the parent firm. All their investments of time, sweat, and heartache were made in the home office, and their strong allegiance to that office is largely a function of expecting a return on that investment.

Two other factors in combination contribute to an expatriate's lopsided allegiance in favor of the home office. The first is poor adjustment to the host country and culture, a problem that is encouraged when expatriate selection processes are primarily based on domestic track records. Someone who cannot relate to the local culture will probably have difficulty developing a commitment to the local operation. The second factor is the formal tie to the home office that expatriates have when a sponsor is assigned to them; when this tie is combined with many years of experience in the parent firm, expatriates may easily focus their attention and allegiance away from the local operation and toward the parent firm.

One of the negative effects a company may experience through expatriates with a high-parent/low-local commitment pattern are early returns from overseas assignments, which are costly and disruptive. Earl Markus indicated that he wanted to return home several times during his first year in Belgium. He stayed overseas because of a fear of negative career consequences more than anything else.

Organizations also incur other costs because of expatriates who have left their hearts with the home office. Since they fail to understand the local operation, culture, or employees, such expatriates often try to implement and enforce programs that are inappropriate for the local operation. Or they implement them in a way that offends the local-national employees, customers, or suppliers. Earl Markus's attempt to implement the inventory system is one such example. His effort antagonized employees, making them unreceptive to other programs and changes he subsequently tried to initiate.

Not all the consequences of having expatriates with a high commitment to the parent firm are bad. Such employees generally want to stay with the parent firm after their repatriation back to the United States. Thus, they offer headquarters some expertise concerning business overseas. (Unfortunately, the expertise may be minimal, since low commitment to the local operation also reduces knowledge about the foreign country.)

These expatriates can provide another extremely important advantage, however. They often facilitate headquarters' efforts to coordinate activities with the subsidiary. In Earl's case, the corporate purchasing agent for the new European offices was able to take full advantage of the buying powers of headquarters' centralized purchasing network. This coordinated effort resulted in substantial savings over prices that the European operations would have gotten on their own.

The ability to coordinate easily with the home office is particularly beneficial for firms at the export stage of globalization. Since the goal generally is to sell products manufactured at home in foreign markets, the primary flow of information is from the parent firm to the local operation. Having someone who can easily work with headquarters is necessary because of the key coordinating role that the home office plays in the exportation process.

Expatriates who see themselves as dual citizens

The final category of expatriate managers is those that have high levels of allegiance to both the parent and the local operations. Our study shows that these expatriates see themselves as "dual citizens." They feel an allegiance to the foreign country and operation as well as to their home country and headquarters. As dual-organization citizens, they feel a responsibility to serve the interests of both organizations.

John Bechenridge directed the Japanese office of a prominent U.S. consulting firm, with which he had spent 13 years. This was his second international assignment. His first was a one-year special-project stint in Singapore that took place seven years before. John was one of the three candidates considered for the job in Japan and his selection was based not only on his past performance but on interviews and assessments by outside consultants of his personal characteristics and the demands of the job in Japan.

Because the job required a high degree of interaction with host nationals from a traditional culture, John was given five months' notice before departing for Japan. During this time the company gave him about 60 hours of cross-cultural training and his wife about ten hours of survival briefing. Four months into the Japan assignment John received another 40 hours of cross-cultural training that concentrated on Japan's culture and business practices. After he arrived in Japan, he also took over 250 hours of language training, which was paid for by the parent firm.

John was fortunate, too, because from the start he had a clear set of objectives for his assignment in Japan. His consulting firm's Japanese office had been established to serve the Japanese subsidiaries of the parent firm's U.S. clients. John's mission was twofold: (1) to increase the growth potential of the Japan office by bringing in Japanese clients, and (2) to promote the growth of domestic operations by facilitating the recruitment of the U.S. subsidiaries of the new Japanese client firms.

John found, to his advantage, that the expectations placed on him by the parent firm conflicted little with those required by the local operation. Furthermore, the home office understood enough about doing business in Japan to realize John would have to spend money and time developing strong local relationships. Unlike some of his friends in other firms, John did not feel the tension between corporate "bean counters" who went crazy over entertainment expenses in Japan and local staff members who constantly proposed new contact opportunities. Fortunately, too, John understood from the beginning how the Japan assignment fit into his career path and how his repatriation would be handled. He was not guaranteed a specific position upon repatriation, but he knew what general opportunities would be his if he met his objectives while in Japan.

Perhaps most important, John was given a great deal of autonomy and discretion on how to achieve the objectives that were set. John felt he had the flexibility he needed to deal effectively with the inevitable conflicts that were bound to arise between the parent firm and its subsidiary. When asked about his allegiance, John commented, "I feel a strong sense of allegiance to both companies [local operation and parent firm]. Although they sometimes have different objectives, I try to satisfy both whenever I can." When objectives or expectations were in conflict between the two organizations, John generally worked to bring them together, rather than simply follow one or the other.

The personal and organizational consequences of John's dual citizenship are primarily positive. John said he was sometimes torn in two directions by the separate needs of the parent firm and the local operation. Nevertheless, the clarity of his objectives, the latitude he had with which to pursue them, and the relative infrequency and insignificance of the conflicts between the two organizations made the experience rewarding for him and beneficial for both organizations. John did so well in his five-year assignment that he received a substantial promotion on repatriation. Furthermore, he was placed in a position in which some of what he learned in Japan was used in his firm's expansion plans, both at the domestic and international levels.

To the benefit of the organization, John's dual allegiance resulted in solid relations with Japanese clients as well as government officials. It also facilitated the home office's efforts to establish relationships with the U.S. subsidiaries of the new Japanese client firms. John felt his dual focus gave his firm other advantages as well, including a strong ability to recruit high-quality Japanese employees (a skill competitors unsuccessfully struggled to acquire).

Our research found that roughly one fourth of our sample of American expatriate managers have high levels of commitment to both the local operation and parent firm. Although difficulties sometimes arise with dual-allegiance expatriates, they are more likely than other types to perform positively on all fronts – namely, to stay in their foreign assignments the expected length of time, to stay with the firm on repatriation, and to adjust well during their stay overseas. Dual-citizen expatriates are therefore desirable for any firm at any stage of globalization. They are most necessary, however, for those firms that require extensive coordination between subsidiaries as well as between the parent office and each subsidiary.

The dual-allegiance expatriates we interviewed talked of trying to understand the needs of both the parent firm and local operation to find solutions to benefit both organizations. Generally, they were able to effectively implement home-office policies in the local operation, while passing information from the local operation to corporate that would shape effective strategy and policy development for that foreign operation and other foreign operations as well.

Role conflict is one of the greatest impediments to the development of an expatriate's commitment to both the parent firm and the local operation. Interviews with expatriates indicate that the single most common source of role conflict arises when expatriates clearly understand what is expected of them, but the expectations of the parent and local organizations differ. The greater the conflicts, the less expatriates feel responsible for the outcome of their actions and the less they feel a sense of commitment to either organization. As one expatriate explained, "It's hard to feel responsible for what happens when you are being torn in opposite directions." In contrast, the greater the consistency of demands, expectations, and objectives between the parent and local organizations, the more expatriates feel responsible for what happens and the more committed they feel to both organizations.

Role ambiguity is similar to role conflict in its dynamic. However, in contrast to role conflict, which involves clear but conflicting expectations, role ambiguity occurs when neither organization has clear expectations. Interviews with expatriates reveal that poor coordination between the parent firm and the local operation often results in role ambiguity. When we asked one expatriate manager how much responsibility he felt for what happened on his job, he replied, "How can I feel responsible, when I do not really even know what I am supposed to do or what is expected of me?" Generally, the greater the role clarity – provided too much conflict is not involved – the more expatriates feel responsible for what happens at work and the more they feel committed to both the parent firm and the local operation.

Another factor related to high allegiance to both the parent firm and the local operation is a *clearly defined repatriation program*. Unfortunately, over 60 percent of American firms have no systematic or formal repatriation programs. However, when they do exist, and are clearly defined, many expatriates are freed from worries about returning home and can focus on the job at hand. Expatriates are also likely to develop an allegiance to the local operation when a clearly defined repatriation program is combined with clear, nonconflicting job expectations. At the same time, well-communicated repatriation programs tend to make expatriates feel that the parent firm is taking care of them, so their sense of obligation and commitment to the parent firm is heightened.

The most powerful factor for expatriates in developing dual allegiance is *role discretion* – the freedom to decide what needs to be done, how it should be done, when it should be done, and who should do it. The more discretion expatriates have, the more they feel responsible for what happens at work, and the more they feel committed to the local operation. Furthermore, because they usually consider the parent firm responsible for the amount of freedom they enjoy, a high level of role discretion translates into an increased sense of obligation and commitment to the parent firm. Discretion is the most important factor in developing dual allegiance, largely because most expatriates do experience a certain level of role conflict and ambiguity. A high level of role discretion gives the expatriate the flexibility and freedom he or she needs to resolve conflicting expectations in a way that benefits both organizations.

What are the policy implications?

Most multinational firms and their executives are aware of the phenomenon of expatriate allegiance. Nevertheless, few expatriates in our study said that their firms understood the causes and consequences of the different allegiance patterns or had a systematic means of developing dual-citizen expatriates. Instead, many firms try to counterbalance expatriate tendencies to be overly committed to one organization or the other. In the next few pages we will explain what some firms are actually doing to counterbalance "lopsided" allegiance. Then, on the basis of our research results, we will outline steps that employers can take to develop dual-citizen expatriates with balanced and high levels of allegiance.

Strategy 1: counterbalancing local allegiance

The expatriate who is most likely to have a high level of allegiance to the local operation at the expense of the parent firm has had several years of international experience and has adapted to foreign cultures in the past. With this information in mind, Honda Motors counterbalances tendencies to go native by having expatriates return home to Japan for a few years before they are sent overseas again. As a result of this periodic repatriation, ties between the expatriate and the parent firm are reinforced, and the tendency to go native and become overly committed to the local operation is mitigated. In Honda's view, having a cadre of career internationalists who move from one foreign assignment to the next is illogical; no firm can expect expatriates to remain highly committed to the home office when they are constantly kept at a distance.

Another way firms counterbalance tendencies to go native is to send only those employees with long tenure in the parent firm. Executives with long tenure have made an investment in the parent organization and are therefore relatively committed to it. This strategy conflicts with the relatively new policies of such firms as General Motors and Ford, which increasingly use international assignments as developmental experiences for young, high-potential managers.

GE has taken another, broader approach to counterbalance tendencies to go native by developing a system of sponsors. In some GE divisions this system involves a commitment to hire the expatriate manager back into a specific position before he or she even leaves. More often, however, it entails the following: (1) assessing the expatriate's career objectives, (2) choosing a senior manager (often in the function to which the expatriate is likely to return) who is willing to serve as sponsor, (3) maintaining contact between the sponsor and the expatriate throughout the assignment, including face-to-face meetings, (4) clarifying career objectives and capabilities before repatriation, (5) evaluating the performance of the expatriate during the assignment, and (6) providing career advice and help in finding the expatriate a position prior to repatriation.

We received additional advice from executives at several firms that offer sponsorship programs. Overall, they recommended that sponsor assignments be systematic. First, the sponsor should be senior enough to the expatriate to provide a broad view of the organization. Second, the sponsor should be given specific guidelines for keeping in touch with the expatriate. The form, content, and frequency of communications should be clearly defined. Too often a sponsor assigned to an expatriate receives no instruction. In such a case, if the sponsor takes the initiative and fulfills the responsibility, matters go well. Otherwise, the assigned sponsor is a sponsor in name only. Finally, the responsibility of planning for the expatriate's return and of finding a suitable position should not be the sponsor's burden. It should be incorporated into the firm's career development system.

Most U.S. firms do not offer their expatriates cross-cultural training before or after the expatriate's arrival overseas. That is a shame, since our research results indicate that such training counterbalances tendencies to go native. At first one might think that predeparture training would only help the expatriate identify closely with the host culture and therefore increase rather than decrease the probability of going native. Our data show, however, that while cross-cultural training does improve expatriate performance in the host location, it has an even stronger impact on the expatriate's sense of obligation and commitment to the home office; expatriates tend to feel that an organization that provides cross-cultural training is concerned about their welfare.

Firms can counterbalance the probability of going native in several ways, and once the counterbalancing strategy has been undertaken, policies that encourage the development of high levels of dual allegiance can be employed.

Strategy 2: counterbalancing the heart-left-at-home syndrome

Interestingly, many executives in U.S. firms are less concerned by the expatriate tendency to leave the heart at home than they are by the tendency to go native. Our research suggests that the negative consequences associated with an overly strong allegiance to the home office are just as severe as those associated with going native. Consequently, we draw more from our research results than from actual organizational practices in suggesting ways in which firms might counterbalance the tendency to align with the home office.

Generally, the expatriates who are most likely to leave their hearts at home have long tenure with the parent firm and little international experience. In light of this background, one might say that such firms as GE, GM, and Ford, which are sending more and more young managers overseas, are perhaps unintentionally counterbalancing this tendency.

Helping expatriates adjust to the local environment is another powerful counterbalancing force. Senior executives with long tenure are most susceptible to the heart-at-home syndrome. Ironically, they are also the ones who usually receive perks – such as company housing and cars with a chauffeur – that isolate them and inhibit their adjustment to the local culture. One factor that can hasten such an expatriate's adaptation is the successful adjustment of his or her family to the local environment.

A firm's efforts to facilitate the expatriate family's adjustment can have a profoundly positive effect on its expatriate. Ford is one of the few American firms that consistently try to provide training and preparation for the families – especially the spouses – of its expatriates. Although executives at Ford did not have leaving-your-heart-at-home tendencies in mind when they decided to provide such training, our research suggests that they are probably reaping unforeseen benefits in that area.

Family preparation programs are helpful, but they do not necessarily guarantee a smooth adjustment for the newly arrived expatriate and family. What also seems to work is frequent interaction with local nationals. The more expatriates interact with local nationals outside of work, the better their adjustment will be to the local environment and culture. Local nationals understand how to get along in their own culture and environment. Consequently, they are the best sources of instruction and feedback for day-to-day living in the host location.

To ease the adaptation period, therefore, firms can ask local-national employees and their families to help specific expatriates and families adjust to local life and work in the first few months after arrival. Care should be taken to match the sponsoring family's characteristics (number of children, age, etc.) with those of the expatriate family. Several Japanese auto firms use this strategy; they hire Americans who speak Japanese to help their expatriate managers and families adjust to life in the United States.

Strategy 3: Creating dual citizens

The most important steps a firm can take are those that prompt expatriates to develop high levels of dual allegiance. As discussed earlier, role clarity, a high level of role discretion, and low role conflict are the most powerful contributors to high dual allegiance. All a firm need do, therefore, is clearly define the expatriate's job, reduce the conflicts concerning his or her job expectations, and give the expatriate a fair amount of freedom in carrying out the assigned tasks. In the abstract it may seem simple, but the execution of these ideas can be complex.

Let's consider the issue of role clarity. One of the easiest but most rarely used techniques for increasing role clarity is job overlap. That is, the new expatriate and the job's previous incumbent are provided several days or perhaps weeks of overlap time. During this time the incumbent teaches the new entrant "the ropes." The more complex the job and the less experience the new entrant has with the tasks required in the job, the longer the overlap time should be. Theoretically, the incumbent should be able to help clarify all aspects of the job. Several expatriates specifically mentioned that this was a relatively low-cost way to facilitate expatriate adjustment and effectiveness. Expatriates in Japan and Korea also mentioned that overlap was necessary for properly introducing the incumbent's replacement to the local operation.

When overlap is not possible, our research suggests that clarification of the expatriate's job description can encourage a high level of commitment to both the parent and local firms. When job expectations are clarified, however, previously hidden conflicts between the parent and local organizations are frequently revealed. Thus, firms must simultaneously try to increase role clarity while decreasing role conflict. This requires a clear understanding of what is expected of the expatriate manager from both the parent firm and the local operation and a subsequent integration of the two points of view.

Even a firm's best intentions to accomplish this clarification and integration of expectations may not erase ambiguity and conflict. The ultimate safety net, then, is to offer expatriates role discretion so they can have the freedom to integrate the demands of the two organizations according to their best judgment. Companies cannot guarantee that they will immediately resolve all conflicts with their subsidiaries, but they can ease their expatriates' tensions by giving them the power and autonomy to resolve the issues at hand. Because it ensures that expatriates will not be caught in the middle of conflict in a powerless and frustrating position, a high degree of role discretion is the most important factor contributing to dual allegiance.

The solution to allegiance problems seems easy. Simply give expatriate managers a lot of role discretion and freedom. Unfortunately, even this may not be the answer. Too much discretion without clear objectives may cause an expatriate to make poor choices because of lack of perspective. Firms really need to consider all three factors affecting an expatriate managers' allegiance *simultaneously*.

Even though our data clearly indicate that role clarity, a reasonable level of conflict, and role discretion are important factors for creating high dual allegiance, we believe that these aspects of the expatriate manager's job are best thought of not as *targets* of manipulation but as *outcomes* of broader policy and strategic processes. If firms want to make significant, long-term, and effective changes regarding the description of an expatriate manager's job, they can do so by asking themselves the following questions:

1. Why is this particular expatriate being sent to this post? Is it because no local national is capable of doing the job? Or to provide the expatriate with needed developmental experience? Or to accomplish a predefined strategic objective?
2. By what criteria can success on the job be measured? What is really needed from the expatriate in this particular position?
3. Are the objectives and goals of the parent firm and the local unit consistent? Are they consistent between the local unit and the particular department in which the expatriate will work?
4. How much controlled coordination is needed between the parent firm and the local operation? How much freedom and autonomy should be incorporated into the local unit? Is the amount of discretion in the expatriate's position consistent with the coordination needs of the parent and local organizations?

When these questions are not asked, mistakes are easily made. Firms may adjust their expectations to reduce conflict only to jeopardize the overall relationship between the parent firm and the local operation, they may merely clarify severe expectation conflicts between the parent and the local organization, or they may give too much freedom to the expatriate in a situation in which increased amounts of control and coordination are required.

Consequently, adjustments in the job description of an expatriate manager independent of the broader strategy and context within which the job exists are likely to produce positive results that are short term at best and severely negative results at worst. In contrast, an analysis that begins with a broad strategy and context naturally leads to an understanding of what adjustments to the expatriate's job description are appropriate. Thus, the probability of achieving dual allegiance is greatly increased.

References

1. Gregersen, H.B. and Black, J.S. "Antecedents to Communications to a Parent Company and a Foreign Operation," *Academy of Management Journal,* 1992, Vol. 35, pp. 65–90.

2. Black, J.S. "Work Role Transitions: A Study of American Expatriate Managers in Japan," *Journal of International Business Studies,* 1988, Vol. 19, pp. 277–294. Copeland, L. and Griggs, L. *Going International.* New York: Random House, 1985.

3. Black, J.S. and Porter, L.W. "Managerial Behavior and Job Performance: A Successful Manager in Los Angeles May Not Be Successful in Hong Kong," *Journal of International Business Studies,* 1991. Miller, E. "The International Selection Decision: A Study of Managerial Behavior in the Selection Decision Process," *Academy of Management Journal,* 1973, Vol. 16, pp. 234–252.

$\diamond$

5.4 Self-Management Training for Joint Venture General Managers

$\blacklozenge$

Colette A. Frayne
J. Michael Geringer

Joint ventures (JVs) have become an increasingly important element of many companies' competitive strategies. These ventures involve two or more companies (the partners), each of which participates in the decision making activities of the jointly-owned entity. JVs offer the potential for promoting organizational learning and improving a company's competitiveness by reducing risk, promoting economies of scale or scope, and providing access to complementary technologies or other resources. The strategic importance of JVs is intensified since they are usually formed between existing or potential competitors and involve products or markets which constitute the primary or "core" activities of the partner firms.[1]

Although they are increasing in frequency and strategic importance, many JVs perform poorly and fail to achieve their objectives.[2] JV performance problems are often attributed to the complexity associated with the presence of two or more partners, which may be competitors as well as collaborators. In addition to running

Source: Colette A. Frayne and J. Michael Geringer, "Self-Management Training for Joint Venture General Managers," excerpted from *Human Resource Planning*, 1993, pp. 69–85, Vol. 15, No. 4. Reprinted by permission of Human Resource Planning Society.

the venture itself, the JV's general manager (JVGM) must manage relationships with each of these partner organizations, which often have conflicting motivations, operating policies, and cultures. Yet, despite the unique managerial challenges associated with this job, the role of the JVGM and its relationship to the JV performance have largely been overlooked as human resource concerns.[3] There has been essentially no effort to identify variables associated with successful or unsuccessful JVGM performance, or to develop training programs which might enable JVGMs to improve their performance.

Research and practice in clinical psychology and organizational behavior have shown that self-management techniques have had a significant relationship with performance of individuals in a variety of demanding contexts. After interviews with JVGMs and their superiors, it was apparent that self-management practices might also be useful for improving the performance of JVGMs. The potential value of self-management techniques was further reinforced by results of our pilot study examining JVGMs. Therefore, our objective here is to propose a program for training JVGMs to become more effective self-managers, and thus to improve the performance of JVGMs and their ventures. First, we will discuss the challenging nature of the JVGM's role and variables which are associated with JVGM performance. We then introduce the concept of self-management, techniques required for a comprehensive self-management training program for JVGMs, and the anticipated benefits from a self-management training program.

The challenging nature of the JVGM's role

The role of the JVGM typically differs from that of a general manager in a wholly owned subsidiary. Indeed, in our study, 86 percent of JVGMs and 82 percent of executives from the partner companies indicated that the skills required by a JVGM were different from the general management skills required for similar positions in the partners' non-JV subsidiaries. When asked to identify the different skill requirements, the managers commonly mentioned an increased need to communicate with multiple and diverse partner company executives, to negotiate and closely monitor JV performance, and to continuously try to separate the problems associated with managing the JV from those incurred by trying to satisfy the preferences of multiple partners. Further, 74 percent of JVGMs and 58 percent of partner company executives indicated that the requirements of the JVGM position were more challenging than those of similar GM positions in the partners' non-JV businesses. None of the JVGMs and only 6 percent of partner company executives indicated that the JVGM position was less challenging than similar non-JV positions.

As several executives in our study remarked, the additional challenges of the JVGM's position are often not readily apparent, particularly for managers who have not previously been involved directly with one of these ventures. Managers identified differences in terms of both the degree as well as the underlying nature of the challenges confronting the JVGM. Overall, the contextual challenges associated with the JVGM's role include the following issues: (1) the presence of multiple partner companies, (2) the existence of divided loyalties, (3) the need for operating independently, and (4) responsibility which exceeds authority.[4]

Conclusions and implications regarding the JVGM's role

Given the job's challenging context, the JVGM represents a critical variable to the effective control and performance of the JV. Their posting to the JV was viewed by the vast majority of the JVGMs as being of major importance to their personal and career development, as well as to implementation of the partners' strategies. To succeed despite the challenges of the position, the new JVGM is forced to be more flexible and self-reliant than in a corresponding intrafirm job. Interviews revealed that many JVGMs and executives from the partners felt that, to be successful, JVGMs need a varied skill set. Desired skills included effective leadership skills, networking and interpersonal skills, a vision of where the JV should be going, an ability to manage the needs of the partner companies as well as the venture, and a high degree of perceived self-efficacy and task accomplishment. In addition, the JVGM must be able to set realistic goals, monitor performance of the JV, and respond to changes in the market or in preferences of the JV's board of directors through goal readjustment and evaluation. These attributes are consistent with the concept of self-management. Anecdotal evidence gathered from our interviews suggested that JVGMs who have performed best have been those who were effective self-managers, while those with poor self-management skills were more prone to performance problems.

Self-management: Its theory and application

The concept of self-management is based on social cognitive theory.[5] Social cognitive theory represents a unified theoretical framework for analyzing and explaining human behavior. In essence, this theory states that a person's cognitions, behavior, and environment are reciprocal determinants of one another. Thus, people respond both proactively and reactively to external influences, and the external influences themselves can be altered as a result of an individual's responses.

Sometimes called self-control or self-regulation, self-management represents an individual's attempt to exert control over certain dimensions of his or her decision making and behavior. The objective of self-management training is to teach an individual to assess what the problem is, establish one or more specific goals, monitor the ways in which the environment may be hindering the attainment of these goals, determine whether the plan is successful, and refine or change the trainee's tactics when necessary. For self-management to be effective, the trainee must first identify and commit to specific goals. Otherwise, self-monitoring, which is a pre-condition for self-evaluation, will have no effect on behavior. Written contractual agreements are frequently used to increase goal commitment by specifying the reinforcing conditions for acceptance of the self-set goal. Obviously, while many individuals may practice self-management, not every individual is an effective self-manager.

Researchers have developed a model for self-management, one which is based on a negative feedback loop.[6] This model shows that self-management behaviors are initiated when an individual confronts a choice point. These points occur when the individual's attention is directed toward a specific behavior (e.g., a partner company executive tells the JVGM that continued inability to achieve performance objectives is likely to result in the loss of his or her job), or because of changes in reinforcement contingencies (e.g., the JVGM's written memos and reports to a foreign partner company formerly received no feedback, now they are reinforced through regular verbal and written communications), or when expected outcomes are no longer forthcoming (e.g., informal sessions with visiting members of the JV's board of directors cease to be enjoyable). When there is an interruption of these activities or when these activities fail to produce the effects which the person anticipated, the self-management process begins.

Self-management involves three distinct stages. First, self-observation or self-assessment provides the individual with a baseline against which future changes can be evaluated. On the basis of the individual's past experience and his or her expectations regarding what is likely to happen in a given situation, specific performance goals are set. Second, the person compares information obtained from continued self-observation with the goals for the given behavior. It is at this stage that the individual engages in self-monitoring. If there is a discrepancy between observed behavior and goals, and if the individual's behavior exceeds the goal, higher goals are usually set. The third stage involves the self-administration of reinforcers or punishers, contingent upon the degree to which the behavior has diverged from the performance goals.

Applying self-management techniques to JVGMs

The specific techniques comprising a self-management training program provide a means for JVGMs to direct their behavior toward the most critical management activities and free them to use creative management judgment in establishing a direction for the JV's operations. The net result should be the development and implementation of effective strategies for managing the venture. The six components required for a comprehensive JVGM self-management training program are (1) self-assessment, (2) goal setting, (3) self-monitoring, (4) self-evaluation, (5) written contracts, and (6) maintenance.

1. Self-assessment

Self-assessment provides the foundation for self-management. This technique involves systematic data gathering by the trainee about his or her own behavior. This assessment establishes a basis for self-evaluation, which in turn provides information on which to base self-reinforcement. The aim of self-assessment is to identify when, why, and under what conditions a person behaves in certain ways and achieves certain levels of performance. For example, the JVGM from an American-Japanese JV began receiving complaints that he was unfriendly and aloof with his employees, and that he was not being an effective manager. Through analysis of his own behavior, he discovered that, due to his own impatience and frustration arising from language and cultural differences, he had unconsciously eliminated almost all direct oral communication between himself and his Japanese management team members. This behavior had created a barrier between himself and his subordinates. To manage this situation, he began to record the number of interactions he had each day with his Japanese managers, and how he responded to each encounter. In this way, he established a basis for self-evaluation and reinforcement as well as possible insight regarding the causes of his behavior. A manager should record key behaviors such as these over a period of time in order to obtain a useful benchmark measure of behavior. Self-assessment activities such as this can help JVGMs to better understand their past behavior and provide insight into how they can better manage themselves in the future.

2. Goal-setting

Goal-setting is another essential component of effective self-management programs. After determining which behaviors need to be changed, as identified during the self-assessment session, the JVGM can develop self-established goals. Goals provide direction for a manager's efforts that might otherwise be characterized by sporadic, reactionary activity that has no consistent, purposeful basis. This technique also allows the individual to set both proximal (short term) and distal (long term) goals for improving his or her performance. For example, many JVs encounter difficulties in technology transfer and product development due to an "us-them" environment between employees originating from the individual partner companies. Anticipating that this problem might occur, the JVGM of a Canadian-Italian JV established goals regarding the type and frequency of interactions he wished to promote between employee groups (e.g., weekly meetings, monthly review reports), as well as the nature and frequency of his own participation in these interactions. The driving force for establishing these goals was the need to enhance effective technology transfer from the foreign partner and, ultimately, to promote employee identification with the JV rather than with one of the partner firms. Similarly, a French JVGM who was unfamiliar with the operations, resources, and personnel of his venture's Quebec partner established clear goals regarding the number and frequency of contacts which he would cultivate within that firm, particularly during the JV's start-up phase.

Unfortunately, a lack of consistency among JV partners' goals is quite common and tends to be a significant source of friction. In addition, JVGMs in international JVs often exhibit fundamentally different cultural "frames of reference" than the partner firms, thus impeding the process for developing goals for the JV. While these types of issues may also arise in purely domestic JVs, they tend to be more pronounced in international JVs. Thus, the importance of setting goals and managing the development and execution of these goals becomes even more critical for those managers who are operating in international settings. How challenging should the goals be? Given that a particular goal is accepted by the JVGM and the partners, goal-setting theory states that a specific, challenging goal leads to higher levels of performance than is the case for nonspecific, do-your-best, or easy goals.

3. Self-monitoring

Self-monitoring is the process by which trainees record their behavior, including when, where, or for how long the focal behavior occurs or does not occur. The type of behavior to be monitored (e.g., interactions with JV engineers involved in the technology transfer process, or contacts with partner company managers regarding progress in effecting technology transfer), as identified during the goal-setting session, represents the critical variable in determining what self-monitoring system should be employed. Critical to the effectiveness of this technique is training the JVGM on both the selection of a measurement instrument (e.g., wall graphs, charts, diaries, performance reports), as well as the need to record behavior in a timely, accurate manner (i.e., daily, weekly, as close in time to the occurrence of the behavior as is practical). Although it may initially appear to be a nonessential, time-consuming activity to a busy manager, this self-monitoring activity is critical. Indeed, research and training experience have shown that goal-setting in the absence of self-monitoring has minimal effect on behavior. Yet, when used alone, the effects of self-monitoring are at best short-lived.

4. Self-evaluation

Self-evaluation, which leads to either self-reinforcement and/or self-punishment strategies being enacted, is a powerful method for enhancing the effectiveness of self-management techniques. Self-reinforcement involves the self-delivery of rewards after the occurrence of desired behavior. By providing oneself with rewards for desirable behavior, a positive influence on future actions can be exerted. These self-administered consequences may, but need not, be tangible (e.g., they may consist of the trainees simply giving themselves a "pat on the back" or leaving the JV's site before 6 p.m. in order to spend the evening with their families).

Self-punishment, which attempts to reduce undesired actions or behavior by self-administering aversive consequences, does not seem to yield the same high level of effectiveness as self-reinforcement. Successful use of self-punishment requires the "penalty" to be sufficiently aversive to suppress undesired behavior, yet not so aversive that it will not be used. For example, consider the case of a JVGM in an Indonesian venture. This JVGM had not achieved his self-set goals regarding the frequency or quality of interactions he wished to have each month with managers from the JV or the partner company. His chosen penalty was to devote a specific proportion of his lunches and dinners over the ensuing month solely to business purposes with these target managers. He reasoned that this self-set "penalty" would represent a more effective and motivating self-punishment than requiring himself to relinquish one of his weekend recreational trips with his family.

The importance of the self-reinforcement and punishment strategies is that it gives the JVGMs the opportunity to reinforce or punish their own behavior using reinforcers that are important and motivating to them, eliminating the need for organizations to constantly seek reinforcers of motivating importance. This is a particularly relevant consideration for JVGMs operating with cross-cultural settings, where more traditional rewards and punishments might prove to be inappropriate for certain individuals, due to the JVGMs' different cultural backgrounds. In conclusion, although JVGMs can learn the required management skills for success, they must also be motivated to spend time applying these skills to the appropriate management tasks.

5. Written contracts

Written contracts are another integral part of self-management training. A written contract is an agreement with oneself that specifies expectations, plans, and contingencies for the behavior to be changed. The purpose of the contract is to specify, in writing, (1) the goals that are set, (2) the actions that the trainee will take to attain these goals, and (3) the contingencies for self-administering the rewards or punishers. The contract is a precursor to the implementation of a self-management program. It serves to prompt the JVGM to follow through on the planned course of action, as well as serving as another form of goal commitment. Contracts for self-management programs are basically contracts with one's self, although the participation of another person (e.g., a partner company manager or a member of the JV's board) may improve the contract's effectiveness in terms of influencing behavior.

6. Maintenance

Maintenance is a critical test of the usefulness of self-management training. The desired behavioral change is most likely to occur and to remain in effect over time if the JVGMs have been allowed to practice the desired skills during the training program, if they are encouraged to practice these skills in different situations on the job, and if they continually self-monitor their performance of these new behaviors.

Maintenance strategies include training the JVGM to recognize common problems and pitfalls in applying self-management techniques as well as developing strategies for effectively overcoming these challenges. The objective of this technique is to minimize relapses by having the JVGM trainees identify high-risk situations, plan ahead for such situations, and utilize coping strategies to deal with these potentially problematic situations when they occur. For the JVGM, this skill is imperative. For example, the JVGM in one of our study's ventures anticipated that product developments critical to the JV's success might be delayed due to complications in effective transfer of technology from the German partner company to the venture. By anticipating the possibility of such an outcome, the JVGM was able to focus his efforts on identifying and managing variables critically influencing the extent of such complications (e.g., clashes of national or corporate culture among the JV and partner firm employees), as well as on developing contingency plans (e.g., identifying alternative means of accessing and transferring the technology from the partner company, and arranging for importation of products until JV production began) for effectively responding to problems if and when they might occur.

The benefits of self-management training

Training in self-management can lead to improved performance by enhancing expectations of personal efficacy. Self-efficacy is a cognitive variable which reflects an individual's conviction that he or she can successfully execute the behavior or behaviors required in a given situation. Such expectations are assumed to influence the acquisition of coping behavior as well as the effort that a person will expend to maintain coping behavior in the face of real or perceived obstacles. People who judge themselves as ineffective in coping with environmental demands perceive that their difficulties (e.g., the existence of multiple partners, organizational barriers to partner-JV resource sharing) are more formidable than they are in fact. In contrast, people who have a strong sense of self-efficacy focus their attention and effort on the demands of the situation (e.g., maintaining high performance in the JV). When confronted with perceived obstacles, people with high self-efficacy are motivated to increase their efforts.

Our basic proposition in this paper is that JVGMs who are successfully managing a JV tend to be those individuals who are able to effectively use self-management skills to overcome the personal obstacles, as well as the situational demands, which affect their ability to perform effectively. JVGMs who are unable to manage the JV successfully may be those who perceive that they are unable to overcome problems that interfere with JV performance. That is, they have low self-efficacy. This relationship received support from our study's results, as discussed earlier. This argument also receives indirect support from an earlier study's discovery of a JV "failure cycle." A common pattern of decline in JVs, this "failure cycle" often is triggered by the JVGM being subjected to increasingly close monitoring by the partner companies and it may eventually destroy the JVGM's ability or perceived ability to manage the operations effectively.[7] This tendency to increase the frequency and scope of performance evaluations can substantially reduce a JV's prospects for success. Interviews with JVGMs in our study suggested that an increase in the frequency and detail of performance evaluations commonly occurred when one of the partners had concerns regarding how the JV was being managed or was performing, or when the JVGMs themselves demonstrated that they were not skilled in effectively setting goals for their own performance as well as that of the JV. Consistent with these concepts, recent studies have prescribed that one way to manage JVs successfully is to hire an independent-minded, strong-willed individual to run the JV from the outset, and to grant substantial decision making autonomy to that manager.[8] The JVGM should possess strong self-management skills, however, in order to justify a high level of autonomy.

Training in self-management is offered as one approach to improving the effectiveness of JVGMs by providing these managers with techniques designed to help them manage their own behavior. While self-management training programs vary in length and content, our experience has demonstrated that performance of trainees may be significantly increased based on a straightforward, 12-hour self-management training program consisting of group and individualized sessions.[9] The content in this latter study's training program consisted of lectures, group discussions, case studies, and the individualized sessions. Thus, with proper design and a skilled trainer, effective self-management training programs for JVGMs can be simple, flexible, and not time-intensive. This is a critical consideration given the chaotic nature of the JVGM's position and the frequent demands for quick performance after the manager's assignment to the venture.

Conclusions

As domestic and international joint ventures and other forms of alliances are increasingly used for achieving strategic objectives, and as the subsequent demands on JVGM performance intensify, there is a growing need for effective self-management techniques. In response, this paper attempts to supplement the tools available to human resource management professionals by extending existing training theory and practice to a challenging new context: joint ventures. The concepts we have presented are particularly valuable since, in contrast to many human resource training proposals which may apply to only a limited range of operating contexts, self-management appears to have the potential for application across a diverse array of industrial and cultural environments. The range of strategies available for practicing effective self-management skills should further increase the attractiveness of these techniques to managers such as JVGMs who must largely manage their own behavior rather than relying extensively on outside sources for direction and motivation.

Overall, we have tried to show that training JVGMs in effective self-management techniques represents a promising option for enhancing performance of these managers and their ventures. Nevertheless, it is naive to assume that self-management and external forms of control are mutually exclusive. Indeed, managers must always exercise some degree of self-management, even in situations which involve the most intensive levels of external control. Yet, even when self-management is deliberately encouraged, some external control by the partner companies – whether focused primarily on output measures, resource allocation, or at the task boundary – will commonly be found and will typically be encouraged by the JVGMs. The essential tasks of each of the partner companies is to provide the JVGM with clear task boundaries within which discretion and knowledge can be exercised.

In general, we are suggesting that JVGMs with strong self-management skills should be loosely supervised in terms of the specific activities undertaken as part of their role, but more closely in terms of clarifying the boundaries of their positions and discretionary supporting activities which the JVGM may undertake. In addition, external reinforcement of self-management training by the partner companies is necessary in order for the training to be successful and performance of the behaviors to be maintained. By proposing training programs that include self-management skills as well as organizational support, the effectiveness of the training – as well as the resulting performance of the individual JVGMs and their organizations – may be enhanced.

Endnotes

1. For example, see Harrigan, K. R., "Joint Ventures and Competitive Strategy," *Strategic Management Journal,* 9 (2), 1988, pp. 141–158; Geringer, J. M. and Woodcock, C. P. "Ownership and Control of Canadian Joint Ventures," *Business Quarterly,* Summer, 1989, pp. 97–101.

2. Issues regarding the strategic orientation and performance problems of joint ventures are reviewed in Geringer, J. M. and Hebert, L., "Control and Performance of International Joint Ventures," *Journal of International Business Studies,* 51, 1989, pp. 235–254; Geringer, J. M. and Hebert, L., "Measuring Performance of International Joint Ventures," *Journal of International Business Studies,* 22 (2), 1991, pp. 249–263; Geringer, J. M., *Joint Venture Partner Selection: Strategies for Developed Countries* (Westport, CT: Quorum Books).

3. For example, see Frayne, C. A. and Geringer, J. M., "Joint Venture General Managers: Key Issues in Research and Training," in K. M. Rowland, B. Shaw, and P. Kirkbride (eds.), *Research in Personnel and Human Resource Management* (Greenwich, CT: JAI Press, 1993); Geringer, J. M. and Frayne, C. A., "Human Resource Management and International Joint Venture Control: A Partner Company Perspective," *Management International Review,* 30 (special issue), 1990, pp. 103–120.

4. Frayne, C. A. and Geringer, J. M., "Training Managers for International Ventures: Topics and Techniques," *Journal of Management Education,* December (special issue), 1992, pp. 93–114.

5. Bandura, A., *Social Learning Theory,* Englewood Cliffs, NJ: Prentice-Hall, 1977; Bandura, A., *Social Foundations of Thought and Action: A Social Cognitive Theory* (Englewood Cliffs, NJ: Prentice-Hall, 1986).

6. Karoly, P. and Kanfer, F. H., *Self-management and Behavior Change: From Theory to Practice* (New York: Pergamon, 1982).

7. Killing, J. P., *Strategies for Joint Venture Success* (New York: Praeger, 1983).

8. For example, see Deloitte, Haskins and Sells International, *Teaming Up for the 90s – Can You Survive Without a Partner?* (New York: Deloitte, Haskins and Sells International, 1989).

9. This program and its results are reviewed in Frayne, C. A., *Self-Management in Organizations* (Westport, CT: Quorum Books 1991); Frayne, C. A. and Latham, G. P., "The Application of Social Learning

Theory to Employee Self-management of Attendance," *Journal of Applied Psychology*, 72, 1987, pp. 387–392; Latham, G. P. and Frayne, C. A., "Self-management Training for Increasing Job Attendance: A Follow-up and Replication," *Journal of Applied Psychology*, 72, 1989, pp. 411–416.

Part II:

◇

Managing Within Different Cultures

◆

Section 6: The Meaning of Work and Personal Values

Work takes on different meanings in different cultures, and its relationship to personal values can vary. In many cultures, people often experience stress due to conflicting demands from work and other important aspects of life. In **Action Will Be Taken: An Action-Packed Story**, work is not the central focus of a German man who confesses to being "inclined more to pensiveness and inactivity than to work." However, knowing that hard workers are highly valued, he is puzzled when his fellow factory workers keep saying that "action will be taken," but never actually taking any action. When the factory owner dies, he unexpectedly finds the perfect profession to take advantage of his pensiveness and inactivity.

In **The Charcoal-Makers**, two Argentinians work long, hard days in the hills building a charcoal-making machine in 1914. Driven not by money, but by the challenge of seeing their experiment work, they are undaunted by the limited resources they have to become economically independent. But their dream is destroyed when parental duties take priority over work, when a father becomes "fully aware of how huge a place in his heart was occupied by that poor little thing left over from his marriage."

Work is such a fundamental part of a Russian accountant's life that she is at loose ends when told she must retire. **The Retirement Party** records the pain of a woman for whom "that fateful hour strikes" after a forty-year career in which she had "healed herself with work." Now she is alone and has little to occupy her time. Like

165

the bartender in **Home Sickness**, she wonders about the meaning of her life and where she belongs.

Section 7: Power and Authority

Power and authority are typically distributed unevenly in society and organizations. The power of corporate board members is clearly evident from the obsequious behavior of an unidentified employee in the Austrian story, **Welcoming the Board of Directors**. Yet, his repeated assurances that "the structure of the company is not creaking," and that "the executive board is unimpeachable" appear highly suspect in light of the extreme conditions in which the meeting is held. The board's power indeed seems about to be abruptly cut short.

An unconventional way of gaining power, at least to Western eyes, is described in **Government by Magic Spell**. A young girl in Somalia is possessed by a spirit that gives her "a feeling of power, as though she could do things beyond the reach of ordinary human beings." Her family and clan put great faith in her ability to do good, and summon her to the capital. However, her people control the government and use her special powers to enrich themselves at the expense of the rest of the population.

Occasionally, people with little power have the opportunity to retaliate against their exploiters. In **One of These Days**, an impoverished Latin American dentist without a degree devises a way to make the corrupt and powerful mayor "pay for twenty dead men." Revenge against social injustice takes precedence over medical ethics, in a case of the powerful being at the mercy of the powerless.

In **The Experiment**, a young Russian laboratory director is disturbed when a scientist from another institute challenges her authority. He wants her to authorize money for him to conduct an experiment, but refuses to fill out the necessary paperwork or disclose the nature of the experiment. The director does not want to appear "an insensitive bureaucrat," but insists on following procedures despite the scientist's urgings to trust him. Unwittingly, she soon becomes involved in the unusual experiment.

Section 8: Status and Hierarchy

Personal relationships can range from hierarchical and authoritarian to egalitarian and consensual. As shown in **No One to Yell At**, virtually any type of relationship can be effective between superiors and subordinates as long as people have a common understanding of their roles and status. An importer of crystal giftware who immigrated from Turkey to Canada is frustrated that women employees would rather quit than fetch him coffee. He remembers fondly that his employees in Turkey "knew how to be errand boy and clerk" and he "knew how to be boss." They were always there for him to yell at when things went wrong, and never challenged his authority.

Saving face is crucial for honoring status differences and maintaining harmonious relationships in many cultures, particularly in Asian countries. The Chinese story, **The Explosion in the Parlor**, highlights the importance to both host and guest of saving face for each other. Although the relative status of the two individuals is unknown, and the nature of their relationship unspecified, both are eager to smooth over an accident involving a broken dish.

In the Footsteps of a Water Buffalo depicts human beings as having lower status and value than water buffalo in communist-controlled Vietnam. Collective farm workers toil "like beasts of burden, yet nobody dared emit one peep in their defense." Since the all-powerful party secretary controls everyone's fate, "the best thing is to sit still, and the next best thing is to say yes." A conscientious elderly couple suffer great hardship and indignity to gain favor with the party secretary.

The Costa Rican workers gathered in **The Meeting** are also in a desperate situation. Their boss is being sued, leaving them with no work and nothing to eat. They are dependent on him and feel powerless to help themselves: "We're too accustomed to giving in, we can't even ask for what belongs to us any more." All they want is to work, but their passivity leads them to think that, "The thing about being poor is that no matter where we go we're always in a bad way."

Section 9: Managerial Insights

While differences in values, attitudes and behaviors are more readily apparent between dramatically different cultures, they also exist in cultures having a common ancestral heritage. **Business Mindsets and Styles of the Chinese in the People's Republic of China, Hong Kong, and Taiwan** shows how the political, social, and economic environments of these countries have contributed to different values and ways of doing business. For instance, a straightforward, bottom-line approach to business is appropriate with Chinese in Hong Kong. However, in the People's Republic of China, where **The Explosion in the Parlor** depicted the importance of face saving, such an approach would be considered aggressive and antagonistic, just as it would in Taiwan.

Management Styles Across Western European Cultures compares and contrasts business practices in fourteen countries. Topics include decision making styles, risk, innovation, pragmatism, performance, individualism and conflict. Austrian managers, perhaps like the ones depicted in **Welcoming the Board of Directors**, are described as often having a "bureaucratic and hierarchical style," and "intellectual independence and autonomy of decision making are not desired." German managerial style is more participative, yet, as evident in **Action Will Be Taken**, Germans favor rules and precise job descriptions, and demonstrate group solidarity.

Social and political conditions have been blamed for the poor record of public sector management in Africa. The government corruption depicted in **Government by Magic Spell** is such an obstacle. Yet, **The Secrets of Managerial Success** describes characteristics of four Kenyans who were successful in managing rural development projects, initiatives notorious for failure. Political connections and access to resources are understandably essential for success, but must be accompanied by professional competence and integrity, risk taking, and drive. As is the case everywhere, "people with exceptional careers are usually exceptional."

Thinking of a Plant in Mexico? provides advice to foreign companies in managing a Mexican work force. Employees are accustomed to showing loyalty and obedience rather than initiative and independence, and expect managers to fulfill their paternalistic social obligation in return. In Mexico, managers also gain respect by keeping a formal distance from employees and being sensitive to "Latin honor." Saving face is extremely important at all levels of society, and "the sense that 'all is well' occurs when every rank, from the top down, is in its place, working harmoniously."

The Retirement Party and **The Experiment** depict Russians working under the communist regime. At that time, following rules and regulations and meeting plans set by central authorities were the mark of a good manager, while ambition and initiative were disparaged. Success in Russia's emerging market-oriented economy requires a vastly different set of managerial traits. **Understanding the Bear: A Portrait of Russian Business Leaders** analyzes Russian managerial traits in three eras: traditional Russian society, the communist period, and the market economy. Guidelines for Western managers emphasize the need to understand the Russian mindset which often construes ambitious people as "being the object of envy and resentment," and considers "not rocking the boat" a means of self-preservation.

Section 6: The Meaning of Work and Personal Values

◇

6.1 Action Will Be Taken: An Action-Packed Story

◆

Heinrich Böll

Probably one of the strangest interludes in my life was the time I spent as an employee in Alfred Wunsiedel's factory. By nature I am inclined more to pensiveness and inactivity than to work, but now and again prolonged financial difficulties compel me – for pensiveness is no more profitable than inactivity – to take on a so-called job. Finding myself once again at a low ebb of this kind, I put myself in the hands of the employment office and was sent with seven other fellow-sufferers to Wunsiedel's factory, where we were to undergo an aptitude test.

The exterior of the factory was enough to arouse my suspicions: the factory was built entirely of glass brick, and my aversion to well-lit buildings and well-lit rooms is as strong as my aversion to work. I became even more suspicious when we were immediately served breakfast in the well-lit, cheerful coffee shop: pretty waitresses

Source: Leila Vennewitz, "Action Will Be Taken," *Eighteen Stories,* Heinrich Böll, translated by Leila Vennewitz, 1966, pp. 94–97. Reprinted by permission of Verlag Kiepenheuer & Witsch, © 1966 by Heinrich Böll and Leila Vennewitz.

brought us eggs, coffee and toast, orange juice was served in taste-fully designed jugs, goldfish pressed their bored faces against the sides of pale-green aquariums. The waitresses were so cheerful that they appeared to be bursting with good cheer. Only a strong effort of will – so it seemed to me – restrained them from singing away all day long. They were as crammed with unsung songs as chickens with unlaid eggs.

Right away I realized something that my fellow-sufferers evidently failed to realize: that this breakfast was already part of the test; so I chewed away reverently, with the full appreciation of a person who knows he is supplying his body with valuable elements. I did something which normally no power on earth can make me do: I drank orange juice on an empty stomach, left the coffee and egg untouched, as well as most of the toast, got up, and paced up and down in the coffee shop, pregnant with action.

As a result I was the first to be ushered into the room where the questionnaires were spread out on attractive tables. The walls were done in a shade of green that would have summoned the word "delightful" to the lips of interior decoration enthusiasts. The room appeared to be empty, and yet I was so sure of being observed that I behaved as someone pregnant with action behaves when he believes himself unobserved: I ripped my pen impatiently from my pocket, unscrewed the top, sat down at the nearest table and pulled the questionnaire toward me, the way irritable customers snatch at the bill in a restaurant.

Question No. 1: Do you consider it right for a human being to possess only two arms, two legs, eyes, and ears?

Here for the first time I reaped the harvest of my pensive nature and wrote without hesitation: "Even four arms, legs and ears would not be adequate for my driving energy. Human beings are very poorly equipped."

Question No. 2: How many telephones can you handle at one time?

Here again the answer was as easy as simple arithmetic: "When there are only seven telephones," I wrote, "I get impatient; there have to be nine before I feel I am working to capacity."

Question No. 3: How do you spend your free time?

My answer: "I no longer acknowledge the term free time – on my fifteenth birthday I eliminated it from my vocabulary, for in the beginning was the act."

I got the job. Even with nine telephones I really didn't feel I was working to capacity. I shouted into the mouthpieces: "Take immediate action!" or: "Do something! – We must have some action – Action will be taken – Action has been taken – Action should be taken." But as a rule – for I felt this was in keeping with the tone of the place – I used the imperative.

Of considerable interest were the noon-hour breaks, when we consumed nutritious foods in an atmosphere of silent good cheer. Wunsiedel's factory was swarming with people who were obsessed with telling you the story of their lives, as indeed vigorous personalities are fond of doing. The story of their lives is more important to them than their lives, you have only to press a button, and immediately it is covered with spewed-out exploits.

Wunsiedel had a right-hand man called Broschek, who had in turn made a name for himself by supporting seven children and a paralyzed wife by working night-shifts in his student days, and successfully carrying on four business agencies, besides which he had passed two examinations with honors in two years. When asked by reporters: "When do you sleep, Mr. Broschek?" he had replied: "It's a crime to sleep!"

Wunsiedel's secretary had supported a paralyzed husband and four children by knitting, at the same time graduating in psychology and German history as well as breeding shepherd dogs, and she had become famous as a night-club singer where she was known as *Vamp Number Seven.*

Wunsiedel himself was one of those people who every morning, as they open their eyes, make up their minds to act. "I must act," they think as they briskly tie their bathrobe belts around them. "I must act," they think as they shave, triumphantly watching their beard hairs being washed away with the lather: these hirsute vestiges are the first daily sacrifices to their driving energy. The more intimate functions also give these people a sense of satisfaction: water swishes, paper is used. Action has been taken. Bread gets eaten, eggs are decapitated.

With Wunsiedel, the most trivial activity looked like action: the way he put on his hat, the way – quivering with energy – he buttoned up his overcoat, the kiss he gave his wife, everything was action.

When he arrived at his office he greeted his secretary with a cry of "Let's have some action!" And in ringing tones she would call back: "Action will be taken!" Wunsiedel then went from department to department, calling out his cheerful: "Let's have some action!" Everyone would answer: "Action will be taken!" And I would call back to him too, with a radiant smile, when he looked into my office: "Action will be taken!"

Within a week I had increased the number of telephones on my desk to eleven, within two weeks to thirteen, and every morning on the streetcar I enjoyed thinking up new imperatives, or chasing the words *take action* through various tenses and modulations: for two whole days I kept saying the same sentence over and over again because I thought it sounded so marvelous: "Action ought to have been taken;" for another two days it was: "Such action ought not to have been taken."

So I was really beginning to feel I was working to capacity when there actually was some action. One Tuesday morning – I had hardly settled down at my desk – Wunsiedel rushed into my office crying his "Let's have some action!" But an inexplicable something in his face made me hesitate to reply, in a cheerful gay voice as the rules dictated: "Action will be taken!" I must have paused too long, for Wunsiedel, who seldom raised his voice, shouted at me: "Answer! Answer, you know the rules!" And I answered, under my breath, reluctantly, like a child who is forced to say: I am a naughty child. It was only by a great effort that I managed to bring out the sentence: "Action will be taken," and hardly had I uttered it when there really was some action: Wunsiedel dropped to the floor. As he fell he rolled over onto his side and lay right across the open doorway. I knew at once, and I confirmed it when I went slowly around my desk and approached the body on the floor: he was dead.

Shaking my head I stepped over Wunsiedel, walked slowly along the corridor to Broschek's office, and entered without knocking. Broschek was sitting at his desk, a telephone receiver in each hand, between his teeth a ballpoint pen with which he was making notes on a writing pad, while with his bare feet he was operating a knitting machine under the desk. In this way he helps to clothe his family. "We've had some action," I said in a low voice.

Broschek spat out the ballpoint pen, put down the two receivers, reluctantly detached his toes from the knitting machine.

"What action?" he asked.

"Wunsiedel is dead," I said.

"No," said Broschek.

"Yes," I said, "come and have a look!"

"No," said Broschek, "that's impossible," but he put on his slippers and followed me along the corridor.

"No," he said, when we stood beside Wunsiedel's corpse, "no, no!" I did not contradict him. I carefully turned Wunsiedel over onto his back, closed his eyes and looked at him pensively.

I felt something like tenderness for him, and realized for the first time that I had never hated him. On his face was that expression which one sees on children who obstinately refuse to give up their faith in Santa Claus, even though the arguments of their playmates sound so convincing.

"No," said Broschek, "no."

"We must take action," I said quietly to Broschek.

"Yes," said Broschek, "we must take action."

Action was taken: Wunsiedel was buried, and I was delegated to carry a wreath of artificial roses behind his coffin, for I am equipped with not only a penchant for pensiveness and inactivity but also a face and figure that go extremely well with dark suits. Apparently as I walked along behind Wunsiedel's coffin carrying the wreath of artificial roses I looked superb. I received an offer from a fashionable firm of funeral directors to join their staff as a professional mourner. "You are a born mourner," said the manager, "your outfit would be provided by the firm. Your face – simply superb!"

I handed in my notice to Broschek, explaining that I had never really felt I was working to capacity there; that, in spite of the thirteen telephones, some of my talents were going to waste. As soon as my first professional appearance as a mourner was over I knew: This is where I belong, this is what I am cut out for.

Pensively I stand behind the coffin in the funeral chapel, holding a simple bouquet, while the organ plays Handel's *Largo*, a piece that does not receive nearly the respect it deserves. The cemetery café is my regular haunt; there I spend the intervals between my professional engagements, although sometimes I walk behind coffins which I have not been engaged to follow, I pay for flowers out of my own pocket and join the welfare worker who walks behind the coffin of some homeless person. From time to time I also visit Wunsiedel's grave, for after all I owe it to him that I discovered my true vocation, a vocation in which pensiveness is essential and inactivity my duty.

It was not till much later that I realized I had never bothered to find out what was being produced in Wunsiedel's factory. I expect it was soap.

◇

6.2 The Charcoal-Makers

◆

Horacio Quiroga

The two men set the sheet-metal contrivance on the ground and sat down on it. From the place where they were to the trench it was still thirty meters, and the big box was heavy. This was their fourth halt – and last, since close-by the trench cast up its scarp of red earth.

But heavy too was the midday sun on the bare heads of the two men. The harsh light bathed the landscape in a livid eclipse-like yellow, with no shadows or contours. Light from a noonday sun, a Misiones sun, in which the two men's shirts were gleaming.

From time to time they looked back toward the route they had covered, then instantly lowered their heads, blinded by light. One of them, moreover, displayed the stigma of the tropical sun in his premature wrinkles and the intricate crow's-feet about his eyes. After a while they both got up, took hold of the four-handled barrow again, and step by step arrived at last. Then they slumped down on their backs, in the peak sunlight, and shielded their faces with their arms.

The contrivance was really heavy, the weight of four galvanized sheets fourteen feet long, held together by fifty-six feet of L and T irons an inch and a half thick. The product of a difficult craft, but one

Source: Horacio Quiroga, *"The Charcoal-Makers," THE EXILES AND OTHER STORIES,* translated by J. David Danielson, 1987, pp. 55–69. Reprinted by permission from *THE EXILES AND OTHER STORIES* by Horacio Quiroga, translated by J. David Danielson, copyright © 1987 by the University of Texas Press.

176

that was etched to the core of our men's minds, for the contrivance in question was a furnace for making charcoal that they had built themselves, and the trench was nothing other than the circular-heating oven, also a result of their work alone. And by the way, though the two men were dressed like laborers and spoke like engineers, they were neither engineers nor laborers.

One was called Duncan Drever and the other Marcos Rienzi – of English and Italian parents respectively, though neither of them had the slightest sentimental predilection for the stock he came from. They thus personified a type of South American that has appalled Huret, along with so many others: the son of Europeans who makes fun of his inherited motherland as boldly as he does of his own.

But Rienzi and Drever, stretched out on their backs with their arms over their eyes, weren't laughing on this occasion, because they were fed up with working for a month from five in the morning on, more often than not in cold that had dropped to the freezing point.

And this was in Misiones. At eight o'clock, and till four in the afternoon, the tropical sun had its way; but no sooner did the sun go down than the temperature started to drop along with it, so fast you could follow the mercury's fall with your eyes. At that hour the region would begin to freeze, and literally; so that the thirty degrees centigrade of noon were reduced to four at eight in the evening, and then at four in the morning came the galloping descent to one below, two below, three below. The night before it had gone down to four below, with the resulting disarray of Rienzi's geographical knowledge, for he couldn't manage to get his bearings in that carnival climatology – which had little to do with weather reports.

"This is a subtropical country with sweltering heat," Rienzi would say, tossing away the tin-snips scorched with cold and going off to take a walk. Because before the sun comes out, in the glacial twilight of the frosted countryside, working with bare steel tears the skin off your hands quite readily.

Nevertheless, not once in all that month did Drever and Rienzi abandon their furnace, except for the rainy days, when they studied modifications on the blueprint, freezing to death. When they decided on distillation in a closed container, they already knew just about what to expect in connection with the various systems of direct firing – including that of Schwartz. Once they were firmly committed to their furnace, the only thing that never varied was its capacity in cubic centimeters. But its form and fit, lids and condenser, the diameter of the smoke-pipe – all that had been studied and restudied a hundred times. At night, when they retired, the same scene was acted out again and again. They would talk in bed for a while about this or that, whatever had nothing to do with their current task. Then the conversation would cease, because they were sleepy. At least they thought they were. After an hour of deep silence, one of them would raise his voice:

"I think seventeen ought to be enough."

"I think so too," the other would answer right away.

Seventeen what? Centimeters, rivets, days, spaces, anything at all. But they knew perfectly well that the topic was their furnace, and what it was they were referring to.

II

One day, three months earlier, Rienzi had written to Drever from Buenos Aires, telling him that he wanted to go to Misiones. What could they do up there? It was his idea – despite the public hallelujahs about the industrialization of the country – that a small industry, properly conceived, could work out well, at least during the 1914 war, which was then in progress. What did he think of that?

Drever answered: "Come on up, and we'll look into the matter of charcoal and tar."

To which Rienzi replied by getting on the boat for Misiones.

Now the distillation of wood by firing is an interesting problem to resolve, but one requiring at lot more capital than Drever could have at hand. To tell the truth, his capital consisted of the firewood on his land and what he could do with his tools. With this, as well as four sheets of metal left over from when he put up his shed, and the help of Rienzi, it was possible to give it a try.

So they tried. Since when wood is distilled the gases don't work under pressure, the materials they had were good enough. With T-irons for the frame and L-irons for the openings, they assembled the rectangular furnace, about fourteen feet long by two and a quarter wide. It was tedious and dogged work, since on top of the technical difficulties they had to deal with those resulting from the lack of materials and some of the proper tools. The first fitting, for example, was a disaster: there was no way to match those brittle, jagged edges. So they had to put it together with rivets, at one per centimeter, which amounts to 1,680 just for joining the sheets lengthwise. And since they didn't have any rivets they cut 1,680 nails – and a few hundred more for the frame.

Rienzi riveted from the outside. Drever, squeezed inside the furnace with his knees at his chest, sustained the blows. It's no secret that to flatten nails you need a lot of patience – and there inside the box Drever ran out of his with bewildering speed. Every hour they would change places, and as Drever came out cramped and bent, rising jerkily to his feet, Rienzi would get in to put his patience to the test against the skidding of the rebounding hammer.

That's the way they worked. And the two men were so set upon doing what they wanted that they didn't let a day go by without bruising their fingernails. With the usual adjustments on days when it rained, and the inevitable commentaries at midnight.

During that month they had no recreation – this from the urban point of view – but to penetrate the woods on Sunday mornings with their machetes. Drever, who was used to that life, had a firm enough wrist to cut only what he wanted to; but when Rienzi was the one who was breaking the trail, his comrade was very careful to stay four or five meters back. Not that Rienzi's grip was bad; but it takes a long time to learn to use a machete. Then again, they had the daily distraction provided by their helper, Drever's daughter. She was a five-year-old blonde, and motherless, because after three years in the region Drever had lost his wife. He had raised her by himself, with infinitely greater patience than that demanded by the furnace rivets. Drever wasn't a mild-mannered person, and he was hard to get along with. Where that rugged man had gotten the tenderness and patience needed to raise his daughter alone and come to be idolized by her, I don't know; but the truth is that when they were walking together at twilight, one could hear dialogues like this:

"Daddy!"

"Sweetheart . . ."

"Is your furnace going to be ready soon?"

"Yes, sweetheart."

"And you're going to distill all the firewood in our woods?"

"No; we're just going to see what we can do."

"And you're going to make some money?"

"I don't think so, baby."

"Poor darling daddy! You can never earn much money."

"That's the way it is . . ."

"But you're going to run a nice test, daddy. Nice like you, dear little daddy!"

"Yes, honey."

"I love you very much, very much, daddy!"

"Yes, sweetheart . . ."

And Drever's arm would come down over his daughter's shoulder, and the child would kiss her father's rough and broken hand, so big that it covered her whole breast.

Rienzi wasn't one to waste words either, and the two could easily be regarded as unapproachable. But Drever's little girl was pretty familiar with that sort of people, and she'd burst out laughing at Rienzi's terrible scowl, every time he tried, by frowning, to put an end to his helper's daily demands: somersaults on the grass; piggy-back rides; swings, trampoline, teeter-totter, cable-car – not to mention an occasional pitcher of water on her friend's face when he stretched out on the grass in the sun at noon.

Drever would hear a curse and ask what caused it.

"It's that damned little scamp!" Rienzi would shout. "All she can think of is . . ."

But faced with the prospect – remote as it was – of an injustice on his own or her father's part, Rienzi would hasten to make peace with the child, who, from a squat, would make fun of Rienzi's face – washed as clean as a bottle.

Her father played with her less; but with his eyes he would follow his friend's lumbering gallop around the meseta, toting the little girl on his shoulders.

III

It was quite a strange trio – the two long-striding men and their blonde, five-year-old assistant, who went out and came back and went out again, from the meseta to the oven. Because the girl, raised and taught without leaving her father's side, knew all the tools one by one, and more or less how much pressure you need to split ten coconuts all at once, and what smell could rightly be called that of pyroligneous acid. She knew how to read, and everything she wrote was in capital letters.

Those two hundred meters from the bungalow to the woods were crossed time and again while the oven was being built. With firm steps at dawn, or sluggish at noon, they came and went like ants along the same path, with the same winding course and the same bend to avoid the outcropping of black sandstone just above the grass.

If their choice of heating system had been difficult, getting it to perform went far beyond what they had imagined.

"It's one thing on paper and another in the field," said Rienzi with his hands in his pockets, every time a painstaking calculation – of the gas volume, air-intake, surface of the grate, or firing chambers – turned out to be useless on account of their poor materials.

Naturally, what they'd decided upon was the riskiest course possible in that order of things: spiral heating in a horizontal furnace. Why? They had their reasons, and we'll let them be. But the truth is that when they lighted the oven for the first time, and right away the smoke came out of the chimney, after having been forced down under the furnace four times – when they saw this the two men sat down for a smoke in silence, watching it with a rather distracted air, the air of men of character viewing the success of a hard job to which they've given all their effort.

It was finally done! The accessory installations – the gas-burner and tar-condenser – were child's play. The condensation was assigned to eight wine-casks, since they had no water; and the gases were conveyed directly to the hearth. So Drever's little girl had the chance to marvel at that thick stream of fire coming out of the furnace, where there was no fire.

"How pretty, daddy!" she'd exclaim, standing still with surprise. And planting kisses on her father's hand, as she always did:

"You know how to do so many things, my darling daddy!"

Whereupon they'd go into the woods to eat oranges.

Of the few things that Drever had in this world – apart from his daughter, of course – the most valuable was his orange grove, which earned him no income at all, but was a delight to behold. Planted originally by the Jesuits, two hundred years before, the grove had been invaded and overgrown by the forest, and in its underbrush the orange trees went on sweetening the air with the scent of their blossoms, which at twilight spread all the way to the paths of the open countryside. The orange trees of Misiones have never met with any disease; it would be hard to find an orange with a single blemish. And for beauty and delicious flavor, that fruit is beyond compare.

Of the three visitors to the grove, Rienzi had the biggest appetite. He could easily eat ten or twelve oranges, and when he went back to the house he always carried a loaded sack over his shoulder. Up there people say that a frost favors the fruit, and just then, at the end of June, they were already sweet as syrup, a fact that somewhat reconciled Rienzi to the cold.

This Misiones cold – which Rienzi hadn't expected, and had never heard tell of in Buenos Aires – hindered the firing of the first batches of coal, causing an extra-large expenditure of fuel.

In the interests of good organization, they would light the oven at four or five in the afternoon. And since the time required for complete carbonization of wood is normally no less than eight hours, they had to feed the fire till twelve or one in the morning, down deep in the pit before the red mouth of the hearth, while behind them a mild frost was settling in. Though the heating was impaired, the condensation proceeded wonderfully in the icy air, and this enabled them to get a 2 percent yield of tar on the first try, which was very gratifying in view of the circumstances.

Either one or the other had to oversee the process constantly, since the casual laborer who cut their firewood persisted in his ignorance of that way of making charcoal. He would intently observe the various parts of the apparatus, but shake his head at the least allusion to putting him in charge of the fire.

He was a mestizo, a big lean fellow with a sparse moustache, who had seven children, and would never answer a question, however easy, without first consulting the sky for a while, whistling aimlessly. Then he'd reply: "Could be." In vain had they told him to add fuel without worrying, till the opposite lid of the furnace sputtered when he touched it with a wet finger. He laughed heartily, but wouldn't accept the job. So the come-and-go from the meseta to the woods continued at night, while Drever's little girl, alone in the bungalow, amused herself behind the windowpanes trying to make out, in the flashing of the hearth, whether it was Rienzi or her father who was stirring up the fire.

At one time or another, some tourist going by at night toward the port, to board the steamboat that would take him to the Iguazú, must have been more than a little surprised at that glare coming up from underground, amid the smoke and steam from the exhaust pipes: a lot of solfatara and a bit of hell, which would soon afflict the imagination of the native laborer.

The latter's attention was keenly attracted to the selection of the fuel. When in a certain sector he discovered a "noble wood for burning," he would take it to the oven in his wheelbarrow, as impassive as if he were unaware of the treasure he was conveying. And faced with the stoker's delight, he would turn his head aside indifferently – to smile to his heart's content, as Rienzi liked to say.

There thus came a day when the two men found themselves with such a stock of highly combustible woods that they had to decrease the intake of air at the hearth, air that now came in whistling and vibrated under the grate.

Meanwhile, the output of tar increased. They recorded the percentages of coal, tar, and pyroligneous acid obtained from the most suitable woods, though it was all done *grosso modo*. On the other hand what they took down very carefully – one by one – were the disadvantages of circular heating for a horizontal furnace; on this they could admit to being experts. The expenditure of fuel didn't interest them much – and besides that, with the temperature at the freezing point most of the time, it wasn't possible to make any calculation at all.

IV

That winter was extremely harsh, and not only in Misiones. But from the end of June onward things began to look really strange, and the region suffered to the very roots of its subtropical being.

In fact, after four days of mugginess and threats of a massive storm, settling into a drizzle of sleet with clear skies to the south, the weather grew calm. Then the cold began, a quiet and piercing cold, barely perceptible at noon, but already nipping the ears at four o'clock. Without transition the country passed from the whiteness of daybreak to the almost dizzying splendor of a winter noon in Misiones, only to freeze in the darkness of the first hours of night.

The first of those mornings, Rienzi, half-frozen with cold, went out for a walk at dawn and came back in a little while as frozen as before. He looked at the thermometer and spoke to Drever, who was getting out of bed.

"You know what temperature we've got? Six degrees below zero."

"It's the first time that's happened," Drever answered.

"So it is," agreed Rienzi. "Everything I see here is happening for the first time."

He was referring to his mid-winter meeting with a pit-viper, and where he least expected it.

The next morning it was seven below zero. Drever began to doubt his thermometer, and got on his horse to go verify the temperature at the home of two friends, one of whom tended a small official weather station. There was no doubt about it: it was actually nine below zero; the difference from the temperature recorded at his house was due to the fact that Drever's meseta, being very high above the river and open to the wind, was always two degrees warmer in winter – and two degrees cooler in summer, of course.

"We've never seen anything like this," said Drever on his return, unsaddling his horse.

"That's right," confirmed Rienzi.

The next day, as dawn was breaking, a boy arrived at the bungalow with a letter from the friend who tended the weather station. It read as follows:

"Please record the temperature on your thermometer today when the sun comes out. The day before yesterday I sent in the figure we noted here, and last night I got a request from Buenos Aires to correct the temperature I transmitted. Down there they're scoffing at nine below zero. What's your reading now?"

Drever waited for sunrise, and wrote in his answer: "27th of June: nine degrees below zero."

The friend then telegraphed the figure recorded at his station to the main office in Buenos Aires: "27th of June: eleven degrees below zero."

Rienzi saw something of the effect such cold can have on almost tropical vegetation; but fully confirming it was kept in store for him till later on. In the meantime, his and his friend's attention were cruelly drawn to the illness of Drever's daughter.

V

Since a week earlier the girl hadn't been feeling well. (This, of course, was noted by Drever afterward, and became one of the distractions of his long periods of silence.) She'd been a bit listless, very thirsty, and her eyes smarted when she ran.

One afternoon, when Drever was going out after his midday meal, he found his daughter lying on the ground, exhausted. She had a fever well above normal. A moment later, Rienzi arrived and found her in bed, with burning cheeks and her mouth wide open.

"What's the matter with her?" he asked Drever in surprise.

"I don't know . . . a fever of 39 plus. . . ."

Rienzi bent over the bed.

"Hi, little lady! It looks like we won't play any cable-car today."

The little girl didn't answer. It was typical of the child, when she had a fever, to shut out all pointless questions and just barely respond with curt monosyllables, in which you could spot the character of her father for miles.

That afternoon Rienzi took care of the furnace, but came back every now and then to see his helper, who was then the tenant of a little blond nook in her father's bed.

At three o'clock the girl's temperature was 39.5, and 40 at six. Drever had done what you have to do in such cases, even giving her a bath.

Now, bathing, nursing, and caring for a five-year-old child, in a house made of planks and put together worse than a furnace, during icy-cold weather, is no easy task for two men with calloused hands. There are questions of little shirts and other tiny clothes, drinks at set times, details that lie beyond the powers of a man. Nevertheless, with their sleeves rolled up their hardened arms, the two men bathed the child and dried her. Of course they had to heat the room with alcohol, and later change the cold-water compresses on her head.

The little girl had yielded a smile as Rienzi was drying her feet, and this seemed to him a good omen. But Drever feared a stroke of pernicious fever – the end of which one never knows in lively temperaments like hers.

At seven her temperature rose to 40.8 . . . , dropping to 39 for the rest of the night and climbing again to 40.3 the next morning.

"Bah!" said Rienzi with a carefree air. "The little lady is tough, and it won't be this fever that'll cut her down."

And he went off to the furnace whistling, because it was no time to start thinking foolishness.

Drever said nothing. He walked back and forth in the dining room, pausing only to go in and see his daughter. The girl, consumed by fever, persisted in her curt, monosyllabic responses.

"How do you feel, little one?"

"Fine."

"Aren't you hot? You want me to pull down the bedspread a bit?"

"No."

"You want some water?"

"No."

And this without deigning to turn her eyes in his direction.

For six days Drever slept a few hours in the morning, while Rienzi did the same at night. But when the fever stayed threateningly high, Rienzi would see the father's silhouette looming motionless beside the bed, and at the same time realize that he wasn't sleepy. Then he'd get up and make coffee, which the two men drank in the dining room. They would urge each other to rest a while, but a mute shrug of the shoulders was their common response. After which one of them would start looking over the titles of the books for the hundredth time, while the other stubbornly rolled cigars at a corner of the table.

And always the baths, the heating, the cold compresses, the quinine. The girl fell asleep sometimes with one of her father's hands in hers, and no sooner did he try to withdraw it than the child felt his move and tightened her fingers. So Drever would remain sitting motionless on the bed for a good while, and – since he had nothing to do – gazing constantly at the poor little wasted face of his daughter.

Then from time to time a delirium, with the child suddenly propping herself up on her arms. Drever would quiet her down, but the girl rejected his touch, turning the other way. After that her father would resume his walking, and go drink some of Rienzi's ever-present coffee.

"How is she?" asked the latter.

"About the same," answered Drever.

Sometimes, when she was awake, Rienzi came in and strove to lift everyone's spirits with jokes about the little scamp who was playing sick and had nothing wrong with her. But even when she recognized him the girl stared at him gravely, with the sullen fixity of high fever.

The fifth afternoon Rienzi spent at the oven working – which served as a good distraction. Drever called him in for a while and went to take his turn at feeding the fire, automatically throwing stick after stick of firewood into the hearth.

At daybreak the fever went down more than usual, went down still more at noon, and at two in the afternoon, with her eyes shut, the child was lying motionless, except for an intermittent contraction of the lip and little tremors that sprinkled her face with tics. She was cold, her temperature below normal now at only 35 degrees. . . .

"An attack of cerebral anemia, almost for sure," replied Drever to a questioning look from his friend. "Some luck I've got . . ."

For three hours, on her back, the girl continued her feverish grimaces, surrounded and singed by eight bottles of boiling water. For those three hours, Rienzi walked very quietly around the room, watching with a frown the image of the father sitting at the foot of the bed. And in those three hours Drever became fully aware of how huge a place in his heart was occupied by that poor little thing left over from his marriage, and whom the next day he would probably take out to lie beside her mother.

At five o'clock Rienzi, in the dining room, heard Drever getting up; and with a still more wrinkled brow he went into the bedroom. But from the door he could see the gleaming forehead of the girl, who was drenched in sweat – and out of danger.

"Finally . . . ," said Rienzi, with his throat foolishly contracted.

"Yes, finally!" murmured Drever.

The girl was still literally bathed in sweat. When after a moment she opened her eyes, she looked for her father, and when she saw him extended her finger toward his mouth. Then Rienzi drew near:

"So? . . . How we doing, little lady?"

The girl turned her eyes toward her friend.

"You recognize me, now? I bet you don't."

"Yes."

"Who am I?"

The child smiled.

"Rienzi."

"Fine! That's what I like . . . No, no. Go to sleep now . . ."

At last they went out to the meseta.

"What a little lady!" said Rienzi, making long lines in the sand with a stick. Drever (six days of nervous tension capped by those three final hours is too much for a father by himself) sat down on the teeter-totter and dropped his head on his arms. And Rienzi withdrew to the other side of the bungalow, because he saw his friend's shoulders were shaking.

VI

Her recovery was really swift from then on. Over cup after cup of coffee on those long nights, Rienzi had come to the conclusion that, unless they replaced the first two condensation chambers, they would always get more pitch than necessary. So he decided to use two large casks in which Drever had prepared his orange wine, and with the help of their laborer had everything ready by nightfall. He lit the fire, and after entrusting it to the care of the native went back to the meseta, where from behind the panes of the dining room the two men gazed with rare pleasure at the reddish smoke which again rose up in peace.

They were in conversation, at midnight, when the half-breed came to tell them that the fire was coming out another way, that the oven had buckled in. The same idea came to both of them at once.

"Did you open the air intake?" Drever asked him.

"I did," replied the native.

"What firewood did you put in?"

"The load that was right there . . ."

"*Lapacho?*"

"Yes."

Rienzi and Drever exchanged a look, and then went out with the laborer.

It was all very clear: The upper part of the oven was covered with two layers of sheet-metal on L-iron supports, and as insulation they'd spread two inches of sand on top. In the first firing section, which was licked by the flames, they'd shielded the metal with a layer of clay over wire mesh; reinforced clay, let's call it.

Everything had gone well as long as Rienzi or Drever kept watch over the hearth. But the laborer, in order to speed up the heating for the good of his bosses, had opened the door of the ash-pan all the way, just when he was feeding the fire with *lapacho*. And since *lapacho* is to fire as gasoline to a match, the extremely high temperature attained had swept away the clay, the wire mesh, and the metal top itself – leaving a hole through which the blaze arose, compressed and roaring.

That's what the two men saw when they got there. They pulled the firewood out of the hearth, and the flaming stopped; but the breach was still vibrating, white-hot, and the sand fallen onto the furnace was blinding when stirred up.

There was nothing more to do. Without speaking, they headed back toward the meseta, and on the way Drever said:

"To think that with another fifty pesos we could have built a really good oven . . ."

"Bah!" countered Rienzi after a moment. "We did what was right to do. With a perfect installation we wouldn't have found out a lot of things."

And after a pause:

"And maybe we'd have built something a little bit *pour la galerie* . . ."

"Could be," agreed Drever.

The night was very mild, and they sat for a long while smoking at the doorway into the dining room.

VII

The temperature was *too* mild. The weather broke up, and for three days and three nights it rained out of a storm from the south, which kept the two men shut up inside the swaying bungalow. Drever took advantage of the time to finish off an essay on *creolina* – which as a killer of ants and parasites was at least as strong as its namesake derived from pit-coal tar. Rienzi, apathetic, spent the day going from one door to another to look at the sky.

Till on the third night, while they were in the dining room, and Drever was playing with his daughter as she sat on his knees, Rienzi got up with his hands in his pockets and said:

"I'm going to leave. We've already done what we could do here. If you can raise a few pesos to work on the project, let me know and I can get you what you need in Buenos Aires. Down there at the spring, you could set up three furnaces . . . Without water you can't do anything. Write me, when you manage that, and I'll come up to help you. At least" – he concluded after a moment – "we can have the pleasure of being sure that there aren't many guys in the country who know what we do about charcoal."

"I think so too," confirmed Drever, still playing with his daughter.

Five days later, under a radiant noonday sun, and with the sulky ready at the gate, the two men and their helper went to take a last look at their work, which they hadn't approached since the accident. The laborer took off the top of the oven, and like a scorched cocoon the furnace appeared, dented and twisted in its sheath of wire mesh and grey clay. From the oxidation of the fire the sheets removed were quite thick around the breach opened by the flames, and at the slightest contact their surface peeled off in blue scales, with which Drever's little girl filled the pocket of her apron.

From right where he was, along the entire border of the adjacent and surrounding woods and into the distance, Rienzi could assess the effect of nine-below cold on tropical vegetation with warm and shiny foliage. He saw the banana plants rotted into chocolate pulp, collapsed within themselves as though inside a pillowcase. He saw *yerba* plants that were twelve years old – thick trees, in short – scorched to their roots forever by the cold white fire of the frost. And in the orange grove, which they entered for a final gathering of fruit, Rienzi looked in vain overhead for the usual glitter of gold, because the ground was totally yellow with oranges. On the day of the great freeze they had all fallen when the sun came out, with a muffled thumping that pervaded the woods.

So Rienzi was able to fill up his sack, and since time was running short they headed for the port. The girl made the trip on Rienzi's lap, keeping up a very long dialogue with her friend.

The little steamboat was already leaving. Face to face, the two men looked at each other, smiling.

"*A bientôt,*" said one.

"*Ciào,*" answered the other.

But the parting of Rienzi and the girl was a lot more expressive. When the steamboat was already veering downstream, she still cried out to him:

"Rienzi! Rienzi!"

"What, little lady?" they could manage to hear.

"Come back soon!"

Drever and the girl remained on the beach till the little steamboat was hidden behind two massive outcroppings of the Teyucuaré. And as they were slowly going up the bluff, Drever in silence, his daughter held out her arms for him to pick her up.

"Your furnace burned out, poor daddy! . . . But don't be sad . . . You'll invent a lot more things, my darling little engineer!"

6.3 The Retirement Party

◆

Natalia Baranskaya

The ceremony was taking place in the auditorium. The narrow auditorium was almost empty. Some twenty people sat in the first rows, and three on stage. The stage was separated from the auditorium by an arch of three red calico curtains. White diamond patterns wound around them. Under the arch was a table with a plush tablecloth, a carafe and a pale pink hydrangea in a flowerpot. At the table sat a broad-shouldered man with an affable face – the director – and a heavy young woman in a bright green jumper – the union representative.

Nearby, in an old office armchair, sat a thin homely woman with deep-sunken eyes and a halo of permanent over her bulbous forehead. She sat erect, unmoving; only her thin hands twisted and untwisted a handkerchief.

They were celebrating Anna Vasilevna Kosova's retirement. The entire bookkeeping staff was assembled, as well as several of the oldest workers in the company – everyone who knew her. She was mild-mannered, taciturn, and had sat for almost twenty years hunched over the records, abacus and accounts on her desk. There weren't many who knew her.

The union representative spoke first. She said that comrade Kosova was one of the most senior workers in the company, always distinguished for her diligence, never late, never needed to be disci-

Source: Natalia Baranskaya, "The Retirement Party" *Russia According to Women,* edited by Marina Ledkovsky, 1991, pp. 67–77. Reprinted by permission of Hermitage Publishers.

plined, in fact had received two commendations, and that it was from workers like her that one could learn a conscientious attitude towards work.

"You are leaving for a deserved rest, comrade Kosova," she concluded. "And we hope it goes well for you. The administration and the union extend their official gratitude for your long years of honest service, and your comrades tender you this precious gift." And she lifted a sheet of paper covering six teacups painted in yellow and violet.

There was scattered clapping. Anna Vasilevna raised her handkerchief to her lips and began to blink, suppressing the tears she had long been on the brink of.

The director raised a pudgy hand with a wedding ring on it. He asked for attention. He rose, and leaning on the table, spoke quietly, in a mild voice:

"Dear comrade Kosova, today we are sending you off to a deserved rest, as was rightly said. You have been spoken of as a good worker. I would like to add some words about you as a person." He paused a moment and continued: "You worked in the company twenty years – more precisely twenty-one years and eight months. I came here, as you know, two years ago. In the years that you have worked as an accountant, there have been four directors. What does that speak of, comrades? It speaks of the enviable human quality of Anna . . ." ("Vasilevna," the union representative prompted), "Yes, Anna Vasilevna, of her constancy."

He looked around the auditorium at the attentive faces and continued:

"Believe me, it's hard to part with such a person, comrades, but in each of our lives, as they say, that fateful hour strikes. We aren't saying farewell, Anna Vasilevna, we're saying 'till we meet again.' We hope to still work with you from time to time, at our mutual need."

He concluded to loud, friendly applause. Anna Vasilevna's lips trembled, and for a long time she pressed the handkerchief to her mouth. "How well they speak, and how well they all think of me," she thought, flustered. "I wish they'd finish, I can't take any more."

But the chief accountant asked to say a few words. He mounted the stage with difficulty, drew a handkerchief from his pocket, wiped his glasses, started to put them in his pocket, then put them on again over his large nose and said in his sad, soft voice:

"My esteemed Anna Vasilevna, we worked many, many years together. You are a very good worker. And a very, very good comrade. . . . He stopped, then added very softly: "excuse me, please," and returned to his seat.

Anna Vasilevna looked at him in alarm. But then a short-legged red-haired girl with a flushed, freckled face and carrot-colored curly hair jumped up on stage, shook her head, shot the director a quick look and shouted gaily to the auditorium:

"Our union committee invites you all to tea, on its own behalf . . . and Aunt Annie's, of course, so we ask you to come to the Accounting Office, all of you . . ." She looked at the director again, giggled, jumped down wiggling her thighs, and finished on the run: "The samovar won't boil, the teapot's tee'd out – bring the new cups, we don't have enough!"

Everyone got up, started to talk all at once, crowded around Anna Vasilevna and in a decorous procession with flowered cups and saucers in hand filed out of the auditorium.

The director excused himself on the way – business, he said – and went home. "That redhead is hot," he thought, grinning.

Tea didn't last long. The women glanced at the clock and at their bags filled with things they'd bought during dinner break. Anna Vasilevna wanted to go home too. She was tired and hot in her woolen off-duty dress. They hurriedly rinsed out cups, packed the new ones in the cake box, took "Bologna" coats from the coatrack. They went outside together, then began to say goodbye. Some went left, others straight across to the streetcar stop. Anna Vasilevna went right.

Her friend Marya Petrovna went with her. They had known each other a long time. They worked in a sewing shop during the war, sewing quilted jackets for the army. They had both been soldiers. And in the same year they both lost their husbands. Panteleeva was left with two children, Kosova with one. The former had grandchildren now, the latter had nobody.

"Don't get upset, Nyura," said Marya Petrovna, looking into her friend's sunken eyes. "Think of your health."

"What good is it to anyone, my health," Anna Vasilevna replied.

"What can you do, it's all in God's hands."

Anna Vasilevna only sighed in reply. She didn't believe in God. In that terrible year when both had been felled by grief, Maria

Petrovna found consolation in the church. Anna Vasilevna didn't. She healed herself with work.

She loved her uncomplicated profession. She never talked about it. What was there to talk about? It was funny. She simply never complained, never moaned like the others, never cursed her humble lot. She worked eagerly, adroitly, efficiently. No one could more quickly discover an error, find some damned kopeck that everyone was in a fever about at the end of the quarter. And everybody constantly came to her with requests – to check, to finish, to help. She never refused. She worked, and that was it.

She worked until that year, that month, when she was fifty-eight years old. And today they had given her a retirement party, and she was going home for the last time. How did all this happen?

This is how it was. First Masha Panteleeva said, as she had heard secretly from the typist, that they wanted to retire her, that is, Kosova. Masha didn't know if it was true. The typist didn't say where she got this information. They talked about it, and calmed down a bit: people would blather about anything. Still, from that day on, something came over Anna Vasilevna – she felt tight inside and couldn't breathe easily. When the union representative Antonina Rozhnova called her, she thought: "Well, so it's true," and her heart started to beat, and her throat was tight.

Rozhnova asked Anna Vasilevna how many years she had worked in the company, then inquired about her length of service as a whole. Anna Vasilevna began to count and counted almost forty years, maybe even forty-one. She was still a girl when she started working. The conversation proceeded in a casual way, as if Rozhnova was simply interested in Anna Vasilevna as a co-worker. Then all at once Antonina said:

"Comrade Kosova, the administration suggested that I clarify some questions concerning you, since there is a feeling that you ought to be recommended for retirement."

"What, Tonya, do I work any worse than the young ones? As far as I know no one's complained about me."

"No one's suggesting that you work any worse. You're just a lot older. They haven't reached retirement age, and you have."

"Then why do I have to leave, if I don't work any worse than they do, explain to me, Tonya?"

"Well what in the world do you want me to say?" Rozhnova flared up. "I didn't say you were worse. We aren't even comparing at all whether you work better or worse. We're talking about something else entirely. You've worked forty years, while the others, the younger ones, haven't yet. So give them a chance to work too."

In the face of this argument, as irresistible as a gravestone, Anna Vasilevna was silent. What could she say in reply to it? Antonina was probably right. Still, she expressed her desire to speak with the chief accountant – he understood her work.

"Don't make him go against regulations, Kosova. You can see the man can barely walk, he's clutching at his heart. Of course it's your right to talk to the administration. By the way, the director said: 'If she – meaning you – doesn't want to submit her request, bring her to me.' You may not agree with him, you may even have a grievance with him, but personally I wouldn't advise raising a ruckus."

Anna Vasilevna went back to her desk in accounting, wrote a request and took it right away to personnel. That was two weeks ago.

Three went to the left – the chief accountant Yakov Moiseevich Zuskin, the accountant Lyudmila Kharitonova and the bookkeeper Lelka Morkovkina. Lyudmila, calm and thorough, never hurried, while the redhead Lelka, or Carrot-top Lelka, was always in a rush, always late, always running. Now it was costing her a great effort to walk along with her companions. But today was a special day, and she felt sorry for Yakov Moiseevich: the old man was thoroughly out of sorts, that was a fact. Lelka listened out of one ear to his complaint and Kharitonova's sympathetic yeses, while she avidly thought over her own affairs.

"It'll be fine if Yurka has already run after Alka in the garden. But what if Yurka forgot about it playing? Which would be better – to look around the courtyards for Yurka or to run after Alka myself? I can make dinner in a jiffy: fry some chops, boil some noodles – it'll only take a minute. Benjamin isn't playing tonight, I think. Or maybe he is? Is he or isn't he? I forget . . . my memory's going! The fact is, I won't have time to iron him a white shirt. It's awful, the way he sweats at work! And they keep on saying: 'Some job – blowing a trumpet!' They ought to try blowing one themselves. . . . There'll be hell to pay if I don't have a shirt ready!"

Lelka's husband tormented her with two passions – clean shirts and jealousy. She cursed the first and welcomed the second. Jealousy wafted her an air of romance over the horror of everyday life. Lelka remembered the director. She would have to tell Benny about his syrupy glance . . . and how afterwards . . . when they were serving tea, the director put his hand on the back of her chair and whispered to her: "Pour me some tea – it's sweeter from your hands . . ." No, not that. "In your hands tea turns into wine. . . ." Or maybe: "Your tea makes me drunk when I look at you." Aha, that was it!

Finally, her corner! Still, on parting she tried to comfort Yakov Moiseevich:

"It won't help for you to carry on about Anna Vasilevna like someone who's died. It's not even good. A person has retired . . . why, that's happiness! If right now I was given fifty rubles and told: 'You're free, comrade Morkovkina,' why, I'd. . . ."

"Don't talk nonsense," Lyudmila interrupted her, "We'd do better to arrange with the whole accounting office to go visit her next week."

"Sure," Lelka said cheerfully. "See you later."

Soon Kharitonova turned off as well. Yakov Moiseevich went on. As soon as he was alone, his thoughts returned to that day in May.

Right after the May holidays the director of the company Shavrov called Yakov Moiseevich in.

"Good day, Yakov Moiseevich," the director greeted him, extending his hand and pushing a silver cigarette case towards him. "Have a smoke!"

"Thank you, Pavel Romanovich, I don't smoke," answered Yakov Moiseevich, touching two fingers to the left side of his chest, which meant, his heart wouldn't allow it.

"I wanted to ask you, Yakov Moiseevich, are there any employees of retirement age in the accounting office? Naturally I don't mean you." The director smiled; he was joking. The company couldn't do without Yakov Moiseevich; the director himself called him "the high-flying accountant."

"So what about the old ladies in your harem, eh?"

Yakov Moiseevich averted his eyes. He didn't want to talk about that. He tried to joke his way out of it.

"They're all young in my harem, the old ones are even younger than the young ones," he said despondently.

But the director was no longer disposed to joke. Glancing at some sheet of paper, he got down to business:

"You have a bookkeeper named Kosova, born in 1907. I think it's time she had a rest. What's her salary, seventy? Well, she'll lose a little, fifteen or eighteen rubles."

"She's a good worker," the chief accountant rejoined.

"We don't have any other kind, if I know you. And if we do, let's get rid of them. Is there someone in particular we could do without?"

Yakov Moiseevich was silent.

"Well, we'll just have to grin and bear it," the director said soothingly. "As far as I can see, Kosova is the most suitable candidate. It's time she had a rest! She can bake pies for her old man, look after her grandchildren."

"Her husband died in the war."

"And how long ago was that! The war has been over for twenty years. She must have found another one ages ago."

"She doesn't have anybody. Neither children nor grandchildren. And she's a good worker, an excellent worker."

"Please, Yakov Moiseevich, don't let's quarrel." Shavrov began to drum his fingers on the table. Everyone in the company knew this sign of oncoming irritation. "How does the song go? 'Our young will always have a way, our old are honored everywhere.' We have to break in new staff."

Yakov Moiseevich asked if the director had a specific candidate in mind.

"We'll see, we'll see," Shavrov answered distractedly, leafing through the papers in his folder. "So, are we agreed?"

"I don't want to hurt a good person," Yakov Moiseevich sighed.

"Don't hurt her, then; throw her the finest party, give her a nice gift. . . . The director took out a zippered purse and rustled some bills. "Here," he said, taking a three-ruble note. "No wait, I have change." And he took a silver ruble out from under the bills. "And see that you don't skimp, either."

"Not now," Yakov Moiseevich objected. "Let the union representative take care of that."

"All right, all right," the director agreed. "Things are agreed with you, for the rest you aren't needed. We'll talk to Kosova without you as well." And he dialed the number of the union representative.

"Hello? Rozhnova? This is Shavrov. Listen Tonya, do you know Kosova from accounting? She was born in 1907. How do you find her? Slow? You hear, Yakov Moiseevich, your Kosova is slow. Okay, okay, stop by my office, Rozhnova, we're having a conference. In ten minutes or so. That's all."

Yakov Moiseevich rose. He wanted terribly to put his hand on his chest; his heart ached. But he restrained himself.

"Yes, Yakov Moiseevich, I've read your request. I'll talk it over with Rozhnova shortly. I want to accommodate you, but we can't forget about business either, of course."

This was a request for additional leave without pay. Yakov Moiseevich had long been waiting for a decision.

"Oh, how unpleasant, how bad," thought the chief accountant, descending the steps. "I've gotten old, really old."

And on his way he passed Rozhnova, smoothing her jumper, which was rising along her stout flanks.

Anna Vasilevna arrived home, sat down on a chair and sat for a long time without moving or thinking of anything. Afterwards she felt like having potatoes with green onion. She hadn't eaten since morning. She hadn't even been able to eat the cake – her stomach was too upset.

Anna Vasilevna took off her good dress, put on a robe and went into the kitchen. It was empty there. She was overjoyed: she didn't feel like talking. Anna Vasilevna ate, drank tea and washed the dishes. She thought about darning socks or reading a newspaper, but she was so sleepy that she barely had the energy to make the bed.

She lay down on her old bed with the sagging springs, put out the light, settled herself more comfortably on her right side and, sweetly sighing, closed her eyes. Through her head ran all sorts of trivialities, as always before sleep. Whether Carrot-top Lelka wouldn't forget to redo the account for payment of the trimmings . . . a burning smell was coming from the kitchen; that fat woman was always smoking up the apartment . . . where was her handkerchief? It wasn't in her bag – she must have lost it, too bad. . . . It would be interesting to know if Benjamin would be jealous tonight because Lelka was late. She'd tell about it tomorrow – a whole romance. . . .

But now it hit her like an electric shock – she wouldn't see Lelka tomorrow! She wouldn't be going to work tomorrow!

Anna Vasilevna tossed over on her back so that the springs nearly threw her on the floor. Anxieties – large and small – welled up in her. How would she live now? What would she do? How would she kill the time?

She hadn't mended her coat last year, she had gone on vacation. Now the coat was probably beyond her strength. If she set aside so much for food each day . . . and Anna Vasilevna began to think about her new budget. Then she was sorry that she hadn't saved money, she had spent it all. True, she never did have much to save. If earlier, when she had lived with her husband . . . but had they lived together long?

She had married late. She wouldn't have married at all, had she not met a man as modest, quiet and unsettled as herself. His first wife was disappointed in him because he didn't earn a good living, divorced him, sued him successfully for half a room, and afterwards drove him out altogether. He let a corner from the old woman in this very apartment. Anya lived then with her mother in the large room. At that time her room was only a piece out of the large one. The window was even somewhere in the corner.

She looked out the window – the sky was already getting light. She told herself sternly: "Better sleep, it's almost morning." But sleep didn't come.

In the predawn twilight Anna Vasilevna looked around at her room, as if she was seeing it for the first time. It was narrow and crooked. It was wider at the head, narrower at the feet. . . . "What is it, it's like a grave, really, it is." She was frightened. It seemed like the walls were pressing in, the ceiling was lowering onto her chest. It was hard to breathe. And there on a poplar under the window a crow woke up and cawed three times in a rusty voice.

"That's a bad omen, a very bad omen," she thought miserably. She felt on the brink of tears again. But her thoughts again kept her from crying. She remembered the last wearisome days.

In the accounting office they had talked a lot about Anna Vasilevna's leaving, made various speculations, pitied her, tacitly blamed Yakov Moiseevich and cursed Rozhnova. At first this made Anna Vasilevna feel better, as if the hurt were beginning to pass away. But these conversations quickly became unbearable to her – she was heartsick. There was still time left – let the days not pass, that was all.

Later everyone got tired of feeling sorry for Anna Vasilevna, and talked about the other one – whoever it was God would send them.

"The administration knows who God will send," Lelka giggled.

They began to think and guess what she would be like, the new co-worker. "Most likely some hoity-toity," said Kharitonova. Lelka began to picture her, this future hoity-toity. She made her lips into a trumpet, forcing her words through them, lisping, walking without bending her knees, on tiptoe, figured the account splaying her fingers out, and said, sadly rolling her eyes: "We have a total of a million kopeks and a hundred thousand rubles." Everyone laughed; things were never boring with Lelka around. But Anna Vasilevna's heart ached. They were already forgetting about her.

She fell asleep in the early morning. The top of the poplar was lit – the sun was up. The birds woke, and the yard was filled with twittering, singing, chirping. Loud sounds were heard, a child's crying, and somewhere the roar of a motorcycle. A woman shouted impatiently: "Vanya, are you coming?" People were going to work. Anna Vasilevna slept.

She was awakened by a loud ringing. The alarm clock had gone off – cheerfully, desperately, knocking its metal legs on the table and slowly turning its round body.

"Are you out of your mind?" She asked it tenderly, in a sleepy voice. She never set the alarm; she always woke up on time. But the hands already pointed to eight o'clock. "I'm late?!" she groaned and quickly sat up, immediately sliding her feet into her slippers.

And only then did she remember: she didn't have to go anywhere. There was no need to get up. There was no need to do anything.

She sat on the edge of the bed, with her hands hanging limp. The alarm clock rang and rang. It seemed as though that useless sound would never end.

Section 7: Power and Authority

◇

7.1 Welcoming the Board of Directors

◆

Peter Handke

Gentlemen, it's rather cold in here. Let me explain the situation. An hour ago, I called from the city to ask if everything had been prepared for the meeting, but no one answered. I immediately drove here and looked for the porter; he was neither to be found in his booth, in the basement near the furnace, nor in the auditorium. But I did find his wife there; she was sitting in the darkness on a stool near the door, her head bent, her face in her palms, her elbows resting on her knees. I asked her what had happened. Without moving, she said that her husband had left; one of their children had been run over while sledding. That is the reason that the rooms were unheated; I hope you will take this into account; what I have to say won't take long. Perhaps you could move your chairs a bit closer so I won't have to shout; I don't want to make a political speech; I merely want to report on the financial situation of the company. I'm sorry that the windowpanes have been broken by the storm; before your arrival the porter's wife and I covered the spaces with plastic bags to keep the snow from coming in; but as you can

Source: Peter Handke, "Welcoming the Board of Directors," *Bergrussung des Aufsichtsrats,* translated by Hebert Kubner, 1967, pp. 111–116. Reprinted by permission of Residenz Verlag.

see, we weren't entirely successful. Don't let the creaking distract you as I read a statement on the net-balance of this business year; there is no reason for concern; I can assure you that the executive board is unimpeachable. Please move closer if you have difficulty understanding me. I regret having to welcome you here under such circumstances; they are due to the child having sledded in front of the oncoming car; the porter's wife, as she was fastening a plastic bag to the window with string, told me that her husband, who had gone down to the basement for coal, howled; she was arranging chairs in the auditorium for the meeting; suddenly she heard her husband howl from below; she stood riveted to the spot where she heard the scream, she told me, for a long time; she listened. Then her husband appeared at the door, still holding a bucket of coal in his hand; in a low voice, his eyes averted, he told her what had happened; their second child had brought him the news. Since the absent porter has the list of names, I will welcome you as a group and not individually. I said, as a group and not individually. That's the wind. I thank you for coming in the cold through the snow to this meeting; it's quite a walk from the valley. Perhaps you thought you would enter a room where the ice on the windows would have melted and where you could sit by the stove and warm yourselves; but you are now sitting at the table in your overcoats, and the snow which fell from your shoes as you came in and took your seats hasn't even melted; there is no stove in the room, only a black hole in the wall where the stove pipe had been when this room and this empty house were still inhabited. I thank you for coming in spite of all the difficulties: I thank you and welcome you. I welcome you. I welcome you. Let me first welcome the gentleman sitting near the door where the farmer's wife had sat in the darkness; I welcome the gentleman and thank him. Perhaps when he received the registered letter a few days ago informing him of this meeting at which the accounts of the executive board are to be reviewed, he didn't think it imperative to attend since it was below freezing and snow had been falling for days; but then he thought that perhaps everything wasn't as it should be in the company; there was a suspicious creaking in its structure. I said that perhaps he thought that its structure was creaking. No, the structure of the company is not creaking. Pardon me, but what a storm this is. Then he got into his car and drove from the city in the cold through the snow to this meeting. He had to park the car in the village below; a narrow path is the only way up to the house. He sat in the tavern reading the financial section of the paper until it was time to leave for the meeting. In the woods he met another gentleman who was also on his way to the meeting; the latter was leaning on a wayside crucifix holding his hat in one hand and a frozen apple in the other; as he ate the frozen apple snow fell on his forehead and hair. I said that snow fell on his forehead and hair as he ate the frozen apple. As the first gentleman approached him, they greeted each other; then the second gentleman put his hand in his overcoat pocket and brought out a second frozen apple which he gave to the first gentle-man; at that the storm blew his hat off and they both laughed. They both laughed. Please move a little closer, otherwise you won't be able to understand me. The structure is creaking. It's not the structure of the company that's creaking; you will all receive the dividends that are due to you in this business year; I want to inform you of that in this unusual meeting. As the two men trudged through the snow in the storm, the limousine with the others arrived. They stood in their heavy black overcoats next to the car, using it as protection against the wind, and tried to make up their minds whether or not to climb up to the dilapidated farmhouse. I said: farmhouse. Although they had their doubts about making the climb, one of them persuaded the others to overcome their fears and reminded them of the grave situation that the company was in; after reading the financial news in the tavern, they left and trudged through the snow to this meeting; they were sincerely concerned about the company. First their feet made clean holes in the snow; but eventu-ally they dragged their feet, making a path in the snow. They stopped once and looked back at the valley: flakes floated down on them from the black heavens; they saw two sets of tracks leading down, one set was faint and almost covered with snow; they had been made by the farmer when he had run down after hearing of the child's accident; he often fell on his face without trying to break his fall with his hands. He often found himself buried in the icy snow; he often dug himself in with his trembling fingers; when he fell, he often licked the bitter flakes with his tongue; he often howled under the stormy skies. I repeat: the farmer often howled under the stormy skies. They also saw the tracks that led to the dilapidated farmhouse, the tracks of the two gentlemen who discussed the situation of the compnay and suggested that the capital should be increased by distributing new stocks and ate glassy pieces of the green apples as they trudged through the storm. Finally, after night had fallen, the rest of you arrived and entered this room; the first two gentlemen were sitting here, just as they are now, with their notebooks on their knees holding pencils in their hands; they were waiting for me to deliver my welcoming address so that they could take notes. I welcome all of you and thank you for coming; I welcome the gentlemen who eat the frozen apples as they write my words down; I welcome the other four gentlemen who ran over the farmer's son with their limousine as they sped over the icy street to the village: the farmer's son, the porter's son. The structure is creaking again; the roof is creaking, the creaking being caused by the heavy weight of snow; it isn't the structure of the company that's creaking. The balance is active; there are no irregularities in the business management. The beams are bending from the pressure on the roof; the structure is creaking. I would like to thank the farmer for all that he has done for this meeting: for the last number of days he climbed up to the house from the farmstead, carrying a ladder so that he could paint this room; he carried the ladder on his shoulder, holding it in the crook of his arm; in his left hand he carried a pail with whitewash with a broken broom in it. With this he painted the walls after his children had removed the wood that lay piled up to the window sills and had carted it to the farmyard on their sleds. Carrying the pail in one hand and holding the ladder with the other, the farmer walked up to the house to prepare this room for the meeting; the children ran shouting in front of him carrying their sleds, their scarves fluttering in the wind. We can still see the overlapping white rings on the floor where the farmer placed the pail when he climbed the ladder to paint the walls; the black rings near the door where the powdery snow is now coming in are from the pot with the boiling soup which the farmer's wife brought at mealtimes: the three of them sat or squatted on the ground and dipped their spoons in; the farmer's wife stood at the door, her arms crossed over her apron and sang folk songs about snow; the children slurped the soup and rhythmically swayed their heads. Please don't worry: there is no reason for concern about the company; the creaking you here is in the structure of the roof and is being caused by the weight of the snow which is causing the structure to creak. I thank the farmer for everything he has done; I would address him personally if he weren't down in the village with the child that has been run over. I would also address the farmer's wife and I would thank her, and I would address the children and give them my heart-felt thanks for everything that they have done for this meeting. I thank all of you and welcome you. I beg you to remain seated so that your movement doesn't cause the structure to collapse. What a storm! I said: What a storm. Please remain seated. I thank you for coming and welcome you. It is only the structure that is creaking; I said that you should remain seated so that the roof doesn't cave in. I said that I said that I said that you should remain seated. I said that I said that I said that you should remain seated! I welcome you! I said that I said that I welcome you. I welcome all of you who have come here to be made an end of! I welcome you. I welcome you.

◇

7.2 Government by Magic Spell

◆

Saida Hagi-Dierie Herzi

At the village

When she was ten, Halima learned that she was possessed by a jinni. The diagnosis came from the religious healer of the village, the Wadaad. Halima had been ill for several months. The Wadaad had tried all his healing arts on her till he had understood that there could be no cure: Halima was not ill in the ordinary sense of the word; she was possessed – possessed by the spirit of an infant, which she had stepped on by accident, one night in front of the bathroom. Fortunately for Halima, the sage expounded, the jinni was of the benevolent sort, one that was more likely to help than to harm her. But it would never leave her – not leave her voluntarily, not even yield to exorcism. And it would forever be an infant jinni.

With that Halima became famous. The story of her jinni was known from one end of the village to the other within hours after the Wadaad had told her mother. Everyone talked about Halima and her jinni – what it might do and what it might be made to do, for her and for the village. In no time at all, the villagers had convinced themselves and each other that Halima had the power

---

Source: Saida Hagi-Dierie Herzi, "Government by Magic Spell," *The Heineman Book of Contemporary African Short Stories,* edited by Chinua Achebe and Lynn Innes, 1992, pp. 94–99. Reprinted by permission of Saida Hagi-Dierie Herzi.

to foretell the future and to heal the sick. And it was not long before Halima herself was convinced.

Before long, Halima began to act the part. At times she would sit staring off into space. People assumed that she was listening to her jinni. Or she would actually go into a trance – she would talk, though no one was there to talk to; she would shout at the top of her voice and sometimes she would even cry. Those who witnessed these scenes were filled with holy dread. All were careful not to disturb Halima, during those moments or at any other time, for fear that they might offend the jinni. If people talked about Halima they did so in whispers, behind her back.

Halima made believe that the spirits of the infant's parents visited her during those moments of trance. They came to enquire of the infant, she told people, came to teach her how she could make the jinni happy. At the same time, Halima affirmed, they told her all manner of things about life in general, about the people of the village, things past, things present and things yet to come.

A question that was on the minds of many people in the village was who was to marry Halima when she reached the marriageable age. No one doubted that she would marry. It was what women were for – marriage and childbearing. But there was the problem of the jinni. Wouldn't it be dangerous to be married to a woman possessed? Would there be men brave enough to want to marry Halima?

When Halima did reach the marriageable age, a problem presented itself which no one had anticipated. Halima did not *want* to get married. There were indeed men brave enough to want to marry her, but Halima turned them all down. The Wadaad himself proposed to her. He, people thought, would have been the ideal husband for Halima: he, if anyone, should have been able to cope with a woman possessed. But Halima turned him down too.

Not that possession by a jinni spirit was something unusual in Halima's village. Stories of jinnis abounded – of people who were actually possessed by jinnis, of people who had jinni spirits that were like invisible twin brothers, or people who had jinni spirits as servants. It was common knowledge that one of Halima's own forefathers had had a jinni twin brother called Gess Ade, and one of her mother's grandfathers had had, in addition to a jinni twin brother, three devoted jinni servants called Toore, Gaadale, and Toor-Ourmone respectively. When Halima's mother had problems, she called on those three for help and protection. The ancestors of several clans were believed to have been born twins, a jinni being the twin partner of each of them. The tribe of Halima's brother-in-law had a twin jinni by the name of Sarhaan.

When animals were sacrificed, the jinni twins had to get their share. In return, the jinnis were expected to give support and protection to the clan. First the animals would be butchered. Then, the ritual songs having been sung, the carcasses would be cut open and the inner organs removed. These were to be given to the jinnis. Admonitions would be mumbled such as "Let's not forget Gess Ade's share; or Toore's, Gaadale's, Ourmone's . . ."

The parts set aside for the jinnis would be taken to a remote place up in the hills, and, because they invariably and mysteriously disappeared, the villagers were sure that the jinnis devoured them. No one, therefore, would dream of cheating the jinnis of their share. This had been so for generations and would continue to be so. Children were made to memorize the ritual songs so as to keep the ancestral rites intact from generation to generation.

When Halima was under the spell of her spirits, all her emotions seemed intensified. She experienced a feeling of power, as though she could do things beyond the reach of ordinary human beings. She felt good then. Moreover, whatever she undertook, her spirits seemed to lend a helping hand. Because the fortunes of her family, indeed those of the whole clan, prospered at the time, Halima as well as other people assumed that it was the spirits' doing. In time, Halima came to be regarded as a blessing to her family, an asset to the whole clan. And she gloried in the special status her spirits gave her.

To the capital

It was because of her special powers that Halima was summoned to the capital. A big part of her clan was there. The most important and the most powerful positions in the government were held by people of her clan. It had all started with one of their men, who had become very powerful in the government. He had called his relatives and found big government jobs for them. They in turn had called relatives of theirs till the government had virutally been taken over by Halima's people. And that had meant quick riches for everyone concerned. Nor had they been very scrupulous about getting what they wanted: anything that had stood in their way had been pushed aside or eliminated. At the time when Halima was summoned, her clan controlled the government and with that the wealth of the country so completely that no one dared to challenge them any more and they could get away with murder. Still they wanted to secure for themselves the extra protection of Halima's supernatural powers.

They had tried to get Halima's father to come to the capital as well. He was a man of stature, whose presence would have done honor to the clan. But he did not want to go. Old and resentful of change, he did not want to leave the peace and security of his village for the madness of the big city. But he was also afraid for his reputation. It was solid in his village but joining this gang might tarnish it, something he did not want to risk so near the end of his life. However, though he did not want to go himself, he had no reservations about sending his son and his daughter there. On one hand he hoped that they might get a slice of the big pie for themselves and so for the family. On the other hand he thought it would do no harm to have Halima there to protect the clan and to ensure its continued domination. Perhaps she could come to a deal with her spirits – she to continue looking after their infant and they to look after the welfare of the clan.

Halima did let herself be persuaded to go, but, before she went, she consulted her spirits. They asked her to perform two rituals. One was to prepare "Tahleel," a special type of water, over which certain rituals were performed. People drank it or bathed in it to benefit from its powers. The second was to perform daily annual sacrifices to Gess Ade, the clan's twin spirit. Select parts of the innards of thousands of animals – hearts, kidneys, intestines and others – were to be offered to him every day on the eastern shore.

When Halima and her brother were ready to go, a cousin of theirs came from the big city to fetch them. From this cousin, who was an important government official, the two learned many things. They learned about the great privileges their people enjoyed in the city. They got an idea what wealth they had amassed since the clan had come "to power." They found out how completely the clan was in control of the government. They were awed, the more so when their informant told them that the clan had "achieved" all this greatness in ten short years and that most of the people who now held important government positions were illiterate.

In the big city

In the city, the two were given a beautiful villa complete with lots of servants and security guards. Within days, Halima's brother obtained an important government position of his own. He was made the head of the department that handled the sale of all incense, both inside and outside the country. Its official name was Government Incense Agency.

And Halima wasted no time carrying out the two requests of her spirits. She asked two things from the leaders of the clan. She asked them to bring all the water resources of the city together in one central pool to facilitate the performing of the "Tahleel" and she requested the building of a huge slaughterhouse at the eastern shore. The leaders readily granted her requests since they were convinced that Halima's ministrations were of crucial importance for the continued success of the clan.

To centralize the city's water system, two huge water reservoirs were created, one in the eastern half and one in the western half of the city. Eventually all the wells of the city were destroyed, even the ones in private houses, and all water systems were connected to the two reservoirs. This way all the water consumed in the city came from the same source, and when Halima put the spell of her "Tahleel" on the two reservoirs, it reached everyone.

One of the effects of the "Tahleel" was to cure people of curiosity. Those who drank it stopped asking questions. Above all they stopped wondering about the actions of the clan's leading men. They became model subjects doing without questions, without objection, what they were told to do. And Halima kept putting ever new spells on the water, faster than the old ones wore off. Though no one but she herself knew what kind of magic she put on the water, rumors abounded. One rumour had it that she performed certain incantations over the bath water of the leader and then released it into the reservoirs. There was no doubt in her mind and in the minds of the leaders that as long as everyone drank the water that carried her "Tahleel" everything would go according to their plans.

When the new slaughterhouse went into operation, all other slaughterhouses were closed down. Unfortunately the new slaughterhouse was close to the Lido, the most popular of the city's beaches. In no time at all, the waters off the Lido swarmed with man-eating sharks, drawn there by the waste of blood and offals discharged by the slaughterhouse. After a number of people had been killed by the predators people stopped going to the Lido. There was no comment from the government. Quite obviously the slaughterhouse, where the sacrifices to Gess Ade were performed, was more important to the rulers of the country than the beach.

Every so often Halima would come to the slaughterhouse to check on the performance of the animal sacrifices. Here too she modified the rituals periodically to strengthen their effect.

As things kept going well for the tribe and her, Halima became more and more sure that she was the cause of it all. The clan's leaders too were convinced that they owed their continued success to Halima and her spirits. They heaped honors on her. They consulted her on all important issues and her counsel often proved invaluable. It was Halima, for instance, who thought up the idea of the shortages to keep the common people subdued. Shortages of all basic commodities were deliberately created and they kept people busy struggling for bare survival. They did not have time or energy to spare worrying about the goings-on in the government. The leaders of the clan felt more secure than ever.

Nearly twenty years have passed since Halima first went to the city. She is still performing her rituals, and the affairs of the clan are still prospering. Its men still hold all the important posts in the government and they still control the wealth of the country. As for the rest of the nation – they are mostly sruggling to make ends meet, something that's becoming more and more difficult. And if there should be a few that might have time and energy left to start asking questions, Halima's Tahleel and her various other forms of magic take care of them. The men of the clan continue to govern with the help of Halima's magic spell.

◇

7.3 One of These Days

◆

Gabriel García Márquez

Monday dawned warm and rainless. Aurelio Escovar, a dentist without a degree, and a very early riser, opened his office at six. He took some false teeth, still mounted in their plaster mold, out of the glass case and put on the table a fistful of instruments which he arranged in size order, as if they were on display. He wore a collarless striped shirt, closed at the neck with a golden stud, and pants held up by suspenders. He was erect and skinny, with a look that rarely corresponded to the situation, the way deaf people have of looking.

When he had things arranged on the table, he pulled the drill toward the dental chair and sat down to polish the false teeth. He seemed not to be thinking about what he was doing, but worked steadily, pumping the drill with his feet, even when he didn't need it.

After eight he stopped for a while to look at the sky through the window, and he saw two pensive buzzards who were drying themselves in the sun on the ridgepole of the house next door. He went on working with the idea that before lunch it would rain again. The shrill voice of his eleven-year-old son interrupted his concentration.

Source: Gabriel García Márquez, "One of These Days," *No One Writes To The Colonel And Other Stories,* translated by J. S. Bernstein, 1968, pp. 107–110. Copyright © 1968 in the English translation by Harper & Row, Publishers, Inc. Reprinted by permission of Harper & Row, Publishers, Inc.

"Papá."

"What?"

"The Mayor wants to know if you'll pull his tooth."

"Tell him I'm not here."

He was polishing a gold tooth. He held it at arm's length, and examined it with his eyes half closed. His son shouted again from the little waiting room.

"He says you are, too, because he can hear you."

The dentist kept examining the tooth. Only when he had put it on the table with the finished work did he say:

"So much the better."

He operated the drill again. He took several pieces of a bridge out of a cardboard box where he kept the things he still had to do and began to polish the gold.

"Papá."

"What?"

He still hadn't changed his expression.

"He says if you don't take out his tooth, he'll shoot you."

Without hurrying, with an extremely tranquil movement, he stopped pedaling the drill, pushed it away from the chair, and pulled the lower drawer of the table all the way out. There was a revolver. "O.K.," he said. "Tell him to come and shoot me."

He rolled the chair over opposite the door, his hand resting on the edge of the drawer. The Mayor appeared at the door. He had shaved the left side of his face, but the other side, swollen and in pain, had a five-day-old beard. The dentist saw many nights of desperation in his dull eyes. He closed the drawer with his fingertips and said softly:

"Sit down."

"Good morning," said the Mayor.

"Morning," said the dentist.

While the instruments were boiling, the Mayor leaned his skull on the headrest of the chair and felt better. His breath was icy. It was a poor office: an old wooden chair, the pedal drill, a glass case with ceramic bottles. Opposite the chair was a window with a shoulder-high cloth curtain. When he felt the dentist approach, the Mayor braced his heels and opened his mouth.

Aurelio Escovar turned his head toward the light. After inspecting the infected tooth, he closed the Mayor's jaw with a cautious pressure of his fingers.

"It has to be without anesthesia," he said.

"Why?"

"Because you have an abscess."

The Mayor looked him in the eye. "All right," he said, and tried to smile. The dentist did not return the smile. He brought the basin of sterilized instruments to the worktable and took them out of the water with a pair of cold tweezers, still without hurrying. Then he pushed the spittoon with the tip of his shoe, and went to wash his hands in the washbasin. He did all this without looking at the Mayor. But the Mayor didn't take his eyes off him.

It was a lower wisdom tooth. The dentist spread his feet and grasped the tooth with the hot forceps. The Mayor seized the arms of the chair, braced his feet with all his strength, and felt an icy void in his kidneys, but didn't make a sound. The dentist moved only his wrist. Without rancor, rather with a bitter tenderness, he said:

"Now you'll pay for our twenty dead men."

The Mayor felt the crunch of bones in his jaw, and his eyes filled with tears. But he didn't breathe until he felt the tooth come out. Then he saw it through his tears. It seemed so foreign to his pain that he failed to understand his torture of the five previous nights.

Bent over the spittoon, sweating, panting, he unbuttoned his tunic and reached for the handkerchief in his pants pocket. The dentist gave him a clean cloth.

"Dry your tears," he said.

The Mayor did. He was trembling. While the dentist washed his hands, he saw the crumbling ceiling and a dusty spider web with spider's eggs and dead insects. The dentist returned, drying his hands. "Go to bed," he said, "and gargle with salt water." The Mayor stood up, said goodbye with a casual military salute, and walked toward the door, stretching his legs, without buttoning up his tunic.

"Send the bill," he said.

"To you or the town?"

The Mayor didn't look at him. He closed the door and said through the screen:

"It's the same damn thing."

◇

7.4 The Experiment

◆

Rimma Kazakova

"Hello! I'm Arkadii Andreev. I've been sent to you to conduct an experiment."

"What kind?" Mariana inquired unhurriedly but insistently.

"Oho! So you like to take charge! Well, that's just what I can't tell you."

"Cute, but not very informative."

Andreev smiled charmingly, "Believe me!"

"I believe you."

"Will you give me an authorization for some money?"

"No."

Andreev burst out laughing.

"Are you enjoying yourself?"

"Immensely!"

"I think we've finished our introductions."

"Are you chasing me out?"

"I can offer you some tea."

As he stirred in the sugar with his spoon, Arkadii said pensively: "I like your city a lot. It's too bad I'll have to leave as soon as the experiment is over."

Mariana politely remained silent.

"They'll finish reequipping the institute in a week. So, as you see, I have only one week. . . ."

Source: Rimma Kazakova, "The Experiment," *Balancing Acts: Contemporary Stories by Russian Women,* edited by Helena Goscilo, 1989, pp. 164–173. Reprinted by permission of Indiana University Press.

"I can count."

"Will you authorize some money?"

"No. And you can't use our facilities."

"How old are you?"

"Twenty-two. I've been lab director for two years. More tea?"

"Mariana," he said simply and seriously, "I'll try to be honest. It's not because they've shut down the institute. I've thought up the most fantastic idea. I want to give my boss a present. The old boy will be so pleased! I'll. . . ."

Mariana brusquely pulled out the desk drawer and slapped the procedure manuals down on the desk.

"Interesting little books. Have you read them?"

Arkadii said unemotionally and dully, "Please forgive me. The fellows in Section Seven have my proposal. I'll go have a talk. . . ."

"And you please excuse me for a certain lack of cordiality. I'm truly sorry."

The back of his neck was strong and blond. The door closed noiselessly behind him.

That night Mariana dreamed of Arkadii. Throughout the dream – like the shadow of a boat along a river – was his sad, half-familiar face: grey eyes with blue flecks, firm lips, rather coarse blond hair, a movie star's smile. At first it was almost as if he weren't even there, and there was only a feeling of something familiar, like him, which vaguely irritated her: he made Mariana simultaneously feel both friendly and hostile. She was angered by his open desire to win her over for the sake of this mysterious experiment.

The dream wavered and trembled with a watery rippling. Arkadii's face appeared to her sometimes elongated, distorted, and unpleasant, and sometimes calm and serious.

When she got to the lab, the first thing Mariana did was send for Arkadii.

"I didn't understand you very well yesterday. What's going on? Why don't you want to submit an official request? Is this some kind of a joke?"

"No, I wasn't joking."

"What? Really, what is this? Do you know what you're suggesting?"

"Yes, I know."

"Then what do you want?"

"I want you to break the rules."

"Listen, Andreev. It's not just a matter of procedure; understand that. I really don't want you to think that I'm an insensitive bureaucrat. Stop playing your little games. You're not some lovesick girl; you're a scientist. Here's the form. Take a dictaphone and read your request. We'll discuss it. . . ."

"Oh, yes, and by tonight Lipiagin will know everything, right down to the exact wording! Thanks, but no thanks."

"Really? And how would he find out?"

"I don't know! It would seep through the walls. My boss is a genius. All he needs is a hint. He let me off to kick up my heels, to have some fun with people my own age – as you know, there aren't many at the institute under fifty."

"Arkadii, I won't allow an unauthorized experiment. That's final – period!"

"Here I had hoped to move a period, and it turns out the period – such a tiny speck – is heavier than a tombstone."

"Let's not talk about it anymore. I like your attachment to your boss, and there's something to your madness. . . . But after the disaster at Karai. . . ."

"Yes, fine. . . . So, all right, if that's how it has to be."

"How are the fellows in Seven?"

"Charming. Naive and talented, like ancient Greek gods."

"I'm leaving today," said Mariana, as she stepped onto the round platform of the elevator. "Have a good day."

And she pushed the button.

That night she dreamed of Arkadii again. They were walking in a meadow strewn with daisies. Arkadii picked a flower and started mumbling something. "What are you doing?" "It's an old counting rhyme. I learned it from my grandma." "Well, go ahead. . . ." "She loves me – she loves me not, she'll spurn me – she'll kiss me, she'll hug me to her heart – she'll send me packing. . . ." "Charming! Now, how does it go? . . . She loves me – she loves me not. . . ." It was quiet and warm. The daisies had a delicate smell. Like grains of pollen on a butterfly's wings, they rested on the soft, warm ground. Arkadii suddenly threw away the daisy. "Mariana, I want to have a serious talk with you about what's really important. Please try to understand. You know, the disaster at Karai. . . . Do you really think that humanity can be safeguarded against human sacrifices? Of course, it's better when there aren't any. No one disagrees! But you know, we're all walking along the edge. We're invading such a sanctum of nature that there are simply no guarantees of our safety. . . ." His face was sweet, sincere; his words, silent in the dream, had no sound, but were simply absorbed by her, the way skin absorbs sunlight, and with them came a feeling of sympathy and inexplicable joy. "And these regulations. . . . For two centuries now we've been saying that humanity is responsible for each individual, and each individual for humanity. In this respect there's no difference between me and an official committee. So, then, why can't I decide for myself the fate of the experiment? Why such a lack of trust? If I were an illiterate tradesman, they wouldn't have given me a diploma. But this way. . . . I didn't tell you the truth about my boss. My boss urbanely and skillfully hides from us his desire to elevate himself to inaccessible heights. Our boldness frightens him, and here the regulations help. . . ." Mariana listened, picking at the petals, and his words were enveloped in something vague and measured, like the pulsation of blood: "He loves me – he loves me not; he loves me – he loves me not. . . ." "Mariana, and you yourself? You're intelligent, and the fellows adore you, but it's not just tea drinking and official prodecures that give meaning to your existence, is it? And what can you do? . . ." "He loves me – he loves me not; he loves me – he loves me not. . . . And how does it go then? . . . He'll spurn me . . . he'll kiss me. . . ." "You're a slave to the regulations too, a slave of the committee, and of two other committees. There are three committees between you and humanity, and this is considered reasonable, such a censorship of thought, of one's very soul! . . ." "He'll hug me to his heart – he'll send me packing . . . he'll call me his own. . . . Funny boy, terribly funny boy. Who's he saying that to? As if I didn't think the same thing. Help him. . . . Only I'm still not ready. It's not all clear. Of course, there are plenty of old fools on the committees. But reckless young daredevils . . . like me . . . we're not really such daredevils. . . . No, no, I can't. This is too serious. Something's holding me back. Maybe we still aren't mature enough for all this. . . ." "Maybe we're still not mature enough for all this? Nonsense! The disaster at Karai occurred after all the plans had been approved and checked three times. False deductions from natural events. . . ." He took her by the hand; she didn't pull it back. "Mariana! I've wanted so badly for you to understand me! I'm sure that you'll agree with me! Let me do the experiment. You know me well enough for that. And the risk? So what risk? I can only tell you that it won't endanger anyone's life. If everything works out. . . ." "And if it doesn't?" "It will! But that's not the point. If it doesn't work out for me, it'll work out for someone else. What's important is the principle. To hell with routine! Mariana, tell me that you agree. Well, Mariana! . . ."

When she woke up, just one thing struck her: she had never before heard this "He loves me – he loves me not. . . ."

Mariana spent Wednesday at the expedition in the mountains. She got tired, went to bed late, and didn't dream at all that night.

The following day there was a conference in Section Seven. Mariana greeted everyone with a single nod, but was glad to see Arkadii near the vacuum chamber. He was standing with his back to her saying something to the technician. The conference ended quickly, and over the noise of the departing elevators, Mariana gaily shouted to Arkadii, "Well, how about it? Am I a good organizer? I've chased everybody away. The fellows from Section Seven have gone to the mountains for a couple of days."

Arkadii, twisting the chain with the key to the aircar, accompanied Mariana to her office.

"You going to town?" asked Mariana.

"Yes, I am. Want to come along?"

"I'd love to, but I can't. In half an hour I'm flying to the expedition. If you get terribly bored, come join us, but it's not really worth it. We're packing up to come back. . . . You know, Arkadii. . . ."

"What?" he asked intently, sensing something new in her voice.

"I wanted to tell you that our last conversation somehow . . . just that I'm awfully sorry that I can't help you at all. . . ."

"Give me the go-ahead – and you'll stop feeling sorry."

"No, we've already definitely made that decision. It's out of the question! I can't do it. Although my heart tells me. . . ."

"You should follow your heart."

Mariana was embarrassed. He was looking at her pleasantly, honestly, and a little sadly.

"I'll do that . . . after you write a paper entitled 'Physics and the Heart.' "

"People have been working on that for centuries."

"All right. Time to get to work."

Mariana jumped up on the escalator step and touched the familiar button, on which she knew every scratch, but suddenly, remembering something, she called Arkadii's name. He slowly walked back.

"Listen, you wouldn't happen to know this old poem, would you: 'He loves me – he loves me not'? . . ."

" 'He'll spurn me – he'll kiss me, he'll hug me to his heart. . . .' I know it, why?"

"No reason. It just got stuck in my mind. I heard it somewhere – can't remember where. . . ."

She pushed the button.

She wanted to have another dream. She got into bed expecting it. She told herself she would have a dream. And she did. This time it was completely without sound, without conversation – like a silent movie. She saw everything that happened distinctly, and at the same time she realized that it was just a dream, created by her own will, and, if she wanted it to, it would stop completely or do something different. It was her own dream, the way she wanted it, and so it was a wonderful, pleasant dream.

Mariana and Arkadii were sitting on a bench in front of the laboratory windows. Yellow autumn leaves were floating down, and there was a smell of damp, moldy earth. The windows were hidden by the tree branches, and the blinds were pulled down. It was late afternoon; the sun warmed them feebly but affectionately. Mariana's right hand felt Arkadii's cool, firm hand. Her whole being was jubilant and radiant. They sat like that for a long, time, and then he put his arms around her and kissed her. The kiss was also long – infinitely long. It was hard for her to pull away from him; she was afraid to pull away, because she knew, she felt, that the dream would immediately end. How long did it last? A minute? An hour? The whole night? The falling leaves quivered; the warm air shimmered; the warm lips trembled, gently and lightly pressing lips.

The next day Arkadii called on the videophone and asked to see her. When he came into her office, Mariana greeted him radiantly.

"You in a good mood?"

"Wonderful."

"Well, mine is just the opposite."

"Never mind. It'll soon change."

"Not really . . . I have to leave tomorrow."

"Well, so you see, there isn't time for the experiment anyway."

"There will be, if you let me! I'll call the institute and talk them into it. Well . . . I'll break my leg, damn it! I'll think up something."

"You're really positive that the experiment doesn't threaten you in any way?"

"Absolutely."

"Except maybe I'll lose my job. . . ."

"Well, to hell with your job! . . . That is, excuse me, I meant. . . . Well, what do you care for this mechanized saucepan? We'll go to Tulavi; I've read your résumé. You're not just a theoretician. You need real life, room to work, real machinery. . . ."

"Arkadii, let me think till tomorrow."

"It's a deal."

"I'm not making any promises."

"I'm hoping."

He left, but the holiday mood, the feeling of elation, didn't leave.

That night their conversation was repeated word for word. The only difference was that she agreed. When he was about to dissolve, Mariana pulled him by the hand and kissed him herself.

Saturday came. Mariana finished all her urgent tasks before ten and resolutely pushed the intercom button and asked for Arkadii. The person at the desk told her that Arkadii wasn't there. He hadn't come yet. He was getting ready to leave town. "That's strange," thought Mariana. Not hearing any response to this information, the man started to praise Arkadii: "Really got a head on his shoulders, that one. We could use someone like that! Can't you talk him into staying? Even for a month. . . ."

But right then the bell rang, Mariana nodded, and Arkadii walked in.

"Hello. I'll tell you right off: I agree. To be honest, I've been thinking about it myself for a long time. Let everything go topsy-turvy; you're right! How much money do you need?"

"Mariana," he said, cautiously and apparently with great effort lowering himself into the armchair, "I thank you from the bottom of my heart, but I don't need anything. I came to say goodbye."

"What? And the experiment?"

"It's been completed. Everything's in order."

"What do you mean?"

"You see . . . only please don't get angry. Our institute is testing a device which can affect human beings while they're asleep. . . ."

"What?!"

"Just don't think anything bad! The program was developed and approved by all. . . ." He smirked. "By all three committees, and I followed the program exactly. My task was to persuade you, contrary to regulations, to give your permission for an experiment. . . . You see. And exactly per the procedure manual! . . ."

"Exactly per the procedure manual?"

"Yes, of course. Piatkin and Selko were monitoring the procedure. By the way, I'm to thank you in the name of the association for your enormous contribution to science. I don't think it should affect your health in any way, but in September you and another group of participants in the experiment – it was conducted simultaneously on seven subjects – will be invited to Tulavi for the congress. If I'm not mistaken, this is your third paper for the association?"

"Yes," said Mariana distractedly, "my third. This is all very interesting. . . ." She still hadn't recovered.

"I'll leave you the technical write-up, and in a couple of days I'll send a technician and some more background material. Mariana, my dear, believe me, although this is all legal and you were aware of what you were getting into when you joined the association, I still feel like a fool! Our life is so complicated. . . ."

But Mariana was thinking about something.

"Mariana, what are you doing? Say something!"

"Tell me, Arkadii, was it you who recorded that murmuring 'He loves me – he loves me not'?"

"It was, and I was very glad that the signal got through. Otherwise I would have been left in complete ignorance until the end of the week."

Mariana blushed.

"But don't think that it was my own creation! My boss dug up the counting rhyme; you'll find it in the write-up. . . . It's a curious thing, from that ancient time of fortune telling and beliefs in God knows what, but interesting. . . . There's still so much we don't know about human beings."

Mariana finally got up her courage. "You're probably very tired. I don't know the technology, but every night. . . ."

"What! Not every night! There were three sessions."

"Monday, Tuesday, and Friday?"

"There, you see, the experiment really did work!"

"It did. . . . But about human beings – you're right – oh, how little we still know! Not much more than the people with the daisies: 'He loves me – he loves me not. . . .' One more question. In the dream you instilled in me the resolution to disregard the regulations. But, to the best of my memory, didn't we also talk about that when I was conscious?"

"I followed the program. My task was only reinforcement. In other places the experiment was conducted somewhat differently. In two cases, to the best of my knowledge, there was just suggestion, without any direct contact with the subject. . . ."

"And how do you explain such a strange choice of subject?"

"Committee Two is familiar with your report on the work of Class B laboratories. We sort of nudged your thoughts up to the final conclusion, which you weren't quite ready for."

"Oh . . . and generally, what do you think about the regulations and the three committees?"

"Oh, come on, my dear! That's all well and good for an experiment." Arkadii leaned confidingly across the desk toward Mariana. "But in real life. . . . You can imagine what a mess there'd be if you gave the labs free rein!"

Arkadii saw Mariana's frown and interpreted it in his own way.

"I don't think that anything threatens you personally. They'll send you an answer to your memorandum and that'll be the end of it. There won't be any difficulties! You're solid; I can vouch for that, and if it hadn't been for the device. . . . Besides, the association will protect you. It needs you. . . . And now, sad to say, I must say goodbye. They're waiting for me."

Arkadii got up and offered Mariana his hand.

"Wait! Just a minute. . . ."

"What?"

"No, never mind. . . . Goodbye! See you in September! It's been a long time since I was in Tulavi. But, you know, it's not bad here either, is it? Especially our park. And the bench under the oak tree – opposite my windows. . . ."

"I never had the time to get out to your park. So I'll be sure to come back again and sit on your little bench. . . . Excuse me again and – thank you!"

"Well, have a good flight, if that's how it is. Just one more thing. All this time, I had a better opinion of you than I do now. I want you to know that. I even feel sad. The fellow who sent the regulations to hell, and was even ready to break his leg . . . I liked him better. That's what I wanted to tell you."

"Oh, Mariana, my dear, you're amazing. I'd say – old-fashioned. Why, that's charming!"

When the door slammed shut behind Arkadii, Mariana started to swear in a way that wasn't at all old-fashioned.

Section 8: Status and Authority

◇

8.1 No One to Yell At

◆

Ilyas Halia

Kazim Aga from Kayseri was mad as a hornet. He was cursing everything from hell to breakfast. "Damn country!" he yelled. "It's not a country, it's an insane asylum! Nobody has any brains! Something goes wrong and they don't even care! These dull, cowardly dogs, by God! The bastards have no guts! Like a bunch of blockheads. No love, no enthusiasm! If their pants caught fire, they wouldn't put it out without permission from their wives, the idiots! Everything is carefully calculated. Damn such a life! Our money disgraces us. There's no pleasure or charm! Does living here have to be like this? Man, we have everything; we should live like pashas. But we've become coolies wearing ties! In Adana, even my clerk had more pleasure and fun. At least, on holidays, I gave him some spending money and sent him to a bar to enjoy himself. And he knew how to be a clerk; on occasion he came, kissed my hand, and asked after my health. Is it like that in this damn country? Just look at that old guy sitting over there! Has anyone ever seen him grin? Not on your life!

"I go to the bank and deposit wads of money; I withdraw money. Does that insensitive fool, that so-called director, ever offer me tea or coffee, or even a Coke? Never, never!"

Source: Ilyas Halia, "No One to Yell At," *Unregulated Chicken Butts and Other Stories,* 1990, pp. 35–38. Reprinted by permission of The University of Utah Press.

225

In Old Montreal, on a street below the great Notre Dame Cathedral, stands the business place belonging to our Kazim Aga. He wholesales imported crystal giftware from Eastern-European countries. His business seems to go well, but whenever I go to see him, he complains about the situation. Sometimes he plays backgammon with his Lebanese neighbor, a carpet man. When he loses, he's mad at losing, and when he wins, he's mad because he can't make a rural Arab angry. "I can't get a fellah mad," he complains, swallowing his anger.

It was as if the city were on fire that last week in June. The sun blazed in the sky. Narrow streets were filled with idly wandering tourists and young secretaries from neighboring banks. From time to time, the sound of steamships came from the harbor. This area is back of Old Montreal's harbor. The buildings are old and dirty, their walls thick. Wholesalers have occupied this part of the city from way back. However, now, with help from the Montreal city government, a restaurant has been opened on every corner.

A phaeton was parked at the door. It was a one-horse, pretty coach with a fold-down top. Kazim Aga rushed to the window to look at the vehicle. "I love that coach. When I look at it I'm cheered up. If I could, I'd ride it from home every day. But it's expensive! The guy drove me once and took me for fifteen dollars. I swore never to ride it again."

When I came in, Kazim Aga had stopped yelling. I go to visit him during noon-hour from time to time. He's a pleasant man, easy to talk with. Though he appears ignorant, he's really a sharp country boy with lots of common sense. When it comes to money business, or people, he rarely makes a mistake.

Upon seeing me, he said, "Come in and have a coffee. There's something I want to tell you." He sent one of the employees working beside him, to a nearby coffee man to get two Turkish coffees. The young woman left with a sour look on her face.

"Did you see that hussy?" he said, "I pay these people lots of money but they don't want to take two steps to fetch a cup of coffee. That slip of a girl complained to the accountant about me. 'I'm no coffee girl,' she said. 'If he's going to send me for coffee all the time I won't work here.' I told the accountant, 'You tell that girl that I'll not only send her, but the accountant himself if I want to.' Nonsense! If we take jobs, we all must work. If I want, I'll even have her sweep the shop. But, after all, I don't want to judge the young woman. You see all these sons-of-bitches! Spend a wad of money on them, give them jobs, and they all defy you. We couldn't find even one good Moslem to hire. This is the third girl we've tried. Women don't stay long. And I pay them plenty, too! I don't cut their pay the way those other Greek Turks do. Shall I tell you something, sir? 'Life here doesn't suit me! It's empty, cheerless! As my father used to say, 'Life has to have some charm and pleasure!'

"In Adana, I had a little store with a clerk and errand boy. I used to send my errand boy, little Kürt Hasso, to the market to get food and vegetables for the house. Every evening, he swept the store, too. You know, those two were the charm of my life. Sir, we worked together all those years and I didn't offend them even once. We got along together like a big family. They knew how to be errand boy and clerk and I knew how to be boss. On holidays, they came to kiss my hand and I never failed to open my wallet and pay them a bonus. With that life, they were happy, I was happy! When things went wrong, at least I had someone to yell at and curse. If I was upset, I swore at Hasso; I yelled at Hasso. And he would say, 'Good health to you, boss, get mad at me rather than a stranger,' and pacify me, the son-of-a-bitch. I swore at Hasso over little things. If big things went wrong, and I needed someone bigger to curse, I yelled at the clerk, Emin Effendi. He didn't usually answer. He didn't say 'thank you' or 'to your good health.' Perhaps the man hid his anger. Anyway, he never forgot his gentlemanly behavior; he knew his place and, if unwillingly, accepted the cursing with good manners. Never, at any time, did either of them abandon his gentlemanly behavior because I got mad and cursed them. Neither ever stopped me or gave me a cross answer. Being a well-bred man is really something, my friend! Look at the dirty fellows around here! Do they have even a trace of courtesy? Doesn't it ever occur to them to say, 'This is the boss, the owner; naturally he swears, he has a right to.' No one says, 'Let's be a little help to a man who takes all these troubles on his shoulders. Let's tolerate the poor guy's being all upset.' These infidels are ungrateful, by God! They jabber away, but I never listen! I swear the way I know how, in Turkish! But I don't get the same flavor out of it, because they don't understand.

"You know what I decided to do? I've decided to bring Hasso over here. Yesterday, I sat down and wrote him a letter and invited him. 'Come!' I said, 'I'll give you a good monthly salary, bed and board is on me, and I'll pay your doctor bills. I'll pay for your clothes, too.' I told Hasso, 'It's your day again, Hasso. You son-of-a-bitch, come over and see a little country!'

"I'm truly pleased that Hasso is coming. I'll have someone around to curse and yell at. At least, when I swear, the guy has to know, to understand what I say. He mustn't just stare at me stupidly. As far as I'm concerned, Hasso is used to swearing. He couldn't stand not being sworn at. One time, I didn't curse Hasso for a whole week. Whether I was very busy or sick I can't remember. Anyway, I hadn't found a chance to yell for a week. You'll like what Hasso told me that weekend: 'Boss, it's clear you are sick! You haven't opened your mouth and said anything all week. You haven't sworn! Swear, swear and relax, boss, don't stay upset like that!' Have you ever seen such an intelligent man? He can ask me for anything he wants; I'd give my life to one like that. But, he must always know his place. . . ."

◇

8.2 The Explosion in the Parlor

◆

Bai Xiao-Yi

The host poured tea into the cup and placed it on the small table in front of his guests, who were a father and daughter, and put the lid on the cup with a clink. Apparently thinking of something, he hurried into the inner room, leaving the thermos on the table. His two guests heard a chest of drawers opening and a rustling.

They remained sitting in the parlor, the ten-year-old daughter looking at the flowers outside the window, the father just about to take his cup, when the crash came, right there in the parlor. Something was hopelessly broken.

It was the thermos, which had fallen to the floor. The girl looked over her shoulder abruptly, startled, staring. It was mysterious. Neither of them had touched it, not even a little bit. True, it hadn't stood steadily when their host placed it on the table, but it hadn't fallen then.

The crash of the thermos caused the host, with a box of sugar cubes in his hand, to rush back from the inner room. He gawked at the steaming floor and blurted out, "It doesn't matter! It doesn't matter!"

The father started to say something. Then he muttered, "Sorry, I touched it and it fell."

"It doesn't matter," the host said.

Source: Bai Xiao-Yi, "The Explosion in the Parlor," *Sudden Fiction International*, Robert Shapard, translated by Ding Zuxin, 1989, pp. 289–90. Reprinted by permission of the translator.

Later, when they left the house, the daughter said, "Daddy, *did* you touch it?"

"No. But it stood so close to me."

"But you *didn't* touch it. I saw your reflection in the windowpane. You were sitting perfectly still."

The father laughed. "What then would you give as the cause of its fall?"

"The thermos fell by itself. The floor is uneven. It wasn't steady when Mr. Li put it there. Daddy, *why* did you say that you . . ."

"That won't do, girl. It sounds more acceptable when I say I knocked it down. There are things which people accept less the more you defend them. The truer the story you tell, the less true it sounds."

The daughter was lost in silence for a while. Then she said, "Can you explain it only this way?"

"Only this·way," her father said.

8.3 In the Footsteps of a Water Buffalo

◆

Nhat Tien

When the production unit assigned him the task of harrowing the little patch of rice field along the creek flowing past Cong Quan, Vinh was beside himself with joy. At least that was a less punishing job than carrying baskets of clay from the ends of a shoulder pole for the local brick-making cooperative.

But Vinh had not reckoned with the abnormal sluggishness of the water buffalo. Admittedly, it was an old, old beast – a scrawny thing, weaker than the other fourteen buffalo belonging to their February 3 agricultural cooperative, but a water buffalo balking at the plow or harrow – that was unacceptable behavior. So Vinh made maximum use of the bamboo whip, lashing at the beast's ash gray skin while blustering and shouting himself hoarse. The torrid sun had him sweating profusely, and his eyes were blurry. Under his feet, the paddy slosh that had been baking since daybreak was scorching hot. And the water buffalo kept plodding on his way ever so slowly and wearily. Vinh could hear its labored breathing through the gaping mouth dribbling saliva and froth. Its entire skeleton jutted against wrinkled skin, and he could count every rib.

Apparently, Old Man Thuoc had once warned everyone against overworking the water buffalo. The creatures were always being

Source: Nhat Tien, "In the Footsteps of a Water Buffalo," *To Be Made Over*, translated by Huynh Sanh Thong, 1988, pp. 214–225. Reprinted by permission of the translator.

called upon to do this or that. Plowing. Harrowing. Hauling lumber. Transporting goods. Carrying tons of brick. Old Man Thuoc had spoken up at a general meeting: "You comrades should go easy on the buffalo if you want them to work for many years. Overtax their bodies and they'll give out on you in no time."

Thuoc had spoken without malice or innuendo. He only worried about the draft animals, and far from his mind were all those aged humans on whose wizened backs were saddled sundry chores in the cooperative. To his simple way of thinking, water buffalo represented the most precious capital: when one fell sick it was cause for grave concern. If a man was ill, well, that was different: he could get back to work in a few days.

The secretary of the Party branch, however, chose to interpret Thuoc's guileless words in a completely different manner. At a restricted session of the village council, which included leaders of various groups – workers, women, youth, and the supervisory board of cooperatives – he pronounced his verdict: "Old Man Thuoc holds the most reactionary views possible. All of you, comrades, must maintain your vigilance and keep to a minimum his remarks in public on any subject."

All present understood. While innocent enough, Thuoc's words unwittingly reflected the truth of their lives. Old men and women had to bend their shrunken backs hauling bricks, pushing carts, and lugging baskets of dirt with shoulder poles like beasts of burden, yet nobody dared emit one peep in their defense. Why contradict the most powerful voice in the village and court trouble? "The best thing is to sit still, and the next best thing is to say yes." So went proverbial wisdom at meetings under the socialist regime.

Thuoc's incident eventually blew over, and he avoided pursuing the issue any further. On the contrary, both he and his wife eagerly took on any task entrusted to them. So later, when their son signed up for military service, no matter how vigilant the village council wished to appear, it was obliged to offer one of its "progressive family" certificates of merit to Thuoc and his wife. Thuoc was promoted to foreman of the production unit at the brick kiln, and his wife was admitted to the Association of Elderly Women and put on the advisory committee, even though she never opened her mouth or ventured a single opinion at any meeting. From start to finish, she could be seen lifting her apron to her rheumy eyes and dabbing at them all the time.

Then one day, from out of the blue, a warrant from the district came for the arrest of Thuoc's son for desertion. Now, if a young man fell for the "artificial prosperity" of Saigon, or flinched from his international proletarian duty in fraternal socialist Kampuchea, he would hardly be so foolish as to return to his native village. In all probability, the boy had disappeared into the corrupt society of the South, but the comrades of the security police intended to carry out the directives of the district Party committee to the letter and in earnest. Flourishing their weapons, they stormed Thuoc's house as if they were hunting enemy troops. The hut was virtually bare of furniture, and there was not much worth rummaging through, but, all the same, the gang went through the motions of searching, strutting back and forth and turning the place upside down for a whole hour. During all that time Thuoc's wife sobbed and blubbered, crying again and again, "O my son! Where have you gone? Why have you left your ma?"

As for Thuoc himself, he simply squatted at the foot of a post and hugged his knees in stony silence. He was very angry with his boy. The brat might have found a refuge somewhere for himself, but he had brought disaster down on both his father and his mother. In a twinkling their so-called revolutionary contribution to the cooperative, what they had achieved over many years, went up in smoke. Thuoc and his wife would lose their positions in the community and their jobs. They would be ostracized and punished not only in reprisal but as a pointed warning to any other youngsters who might feel tempted to follow their son down the reactionary road to decadence and hooliganism.

All of a heap, man and wife became outlaws and pariahs, doomed to live apart from society. When they met someone out on the road and ventured a hello, that person would look the other way, feigning nonrecognition. A few friends or acquaintances in whom persisted some shreds of decency might bestow on them a commiserative glance, but they would at once look around nervously, as if they had committed a crime and were afraid of being observed.

What they had dreaded, and what hurt most was that from now on Thuoc and his wife would be cut off the ration-coupon system. With ration coupons they had found it possible to buy staples at official prices. Without the coupons, they would consider themselves evicted for good from the community dining table, even if what was spread upon the board was nothing more than potato and cassava.

Thuoc now had to journey all the way to the next village and beg better-off families for work on mutual-help teams. His wife was forced to search through the mire of flooded fields and creeks for crabs and snails to help eke out their meager fare. Both came to look like woebegone souls risen out of the mud. Their plight gave the Party branch secretary much occasion for gleeful gloating. He kept repeating, as if to drill a lesson into the village folks, "This is what will befall all those who go against the Party line and state policy! It's historical necessity – there's no getting around it."

At the very moment when Vinh was struggling with his old water buffalo in the slush of the rice field, Thuoc's wife was floundering in the creek with a basket for collecting snails hung on her back. She clearly heard Vinh curse the beast. She clearly saw his hand wave the bamboo whip and lash repeatedly at its wizened skeleton. But instead of hastening its pace, the buffalo slowed down little by little until it came to a standstill, trembling all over. Utterly exhausted, it seemed unable to pull its foot out of the mire for even one more step. The harrow stuck fast. The steaming paddy slosh beneath burned at Vinh's feet and drove him close to frenzy. He flogged the beast so hard he drew blood from its flank, yet still the buffalo would not budge. Its body was bathed in sweat when, stretching out its neck and rearing its head, it exhaled something like a soft moan. Then the whole mass slumped down. The decrepit animal collapsed in the paddy like some old soldier fallen on the battleground.

This unexpected turn of events stunned Vinh. At first, he stood there staring dumbfounded at the beast asprawl in the field, his every limb numb with fear. Then he flung the bamboo whip down beside the buffalo and rushed off screaming, "Comrades! Comgrades! Come out, take a look – the buffalo is dead!"

As he reached the road running and screaming, Vinh bumped into Thuoc's wife, whose eyes were wide with astonishment. The wretched buffalo had been not unlike a close acquaintance to her and her husband. They knew all about it, when and where it had been born, to whom it had belonged. They knew how many cowlicks there were on its head, how many rinks there were around its horns, even what made it tick. And now it was dead!

Forsaken by kith and kin, Thuoc's wife suddenly realized what the buffalo had meant to her. Never had it glowered at her with contempt or hatred since the day her wretched body had bolted from the army. Never had it averted its gaze when she came up to it and patted it on the back. Thuoc's wife dissolved into tears, mourning a good friend.

Vinh's news struck the cooperative like a thunderbolt. They all dropped whatever they were doing and hurried toward Cong Quan. Water buffalo were more valuable than people. During the war, many people had perished, but no death had ever caused as much consternation as that of this animal.

The person most shocked and astounded was the cooperative chief, a fat, heavy man who never walked quickly, let alone run. Today he broke into a gallop, and younger folks had trouble keeping up with him. His crimson face and eyes glared fury, and in his hand he held a bamboo cane, which he flourished to make his point as he talked to the crowd clustered around him by the paddy: "Which boys are in charge of gathering hay on Team Four? Damn you all, little rascals! You were too busy with your fun and games to feed the buffalo – no wonder it's dropped dead. I'll strip those red scarves off your necks and teach you to love games and sports less!"

In principle, what the cooperative chief had said was a grave offense to the whole Ho Chi Minh Vanguard Youth Corps, an attack on its honor. Had anyone else made the same statement would have provoked an uproar, but the Party branch secretary shared in his comrade's anger completely. Indeed, the two men differed only in the way they expressed their displeasure. While one burst into shouts and curses, the other clamped his lips tightly with a livid look on his face. Children young enough to be the cooperative chief's sons and daughters were too intimidated to make an issue of their corporate pride.

Some boys standing on the fringe of the crowd whispered among themselves:

"Whose turn is it this week to tend the buffalo of Team Four? Is it Nang's group?"

"No. It's Quy's group. And I've seen Quy and his teammates catching crabs up there around the Ong Sung fields!"

A young tattletale, overhearing the conversation, spoke out loud enough to be heard by the cooperative chief: "It's the turn of Quy's team to cut grass for the buffalo!"

The chief swung sharply toward the boy, pouncing on him as if he were a piece of irrefutable proof. On the tip of his tongue was a string of epithets unflattering to Quy's ancestors, which he was just about to rattle off before discovering in time that the culprit was a son of the village security commissioner. As the proverb says: "Before you stroke the face, beware the nose." You don't touch relatives of an acquaintance, let alone one who wields much clout. And so the cooperative chief twirled his cane once more and said, addressing no one in particular, "I don't care whose shift it is! This time I'm going to punish them all. No letters of commendation from me, not even those I've already signed!"

Then he turned to the boys and asked them to carry the beast onto the roadside. Here they found out that the buffalo, while far from well, was not dead: it had simply collapsed from exhaustion.

Relieved, the cooperative chief looked less grim. Somewhat ashamed of his outburst, he now spoke in a more conciliatory tone. "The buffalo is hungry – that's all. Give it a good day's rest and plenty of straw to eat and it'll be back on its feet in a jiffy."

So the water buffalo enjoyed a vacation without benefit of a national holiday to thank. However, the cooperative chief's veterinary assessment fit his own hopes better than it did the facts, soon to transpire, for, on being hauled back to the barn, the buffalo simply lay there like an inert hulk. It was not hungry. A trough full of tender, mouth-watering grass was placed right next to its chops, but it would not even bother to open them. A top whose spinning force runs out will drop to the ground, and the buffalo was like that. There was no way it could pick itself up and go again. It lay there lifeless in the barn, staring stupidly with the glazed vacancy of its eyes, dribbling froth and saliva out of both corners of its mouth.

The deputy chief of the cooperative made a flat statement, mincing no words: "Let's butcher the buffalo."

People who all year round had been dreaming of meat rejoiced, hollering, "That's right! Let's slaughter it now while it's still alive. In a few days we'll have to eat carrion from a dead animal!"

The idea received collective approval. Here was a rare opportunity to forget their starvation diet and feast on meat. Surely, not much more service could be squeezed out of that old water buffalo anyhow, even if it could be cured of whatever ailed it. But, with the buffalo out of commission, the cooperative had to confront and solve another problem, and to talk of butchering the beast at this moment seemed out of place; it smacked of irresponsible gluttony. So the cooperative chief refrained from giving his consent immediately.

That night he convoked an emergency session of the village council to discuss how to replace the sick buffalo. Somebody suggested, "Without the buffalo, a number of our tasks will be crippled. And our cooperative also happens to be in the period of most intense activity. Let's lay out funds and purchase another buffalo."

The cooperative chief dismissed that idea out of hand for this reason: "If the solution were so simple, why hold a special session of the village council at all?"

The truth of the matter was that, deep in his heart, he did not want to spend one damn penny from the budget on anything whatsoever. It had to be further replenished until his cooperative could afford a small automobile. He had always put forward the view that an automobile would be of critical importance to the growth of the cooperative. It would give its chief mobility, allowing him to travel one day to the district seat and the next to the provincial capital. He could keep in touch with various commissions and agencies and arrange trade or exchange for all sorts of products and commodities: seed, fertilizer, gasoline, kerosene, and whatnot. A car would be the magic key to unlock and open wide the door to the world of abundance.

The women had their say too. One comrade recommended that a set of water pumps be purchased to replace the old-fashioned system of irrigation scoops and buckets, all those *gua-dais* and *gau-songs*, which not only did a slow job but also involved a large labor force – made up primarily of women.

She said, "We are living in the age of science and technology. Let's bring science and technology to bear on production!"

But one brother countered the sister's proposal with this heroic argument: "I agree with our sister that it would be better if we could use science and technology. However, let's not forget the words of our communist poet: 'Our hands turn even pebbles and rocks to rice!' "

The sister huffily retorted, "If so, then why don't you take the place of the buffalo and pull the plow yourself, brother? We'll have rice to eat just like when we still had the buffalo!"

That was it! What the sister said in pique struck the cooperative chief as a brilliant idea, a stroke of genius. He slapped his thigh and exclaimed, "Sister Tai is right on target! With determination we can overcome any and all difficulties. Like this problem of the buffalo. I propose that you brothers and sisters discuss the substitution of human strength for animal motive power as a stopgap measure."

In amazement, the sister asked, "You mean somebody will have to pull the plow?"

"What's wrong with that? Years ago, during the war, many agricultural cooperatives took that measure to make up for shortages and to push production."

No one quarreled with the idea that the problem could be solved in that fashion. But the meeting was deadlocked on who was to fill in for the buffalo pulling a plow or harrow. The women, who had always defended equal rights, preferred to forgo this privilege and pass it on to the male members of the Ho Chi Minh Vanguard Youth Corps. But the boys had minds of their own. They would and could do anything only if they cared to. One couldn't lean too hard on them or they might sabotage the cooperative, put it out of business. The cooperative chief knew that. Nevertheless, he made a perfunctory attempt to enlist them, virtually pleading for their help. "Well, let me suggest that the comrades in the Youth Corps hold a separate session and agree among themselves to take turns substituting for the buffalo. I hope that you all will carry out in practice the spirit of your proud motto: "Where they are needed, Youth Corpsmen will be there; where the job is tough, there will be Youth Corpsmen!"

The comrade who represented the Youth Corps realized at once that he'd been given a tough nut to crack. He suspected, and rightly, that none of the boys would take the place of the buffalo and pull a plow. Not that any of them lacked the physical strength and stamina to do it. But once you've played buffalo, how on earth can you face a girl and talk to her seriously? That would be the overriding reason for the boys' inevitable lack of enthusiasm. It was on everybody's mind but went unspoken.

Sure enough, after the local branch of the Youth Corps held two meetings and all means of persuasion were applied, no one volunteered with socialist "joy and zeal" to be cast as a buffalo. A daylong palaver failed to force the impasse.

Meanwhile, Vinh kept a close eye on the buffalo's deteriorating health and reported it hour by hour, minute by minute. The beast could no longer raise its head. It had begun to gasp for breath. Its hind legs had gone into spasms. And he would conclude each account with the refrain "Butcher it now or we'll end up picking the bones of a rotten dead buffalo!"

The next day, Thuoc could be seen cringing and fawning in the cooperative chief's office. The Party branch secretary was also present. It seemed a unique opportunity had arisen for the old man to atone for his son's sins and to earn his way back into the Party's favor. After living as an outcast for almost a year, Thuoc had learned with terror what it meant to lose ration coupons and to suffer social quarantine: the State had cut out all roots, both material and psychic, from under him. Now he begged for mercy and a second chance. "May I submit a request to the two comrades? Though advanced in years, I'm still strong enough to pull a plow. And I have my wife to lend me a hand. She may not look it, but she's as tough and resilient as a leech!"

As he said that, Thuoc glanced outside. Through the wide open window, both the Party branch secretary and the cooperative chief could see Thuoc's wife in the courtyard, squatting under a a tree with her arms clasped around her knees. Beside her there was a basket for crab collecting. She sat there huddled up like a sick cat, gazing fixedly beyond the hedgerow toward a vast field where shadowy figures scurried back and forth lugging stacks of blood-red bricks.

Despite the distance, she could spot friends and acquaintances, even the teenagers as they moved bricks from the kiln to the dirt floor, piling them up in long rows. They looked like ants busily gathering materials for a nest, and they formed a community – a famished and tattered society in which the last ounce of energy was being squeezed out of each of them. But from Thuoc and his wife that society still withheld its ultimate blessing, and hope seemed far beyond their reach.

Over the past year, Thuoc's wife had never had a chance to touch and fondle sheets of ration coupons: this one good for rice, that one for potatoes, another for oil or firewood, for some thread or a needle, and, once in a long while, for a kilo of sugar or a square of cloth. And she had been denied the privilege of standing in line and jostling, of squabbling and fighting outside the state-run store, sometimes in the rain, sometimes under broiling sun, while all around the air was thick with the composite odor, sour and pungent, of many types of sweat.

When Thuoc's wife slogged through the mud for crabs in flooded fields, she often prayed to both Heaven and the Buddha that her prodigal son would come back home after he'd had his lark. At worst he might go to jail, but she would at least still have her boy. Time served, he'd be set free, and the state might then relent and restore the family to the ration-coupon system. She thought long-ingly of the ration-coupon sheet – her pipe dream.

Now she waited for her husband under the tree with all the anxiety and dread of a convict on whom the judge is about to pronounce sentence. As soon as he appeared in the doorway to the cooperative chief's office, she sprang to her feet. She saw him toothlessly grinning from ear to ear. Both Heaven and the Buddha had heard and granted her prayer! Indeed, her husband came run-ning toward her, waving both his hands and shouting jubilantly, "Those gentlemen said yes! We'll take the place of the buffalo!"

◇

8.4 The Meeting

◆

Julieta Pinto

One by one they were entering the little store. It had not rained, and sunbeams fell that the branches of the cedars and the *guanacaste* trees turned aside toward the leaves, tinting them with gold. Step by step the men came forward. The words from the previous week were sounding in their ears: "Starting tomorrow there will be no work. The boss is being sued in town, and we don't have enough money to settle accounts." "What are we going to do now?" one of the laborers' voices had sounded hoarsely against the silence. "I don't know, it's not my affair. They told me to let you know, and so I've done my duty." The overseer had called these last words over his shoulder to them while walking back toward the house.

Some were sitting on the benches in the store, others squatted on the floor.

"Mario, what did they tell you in the city?" asked a heavy man with hunched shoulders and a face covered with wrinkles.

The man spoken to spit out a wad of tobacco and wiped his mouth with the back of his hand.

"They're all a bunch of bastards. They just laughed and came out with "the boss this" and "the lawsuit that" and I didn't know

Source: Julieta Pinto, "The Meeting," *When New Flowers Bloomed: Short Stories by Women Writers from Costa Rica*, Enrique Levi, translated by Leland H. Chambers, 1991, pp. 106–9. Reprinted by permission of the publisher, Latin American Literary Review Press, Pittsburgh, Pennsylvania.

what it was all about, except it was just to say for us to calm down, that they were going to pay us some day."

"But did you tell them we don't have anything to eat?"

"Of course I did, what did you expect me to say? They just said they would send us something to tide us over until they paid us."

"What we want is work," the old man said with an arrogant air that gave a new shine to his deeply wrinkled eyes.

"Oh yeah, when your kids keep asking you for food all the time, you don't care who it is as long as they give you something to eat. I could stick around the yard and survive on a stick of sugar cane and some bananas, but the family won't go along with that."

"Not only the kids, *compadre,* I'd like to see you nibbling on sugar cane and bananas for a whole month straight; the first time a chicken got in front of you you'd stuff it down feathers and all."

"The storekeeper already said he wouldn't give us another day of credit," a redheaded man with blue eyes said as he approached the group. "Fact is, we're just stupid. A lawyer in the city told me we should have complained way last year, when they made us accept the money instead of our benefits."

"Complained? who to?" asked the old man.

"I don't know. To someone. The thing is, now we're not doing anything at all."

"And what do you want us to do? The boss warned us if we didn't accept what he gave us he'd take away our houses. And after living so many years here you can't just go out looking for another job. You love the land, you get to know it, your old lady's gotten attached to the house, and the kids to the yard . . . And what good is it to look for something else if it's going to be the same everywhere you go?"

"Elias is right," another one of the group joined in. "I went down to the Zone year before last, I wanted to get out of this God-forsaken place and make some money, but I got the fever and almost died. And now I don't even have the strength to work. The thing about being poor is that no matter where we go we're always in a bad way."

"Isn't that what I'm telling you? We're just being lazy," the redhead insisted. "It's been days since they told us there wasn't any more work, and we haven't done a thing. The most we did was we sent Mario to the city instead of going ourselves all together so they would pay attention to us. When there's only one person alone they just wave him aside with a flick of their hand and tell him, Just be patient, the law will take care of everything. We ought to go all of us together to the city right now and make them give us work and pay us what they owe us. We're too accustomed to giving in, we can't even ask for what belongs to us any more."

"Juan is right, by myself I couldn't do anything. And when they begin to talk about laws and regulations they get me all mixed up and I can't even answer. That's what happened to me last year when I gave up my social security benefits for just two hundred pesos. You know: the law says this, the law says that, and the boss would be so grateful he'd give me a chance for a better job, and I was so tired I just said "yes" and signed the lousy piece of paper."

The old man had been listening with his head bent over, outlining a strange figure in the dust with his big toe. He straightened up and his phlegmatic voice reached all the listeners.

"Juan is right, Mario is right, but I tell you the devil knows more because of his age than because he's the devil. I've got a lot of years of experience on my back. We've got all these governments, we've got all these laws, these political campaigns where they offer us everything and the only thing we get out of it is a swig of brandy and ten pesos for our vote. You notice that we always come out just the same or maybe worse off than before. That's why I'm telling you that the best thing to do is stay here quietly or go and speak with the boss to see if by chance he'll let us work. You old guys here must remember what happened to Victor. He sued the boss for his wages, with the help of some jailhouse lawyer in the city; the boss didn't want to pay him because he was so young. I told him, 'Wait another year and you'll get paid, and stop all this nonsense about lawsuits.' "

"This blockhead didn't pay any attention to me. That lawyer had just gotten his law degree and was simply waiting for a good case to fall in his lap, and he'd already got Victor's hopes up. So Victor spent two months going back and forth to the city twice a week, with his ticket paid for on credit because he didn't have a job. It's true he won the suit, but do you know who got all the money? The lawyer, of course. And he still claimed Victor owed him money. Victor got screwed, he didn't have a job, he had to haul himself down to the Zone, and he died years ago, wiped out by the fevers."

The men remained silent after the old man's words. The whole sky had become tinted with color, and the reddish light put a grave look on all their faces. The children were playing ball in the street, and one could hear their shouts together with the complaints of the blackbirds begging the cloudless sky for water.

Juan rose to his feet to make his point clear to the cluster of men. As he spoke, he got red in the face.

"We can't let Elias make cowards of us. Times have changed, and we have to be strong. We have to go to the city and speak with whoever is there. If they talk to us about the laws we'll just tell them we don't understand anything but that the kids are hungry and have to eat. So the boss'll fire us? You just heard the man say there isn't any work because the farm is shut down, so we don't have anything to lose."

The men began to react to Juan's final words.

"Well, it's true that they've already let us go."

"Yeah, so we don't have anything to lose now."

"I've got a sick kid, there's no money for medicine."

"Don't tell me about it, my wife is due any day now, and we don't even have enough for a blanket."

"Yesterday the milkman told me he couldn't give me even one more bottle of milk on credit, and the baby needs it because my wife is so worried she can't nurse him."

Their words became whispers. With the last light of the day they began to toy with dreams. "Maybe the farm will start up again soon." "At least they could pay us for the week they owe us and we could get out of debt." "If we all went down together they'd have to listen to us."

The sun was hidden now and only a few lilac-colored clouds could be glimpsed in the sky and around the mountain peaks. The men got to their feet and step by step headed home.

Section 9: Managerial Insights

9.1 Business Mindsets and Styles of the Chinese in the People's Republic of China, Hong Kong, and Taiwan

◆

C. L. Hung

This article examines the business mindsets and styles of the Chinese in the PRC, Hong Kong, and Taiwan focusing upon the differences in their motivation and objectives, personal contacts and rapport, negotiations and decision making, status of women in business, legal contracts and agreements, and business ethics. It will begin with a brief examination of the political, economic, and societal environments in the PRC, Hong Kong, and Taiwan and conclude with cautionary advice for foreign business people.

Political, economic, and societal environments

The Chinese in the PRC, Hong Kong, and Taiwan unquestionably have many cultural similarities in the basic sets of values, social

Source: C. L. Hung, "Business Mindsets and Styles of the Chinese in the P-R-C," excerpted from *The International Executive*, 1994, pp. 218–220. Reprinted by permission of John Wiley & Sons.

organizations, conventions and rituals, and the roles and expectations of individuals in the society. They use the same written language, celebrate in similar fashions the traditional festivities, follow similar protocols, and have similar diets. In doing business with any group of Chinese, one should be aware of these common cultural characteristics. But, notwithstanding these similarities, significant differences in business mindsets and styles have developed in the Chinese as a result of the influences of the respective local political, economic, and societal environments.

People's Republic of China

The PRC has been ruled by a communist regime since 1949. Even though the government has adopted more liberal economic policies in the last 15 years, the PRC economy is still predominantly government directed and controlled with over 80% of the country's industrial production contributed by state-owned enterprises. The private sector, comprised mostly of family owned ventures, is small and plays a very minor role in the country's economy. The government is now intent upon opening the country to foreign investment but the environment for foreign investors is still somewhat restrictive.

The rate of economic growth in recent years has been high, and is impressive even though it has to some extent been inflated by the small economic base. But despite the dramatic progress in many areas such as the Southern and Eastern coastal provinces where special economic zones have been set up, the country is by any standards still lagging economically. This can be attested to by the very low income per capita and the poor quality of infrastructure facilities in transportation, communication, education, health, and public utilities.

Hong Kong

Hong Kong has been a colony governed by the British for more than 100 years. Politically, there has always been freedom and liberty, but no democracy. In sharp contrast to the PRC, the Hong Kong economy has always enjoyed a progressive environment with minimal government intervention. It is completely open and free and is dominated by private enterprises. It is a bastion of unfettered capitalism and has been a prominent example of success for laissez faire. Even though Hong Kong is still officially recognized only as a newly industrialized country, its economy is, by practically all commercial and societal development standards, one of the most advanced in the world in industrial output, in banking, in business services, in communication and transportation, in product innovations, in marketing and distribution, in education, and in technology research. In December 1991, its international reserve of US $28.9 billion was the second highest in the world in per capital terms (US $4,980) next to Singapore.

In short, no two neighboring territories in the world having the same ancestral background can be further apart in their political, economic, and societal environments than the PRC and Hong Kong.

Taiwan

Taiwan is in every respect a composite of the PRC and Hong Kong. Politically, after a decade-long period of gradual liberalization, the country has evolved from single-party autocracy to multiparty democracy, but the parliament is still heavily influenced by the Nationalists who fled mainland China before the Communist take-over in 1949.

Economically, Taiwan is also moving rapidly forward to become another powerhouse in Pacific Asia. Its economic growth in the last 20 years has been phenomenal and it now shares the limelight with Hong Kong, Singapore, and South Korea as the four mini dragons of Asia. Foreign investors are still faced with many artificial barriers, but investment restrictions have been relaxed and business contacts with Western countries have steadily increased in recent years. And like Hong Kong, it has over the past years accumulated a huge international reserve, valued at US $87.3 billion in 1991, that on a per capita basis (around US $4,220), also puts it among the highest in the world. However, more than 20 years of political isolation has kept it from achieving economic maturity as fast as Hong Kong. The infrastructure facilities are modern to adequate in major cities, but in the countryside pockets of underdevelopment can still be found. Its income per capita, although more than 25 times that of the PRC, is only around two-thirds that of Hong Kong.

Business mindsets and styles

Motivation and objectives

Perhaps the most important thing for a foreigner to remember when doing business with the Chinese is what motivates them and what they represent. In the PRC, the people with whom foreigners negotiate and do business rarely represent privately owned businesses. Instead, they represent government owned and controlled organizations. This being the case, the business drive and motivation of these people are different from that of private business people representing their companies. Although it would not be fair to say that the PRC Chinese business people would not bargain for the benefit of their organizations, their primary interest in negotiations may be their positions in the organization. Unlike their foreign counterparts, they do not get much direct personal benefits in business success, commissions, salary raises, and better promotion prospects, for example. In their minds job security is often first in importance, ahead of viability of the organization. In a free enterprise economy, when a company goes under, its employees lose their jobs. In a centrally planned economy, companies are state-owned and seldom, if ever, go under. Hence, their business representatives do not need to worry too much about the survival of the organization. As for its profitability, at best it comes third because profit is an elusive variable and difficult to calculate when production, distribution, and pricing are centrally planned and controlled.

PRC business representatives are also not faced with as many deadlines and targets as their foreign counterparts in achieving a certain sales volume, market share, profit size, or return on investment. This means they can afford to take a long-term view in doing business with foreigners. They do not take many initiatives and are generally very risk adverse because there is no incentive for initiatives or for accepting business risks. Besides, many of the senior executives in PRC business organizations are political appointees and might have ascended to their present positions through party hierarchy and not through the work-place hierarchy. They are not entrepreneurs and entrepreneurial spirit is almost completely lacking in the PRC Chinese. What motivates them in negotiating with foreigners is to secure their jobs and to strengthen their positions in the organization.

Government business organizations in the PRC doing business with foreigners generally have long-term objectives related to national development, modernization, and industrialization. What PRC Chinese negotiators want from foreigners are proposals and agreements that they can bring back to their superiors to show that they have successfully bargained for the benefit of the country and the organization, for example, in getting the necessary supplies at a good price, in attracting foreign investments, in acquiring technology, in generating employment, in securing overseas markets, and in earning hard currencies.

After the liberalization moves in recent years, there are an increasing number of people in the PRC who do business for themselves and are driven by profit motives. They tend to have a much greater entrepreneurial spirit and are willing to take initiatives and some business risks; but their number is relatively small and they rarely do business directly with foreigners.

In Hong Kong, business people with whom foreigners deal usually represent private companies that they personally own or for which they work. They have direct personal interests in the company and do not have a national plan constraining their bargaining positions. They only need to consider the basics in dollars and cents terms and make decisions on a business proposal according to its costs and benefits.

Unquestionably, the single most important environmental factor influencing the motivation of the business people in Hong Kong is the approach of 1997 when the colony will revert to the PRC's control. Even though the PRC government has promised to implement a "one-country-two-system" policy to maintain the status quo of Hong Kong until at least 2047, the local people are skeptical of the PRC's sincerity as well as its ability to keep that promise. Recent events and the squabbles between the PRC and the British government in Hong Kong over the pace of democratization reforms have clearly indicated that the liberty and freedom that the Hong Kong people are now accustomed to will be curtailed when the PRC regains political control. For Hong Kong, 1997 is a "dead"-line. Many local Chinese have already fled Hong Kong since 1982 when negotiations first started, and many others are planning to follow the same path. But before their departure, they will try to make the most of the remaining time so that they can profit as much as possible before they leave. Consequently, many local business people in Hong Kong have a very short-term horizon in their business plans, and they place a heavy emphasis on rapid payback on business ventures. Hence, although the entrepreneurial spirit in Hong Kong is one of the highest in the world and the business people are calculated risk takers, many of them have a very short time frame in business planning, a mindset sometimes referred to as a "grab and run" mentality.

In Taiwan, there are large numbers of government controlled as well as privately owned companies doing business with foreigners. The business motivation depends on whether public or private interest is represented. Those representing government institutions may have drives and constraints similar to those of the Chinese business people in the PRC; but because the reward system is more merit-based, they are generally more profit oriented. Taiwanese doing business on their own or for private companies typically display the same high level of entrepreneurial spirit and risk attitude as the Chinese in Hong Kong. With regard to the time horizon in business planning, Taiwan is midway between the PRC and Hong Kong. Although the country is not faced with a deadline and there are no immediate urgencies to make money quickly, the long-term political outlook of the country is still uncertain.

Personal contacts and rapport

Because business people in the PRC usually represent government organizations, contacts with foreigners are often initiated at the government level in formal settings and in groups, through official introductions, business delegations, trade fairs, or international financing agencies (particularly for capital projects). Initial contacts and introductions through third parties such as other foreign companies with existing business connections in the PRC may also occur, but these are also usually followed by official endorsement by the home government. Individual personal contacts are relatively rare, and whereas personal rapport will help, it is not too important in the PRC because business with foreign companies is not conducted on a personal basis. Moreover, personnel arrangements in the PRC are a variable factor. There are frequent reassignments and changes in the composition of the negotiating teams; and an individual's position and authority in the organization may move up and down with the political wheels of fortune.

In Hong Kong, the government is very seldom directly involved in private businesses. Except for government contracts, all business contacts are at private personal levels. Because business people doing business with foreign companies are usually their own bosses or senior managers with decision making authority, establishing a friendly relationship and personal rapport with these people will not only be helpful, but may even be crucial to a successful business relationship.

In Taiwan the importance of personal contacts depends on with whom the company is dealing, a private enterprise or a government organization. Dealing with a private enterprise will mean that private contacts are sufficient and personal rapport is useful, but dealing with government organizations may require more formal channels and making use of more official intermediaries. The latter scenario appears to resemble that of the PRC, but because the system in Taiwan is more capitalistic and less bureaucratic, private contacts and personal rapport are more helpful in Taiwan than in the PRC even when doing business with a government organization.

Negotiations and decision making

In the PRC, the negotiating process is generally lengthy if not cumbersome. The involved parties may have to touch base on a number of task-related as well as nontask-related matters before serious negotiations take place. There may be numerous exploratory testings, honest enquiries, and not-as-honest pretense from the PRC Chinese to determine what a foreign company can offer and what is its bottom line. Because no single individual in PRC business organizations has undivided authority on a business decision, numerous consultations, referrals, and response delays can be expected. The final decision from the PRC side is frequently a result of consensus and compromises among a group of people at high levels in different interested institutions.

In North American business organizations, there is usually a chief executive officer (CEO) who can readily be identified and who makes the final decisions. There may even be a close association between the CEO's personality and the corporate culture. However, in PRC business organizations, identifying the decision maker is difficult, and there is no way a corporate culture can be associated with an individual's personality. Furthermore, individuals are often subject to multiple authority origins, for example, one from the political bureaucracy and another from the business establishment. No single individual may make a definite yes decision, but business negotiation and progress can be stopped at various levels by people who have the authority to say no or simply refuse to act. And there may be many of them in such a position. Hence, when negotiating with the PRC Chinese, it is essential to identify the power brokers and the vested interest groups.

Because the PRC business negotiators are faced with more constraints, their stance in negotiations can be somewhat inflexible, not in the sense that they are unwilling to compromise, but in the sense that they usually have to refer back and forth before they can come back with a revised position.

Business negotiations and the decision making process in Hong Kong are very different. They are direct and fast paced even by North American standards. There is generally an individual or a small group of individuals with designated authority to conclude a deal. Who owns the business, who is the chairman of the board, who is the head of family, or who is the CEO is readily apparent, and he or she will be the one making the final decision. Thus, there may also be an association between the personality and character of this person and the corporate culture and management style.

Because of the impending arrival of 1997, local business people in Hong Kong, driven by a sense of urgency, are often quite flexible in their stance, and are willing to adapt and compromise in order to reach an agreement quickly. Consequently, business can be concluded after a short negotiation and within a relatively short time period.

In Taiwan, business negotiations and the decision making process are not as fast paced as in Hong Kong, and not as slow paced as in the PRC. When dealing with private businesses, even though the underlying motivation is in dollars and cents terms, the Taiwanese are not driven by any sense of urgency as are the business people in Hong Kong. In government business organizations there is not as much bureaucracy nor as many national constraints as in the PRC; hence, the process may be slow by North American standards, but it is not slow by Asian standards. The two sides in business negotiations need to take time to build understanding and confidence; but once an affiliation and trust are established, business relations can progress rapidly.

Status of women in business

When negotiations involve female executives, there is yet another difference. Women are all active in the work force in the PRC, Hong Kong, and Taiwan, but similar to the situation in North America, they are underrepresented at senior management levels.

In the PRC, even though communist doctrine is based upon equality for the working class, traditional gender roles precede political ideology. Like the situation in practically all Oriental countries, women in the PRC are subordinate to their male counterparts outside of the home. There are very few women who own their own businesses, and because of the lack of competitive environment for them to get ahead, women in the PRC are even less represented at management levels than in Hong Kong and Taiwan. Consequently, it is extremely rare to find Chinese female executives in negotiations with foreign companies in the PRC although many of the interpreters may be women. But this should not be taken to mean that the PRC Chinese are resistant toward North American female executives. On the contrary, the PRC Chinese attitude toward them is quite similar to their attitude toward North American male executives, perhaps because they realize there is gender equality in North America (even though they may not realize that in North America, women executives at senior management levels are also underrepresented). Hence, they generally treat and do business with North American women executives as foreigners first and women second, and do not apply the same rules and attitudes toward them as they do to local Chinese women executives.

In Hong Kong, the free enterprise environment has given many more opportunities for women to be independent and successful in their own businesses, in private companies, and in government. Consequently, women executives are more active and are engaged in business negotiations with foreigners more often. The Chinese in Hong Kong, irrespective of their gender, would treat women executives in business negotiations as they treat male executives, foreign and local alike.

The situation in Taiwan is again somewhere between the PRC and Hong Kong. Because the society is more traditional than that of Hong Kong but more open than that of the PRC, women receive some opportunities to establish themselves in their own businesses or in the companies where they work. The presence of women in business negotiations with foreigners is not uncommon, but it is not as extensive as in Hong Kong. Similar to the situation in Hong Kong, the Chinese in Taiwan would treat foreign women executives essentially in the same way as they treat foreign male executives.

In other words, North American women executives when negotiating and doing business with the Chinese in the PRC, Hong Kong, and Taiwan need not be overly conscious of their gender and feel handicapped because Chinese societies traditionally have a male dominated culture. On the contrary, according to the opinions of many Canadian women executives doing business in Asia, they may actually have an advantage because of certain female characteristics in common with Oriental cultures such as being more flexible, more willing to listen, more cooperative, more ready to interact, having better interpersonal skills, more concern and empathy, less aggressiveness, and being less prone to loss of temper (Industry, Science, and Technology Canada, 1992).

Legal contracts and agreements

North American business people are well known for their legalistic bent. They seldom, if ever, do business without a written contract. At the same time, they are always ready and prepared to go to court for settling disputes.

The Chinese in the PRC are different in their perception of legal contracts and agreements. Even though they realize the importance of a written legal document for foreign companies, the spirit of the agreement is to them more important than the letter of the agreement. They would also try their best to avoid going to court or to have disputes brought out into the open.

North American business people must also recognize that the official language in the PRC is Chinese. Contracts are written in Chinese, and when they are accompanied by English, the English version represents a translation. The Chinese version of a legal contract always takes precedence over the English version if there are discrepancies between the two. Naturally, foreigners are not as adept as the Chinese in mastering the Chinese language and they must be careful. For instance, it would be difficult to argue with the Chinese over a contract term when the Chinese use the Chinese language version as the basis. There have been incidents reported of the PRC Chinese withholding the text of China's laws from the foreigners. Because of this, an American company in a dispute (*Business Asia*, March 1992) was not able to determine whether the disagreement was caused by a discrepancy between the two language versions or because of blatant disregard of the contract terms by the Chinese party, and the company did not know how to launch an appeal.

The legal environment in Hong Kong is similar to the legal environment in North America. Throughout its history as a British colony, Hong Kong has adopted the British common law system and honors formal written contracts and the letter of the agreement. Government laws and business regulations are written in English and translated into Chinese. Similarly, business contracts are mostly in English. When there are discrepancies between the English version of a legal agreement and the Chinese version, the former takes precedence over the latter. This means that foreign companies in Hong Kong, unlike those in the PRC, can be sure of what they have bargained for by looking at the contract in English. Furthermore, because the judicial system of Hong Kong is much more respected for its impartiality and fairness, more business people are willing to use the court to settle business disputes. Hence, whereas foreign companies doing business with the PRC often find no legal avenues to redress complaints and address disputes, the doors to the court in Hong Kong are wide open. But this does not mean that the Chinese in Hong Kong would approach the court as readily as the North Americans. After all, the Chinese in Hong Kong are still very much a people of high context culture (versus the low context culture of North Americans) and would like to avoid the court. (There is a Chinese saying that "If you do not go to the court when you are alive, you do not go to hell when you are dead.") In other words, although the legalistic bent is not as great in Hong Kong as in North America because of traditional Chinese cultural values, legal contracts and agreements in Hong Kong follow the principles and practices of North America more closely.

As far as legal contracts and agreements are concerned, the Taiwanese are more similar to the PRC Chinese in that they place at least as much emphasis on the spirit as on the letter of the agreement. Moreover, the official language in Taiwan is also Chinese. Hence, foreigners have to be sure that the written English version of any agreement and contract they sign with Taiwanese companies has the same meaning in letter and in spirit as the Chinese version. This can be achieved by having someone who is totally proficient in both English and Chinese inspect the translation.

Business ethics

Differences in the political, economic, and societal environments in the last 40 years in the PRC, Hong Kong, and Taiwan have also created somewhat different ethical behavior in some local business people.

The lack of motivation and work incentives under the communist system have for a long time generated a passive attitude in the working population in the PRC. At the same time, the liberalization and increased contacts with the outside world have made the people aware of what they have been missing and how far behind they are in their standard of living. In a not-too-subtle way, a feeling of deprivation and inferiority has developed in many PRC Chinese combined with a sense of rage and urgency to catch up with the rest of the world. But in a communist system in which one is not rewarded according to merit (nor rewarded much anyhow), some PRC Chinese business representatives have an ethical attitude that is a challenge to understand. When representing their government owned organizations in business dealings, they usually negotiate hard on their organizations' behalf and arduously bargain for the best deal. But they may also want to have some reward for themselves. Even the PRC government from time to time admits that corruption is serious and graft is widespread in the country. According to the *People's Daily*, around 7,500 government officials have been prosecuted and jailed for corruption in the last five years. Some Hong Kong businessmen claim that they have to pay, in cash or in kind, all the way up from the lowest level to the highest level to get business from the PRC. The lavish style of dining and partying of the PRC's business representatives in Hong Kong lends support to this claim. A comparison of the level of consumption of expensive consumer goods with the reported income per capita (of only around US$300) provides yet another indication of the size of the underground economy and the extent of corruption in the PRC.

Business ethics problems also exist in Hong Kong, but they are of a different nature from those in the PRC. Whereas corporate fraud is not a problem in the PRC because there are very few private corporations in the PRC that do business directly with foreigners, the situation in Hong Kong is just the opposite. The government of Hong Kong is relatively clean, and after the founding of the Independent Commission Against Corruption (ICAC), corruption, however defined, it now minimal to nonexistent in the government bureaucracy.

However, the same cannot be said of the private sector. Even though the overwhelming majority of business people in Hong Kong are honest, corporate fraud and white collar crime have increased in recent years and are also getting more serious both in terms of value and complexity (*Business Asia*, July 1992). Although this may be considered as an inevitable phenomenon in a booming economy where businesses are flourishing, transactions are internationalized, and money is moved electronically by telegraphic transfers, the number one contributing factor is probably the get-rich-quick mentality developed lately because of the impending PRC takeover in 1997. The consensus is that business ethics in Hong Kong have deteriorated in recent years.

Taiwan is relatively clean by Asian standards, even though North American companies may still consider some of the local business practices ethically dubious. Take nepotism, for example. It is usually considered to be an unfair if not unbecoming practice in North America; it is generally accepted and may even be expected in a closely knit and paternalistic society typical of Asian countries. At any rate, nepotism seldom has a direct effect on doing business with foreigners in the PRC, Hong Kong, or Taiwan.

Conclusions

For a long time business relationships with countries of the West have been very extensive and intimate for Hong Kong. Lately they have also been greatly improved for the PRC and Taiwan. This has resulted in a tremendous increase in personal contacts and interactions between foreigners and the Chinese in order to initiate, negotiate, establish, and maintain business relationships. Presently, there are a few hundred North American companies doing business in the region and it is not uncommon for them to have interests in more than one of these three locations managed by the same group of executives. These executives will encounter Chinese in the PRC, Hong Kong, and Taiwan when they travel there, and because many

PRC organizations and Taiwanese businesses have subsidiaries and representative offices in Hong Kong, they may have to do business in Hong Kong not only with the local Chinese, but with the Chinese from the PRC and Taiwan as well. In this situation, one common mistake would be to use the same business approach and treat the different groups of Chinese in the same fashion without realizing and adapting to their different business mindsets and styles. For example, whereas a no-nonsense, straight-to-the-point, and dollar-and-cents bottom line approach might be effectively employed in Hong Kong, it would be ineffective in the PRC and Taiwan where it would be perceived as aggressive and antagonistic.

Another common mistake is for a North American company to use a Hong Kong Chinese to handle business negotiations in the region and to believe that he will be more effective because of the cultural familiarity. Although this may be true when the Hong Kong Chinese deals with the Taiwanese Chinese, some unique problems may arise when he deals with the PRC Chinese.

A Hong Kong Chinese may be judged by different standards and more harshly than a foreigner for any mistake made because he is presumably knowledgeable about Chinese etiquette and manners and would be expected to fully understand the appropriate social protocol and behave accordingly.

Another problem is that the PRC Chinese may have an ambivalent attitude toward the Hong Kong Chinese (or other expatriate Chinese). If the opportunity arises, the PRC Chinese may use a national-istic appeal for concessions. When this is not accepted, he may be criticized for being unpatriotic. This psychological pressure may compromise his stance in negotiations.

The Hong Kong Chinese may also suffer because of a mutual animosity and negative image in the PRC. Many Hong Kong busi-ness people with investments in the PRC have often criticized the PRC Chinese workers as lazy and apathetic. At the same time, many PRC Chinese perceive the Hong Kong Chinese business people as arrogant, contemptuous, and inclined to overexaggerate their economic importance to the PRC. Sometimes they even criticize them for their subservience to British rule. Even though it is clearly not the fault of the Hong Kong Chinese for being put under the rule of the British colonial government, business people in Hong Kong are sometimes unfairly accused of materialistic opportunism and kowtowing to the British. The PRC government's denial of the legitimacy of the Legislative Council and the Executive Council representing the people of Hong Kong is an unambiguous declaration of China's refusal to recognize the presence of a local government in Hong Kong. Many Hong Kong Chinese business people have complained that the reception and treatment they receive from the PRC are inferior to those given to foreigners.

In conclusion, the Chinese in PRC, Hong Kong, and Taiwan have quite different business mindsets and styles. They do share commonalities because of their ancestral heritage, but the separate developments in the political, economic, and societal environments in the last 40 years in the three regions have generated some notable differences in their business approaches.

Hong Kong will revert to PRC control in 1997 and unofficial negotiations for reunion between the PRC and Taiwan have also been initiated. In the future, there may be a united greater China and the emergence of a Chinese economic zone in Asia embodying all three regions (Lim, 1992). Once under the same environment, the business mindsets and styles of the Chinese may converge and become more similar. This may conceivably happen, but it will take a long time. Meanwhile, the Chinese in the PRC, Hong Kong, and Taiwan will continue to do business in their own ways. It is still one-people-three-systems and North American companies need to understand that they are different even though they are all Chinese.

References

Business Asia (March 30, 1992) "Interkiln Exits China, Citing Major Problems in Four JV Firms."

Business Asia (July 13, 1992) "Corporate Crime in Hong Kong: Complex and Costly."

Industry, Science, and Technology Canada, Canadian-Government (1992) *Canadian Women Doing Business in Asia*, Ottawa.

Lim, L. (1992) "The Emergence of a Chinese Economic Zone in Asia?" *Journal of Southeast Asia Business*, 8(1), 41–46.

$\diamond$

9.2 Management Styles Across Western European Cultures

$\blacklozenge$

Maud Tixier

To study recruitment tools and management styles in Western Europe, two trips at two-year intervals (between 1989 and 1991) in the 14 countries under consideration were necessary. These countries included the 12 countries of the EC (except France) and Switzerland, Sweden, and Austria. For each country 25 interviews were conducted locally and five in France. The individuals interviewed were mainly the managers of large headhunter networks, recruitment agencies, and the human resource directors of large groups. . . .

Management styles across Europe

Employee participation

The first relevant managerial dimension in communication is the degree to which employees participate in the management of a company. The distances that a hierarchy places between individuals can affect the degree of formality in a company, but above all, these distances alter the whole system of internal communication. In this area, the countries of Northern Europe are distinguished from those

---

Source: Maud Tixier, "Management Styles Across Western European Cultures," excerpted from *Academy of Management Executive,* February 1994, pp. 377–391. Reprinted by permission of The Academy of Management.

of Southern Europe (France, Belgium, Portugal, Italy, Spain, and Greece) where hierarchical distances are greater because authority is more centralized and management more autocratic.

The Greeks, for example, have a deep respect for hierarchy. Management in traditional Greek family businesses is conservative and paternalistic, and power is delegated only to a small degree. The Belgians also give much importance to organization charts. In Italy the big, older companies are the most traditional; among them are the banks and insurance companies in which management is particularly bureaucratic and centralized. In Spain there is employee involvement and consultation in the management of a company. This type of monarchical company management is characterized by a very large salary scale, a big distance separating managerial staff from employees, and in training, little weight given to motivation and initiative. Portuguese managers are not inclined toward teamwork. Their culture encourages them to keep information, secrets, and power to themselves and to respect distance and hierarchy, behavior often noted in medium-sized companies where structures remain familial.

At the other end of the spectrum are the Northern European countries like Germany, Sweden, Denmark, and The Netherlands. The German model is often the reference when comanagement or codetermination are mentioned. The management style is democratic and participatory. Not only are employees consulted, but decision making is frequently collective, based on the model of "industrial democracy." Collegiality prevails at every level, and a decision from the top obtained without a consensus is not considered legitimate. If the hierarchy does not weigh so heavily, then the responsibilities are clearly defined at every level. The individual rarely creates a personal job description as is frequently the case in France because the German manager position demands a thorough and precise definition of this role before the appointment to a position.

Swedish management style is characterized as decentralized and democratic. Company organization charts have a generally horizontal structure. There are three times fewer hierarchic levels than in France, and the distances between individuals are therefore smaller. Information is not withheld because the duty to inform is a basic accepted fact and prescribed by Swedish law. This law, called MBL (the "law of concerted decision"), mandates that all important decisions be discussed with employee representatives and negotiated with the unions. All parties affected by a decision must be consulted and all ramifications of a decision must be openly debated before it is finalized. Finally employees must be informed of a decision. Communicating the management intentions becomes a management tool of the management, and failing to prepare subordinates for a decision can result in lowering motivation, even to the point of strikes. Discussions are open and employees express themselves, give their opinions, and make their suggestions. There is trust between management and labor. They listen and exchange ideas. Of course it is a manager who decides in the end. If, however, a union is opposed to this decision, the manager will think twice before taking it. This system creates a climate for good communication and information. If union pressure and power compel management to communicate, then the latter can today use the duty to inform for tactical ends because the decision-making process in Sweden is entirely centered on obtaining results. In fact, the system rests on the observation that better informed and consulted employees are more motivated, more productive, and inclined to carry out company plans. By expressing themselves, employees imply that they understand and support company goals. They have a participatory role to the extent that they adopt the goals of a company. A company head is in direct contact with employees and remains freely available for dialogue, being neither clear nor specific when explaining reasons for a decision because of the process of "grounding it in" the employees, and talks a lot about the decision before finally making it. More than simply being clear, the behavior of Swedish company head must be predictable and without surprises for the employees.

Similarly, in Denmark managerial values are based on a democratic and egalitarian system. The organization charts are very flat and the hierarchical distances between individuals are not very great. Thus the management style is cooperative and participatory. No one receives orders from anybody, and rather than being imposed through the exercise of strong leadership, proposals must be justified. Opinions of individuals are solicited. Orders can be questioned and counter proposals made. Consequently, a Dane has difficulty both in accepting decisions made from above and in exercising authority over subordinates. In Danish culture the notion of responsibility is so internalized that the Danish manager reacts very poorly when not trusted. Similarly the manager does not try to check up on the activities of the staff, those to whom the same trust is granted.

An approach midway between these two is the consultative style, found in Great Britain. The orientation of the decision process is from bottom to top. The final position is usually the result of a consensus. Consulting subordinates is at the initiative of the department head who is entirely responsible for the ultimate decision. Most problems are resolved by negotiations and often informal adjustments.

Finally there are particularities in certain countries like Ireland, Austria, and Switzerland. In Ireland the prevailing management style is more presidential than consensual and, therefore, not very participatory. Middle management opinions are taken into account, but in the end it is the company head who makes the final decision and imposes it. The CEO is more a captain than a coach of the team. The staff generally does not know the company objectives and is informed of decisions after they are made. They do not express their ideas, opinions, or suggestions.

Austria presents a particular case. Being state-owned, the largest companies have a bureaucratic and hierarchical style, that in Germany would be clearly more participatory. The public sector is autocratic; in the private sector different forms of management are encountered depending on the size and field of the companies involved. Nevertheless managers generally have little initiative, and their intellectual independence and autonomy of decision making are not desired.

Switzerland is an exception in Northern Europe to the extent that traditionally Swiss managers run companies in an authoritarian manner based on a model inherited from the army. Swiss managerial culture is today still imbued with military-style management in which notions of hierarchy and order are still valid. Until foreign banks arrived in Switzerland, it was impossible for nonofficers to pursue a career in certain banks. This importance of the military is even stronger in German speaking Switzerland even if, paradoxically, the system is less hierarchical. Today this management model is changing and Crédit Suisse, for example, in 1991 put in place a less hierarchical system with a flatter organization, in this matter following the example of ABB in industry.

Certainly the reality is often more complex and cannot be categorized too tightly in diagrams. Two diametrically opposed management styles often coexist inside the same country. For example, in Greece multinational subsidiaries, often American, function more democratically, and even certain medium-sized companies have set up decentralized structures, often under the influence of second generation owners who have studied abroad. Similarly in Italy, multinationals and companies run by younger individuals have systems leaving more room for the expression of different points of view. In Portugal labor legislation has become more progressive and more participatory. Everywhere the most traditional institutions such as banks and insurance companies and medium-sized firms are the most autocratic in their approach. Consulting firms and service companies generally have a more consensual decision making system and a participatory and cooperative style. The tendency everywhere in Europe is toward dialogue, involvement, and sharing.

The most exceptional situation is in Luxembourg. There, all kinds of management styles mix harmoniously, these styles depending on the nationality of the company. The Luxembourg style itself is difficult to define. In the medium-sized companies the style is generally autocratic and strongly contrasts with the German comanagement-influenced style found in the big industrial companies such as Arbed or the banks. After the steel industry crisis, Arbed went from 29,000 employees to 9,000 without a single layoff or losing a day to strikes. The model later called the "Luxembourg model" has been the basis for very advanced labor policies and legislation in other countries.

Innovation

The second relevant dimension in managerial communication is the degree of innovation by company management in a given country. While the former dimension has an impact on internal communication, the latter has an impact on external communication. Innovation goes together with a certain type of unconventional relationship with people and things, and it can take various forms.

For example it is possible to be inventive, creative, and technically sophisticated like the French or technically innovative and recognized for design like the Swedish. Others like the Portuguese demonstrate their creativity and flexibility by the manner in which they commit themselves to a project. Because of their cultural heritage, Austrians adapt and adjust well to situations and people. Likewise the Greeks, who are naturally positive and optimistic, enjoy the opportunity to be creative and are willing entrepreneurs. The Greeks are quick, shrewd, and overflowing with imagination and resources; they have the reputation for being flexible and adapting to situations, which they understand quickly.

But the prize in Europe for inventiveness, creativity, and business aptitude certainly goes to the Italians. Their remarkable qualities for adaptation as well as their art of compromise have even given them the reputation of chameleons. Enthusiasm, creativity, and dynamism are elements of their character. The Italians, who innovate because they are without any particular prejudices and are open to everything new, appreciate people who have ideas. They are naturally curious and inventive and have a very sophisticated business sense. This entrepreneurship, Italian style, has been exported and is the hallmark of Italian success abroad, the Benetton phenomenon being an example. This gift of Italian entrepreneurs has created a style, and added to that gift are their marked taste for aesthetics, refinement, design, and fashion that attest to their unmatched artistic sense.

The opposite of innovation is tradition and conservatism, but also a certain reliability and predictability. Among European countries where the smallest premium is placed on intuition and imagination are German, Switzerland, Denmark, Luxembourg, and The Netherlands. Because they lack creativity and capacity for innovation, certain Europeans such as the Swiss are in the position of "improvers": they improve what others have created. In these countries, it is generally an arduous task to prepare mindsets for change. This tendency has a very noticeable impact on external communication. German advertising makes little appeal to the imagination because it is supposed to furnish customers with the technical elements to make a choice. For that reason the Austrians, who differ from the Germans on this point, often choose Italian advertising campaigns and adapt them for use in Austria in the automotive field.

Risk

The third managerial dimension having an impact on communication, the attitude toward risk, is linked to the preceding one. The attitude toward risk is related to the qualities of interpersonal relationships, trust, for example, as well as a preference for written or oral communication.

Among Europeans averse to risk are the Swiss, whose caution is legendary, and the Germans, whose attachment to rules and details denotes a strong wish to control uncertainty and the desire to attenuate the unpredictable aspects of a project by building up a store of small certainties. Belgians, especially those of Flemish origin, do not like risk either. When they take risks, they more often do so under compulsion because there is no other choice. It is interesting to note that the typical Belgian manager is not an entrepreneur probably because of a fear of complications or failure. This big difference separates these Europeans from the Italians, the Greeks, and the Austrians who like to innovate, but who paradoxically have a timid attitude toward risk. For the Greeks it is probably because they are brought up with a philosophy of seeking reassurance and, therefore, have difficulty getting started in a project. When all is said and done, the Italians are rather unadventurous because they build for the long term. As for the Austrians, they are too fond of mastering the individual phases of a project to move forward blindly.

Among Europeans the managers most at ease with risk and uncertainty are the British, and this trait has important consequences concerning communication. The English manager is happy to have general control in running the firm and does not expect to be informed in detail of operations.

We should note, however, that individual behavior can be somewhat different when these same executives are managing their careers and not their company. Employment recruiters with Europeanwide networks claim that the French and Italians seem to be the most adventurous. They gladly let themselves be charmed by a company, company image, the charisma and management style of the general director, etc., and can come to an interview without knowing anything about a position. These attitudes contrast strongly with those of British and German executives who want to know everything about the position before going to an interview to discuss it. They thoroughly check out the financial condition of the recruiting organization and appear very particular about the fringe benefits accompanying a salary.

Pragmatism

Another dimension of management already mentioned is the degree of pragmatism of various managers. This dimension contrasts with a preference for manipulating ideas and concepts. It shows an important connection to the pleasure and skill that certain executives have for communicating in their own language.

Realism, rationality, and sometimes empiricism and utilitarianism and an affinity for the concrete are associated with pragmatism. It seems that pragmatism in managment is more particularly the province of the British, the Scandinavians, the Dutch, the Belgians, and the Germans. Conversely the French like great intellectual and abstract theories. The Italians appreciate panache, lively intellect, and quick wit. On one side there are the facts and solutions, however imperfect, and on the other, the philosophy of the problem and the analysis. The Germans, for example, think that the supremacy of theory and conceptualization is detrimental to action. The Swedish like the simplicity of facts on which to found their judgments and are effective without complex demonstrations. Their rationalism and pragmatism are founded on the fundamental values of protestantism. The Belgians claim to be grounded in the land and their pragmatism, as in Switzerland, is akin to traditional peasant values. As for the British, good Anglo-Saxons that they are, their thought has always been empirical, utilitarian, and concrete. With them pragmatism is accompanied by a good sense of timing and skillful diplomacy.

Performance

Much linked to the preceding, the following managerial dimension is concerned with the value placed on performance and on obtaining results in different European countries. This dimension has a strong impact on the style and content of corporate presentations.

Among Europeans, the Germans, the Swedish, the Danish, and the British are focused on performances, objectives, and final results. The Swiss, notably the German speakers, seem to reward the effort and contribution of each employee at intermediate steps of a project. The Swedish have the specific trait of compensation for goals that are not only financial and in this respect the Danish borrow from American managerial values. The Danish have always been much quicker to dismiss unproductive personnel. As for the British they value operational skills, productivity, and knowledge about managing profit centers. In these preferences they are close to classical American management.

Some European countries have a less aggressive management style, either because they have never had to make efforts to sell, the case of Luxembourg for its financial products, or because, as in Belgium, their executives measure themselves by other values more related to power. In this situation, executives at a recruitment interview, for example, describe their professional experience, not in terms of a result described by numbers, but by a long description of assignments and responsibilities taken on and tasks carried out. The emphasis is more often placed on the process and the means than on the result. An executive in this case is sensitive to hierarchical structures and the specific contributions of the position to a company's turnover and, most important, the number of employees answerable. The executive takes pains to indicate the importance of duties, vis-à-vis, the decision-making center.

Other countries simply have not yet integrated performance into their value system. In Greece executives are hardly concerned with decision making in itself and little oriented toward obtaining results. Likewise in Portugal setting goals and sticking to them is difficult. Often long meetings are held without an agenda and the tendency to dissipate effort is strong. Finally there are other countries like Italy and Ireland that have recently incorporated the importance of objectives into their value systems. Today they regard meeting objectives and obtaining results among recruitment and evaluation criteria although this is difficult in Ireland where judging individuals and telling them disagreeable things is not a tradition. Consequently executives are led to overrate unproductive employees. This situation is connected to the attitude toward conflicts that consitutes the next managerial dimension for discussion.

Individualism

Another dimension concerns the respective roles of the individual and the group. According to Hofstede's well-known scales of measurement, certain Europeans are more individualist than others. This is notably the case of the French, the English, the Italians, and the Belgians. Others like the Greeks, the Dutch, the Swedish, and the Germans show more solidarity, be it to the family or another social group. The Greeks, for example, are only individualist psychologically and in appearance. If they do not work well in groups, they also have a weak tolerance for nonconformist behavior and are very dependent on the group. They like socially acceptable behavior and a community spirit. (Unemployment, for example, is less of a bad experience in Greece than it is elsewhere because of the solid family unit which reduces its impact.) The Dutch like to gather together in large groups, which makes them gregarious and noisy in French eyes.

The Germans are, above all, motivated by reactions of belonging to a group (identity, citizenship). They are comfortable in structures of exchanges such as forums and networks. They have a great respect for the community interest. They favor collective success more than individual success and display solidarity among themselves against foreign competitors. This form of national solidarity among German companies excludes overt fratricidal struggles on foreign markets and promotes the choice of German equipment and products in Germany. This same solidarity comes into play when consensual decisions are carried out once individuals have settled their conflicts.

This difference is obvious as far as French and Swedish communication is concerned. Pierre Guillet de Monthoux has noted that a French discussion is a sort of crucible in which individual ideas are melted down to produce new ideas; a Swedish debate is a podium on which the ideas of the group are presented and submitted to a general inspection. What gives credibility to the individual's words is not the logic of argumentation, but the fact they are expressed in the name of the group. Each person waits for a turn to speak, and personal ideas are not expressed (Schnapper and Mendras, 1990). In Sweden people are generally more preoccupied by what others will say and think. For all of these reasons, the Germans, the Dutch, the Flemish-speaking Belgians, and the Swedish work much more comfortably in groups than executives from Latin countries, who are generally more individualist and show less solidarity.

Attitude to conflict

Finally the last dimension taken into account is precisely the attitude toward conflict, and it is closely linked to the tone of communication used by executives in these countries.

The attitude toward conflict can be viewed in two distinct forms: labor conflicts or strained relationships between individuals. In the Nordic countries for example, social-democratic policies are based on the notion of consensus. Codetermination laws have reinforced the collective relationship between employers and employee representatives and have contributed to the creation of a cooperative labor climate. Similarly in Switzerland, management is not accustomed to difficult confrontations. Neither the employers nor the unions like confrontation, and negotiation or consensus are systematically sought.

Similarly, in interpersonal relations the Scandinavians have an attitude toward conflict different from the one found in Southern Europe. In the Nordic countries, conflict is avoided because it is judged to be sterile while the Latin environment is full of conflict, and therefore, difficult for the Danish or the Swedish to decode. In Denmark words are weighed carefully in situations where the French appear aggressive in their vocabulary. Commercial negotiations, which are very important for a trading nation such as Denmark, are also conducted through dialogue and in an atmosphere of mutual respect. The Danish are attached to the win-win model of negotiation. The same is true for Sweden where problems are settled politely and humanely. Swedish executives are supposed to help those experiencing difficulty. They dislike conflicts inside companies. Therefore, disputes are resolved as soon as they arise, with dignity and respect for the individual taking care not to offend or to hurt the feelings of others.

Among the Latins the attitude toward conflict can be markedly different. The Portuguese for example claim to be more peaceable and less conflictual in their relationships than the Spanish. As proof they cite the fact that they are fond of bullfights on horseback that do not put the bull to death. In meetings in Portugal managers avoid direct conflicts as much as possible.

American style influence

Let us end this analysis of the differences of management style throughout Europe by noting the heavy influence of American management that has served as a model for a number of these countries.

This is notably the case for Great Britain, Germany, Italy, Spain, Denmark, The Netherlands, Portugal, Greece, Ireland, and France. The influence of European management styles on one another has generally had a smaller impact: note that of Great Britain's on Ireland's; France's on Belgium's and Portugal's; Germany's on Spain's, Austria's, and the Netherlands'.

The forces, the reputation, or certain managerial characteristics of these countries stem from their culture, but also from their own resources connected to their geographical situation. Production is dominant in Germany and Belgium, and technology in Germany, Denmark, Sweden, France, and Ireland. The ability to sell and to negotiate is favored among the English, the Danish, the Dutch, the Greeks, and the Austrians. Marketing is particularly developed in Italy, Denmark, The Netherlands, and France. The management of human resources, as we have seen, is better among the English, the Danish, the Dutch, the Swedish, and the Austrians. Other countries have developed specific skills in the fields of finance, accounting, or insurance (Great Britain, Luxembourg, Ireland, and Switzerland), and still others have produced very skilled lawyers (like Great Britain and on this point exactly like the United States), who are quite numerous and in demand in Italy, Portugal, and Greece.

Thus certain countries develop general skills in their managers and others prefer managers with specializations, a trend similar to what is happening in the United States. Here again France and Germany furnish good examples of contrasts. The French executive basically has the culture of a generalist and needs to be many-sided to feel comfortable in work, where the German manager is by nature a specialist. In negotiations, Germans prefer to have a team of specialists opposite them. Often they will have opposite them on the French side a brilliant "jack-of-all-trades" incapable of answering detailed questions and who retreats into the upper sphere of strategy.

Conclusion

Management styles differ greatly across Europe. European executives usually deal with the countries closest geographically and are unfamiliar with others. As Europe 1993 makes executive transfers and recruitment easier than before across the EC, it is important to be aware of the various management styles in Western European countries. It is just as crucial for non-EC foreigners dealing with those countries to understand cultural differences and diverse styles of management.

As most managers have been exposed to the American manage-ment style, and sometimes the Japanese style, in the past, the ques-tion may be raised as to whether a European management style is likely to emerge in the future. For example, we recognize the ten-dency everywhere in Europe toward dialogue involvement and shar-ing. We note how humanistic values are shared by most of these countries. Yet it is at present too early to say whether an identifiable European style will actually emerge at some point in the future.

Reference

Schnapper, D. and Mendras, H. (1990) *Six manières d'être Européen,* Paris: Gallimard.

◇

9.3 The Secrets of African Managerial Success

◆

David K. Leonard

It has become fashionable to despair at the quality of African public sector management.[1] Generally the problem is attributed to the social and political context within which governmental activities must be conducted on the continent (see Hyden, 1983; Moris, 1981; Price, 1975). There is no doubt that the environment for public management is frequently inhospitable in Africa.

The environmental argument explains too much, however, and is thereby unduly pessimistic. It implies that almost all public sector activities should fail, since they are all subject to the same unfavorable environment. As Barbara Grosh has shown, a good number of indigenously managed Kenyan parastatals have in fact been successes (Grosh, 1987). The same can be said for many civil service initiatives. In these cases African managers have prevailed despite the inauspicious context within which they worked. Why and how? The answer is important to the developmental future of the continent.

In search of the secrets of African managerial success I am writing the biographies of four Kenyans who have been particularly effective in their management of rural development initiatives, that domain of public activity in which failure is most prevalent (Hirschman,

Source: David K. Leonard, "The Secrets of African Managerial Success," *International Studies of Management and Organization*, 1988, pp. 35–41, Vol. 19, No. 4. Reprinted by permission of *International Studies of Management and Organization*.

1987; Israel, 1987, 18–26). Within their life and career histories I have found some clues as to why they were able to breathe success on many of the enterprises which they led. Of course the resulting insights must be treated cautiously until they have been verified through quantitative research on a systematic sample of managers. I offer them now, not as proven generalizations, but to promote discussion and to strengthen our understanding of some of the forms of managerial behavior that are at least possible on the continent.

The four men whom I have studied are: Charles Kibe Karanja, General Manager of the Kenya Tea Development Authority from 1970 to 1981; Harris Mutio Mule, who moved through the ranks of the Planning Department to become Permanent Secretary of the Ministry of Finance from 1980 to 1986; Simeon Nyachae, Provincial Commissioner from 1964 to 1979, then head of the President's policy staff and finally Chief Secretary from 1983 to 1986; and Ishmael Muriithi, Director of Veterinary Services from 1966 to 1984. I have probed the lives of these men in considerable depth, interviewing them and their families, professional associates, friends and village acquaintances. Altogether I conducted nearly 300 interviews with almost 200 people in pursuit of these biographies.

The four men have varied in the extent and clarity of their success as public servants. The most unambiguous case is that of Charles Karanja. The Kenya Tea Development Authority is an internationally acknowledged success story (Paul 1982:11, 60–2) and Karanja saw it through its period of greatest growth, including its movement into the new and difficult areas of manufacturing and international marketing.

The choice of Simeon Nyachae is more controversial. His service to the President was always impeccable but some of the enterprises with which he was associated during his tenure as Provincial Commissioner did not have a positive developmental impact. (For example, he was chair of the failed Wheat Board.) A change gradually overtook him when he assumed responsibility for national policy, however. Kenya's *Financial Times* wrote of his term as Chief Secretary that he:

> bestrode the Kenya civil service like the Shakespearean colossus. For most of that period, Nyachae's influence permeated every department of government operations and he was the most articulate exponent of most economic policies . . . He was the prime moving force behind

the government's district focus for rural development programmes and its most lucid spokesman (Kisero 1987:4).

I think that he had a major and, on balance, positive impact in this period.

Harris Mule was a quieter, less obtrusive man. Working behind the scenes he was a prime architect of Kenya's Arid and Semi-Arid Lands and District Focus programs (the latter with Nyachae). These were progressive, redistributive programs. He also was responsible with Philip Ndegwa, Governor of the Central Bank of Kenya, for the country's early and courageous economic readjustment in the 1980s, which might be thought of as a conservative policy. One international observer of Kenya's economic policies called Mule "one of the ten best stabilisers in the world." Both Kenyans and foreigners agree that he was exceptionally good at handling donor agencies and their pressures. Mule's internal management of the Ministry of Finance was more mixed; he was criticized for not Africanizing rapidly enough and some departments were not tightly administered.

Ishmael Muriithi presided over a dramatic expansion in Kenya's veterinary services and with it the successful explosion of smallholder dairy production. His iron managerial hand turned limp however, when President Kenyatta died and the expansive public budgets on which he had relied began to run dry. His final years were not effective ones.

All of these men were responsible for important successes, but they had failures as well.[2] Thus the assessment of the managerial attributes of these men that follows is a subtle one, giving greater weight to those factors that are associated with the successes and steering away from those elements that seem to be responsible for their failures. Given the discriminating nature of this analysis and the brevity that is necessary to the *Bulletin* article, full proof will not always be possible for the conclusions that are drawn.

Political connections and organizational autonomy

One of the older pieces of wisdom on public enterprises is that their effective management requires political autonomy. Organizations are expected to prosper to the extent that their leaderships are appointed for their technical, not their political qualifications (Hanson 1959). It is evident from my case studies that this analysis is over simple.

Although all of my subjects were professionally well qualified for the positions that they held, their managerial success and the autonomy of their organizations was critically dependent on their political connections.[3] In 1973 Charles Karanja wanted his Kenya Tea Development Authority (KTDA) to expand vertically into the technically difficult areas of processing and international marketing. He was opposed in this decision by the World Bank, which was KTDA's major financier, and the multinational tea corporations that were then handling these functions for the KTDA. As a consequence, the Minister for Agriculture and his Permanent Secretary decided firmly against the expansion. But Karanja would not be stopped. He sought out an interview with President Kenyatta and asked that he be permitted to take on the new functions and to be fired if he failed. Kenyatta expressed his high regard for Karanja and gave his permission. The other actors then withdrew their opposition and the KTDA successfully assumed these new roles. This action would not have been possible if Karanja had not earlier in his career come to the personal attention of Kenyatta, inspired his confidence and had direct access to him.

The self-assurance which Karanja's presidential connections gave him also provided the KTDA with an impressive degree of autonomy, much *more* than was granted to it by its legal charter. Twice in the 1970's the Kenya Government negotiated a Tripartite Agreement whereby organized labor agreed to a freeze on wages in return for a 10 percent increase in employment by private employers and the state. This agreement proved particularly costly to public organizations because whereas the private firms returned to their previous employment levels relatively quickly through normal attrition in their labor force, the state increased the numbers of its established positions and remained permanently fixed at the higher level. Karanja correctly felt that this agreement would be disadvantageous to the farmers whom the KTDA served, as the increased costs would have to be deducted from the payments made to them. He felt so confident of his personal standing with the President that he never implemented the Agreement, by making seasonal workers permanent. This resulted in no increase in expenditure and protected the health of his organization from a disadvantageous political decision.

When Kenyatta died Karanja lost his direct contact with the President, but was so confident of the importance of the KTDA and of the quality of its management that he continued to act with the same independence and decisiveness. Ultimately this cost him his position. The dénouement came during a time of high tea prices on the world market when packaged tea that Kenya subsidized for its domestic market was being smuggled to Ethiopia. A Cabinet Minister and important supporter of President Moi publicly accused the KTDA of responsibility for the smuggling and the shortage of tea in his constituency. Stung by this questioning of the KTDA's integrity, Karanja held a press conference to point out that the Minister owned the major shop in his constituency which received KTDA tea allotments, implying that if there were smuggling the Minister must be responsible for it himself. The Minister denied he was an agent for tea. As Karanja prepared to reply with documentary evidence of the Minister's role and of smuggling through Nairobi airport, he sought an audience with President Moi to brief him on the conflict. The Minister was able to keep him from seeing the President, and the Government subsequently took tea distribution away from the KTDA and instructed it to divert international supplies to the domestic market, at the cost of small farmers' profits.[4] Although Karanja wasn't dismissed until some time later, his effectiveness as a manager was substantially diminished from this point. He no longer had the contacts necessary to protect his organization.

Part of Ishmael Muriithi's job as Director of Veterinary Services was to protect Kenya's most productive beef herds from Foot and Mouth Disease so that they could be sold in the lucrative European markets. To do this, strict quarantine had to be imposed on the movement of livestock from the infected areas into disease free ones. Well placed individuals would use their influence from time to time to evade the quarantine and reap the considerable profits available from the difference in prices in the two markets. It was particularly difficult for the Veterinary Department to control the problem when people such as senior police officials were the culprits. Muriithi gained the support which he needed to win this critical struggle by going directly to President Kenyatta. He did not have personal connections himself with the President but was able to reach him and gain his confidence through Geoffrey Kariithi, who then held the powerful position of Chief Secretary and had been to high school with Muriithi. This liaison was used by the Director of

Veterinary Services on a number of occasions to obtain critically needed resources and support for his department. When Kenyatta died and Kariithi retired, Muriithi was deprived of his connections with the Office of the President and was unable to protect the Veterinary Services from the conflicts and mindless budget cutting that then undermined its effectiveness. In his final years as Director he lost his characteristic vigor and decisiveness and came near to a despairing lethargy, probably only partly due to his declining health.

Harris Mule never had personal connections with those around the President and his ascension to a permanent secretaryship was delayed partly as a result. When he finally became Permanent Secretary to the Ministry of Finance and Planning under President Moi, he still lacked the direct contacts necessary to obtain the economic policies he regarded as critical. He began by working through his Minister, Vice-President Mwai Kibaki, with whom he had a long-standing and close relationship. However, this became less and less effective as Kibaki's political power began to slip. Mule then allied himself informally with Simeon Nyachae in the Office of the President.

Nyachae is one of the few men to have had the personal confidence of both Presidents Kenyatta and Moi. This is probably because of Nyachae's principled determination always to give priority to the interests of his Presidents and never to act in a way that might diminish them, even at the cost of service to his own home area. Such dogged loyalty gave both Presidents confidence in the advice that they received from Nyachae. As a consequence, on one known occasion Kisii Nyachae was even able to win a showdown with a senior Kikuyu official who was well connected with President Kenyatta.

As allies, Mule and Nyachae were able to achieve a number of important reforms through the President's trust in the latter. Most remarkable was their ability to persuade Moi to accept the politically risky conditions needed for an IMF agreement less than two months after the major coup attempt of August 1982. The great strides made under the District Focus strategy were also a direct result of the three men seeing eye to eye on the policy. On another occasion, when Mule pressed for deregulation of the grain market harder and longer than was politically expedient, it was his relationship with Nyachae and the latter's ties with the President that saved Mule from losing office.

In all of these cases we see that the ability of these public servants effectively to pursue professionally dictated policies and to protect the integrity of their organization against inappropriate political pressures was directly contingent on their personal connections, direct or indirect, with the President. When these relationships of confidence were lost, so was their managerial effectiveness. Thus we see that the autonomy of an organization from undue politicization is not something that can simply be granted to it in a single constitutional act. It has to be earned and then maintained through political connections. Virtually all public organizations need favorable policy decisions and additional resources at critical junctures if they are to prosper (see Mukandala 1988; Grosh 1987). They also need protection from unwise policy initiatives and politicization. All of these requisites, even depoliticization, are achieved as a consequence of political action. In Kenya and most other African states, the relevant political intervention comes from the President.

Effective public servants are able to mobilize support at critical junctures *not* by building independent political bases of support for themselves or their organizations, but from personal access to and the confidence of the President. By and large, these crucial connections were not fortuitous for the four men studied here. They resulted from loyalty and careful network building and are a tribute to their administrative astuteness in an underbureaucratized environment.[5] Thus political considerations are important in the appointment of the most senior public servants if political autonomy and effectiveness are to be maintained.

Professional integrity

Not everyone who has the confidence of a president is going to use it to advance the performance of the organization that he or she leads, however. Those who come to positions of leadership in Africa through a political career or because of their ability to mobilize support in the larger political community are not likely to be effective managers. They are likely to see their positions and the powers which they convey as a reward for the delivery of their support to the president, not as a resource to be used to advance the effectiveness of the organization. Managers with this type of political support tend to sap, not strengthen their units.

The effective managers in our "sample" were committed professionals. Harris Mule and Ishmael Muriithi were trained overseas
respectively as a professional economist and veterinarian. Both men
were deeply committed to their profession and dedicated to maintaining their standards in Kenya. Charles Karanja was trained in
Uganda as a civil engineer. Such a background was quite unnecessary
to the leadership of the KTDA, but it did seem to shape Karanja's
ideas about public service and efficiency. In all three of these cases
professional identity gave these men a strong commitment to the
goals of the organizations they headed and caused them to resist
their use for inappropriate personal gain by themselves or others.

Simeon Nyachae was prepared to be a provincial administrator,
first by his father, Chief Nyandusi, and then by training in Kenya
and England. This background gave him a very strong identification
with the state and a principled determination to serve the interests
of those who hold political power. In his years as a Provincial
Commissioner these values did not give him a particularly strong
commitment to the goals of some of the organizations with which
he was involved, and he was willing to see them taxed to serve the
personal interests of those who held political power over him. When
he came onto the national scene, however, Nyachae increasingly
came to see the interests of the "nation," conceived in a conservative
sense, as coincident with the interests of his President, the state,
and the business class of which he was a part. This broadening of
vision gave him a set of values which made him quite open to the
policies advocated by the economist Mule.

All four men were careful to place the interests of the organizations
that they served above their own personal gain. Although their
conception of what constitutes conflict of interest was more lax than
those applied in the United States today, they definitely had one
and adhered to it. They also differed among themselves. Muriithi's
and particularly Mule's personal ethics were the strictest, and their
personal wealth upon retirement was consequently modest. Karanja
and Nyachae had laxer conceptions and left the public service rich.
Their wealth was due to hard work and business acumen, however,
and probably only to a minor degree to the positions they had held,
particularly for Karanja.

As long as they take care of their organizations well, does it
interfere with their effectiveness if public managers use their positions to advance their personal wealth in Africa? I have concluded
that the answer is yes. Certainly the general political and social

environment of which these men were part was quite unconcerned about corruption, and effectively encouraged it. In much the same way as Robert Price demonstrated for Ghana (Price 1975), the question in the popular mind was never how someone got their wealth but whether they were personally tranferring resources to their relatives and home areas. My interviews revealed, however, that a different set of values usually prevailed *inside* public agencies among the professional subordinates and peers of the managers I studied. The respect and support that a manager of a professional organization received from his subordinates and from his peers in related organizations appears to be heavily contingent on his perceived personal integrity. This does not mean that these subordinates and peers were always behaving with integrity themselves. Unlike members of the general public, however, they understood the concept of conflict of interest and felt that they owed effort and support to those who were faithful to it, even if they were not. Conversely, they felt free to be slack in their duties if they were asked to do something by someone whose integrity they doubted. I am not suggesting that Kenyan professionals always – or even usually – practice what they preach, but they do believe what they preach. Their views on integrity have something of the same status as American views on marital fidelity in presidential politics. Even those who do not practice the ethical code themselves believe that those who break it do not deserve to hold leadership positions. Thus in Kenya, those whose integrity is in doubt are unlikely to be effective managers of professional organizations. Indeed, the decline in the careers of two of the managers in our "sample" can be traced in part to revelations that they had profited from minor conflicts of interest.

I have carefully limited the above generalization about the relationship between integrity and managerial effectiveness to professional organizations. Interviews with Simeon Nyachae's colleagues in the Provincial Administration did not reveal much concern with the conflict of interest issue. Quite possibly this part of the Kenya Government is so closely tied to the regulation and practice of politics that it has no distinct professional code of ethics on such matters.

Access to donor resources

Another attribute that proved critical to managerial effectiveness was the ability to inspire the confidence of international actors.

African economies are relatively small and weak, and international markets and donor transfers are usually important to them. Those managers who are skilled at acquiring these resources are able to use them to gain flexibility in an environment that is usually severely constrained. They also perform a function for the economy that gives them support from other powerful domestic politicians and public servants.

Harris Mule was particularly well known for his skill with donors; this attribute was independently raised by eight quite different interviewees. It is interesting that whereas the foreigners tended to say that Mule "*gets along* well with donors," one of the Kenyan respondents said that "he *handles* donors well," a subtle but significant difference in perspective. Mule was helpful in international economic negotiations because he both understood donor objectives and was able to make them in turn understand Kenyan political constraints. Thus he was invaluable in advancing some of the reforms that donors regarded as important and in getting them to accept that others were unachievable at the time. In this way he was crucial to obtaining IMF, World Bank and bilateral donor resources at critical junctures for the economy. Mule's skill in this regard was immensely aided by and may well have depended on his reputation for professionalism and absolute personal integrity, which made donors trust what he said. One donor even funded a project in Mule's home area to reward him for being incorruptible and thus unable to finance any significant projects himself.

Ishmael Muriithi's professional reputation was similarly responsible for inspiring international confidence in Kenya and thus bringing it advantage. In his case the critical problem was gaining access to the lucrative European beef market, despite the continued presence in Kenya of animal diseases such as Foot and Mouth. European states usually prohibit the import of fresh beef from any country in which these diseases are identified. Kenya gained access to some of the European market by arguing that it would export beef only from zones which were kept free of the offending diseases. For European veterinary officials to accept this argument they had to be convinced that Kenya would indeed enforce a rigid quarantine on cattle movements into these zones, and that only beef that came from these zones would be cleared for export to Europe. To be so persuaded they had to have confidence in the high standards and integrity of Kenya's Veterinary Service. Muriithi's reputation as

Director for being incorruptible and firmly committed to professional standards created that international confidence. In a similar way, the high regard with which he was held in international veterinary circles helped him to bring the International Laboratory for Research on Animal Diseases' and other, even more direct forms of donor assistance, to Kenya.

Charles Karanja's reputation for efficient management of the Kenya Tea Development Authority facilitated its continued access to substantial amounts of assistance, particularly from the World Bank, and thus gave it the resources and flexibility to grow beyond what Kenya's domestic capital constraints would have allowed.[6] The KTDA's size and international reputation in turn gave Karanja weight in many domestic policy struggles.

The only one of our four who was not particularly gifted with the international community was Simeon Nyachae. As a Provincial Commissioner, Nyachae had been one of President Kenyatta's primary instruments for the control of domestic politics (see Gertzel 1970). When Nyachae came to the national policy scene he had very little international experience and was tainted by his past political connections. He and the donors didn't understand each other very well, and they were not certain that they could trust him. It was here that Nyachae's alliance with Mule was of such great importance; just as Nyachae provided Mule with political connections, Mule provided donor access to Nyachae.

Africanization

Frequently there was a down side to donor confidence, one that reduced the loyalty that managers inspired in their own staff. Three of the managers in our "sample" felt that they had to use some non-Kenyan staff in order to maintain high professional standards in their organizations, standards which gave them a strong international reputation. The morale and allegiance of their Kenyan staff depended, however, on a vigorous Africanization program, replacing foreign with local staff.

Only Charles Karanja handled this dilemma well. He concentrated expatriate staff in training positions and in those parts of the organization where new functions were being added. He was able to rally nationalist sentiment for his personnel policies, despite the continued use of foreigners, by externalizing the conflict. He argues that the important issue was not the exact distribution of positions inside the organization but whether it would be the Kenyan-controlled KTDA or the multinational corporations that would control critical aspects of the domestic tea industry. For the technically demanding role of factory manager, he was able to point out that the multinationals did not believe it was possible for any Kenyan African to do the job in the near future. Thus when he hired an expatriate to head the factory division and to train managers, he could argue that he was promoting, not hindering Africanization, and in the process was able to unleash a nationalist determination among his recruits to do their jobs well and prove the multinationals wrong.

Ishmael Muriithi was not so adept. He was under great pressure to replace expatriate veterinarians with Kenyan ones as they became available. He argued that this was a non-issue. As the country had a shortage of vets anyway, both should be employed. But he also felt that his highest priority was to assign African vets to field positions, where they would be able to interact with African livestock producers. This meant that he was seen as keeping expatriates in the highly prized headquarters positions. Consequently he developed a reputation among his Kenyan staff for being insufficiently attentive to their advancement, and lost some of their loyalty. This was tragic, for the circumstances actually closely parallel those in the KTDA where Karanja was able to engender the extra incentive of nationalist competition. The measure of an "Africanizer" may be as much subjective as objective. The manager who is able to give reality to an external promotion standard that he is *helping* his staff to meet will out-perform one who is seen as being the gate keeper himself.

Harris Mule also had trouble with Africanization, a problem which he inherited from his predecessor, Philip Ndegwa. In Finance and Planning the replacement of expatriates with locals in line positions took place relatively rapidly, perhaps too rapidly. For it was then felt that certain critical skills were still in short supply, and foreign advisers were brought in to provide them. Mule's Kenyan subordinates frequently resented the influence that some of these advisers had, and the fact that they often seemed to get the more challenging work. There was something of a vicious circle here, for as Kenyans grew discontented with foreign advisers they sometimes became more lax in their own work and the need for expatriates increased.

Something like Karanja's device for making this competition functional rather than destructive was needed.

Risk taking

A further attribute that emerges from our case studies is the willingness to take risks. All four men occasionally faced circumstances in which they had to put their own careers at stake by taking decisions or advocating policies which were critical to their organizations. Karanja, Mule and Nyachae were willing to do so when they calculated that the political odds gave them some chance of success, and they usually won. Muriithi was a more classically "conservative" bureaucrat, however, and his organization may have suffered at some critical junctures as a result.

It is interesting to ask why these three managers were willing to risk their careers. Karanja and Nyachae both said that it was because they were already well to do and had always intended to make their careers in private business rather than the public sector anyway. Mule had always been dedicated to a public career and his personal property was quite modest, but he too felt that his earning opportunities did not depend on his continued government service. Since he had been incorruptible, he could make more as a private or international executive. Although I think that all three men, in different ways, loved the exercise of power, that love did not outweigh their drive to accomplish certain goals that they had set for their organizations, and they felt that they had the financial independence to take the risk. Business or other executive positions awaited them outside the public sector.

Paradoxically the fact that the Kenyan state does not have a monopoly control over higher income earning positions therefore seems to have given it better service from its managers by making them less risk averse. Muriithi's unwillingness to take the same risks as the other three men may have been due to the extremely limited possibilities for private veterinary practice in Kenya which his own policies had helped to create.[7]

Drive

Finally and unsurprisingly, all four men had extraordinary drive and an ability for hard work that was sometimes of legendary proportions. They worked exceedingly long hours and were extremely self-disciplined. Mule read voraciously and into the early hours of every morning. Nyachae began his day early, worked through lunch, and kept to a rigid schedule of exercise. He was famous for the speed with which he gave written replies to memos. All four were unusual in being extremely temperate in their drinking, although Mule loved bars as a young man; Nyachae believed in total abstinence from alcohol and would not even drink coffee.

Conclusion

"Type A" personality attributes are a common part of the folk-lore of executive success everywhere. People with exceptional careers are usually exceptional. Of greater interest are the attributes of political connections, professional competence and integrity, access to donor resources, and skill at maintaining staff quality and commitment through the trials of Africanization. We see that these attributes have a distinctively African character that is consistent with the universal tenets of organization and social exchange theories, but which could not have been easily predicted from them. Much more work is needed on this fascinating and important topic. I will have more to say as I continue my analysis of my case studies, and I hope that others will join me in research in this area as well.

Endnotes

1. I am grateful for the high quality of research assistance that I have received on this project from Martha Saavedra, Zeverino Mogaka, Kamene Mutambuki, Samwell Ngigi, and Fred Schaffer. Funding for the research was provided by the National Science Foundation (SES-8599532), a Fulbright Fellowship, and the Institute of International Studies, University of California, Berkeley.

2. Mixed records are characteristic of the great American public administrators as well: see Diog and Hargrove 1987:12.

3. It turns out that this is true in the United States as well: see Doig and Hargrove 1987:15.

4. *The Daily Nation* (Nairobi), 12/4/78, p. 10; 12/5/78, p. 1; 12/7/78, p. 4; 12/12/78, p. 5. *The Nairobi Times,* 1/21/79, p. 1; *The Weekly Review,* 1/26/79, pp. 30–31; 2/2/79, p. 24.

5. I owe this observation to Emery Roe.

6. The KTDA's access to Bank funds was *aided* by, but was not *dependent* on Karanja's management. As Rwekaza Mukandala has pointed out to me, other, less well managed tea authorities were getting Bank monies at this time. Of course the popularity of tea as a target of lending was due in large part to the KTDA's success, which in turn was influenced by Karanja.

7. As Emery Roe has pointed out to me, these observations indicate that the brain drain from the public to the private sector in Kenya at least has some compensating advantages.

References

Doig, Jameson W., and Hargrove, Erwin, 1987. " 'Leadership' and Political Analysis" in Doig and Hargrove (eds.), *Leadership and Innovation: A Biographical Perspective on Entrepreneurs in Government*, Johns Hopkins University Press, Baltimore.

Gertzel, Cherry, 1970. *The Politics of Independent Kenya*, East African Publishing House, Nairobi.

Grosh, Barbara, 1987. "Performance of Agricultural Public Enterprises in Kenya: Lessons from the First Two Decades of Independence," *Eastern Africa Economic Review*, vol. 3, no. 1.

Hanson, A. H., 1959. *Public Enterprise and Economic Development*, Routledge and Kegan Paul, London.

Hirschman, Albert, 1987. *Development Projects Observed*, The Brookings Institution, Washington.

Hyden, Goran, 1983. *No Shortcuts to Progress: African Development Management in Perspective*, University of California Press, Berkeley.

Israel, Arturo, 1987. *Institutional Development: Incentives to Performance*, Johns Hopkins University Press, Baltimore, pp. 18–26.

Kisero, Jaindi, 1987. "Lord of a New Realm," *Financial Review*, 29 June.

Moris, Jon, 1981. *Managing Induced Rural Development*, International Development Institute, Indiana University, Bloomington.

Mukandala, Rwekasa, 1988. "The Political Economy of Parastatal Enterprises in Tanzania and Botswana," PhD dissertation, Department of Political Science, University of California, Berkeley.

Paul, Samuel, 1982. *Managing Development: The Lessons of Success,* Westview Press, Boulder (Co.).

Price, Robert, 1975. *Society and Bureaucracy in Contemporary Ghana,* University of California Press, Berkeley.

◇

9.4 Thinking of a Plant in Mexico?

◆

Mariah E. de Forest

The opportunities for American business in Mexico are great. But the actual job of managing a Mexican fabricating or assembly plant is a challenge for even the best of managers – because not only must the production get out on schedule, there is the added twist of dealing with a different culture and language. For example, believing that a good grievance system was the ticket to preventing labor problems from blowing up in his face, one American manager in a steel conveyor plant in Puebla installed a three-stage system in which complaints would go first to the immediate supervisor, then up the chain of command, with strict time limits and the guarantee of prompt management response. Since no grievances had ever arisen from the floor through this new grievance process, the manager was astonished one day when the entire plant walked out. Unlike their more assertive neighbors to the north, Mexican workers typically avoid directly confronting their superiors with complaints because such behavior is considered seriously antisocial in the context of a basically authoritarian society.

In comparison with U.S. workers, Mexican workers may not follow through on tasks, they tend to be activity oriented rather than problem solvers and appear to assume that companies exist to

Source: Mariah E. de Forest, "Thinking of a Plant in Mexico?," excerpted from *Academy of Management Executives*, February 1994, pp. 33–40, Vol. 8, No. 1. Reprinted by permission of The Academy of Management.

provide jobs rather than to make a profit. In most instances, however, these behaviors are simply the result of the French-style, rote-learning Mexican educational system, as well as years of economic protectionism, rather than fatal flaws in the Mexican character. Having grasped this fact, it is a small step to undertake training of Mexican managers and employees specifically designed to teach goal-oriented work, problem-solving skills and the importance of initiative and profitability. Mexican workers and managers welcome their exposure to American business methods, and are eager to adapt when given the opportunity. It is only when Mexicans are asked to adapt to values that conflict with local beliefs, customs, norms of respectable behavior, and views of the proper role of authority that problems inevitably arise.

Job expectations

Mexican firms have tended to reflect the same traditional structure as the government, the church and Mexican society itself. Most have a rigid hierarchy, with power vested in the person at the top, a position often inherited, or acquired through friendships and mutual favors. Most top managers balance competing interests through consensus rather than engaging in open competition. Mexican firms tend to reward submission, direction, and loyal personal service – remember, *personal* service – to the person in authority.

After the Mexican Revolution put an end to the old *patron* system of haciendas and peons in 1922, Mexican labor law endeavored to modernize the old feudal relationship by outlining mutual obligations of employers and workers. Under current law, employers have significant responsibility for the conduct and improvement of workers' lives, assuring their "life, health, dignity and liberty." Moreover, a job is more than just an exchange of money for labor – it is also a social right, just as being an employer is a social and economic obligation.

It is the interrelation of "paternalistic" employer obligations toward workers, together with workers' duties to the employer – rather than a simple economic exchange – that underlie the unspoken expectations in today's Mexican workplace. When Americans accept that Mexican employees, by law, can and do expect from their jobs something other than just a paycheck or a chance to get ahead, and when Americans respect the employer's admittedly paternalistic social obligation, then good labor and community relations, and efficient operations, follow much more easily.

Seeking harmony in the workplace

In the Mexican mind, the sense that "all is well" occurs when every rank, from the top down, is in its place, working harmoniously. Stepping out onto the typical Mexican plant floor, a visitor is immediately impressed by the cordial and good natured atmosphere. This impression is not misleading – characteristically, the Mexican desire is for harmony rather than conflict. Compared to the U.S., there is low tolerance for adversarial relations or friction at work. When selecting among job applicants, Mexican employers typically look for a work history that demonstrates ability to work harmoniously with others and cooperatively with authority. Mexican employers tend to seek workers who are agreeable, respectful, and obedient rather than innovative and independent.

United States business embodies such traditional American values as individualism, self-determination, achievement, future orientation, optimism, curiosity, problem solving, and doing more than expected. But traditional Mexican ideals stress employee/employer *interdependence,* mutual responsibilities and loyalty between boss and worker; age, sex and position ranking orders in the organization; collectivism and continuity rather than individualism and change; belongingness and cooperation rather than competition; and not exceeding the boundaries of doing what you're told. Mexican employers tend to reject workers prone to criticize, who take their complaints to a higher authority, who exhibit competitiveness – because these traits disturb harmonious relations, the social fabric.

Equality in union/management relations is valued by employees, management and the union. This norm is sometimes difficult to understand for Americans who are accustomed to union and management often being adversaries. But under Mexican labor law, union and management roles are often complementary and parallel: both strive to maintain a "fountain of employment," one accountable for workers, the other directing the business – although day-to-day relations often fall short of this ideal. Direct management communications to the workforce are welcomed by unions as a way to cement good relations, and management solicitation of grievances is encouraged. The union cooperates in disciplining workers; management's role is to discipline supervisors. As long as wages do not fall below the legal minimum, supervisors act reasonably and sports or other social activities are available, Mexican employees view peaceful relations between the union and management as normal and desirable, rather than as being coopted.

Ideal working conditions

Mexican workers generally do not place a priority on working conditions where self-expression, wide latitude of action, and independent responsibility are encouraged. Rather, Mexicans value working conditions where supervisors are understanding (*comprensivo*), keep their distance and address workers formally, patiently demonstrate a job, yet are flexible enough to lend a hand once in a while. Mexican workers, looking upward from the lower levels of the organization, respond warmly to formal and dignified treatment – in other words, they appreciate it when authority is not abused. Their paradigm of ideal working conditions is the family model: everyone working together, doing their share, according to their designated roles.

Teamwork and cooperation are compelling ideals in the Mexican workplace, but difficult to achieve in reality. Often there are strong allegiances to fellow workers who may be family members, *compadres,* or neighbors. Nevertheless, Mexican workers respond best emotionally to management exhortations to improve group efficiency or group output, rather than to programs which stress competition with other workers. In practice, Mexican workers often excel when rewarded individually with incentive bonuses.

Minding one's manners

Behavior that is literally counterproductive results from Mexican supervisors' social instincts to mind their manners and preserve the appearance of harmony. For example, maquiladora supervisors may scrap or hide defective work from the preceding department, rather than have to confront another supervisor or report the problem to a manager. Many simply prefer not to get involved. For U.S.-trained maquiladora managers, it goes without saying that relaying information and problem solving are two of the major responsibilities of a supervisor. But failure on the part of American managers to verbalize these priorities often leads to misunderstanding about the supervisor's role.

Social manners in Mexico also tend to be more formal and private. An American manager in Nogales kept inviting other Mexican managers and their spouses to dinner at his home on the Arizona side of the border, but they continued to find excuses for not attending. The Mexican managers reported that they resented being invited to admire the American's home and belongings. This was the only explanation they could think of for the invitations. In Mexico, business associates traditionally entertain at restaurants, reserving their homes only for close friends.

The Face of Honor

The public image, the face of honor, is carefully observed in Mexico. Putting on a good appearance is tremendously important at all levels of society. A child may quit school because his or her family can't afford good shoes; a new salesman's first purchase is often a proper-looking gold watch. Employees will quit in outrage if criticized in public by their bosses.

Keeping face and minding that of others is one of the reasons for what appears to be excessive flattery, flowery language and other obsequious sounding reference in Spanish conversation. Similarly, status considerations lie behind the pervasive custom of calling people by their titles, rather than by their surnames – much less their first names. Thus, showing respect in a business setting involves keeping a proper distance; that is, being formal rather than friendly, casual and intimate.

Unfortunately, Americans in Mexico are generally oblivious to this daily drama of Latin honor and the sensitivity of Mexicans toward anything that calls their honor into question. The need to save face is what makes it so difficult for Mexicans at all levels to accept criticism and to change; many find it humiliating to acknowledge having made a mistake. Maquiladora management staff meetings can founder for the same reasons – in a Mexican firm, staff meetings often serve as a forum for people to receive orders, rather than to report, discuss and problem solve among managers.

Role, place and status

Octavio Paz, the Nobel prize-winning Mexican author and intellectual, pointed out twenty years ago that Mexican thinking is medieval rather than modern; hierarchical and dogmatic rather than pragmatic and open; and ceremonial, formal and ritualized, rather than spontaneous or purposeful. While much has changed since then, it is still often the case that in Mexico's relatively fixed social order people have a particular status and value its observance. Laborers, supervisors, managers, and union officials all honor each other's roles and their relative status or place. Recognizing another's place through symbolic formalities or a bit of flattery is the bedrock of human relations. Whether janitor, hopper-feeder or union leader, one's role must be respected as a legitimate and honorable endeavor. For example, a union president in a Piedras Negras maquiladora was deeply insulted when an American plant manager failed to introduce him to visitors from the home office. The plant manager regarded him as just another worker, whereas the union leader's place was that of commander of the entire labor force, and, under labor law, possessed *equal status* with the employer!

In another case, an American manager in a casting plant in Chihuahua habitually wore jeans and rumpled sports shirts, insisted that everyone call him Jim, and addressed all the Mexican managers by their first names. Because he felt he was doing a good job of reducing the visible economic and status gap between himself and the Mexicans, he was amazed to hear through the grapevine that the local employees and staff considered him uncultured and boorish. In Mexico, one's level in the management hierarchy is reflected in appropriate appearance – the higher in the hierarchy, the more formal the attire, the fancier the wristwatch, the shinier the shoes.

Americans often note that Mexican managers, usually in business attire, seem to be afraid to get their hands dirty, staying away from the factory floor and sending subordinates instead. American managers, on the other hand, find it more natural to mingle and joke with factory employees, and to attend company functions that include workers. In Mexico, American managers run the risk of being criticized as being too familiar. Nevertheless, we have found that maquiladora workers will respond eagerly to any management actions that communicate real interest and respect for them. Workers find acceptable a manager's mingling with them in the local May Day

(Mexican Labor Day) parade, occasionally appearing in the company cafeteria or personally visiting the plant floor from time to time. Such activities, if not overdone, can break down the onerous status distinctions and at the same time correspond to the ideal of harmonious relations in the workplace.

Exercising authority

Mexican workers respond to a person, rather than to any abstract set of work rules, or the exchange of labor for a paycheck. Since workers' lives often amount to being ordered about by people in authority, the desire is that authority be wielded in a kind and sensitive way. Mexican workers typically want to be closely supervised, rather than left alone. If told exactly what to do, they try hard to do it. They, more than their U.S. counterparts, accept their unequal status, simply asking that authority look out for their interests, provide clear instructions and correct them in a civil manner.

Maquiladora workers tend to regard their loyalty bonds with superiors as the key element in job security, rather than any seniority system. These *personal* bonds are what really determine whether or not workers come to work every day, are willing to work overtime, or work industriously when they are at work.

Maquiladora supervisors are as proud to be working for an American company as is the workforce, and this attitude forms a very positive foundation for management-supervisory relations. Supervisors are called *empleados de confianza* (confidential employees), which refers to the personal relationship between them and their superiors, rather than to a specific job function. The Mexican supervisor's role is to exercise authority within the hierarchical system of loyalties, and that power is exercised personally.

In the Mexican experience, power flows down from above; so, whatever other duties a job may entail, what the supervisors actually do tends to be what has been specifically authorized by the boss. It is confusing to maquiladora supervisors if American managers insist that supervisors earn authority and respect from the workers, or show initiative in solving problems. A supervisor's authority cannot be shared (or earned either) – because he or she serves at the pleasure of someone else, whose power flows through them from above. This is what *de confianza* (of trust) really means.

Supervisors see their role as strictly following orders to the best of their ability, neither questioning nor taking matters into their own hands, and this is exactly how they view the proper role of their subordinates. The Mexican supervisor's style is to supervise closely, and look for willing obedience. Opinions expressed by employees are often regarded as back talk. Likewise, supervisors generally find it unnecessary and even a sign of weakness to explain themselves or their orders. To explain is not to have the right to give orders, to not be the boss. Organizational communications in Mexico are normally downward, and usually are in the form of directives. A supervisor rarely explains why something is to be done or even how it should be done.

System, rules and discipline

To the average American, the Latin way of life is comparatively less disciplined at home and work. In general, the Mexican approach to regulations seems to be the rule of men, not laws. Rules tend to be a loosely applied set of guidelines, or an indication of what ought to be, but not necessarily what's done. For example, once across the border, no parking signs are rarely honored. One-way streets frequently have traffic in the opposite direction. It seems as if no Mexican feels compelled to follow disembodied directions. Stop signs, wait your turn signs, injunctions to wear ear plugs or safety glasses, and even attendance or seniority and job-bidding policies simply are not adhered to in Mexico. The person of authority, such as a policeman or boss, is more likely to be obeyed through the strength of his or her ability to affect the life of the individual. Americans emphasize fairness and justice if everyone follows the rules. In Mexico, if there is no strong, cohesive force that has a strong emotional, religious, or authority basis, no one follows the rules.

Time

In contrast to the U.S., time in Mexico seems neither linear nor progressive. History does not advance. Mexican time tends to be either right now or some other time. Dates and meeting times are more flexible – in fact, the entire Mexican notion of what being on time actually means differs from the American interpretation. At a microphone assembly plant in Nogales, a newly arrived American plant manager loudly pounded his desk in frustration because his middle managers never showed up on time for the daily ten o'clock staff meeting. When these tardy managers were queried, it was discovered that none of them even wore a watch. They felt that their gold watches should only be used for special occasions and not for daily use in the factory where they could get damaged.

In Mexico, appointments are often agreed to simply to create a pleasant encounter and avoid any disappointment. Moreover, in Mexico, the first priority is often assigned to the last request, rather than to the first. What often frustrates American managers, and is difficult for their parent companies to understand, is that life is *slower* in Mexico. Frequently, maquiladora schedules are confounded by delays of one sort or another. Basic systems may break down; banks may suddenly not have pesos; phone service can take months to be installed or repaired; obtaining a box at the post office can involve months of negotiations; electricity to the entire plant can fail. The production line of one telephone equipment wiring plant near Monterrey was shut down for half a day, idling about 500 workers, because a truckload of vital parts failed to arrive on time. After some frantic telephoning, the truck was found at the border, awaiting a lost routine Mexican entry permit.

Mexican employees are faced with similar problems almost daily. It can take an entire day to obtain license plates for a car, or several hours in one of the smaller towns to make a long-distance phone call from a special booth in the center of town. Businesses and government offices open and close at all hours, seemingly at random. The town buses bringing employees to the plant may simply stop running, or go somewhere else.

Possibly it is in response to this uncertainty in daily life that factory employees can legally take three days off per month without penalty. Americans who are familiar with local conditions can plan intelligent remedies (such as providing a company bus) rather than wringing their hands over high absenteeism and tardiness.

Compensation

The kinds of wages perceived as fairest in Mexico are based on an underlying sense of quid pro quo. Rather than an impersonal wage scale, Mexican workers tend to think in terms of payment now for services rendered now. A daily incentive system with automatic payouts for production exceeding quotas, as well as daily/monthly attendance bonuses, works well. The paternalistic nature of the employer, as well as the need to keep wages low, leads many employers to add on a series of small but meaningful benefits, such as weekly food baskets, bonuses for quality, free meals, free bus service, free day care.

The preference in Mexico for incentive pay also provides the rationale for establishing rigorous production standards. Unions support standards when those standards form the basis for production bonuses. Higher rates of pay for higher job classifications are a problem, because companies may not, under Mexican law, reduce an employee's wages when downgrading his or her job. Again, companies can avoid this problem by paying one fixed base rate and adding incentives and bonuses which are not considered wages.

Attitudes towards Americans

Mexicans are ambivalent about Americans. The Mexican view of the U.S. is highly colored by history from the Mexican angle: by past invasions by the U.S., excessive American ownership of Mexico's natural resources until foreign ownership was finally outlawed in the thirties, and the daily contrast of a struggling and dependent country with the strongest national power in the world. Some Mexicans also resent the invasion of American pop culture and view with disdain the drug addiction, violence and pornography observed in the U.S. Freedom to Americans is a national religion, but the same term in Mexico often connotes license, and lack of moral standards.

Yet, side by side with this resentment and moral condemnation exist aspirations for the material bonanza lying just across the border. Mexicans have a fascination with the U.S., and MTV has enabled Mexico City to be as fashionably current as anywhere in the world. Mexicans also admire and emulate the same national and open-minded attitudes they criticize. Expectations of American management are extremely high in maquiladoras. In spite of local environmental strains caused by the influx of foreign plants, the maquiladora industry as a whole is viewed by many in Mexico as an economic savior. They trust and respect American know-how. It is almost universally believed that American operations in Mexico benefit local economies, upgrade Mexican industry and pay well.

But, Americans are also feared in Mexico. Strange plant rumors circulate daily in maquiladoras, since few workers have enough real-life experience with Americans to be able to judge with any accuracy the meaning of what American managers do. Unfortunately, lack of fluency in Spanish leads many American managers to scurry through the plant, avoiding any contact with employees. However, quite often, a smile or nod can convey what language cannot.

A final word

Modern management is needed in Mexico and is ardently desired. Mexico as a whole, and particularly in the northern states, understands that the maquiladora industry needs to be able to manufacture and assemble at a level of efficiency and quality that compares favorably with what can be accomplished in the U.S. American managers in maquiladoras must also understand their difficult but fascinating position of being goodwill ambassadors, social luminaries, teachers and educators. In sum, the future holds real promise as long as the culture, beliefs, and customs of Mexico are kept in mind.

◇

9.5 Understanding the Bear: A Portrait of Russian Business Leaders

◆

Sheila M. Puffer

A new entrant has abruptly and dramatically appeared on the international business scene. Hibernating for most of this century in a long winter's sleep induced by the communist regime, the Russian bear has awakened and is now dancing to the beat of capitalism. The bear is looking for a willing Western partner, and many North Americans are eager to be asked for a dance. With the hope that they will have a smooth *pas de deux* and avoid stepping on each other's toes, what follows is a portrait of their potential Russian partners, including their leadership traits in three eras: traditional Russian society, the communist regime, and the developing market economy.

Consider the following descriptions of individuals who made *Moscow Magazine's* 1992 list of the Top 50 business people in Russia:

Evgenii Alekseevich Brakov – Fifty-four years old, married with one daughter and a granddaughter. General Director of the huge ZIL Automobile Factory. Rags-to-riches story: Brakov began as a humble mechanic at ZIL (top-of-the-line Russian limousine) and worked his way to the top. No time for hobbies, he is utterly devoted to turning ZIL into a successful company.

Source: Sheila Puffer, "Understanding the Bear: A Portrait of Russian Business Leaders," *Academy of Management Executive*, 1994, pp. 41–54, Vol. 8, No. 1. Reprinted by permission of The Academy of Management.

Dmitrii Vladimirovich Liubomudrov – Financial director of the industrial finance firm Profiko, founded in August 1990. Thirty years old, married with one child. Hobbies include horseback riding and Amateur Song Club. One of the founders of MosinkomBank. Director of brokers office of Moscow Central Stock Exchange and the Russian Commodity Exchange. Among Soviet and foreign bankers is well-known for being meticulous and hard working. An outstanding horseman, at one time he even trained horses for professional competition. He is also an excellent electrician; a large part of the everyday appliances in his home were made with his own hands.[1]

In some ways North Americans may feel they already know such people. They possess the same hard-driving ambition, boundless energy, and keen ability that are associated with successful business leaders in the United States. Yet, by probing a little deeper, some important differences emerge that, if not well understood, could interfere with Russian and U.S. managers' efforts to work effectively together.

This article draws upon interviews and surveys of Russian managers that I have conducted since 1979 while living and working periodically in Russia and collaborating with a number of Russian and American colleagues. In part, we will explore how the traits that made managers successful under communism compare with those that are needed in the nascent market economy.[2] The framework for this portrait of Russian business leaders will consist of four leadership traits that researchers have identified in effective leaders in the U.S.: (1) leadership motivation; (2) drive; (3) honesty and integrity; and (4) self-confidence.[3] As shown in Exhibit 1, I will first describe how historical influences in traditional Russian society have shaped these traits, and then discuss how these traits apply to Russian managers in two eras: the "Red Executive"[4] of the communist regime which prevailed from 1917 to 1991,[5] and the market-oriented manager who has emerged in the market economy which began to develop after the breakup of the Soviet Union at the end of 1991.[6]

Leadership motivation

Leadership requires first and foremost the strong desire to lead. Leadership motivation includes: (1) the desire to exercise power and be recognized as influential and occupying a position superior to others; and (2) the willingness to assume responsibility.

Exhibit 9.5.1   Russian leadership traits in three eras

Leadership Trait	Traditional Russian Society (1400s to 1917)	The Red Executive (1917 to 1991)	The Market-Oriented Manager (1991 to present)
Leadership motivation			
Power	Powerful autocrats	Centralized leadership stifled grass-roots democracy	Shared power and ownership
Responsibility	Centralization of responsibility	Micro managers and macro puppets	Delegation and strategic decision making
Drive			
Achievement motivation	Don't rock the boat	Frustrated pawns	The sky's the limit
Ambition	Equal poverty for all	Service to party and collective good	Overcoming the sin of being a winner
Initiative	Look both ways	Meticulous rule following and behind-the-scenes finessing	Let's do business
Energy	Concentrated spasms of labor	"8-hour day," 8 to 8, firefighting	8-day week, chasing opportunities
Tenacity	Life is a struggle	Struggling to accomplish the routine	Struggling to accomplish the new
Honesty and integrity			
Dual ethical standard	Deception in dealings, fealty in friendship	Two sets of books, personal integrity	Wild capitalism, personal trust
Using connections (blat)	Currying favor with landowners	Greasing the wheels of the state	Greasing palms, but learning to do business straight
Self-confidence	From helplessness to bravado	From inferior quality to "big is beautiful"	From cynicism to over-promising

Traditional Russian society

The image of Russian leaders as powerful autocrats is legendary.[7] Centralization of authority and responsibility in Russia has a long history. In the peasant village communes of medieval Russia, the board of village elders was entrusted to "find the common will."[8] Villagers would discuss issues in an open forum in such a way that suggestions and criticisms were lost in the din and could not be pinned on any individual. According to a proverb, "No one is responsible for the *mir*" (village commune).[9] It was the elders' task to sort through the comments, define the consensus of the group, and make recommendations to the chief elder (*starosta*). Group members believed that it was not possible to anticipate the elders' wishes, and would wait to be told what to do rather than initiate action themselves. In sum, the village elders who were the leaders in traditional Russian society wielded unchallenged power and bore full responsibility for the welfare of the group. In addition, they behaved paternalistically toward the members of the community, and were addressed as *batiushka* (little father).

The Red executive

Traditional Russian attitudes toward power and responsibility found their way into work organizations in the communist period and resulted in practices that hampered the effectiveness of enterprise managers and their subordinates. According to communist principles, managers were supposed to balance two types of leadership reminiscent of the village commune and the board of elders: one-person leadership (*edinonachalie*) and collective leadership (*kollegial'nost'*). One-person leadership, which denoted the unquestioned authority of the leader, had predominated in the army and in public administration under Emperor Paul I in the late eighteenth century, and was legalized under Lenin in 1923 as the basic management tenet of Soviet enterprises.[10] A few years later, managers were instructed by the party to combine one-person leadership with collective leadership. The leader's task was to identify issues and set goals. The collective was then expected to discuss the issues and submit a proposal to the leader, who in turn made the decision and instructed the collective to implement it. This alternating wave pattern, that our research team labelled "centralized leadership/

grass-roots democracy,"[11] was short-lived. Stalin's totalitarian oppression and managers' critical roles in the rapid industrialization of the country in the 1930s resulted in centralized leadership stifling grass-roots democracy as enterprise managers became more autocratic. During *perestroika,* the 1987 law on the Soviet State Enterprise was intended to redress the imbalance of power and improve economic performance by granting greater participation in decision making to the collective. The law mandated the election of line managers by the workers and the creation of an elected council of the workers' collective in each enterprise to oversee organizational decision making. However, neither initiative had a lasting effect. In 1989, the Soviet government abolished the election of managers in response to protests by influential enterprise managers who argued that the policy was undermining organizational effectiveness. Managers cited instances in which workers elected bosses who made life easy for them rather than those who made tough decisions in the interests of productivity and efficiency. Furthermore, the workers' council was essentially an advisory body to top management who retained final decision-making authority in enterprises.

Wielding virtually all the power within their enterprises, heads of enterprises also bore all the responsibility. They became thoroughly overburdened, and enterprises became paralyzed because no one took action without authorization from their superior as a way of avoiding blame if something went wrong. In fact, Russian executives have marvelled at the way Western executives delegate many tasks, freeing themselves to concentrate on strategic decision making.[12] In contrast, Russian executives were micro managers and macro puppets.

The market-oriented manager

Many enterprise managers have endeavored to retain the autocratic grip on power that they have enjoyed for decades. Now, however, in an attempt to save their enterprises from bankruptcy, they are forced to share power with employees who have become owners, as well as with outside investors and stockholders. These established managers, therefore, must learn to use their power in a more collegial way in order to survive in the new economic environment.

The urgent requirements for restructuring state enterprises and creating new business ventures in Russia call for individuals who have a high need for power and who are willing to assume a high level of responsibility for their work. Some promising signs come from surveys that my colleagues and I have conducted. Many of the forty Moscow entrepreneurs we surveyed in 1992 had created their businesses in order to be their own boss, and were willing to share power and create an atmosphere of participation in their organizations, particularly in small firms staffed by talented professionals.[13] We also found that 120 managers at all hierarchical levels of state-owned enterprises felt considerable responsibility for their work,[14] attitudes that were confirmed by government economic officials.[15] Yet, managers must continue to push responsibility down the hierarchy and teach subordinates to solve problems themselves.[16] Besides delegating routine tasks, senior executives need to learn and practice strategic decision making to make their enterprises competitive and economically viable.

Drive

The second cluster of leadership traits is drive, a set of the following five characteristics associated with expending a high level of effort: (1) achievement motivation, (2) ambition, (3) initiative, (4) energy, and (5) tenacity. High achievers gain satisfaction from performing challenging tasks, meeting high standards, and finding better ways of doing things. Ambitious people have a strong desire to advance in their careers and to demonstrate their abilities. Having initiative means being proactive in making choices and pressing for change. Energetic leaders have great physical, mental, and emotional vitality and stamina. Lastly, tenacity refers to persevering under adversity and pursuing goals that may take many years to accomplish.

Traditional Russian society

In the communal living and farming conditions of traditional Russian society, the well-being of the collective was highly valued, and individuals who showed signs of making themselves better than the group were viewed with suspicion and contempt. Consequently, such individualistic traits as achievement striving, ambition, and initiative were considered to be socially undesirable and destructive for group harmony. The norm was to blend into the group and avoid challenging the standard way of doing things. In fact, farming techniques in Russia remained primitive for so long that grain yields were the lowest in all the long-settled countries, including India.[17] There was an anti-achievement attitude that could be summarized as, "Don't rock the boat."

In a similar vein, ambitious people have long been viewed with resentment, suspicion, and envy, feelings that stem from the deeply rooted view that social justice consists of everyone subsisting at the same level. According to egalitarian principles, no one was supposed to sink too low, nor was anyone to rise too high. People who strived to be better than others were seen as taking away the rightful share of others.[18] One anecdote about Russians' preoccupation with envy involves a peasant to whom God would grant any wish, but would also give his neighbor twice as much. After much thought, the peasant asked God to strike out one of his eyes along with both of his neighbor's eyes.[19] In place of ambition, then, Russians substituted envy, creating "the syndrome of equal poverty for all."[20]

Another characteristic often associated with Russians is caution. The peasant admonition dating from the fifteenth century, "to look both ways," is thought to be associated with the rough terrain and harsh environment.[21] With such a high value placed on cautious behavior, it is little wonder that initiative was not a common feature of traditional Russian society.

The last two elements of drive, energy and tenacity, also bear a unique Russian stamp. Russians are notorious for their bursts of energy, followed by long periods of lethargy. Historians have traced this behavior to peasants who would work feverishly during the spring and summer to bring in the harvest, and then lie idle throughout the long, cold winter months. A nineteenth-century Russian historian boldly concluded: "No other nation in Europe can put forward such concentrated spasms of labor as the Russian."[22]

Russians are a tenacious people. Their ability to endure hardship and survive under adverse conditions is a hallmark of their character. They have persevered through brutally harsh winters, the ravages of war, and severe shortages of basic material goods and comforts that the Western world takes for granted. Many believe that their destiny, reinforced by the teachings of the Russian Orthodox Church, is to endure suffering as a means to a brighter future. Two often-heard refrains are that life is a struggle, and that one must be patient.

The Red executive

Conditions in most enterprises during the communist period were frustrating for managers who had high levels of drive. For instance, their achievement strivings were channelled toward meeting unrealistic deadlines and manufacturing products specified in the plan using insufficient or inferior raw materials, unsuitable equipment, and unmotivated workers. While standards for production volume were often unrealistically high, quality standards were often abysmally low or easily subverted.[23] In short, achievement-oriented managers were frustrated pawns of the central planning authorities.

To be successful, upwardly striving managers had to direct their ambition toward service to the party and advancement of their enterprise's collective good. Their success depended on both talent and political factors, including party membership, protection, connections, and loyalty to superiors.[24] In addition, it was common for managers advancing to top management ranks in enterprises to spend several years on leave working in a communist party organization before returning to a line management position in their enterprise.

During the communist regime initiative was not only discouraged, but was often punished. Officially, managers were rewarded for meticulously following rules and demonstrating loyalty to communist party principles. However, behind the scenes, many managers showed exceptional initiative and creativity by finessing problems in order to meet planned targets. For example, at an electric motor manufacturing plant we studied in 1988, a multimillion-dollar computerized machine tool ordered from Europe by ministry officials turned out to be incompatible with the existing machine tools on the assembly line. Several dozen workers were assigned to perform the operation by hand using outmoded tools – an expensive and labor-intensive process.[25]

During the communist period, conscientious managers had to have the energy to work long hours and be all things to all people. Managers whom our team interviewed in 1988 would joke that they worked an "eight-hour day" – from 8 a.m. to 8 p.m., that is.[26] Heads of enterprises spent most of their time "fighting fires." They were "hands-on" managers who would tour their plants once or twice a day and become involved in operational problems. Unfortunately, the amount of energy required to be successful took its toll on the health of many Russian managers. Heads of Soviet enterprises have been diagnosed as experiencing more stress and health problems than managers in the United States, Japan, and India.[27]

Managers during the communist period struggled tenaciously to accomplish routine tasks. Effective managers persevered under adversity and fulfilled their enterprise's plans in spite of shortages and bureaucratic obstacles. For example, a successful materials manager we interviewed in 1988 had chronic problems getting a supplier to provide copper wire for a new model of motor. First, the manager went several hundred miles to see the supplier. When this attempt failed, the plant used economic sanctions against the supplier who paid them several thousand rubles in fines, yet still sent no wire. Finally, the manager had higher authorities force his counterpart to meet with him at the ministry in charge of wire production. The motor plant finally began receiving the wire, but shipments were consistently at least five percent short.[28]

The market-oriented manager

A growing number of managers and entrepreneurs are exhibiting the five elements of drive that are associated with success in a market economy. For example, according to one recent study, Russian entrepreneurs have as much achievement motivation as their American counterparts.[29] My colleagues and I also found that entrepreneurs sought challenging tasks and had high standards. Many in our study had left the security of the state sector to start new businesses that would allow their scientific and technical expertise to flourish. Moreover, they rated the high quality of their products and services as the number one factor contributing to their firms' success.[30] The spirit of these achievement-oriented individuals is that the sky's the limit.

Although there is no longer any legal restriction on realizing one's personal ambition by starting a private enterprise, there is still tremendous social pressure against ambitious entrepreneurs. As one American journalist observed: "In America, it's a sin to be a loser, but if there's one sin in Soviet society, it's being a winner."[31] In essence, "blind, burning envy of a neighbor's success . . . has become (virtually at all levels) a most powerful brake on the ideas and practice of restructuring [the economy]."[32] Ambitious business people, therefore, must deal with the problem of overcoming the sin of being a winner, and being the object of envy and resentment. The new economic conditions have also sparked a heated debate about social justice in the press, including the legitimacy and morality of private enterprise. In some articles entrepreneurs have been portrayed as latter-day *Nepmen* (entrepreneurs encouraged for a few short years during Lenin's New Economic Plan) and *kulaks* (prosperous peasants who were often accused of exploiting other peasants). Many entrepreneurs recall how such people were persecuted in earlier times, and fear they will suffer the same fate. According to Oleg Smirnov, a Russian representative of Pepsi-Cola: "There is no tradition of law in this country, so some powerful official can strangle a cooperative [private business] in five minutes – there are sixty-four thousand ways to do it."[33]

Many new Russian entrepreneurs are also demonstrating a great deal of initiative, although one study has found them to be more risk averse and less innovative than Americans.[34] Nevertheless, hordes of entrepreneurs, brimming with initiative, have been unleashed in Russia. Their attitude is, "Let's do business." Claimed Herman Sterligov, president of the computerized commodity exchange, The Alysa System, in Moscow: "Every day we have a thousand people who come to our Moscow office saying, 'Please privatize us' or 'I have this idea and I need funding.' "[35]

The new entrepreneurs must also possess energy and stamina to start their own businesses and foster their growth. Some people are pursuing so many opportunities that they seem to work eight days a week. An outstanding example is Sviatoslav Fedorov, who was named Businessman of the Year in 1991 by *Moscow Magazine* in recognition of his ventures that include eye surgery clinics, medical manufacturing plants, and hotels and casinos.[36] Among the most energetic entrepreneurs are young people who have little experience with the communist regime. In Moscow, for example, teenagers could be found recently washing cars and fetching hamburgers for customers unwilling to wait in line. The most enterprising were earning as much as 300,000 rubles a month when the average monthly wage was less than 10,000. Such individuals "were not tainted by all those years of 'Glory to the Communists' " and they represent "the first generation that will have no doubts about the need for a market economy."[37]

Whereas communist managers struggled tenaciously to accomplish the routine, market-oriented managers, who face immense obstacles, struggle to accomplish the new. There is virtually no legal or economic infrastructure to support private enterprise, and venture capital is extremely limited. The Moscow entrepreneurs my colleagues and I queried in 1992 cited the unstable political situation and government regulation as the biggest obstacles to doing business.[38] For example, some laws are so ambiguous or rewritten so frequently that it is difficult for firms to develop long-term business strategies.

Honesty and integrity

Effective leaders are viewed as credible and trustworthy because they behave ethically and exhibit honesty and integrity. Honesty means telling the truth, and integrity refers to being consistent in words and actions.

Traditional Russian society

While there are many basic similarities in the ethical and value systems of Western and Russian people, two important differences stand out. The first one, the dual ethical standard, refers to the way ethics is construed in different situations. In the West, particularly in America, people are expected to employ the same set of ethical standards regardless of the situation. In contrast, in Slavic cultures two sets of ethical standards have developed – one for impersonal or official relationships, and one for personal relationships.[39] In short, there is deception in business dealings, but fealty in friendship. Thus, in Russia, while it would not necessarily be considered unethical to deceive someone in a business transaction to achieve a worthy goal, it would be unethical to deceive a friend or trusted colleague. In contrast, in the United States, deception would be considered unethical in both business and personal relationships.

The second feature of the Russian ethical system is the use of *blat,* informal influence or connections to obtain favors. This practice probably stems from the era of serfdom and bondage that began under Ivan III in 1440 and lasted until The Emancipation Act of 1861. Peasants worked land they did not own, and would curry favor with landowners by bringing them food they had grown.

The Red executive

The dual ethical standard was evident in the distinction made between personal and professional honesty by the managers with whom I studied in Moscow in 1979. They contended that honesty was essential in personal conduct, such as keeping one's word, but that honesty in terms of managing by the rules was considered unrealistic, and even undesirable. The managers agreed that if they tried to abide by all of the 80,000 rules and regulations in an average enterprise, they would not accomplish much and would not be successful in their jobs.[40] This duality of ethics helps explain why, under communism, a great many people routinely engaged in behavior that was in violation of the 1961 twelve-point moral code of the communist party.[41] For instance, the relatively common practice of stealing state property from the workplace was certainly not condoned, but it was viewed by most people as less serious than stealing possessions from an individual. Moreover, workers and professionals would deceive managers about production quality and output, and the managers in turn would deceive ministry officials. Enterprises typically would keep two sets of books, one containing actual results for their own records, the other containing information prepared for the ministry. In this way the enterprise would receive its bonuses, while protecting itself from receiving a tight plan or fewer resources. It was a game in which virtually everyone tacitly participated. Such deception was often a matter of survival, and was viewed as a necessary evil.

Another questionable practice stemmed from the use of *blat* to break through bureaucratic bottlenecks and grease the wheels of the state. Managers would make informal deals to get things done, such as obtain scarce spare parts or obtain authorization for an activity. Personal gifts or needed goods or services produced by the enterprise were the customary methods. Good managers knew the boundary between using *blat* for the legitimate benefit of the organization as opposed to abusing it for personal gain or other corrupt purposes.

In the communist system, then, a good manager was skilled in manipulating the truth as well as in using *blat* for the benefit of the enterprise and the individuals who worked in it. At the same time, a good manager did not betray employees and developed a relationship based on personal trust and honesty with them. Managers and employees were like a family with mutually dependent members whose personal and professional lives were intertwined.

The market-oriented manager

Ethics and morality have come under much public scrutiny since *perestroika* and the disintegration of the Soviet Union. People have expressed their dismay at the decline of moral values which occurred under the communist regime. Professor Dmitrii Likhachev, considered by many to be the spiritual and moral leader of *perestroika,* said that a fundamental failing of the Soviet people is "we became used to a double life: we say one thing, but we do another. We have unlearned how to tell the truth, the full truth."[42] Professor Likhachev attributes this society of deception to the fact that traditional Russian culture was shown disrespect and even destroyed by the communists.[43]

Corruption and unethical behavior are rampant in both business and government. Some entrepreneurs are tenaciously trying to hold onto their businesses and keep them from being overtaken by the criminal element. For instance, some private business owners have formed associations to find ways to deal with threats by organized crime. Similarly, a few years ago, one thousand taxi drivers staged a meeting at Vnukovo Airport to discuss how to avoid paying protection money.[44] Still other entrepreneurs have rebuilt their businesses that were sabotaged or closed down by government officials.[45] Yet, most businesses are at the mercy of the mafia, and murders of business people have been reported in the press.[46]

The pervasiveness of corruption associated with "wild capitalism" in Russia makes it extremely difficult for ethically-minded business people to function. To run their businesses, people are forced to grease the palms of government officials to obtain licenses and permits, as well as of criminal figures who threaten violence if they do not receive a portion of the profits. Furthermore, ethical business people frequently endure unfounded criticism from the general public, many of whom hold the stereotype that all entrepreneurs are dishonest and exploitative. Finally, some people who want to conduct business in an ethical manner are prisoners of their experience in the communist period. According to Ira Tatelbaum, an American partner in a Moscow clothing factory, some of his Russian employees still want to do business the old convoluted, underhanded way. Out of habit they use *blat,* but are learning to appreciate the relative simplicity and straightforwardness associated with standard Western business practices.[47]

Self-confidence

The many demands placed upon leaders require them to have self-confidence in making decisions under uncertainty, directing the work of others, overcoming obstacles, taking risks, and accepting responsibility for mistakes.

Traditional Russian society

Throughout their history, Russians have been portrayed as having self-confidence that ranged from helplessness to bravado. At one extreme, writers such as Dostoevskii and Gogol have depicted Russians as a pessimistic people who see life as gloomy and hopeless and beyond their control. Some scholars believe this mentality has its origins in religious beliefs that a savior will deliver the people from their plight. At the other extreme are writers who portray Russians as highly confident and adept at outsmarting others. For example, in the nineteenth-century short story by Leskov, *The Left-Handed Man,* a cross-eyed left-handed craftsman outdid British metalworkers by making shoes for a steel flea they had made for the Tsar.

The Red executive

As in literature and folklore, extremes of self-confidence can also be found among Russian business leaders. During the communist period managers' self-confidence took a blow from the inferior quality of products they produced, yet they took pride in the "big is beautiful" phenomenon of running some of the biggest factories in the world. Russian managers were also the target of sharp criticism by the public. One frustrated citizen even proposed that the entire power structure be replaced by foreigners in the following letter to the editor of a popular magazine:

"Where, for heaven's sake, is there a sensible distribution? When are we going to be well off? With bosses like we've got now – never. I therefore

propose that we sack all the apparatchiks from leading posts, all the various factory managers, and all the sundry farm chairmen ... and invite managers and administrators from West Germany, asking them to take over. I figure the situation would improve immediately. If we don't, it's no use anticipating any improvements in three years or even ten. If you remember, in Peter the Great's time we invited plenty of foreigners to Russia to serve and work, and they successfully replaced the arrogant grandees and bureaucrats. It worked great."[48]

The market-oriented manager

Among market-oriented managers self-confidence ranges from cynicism about their ability to solve problems, to over-promising what they can actually deliver to their business partners and clients. Low self-confidence may account for the wish that some managers have for others, particularly foreigners, to solve their problems for them. As Vladimir Kachenuyk, a Russian executive, explained:

"[T]he people in the Soviet Union in general have an almost fanatic belief in the United States ... All the American goods, American experience and ideas, American organization and production management, American technology – outstanding! All of these are being perceived as a panacea which will prove to be the salvation of the Soviet Union."[49]

A call for help from foreigners was expressed more seriously by Eduard Shevardnadze, former Soviet foreign minister, in an appeal for Western investment following the dissolution of the Soviet Union: "We are sure that Russia can be saved by foreign business."[50]

In contrast, the power that high self-confidence has in improving managerial performance is illustrated by the success story of the Cheremushkii Sewing Factory. In the late 1980s, with a boost of self-confidence derived from increased pride in their product, enterprise officials succeeded in having Russian women actually purchase some of the 22 million brassieres they manufactured annually, rather than continue to produce them "for the warehouse." The brassieres had been of high quality, but women refused to wear them because of the stigma of Russian-made goods. A retired American businessperson, Harold Willens, conducted an experiment in Moscow whereby he had 50 identical brassieres made in the United States, and then switched half the labels. Those with Russian labels were disparaged by consumers. When the factory managers and ministry officials realized that they offered a high-quality product, they launched a marketing campaign about their "world-class bras" and received an increase in orders as a result.[51]

Despite such successes, some highly ambitious entrepreneurs need to guard against becoming overly confident. With many attractive opportunities to explore, and few laws and regulations to control their business dealings, a number of entrepreneurs have adopted a "Wild West" attitude toward doing business. By cutting corners and acting unscrupulously for quick gains, they tarnish the reputation of private enterprise for everyone.

No more dancing in the dark: some guidelines

The fall of communism and the reconfiguration of the Russian political and economic system have created many promising opportunities for doing business with Russians. This trend is likely to continue. The music of the market is playing, and many North Americans may find themselves dancing with the bear. Whether Russian partners come from established state enterprises or from fledgling entrepreneurial firms, I hope this portrait describes them sufficiently to avoid the feeling of dancing in the dark. However, for those still unsure about taking the first step, let us look at ways that this portrait of Russian leaders can help Western firms build effective business partnerships. The following guidelines should help create a favorable impression on Russians by showing sensitivity to the way Russians perceive themselves and do business. In addition, these guidelines should enable Westerners to develop the appropriate responses and behaviors to make interactions with Russian business leaders go smoothly.

First, relieve Russians of responsibility for unforeseen negative consequences

Power, responsibility, and decision making are typically centralized in Russian organizations, and many executives have difficulty delegating authority. Russian managers at all levels are accustomed to exercising power without being challenged by subordinates, but they hesitate to act, even on trivial matters, if they fear being held responsible for decisions that have not been explicitly approved by the head of the organization or not been prescribed in standard procedures. Consequently, it is easier for Russians to take action if their partners relieve them of responsibility for unforeseen negative consequences. They should be assured that someone else will bear the responsibility. This unconventional approach is part of the risk associated with doing business with Russian partners, and it is important to exercise judgment about the particular situations in which it is appropriate.

Second, avoid appearing exploitative, and respect collectivistic attitudes

Russian business leaders have had much of their drive suppressed by communal traditions and attitudes passed on from peasant society, as well as by the egalitarian principles of communistic ideology and the stultifying bureaucracy of the centrally planned economic system. Three of the five components of drive – achievement, ambition, and initiative – have been denigrated in Russia. People with a high need for achievement have been condemned for being individualistic, antisocial, and enemies of the people. Personal ambition has been met with envy, vindictiveness, and derision. And initiative has usually been received with indifference, at best, and punishment, at worst. Negative attitudes towards these characteristics are so deeply ingrained in the Russian psyche that many Russians who want to realize their ambitions feel pressure from two sources – public scorn and their own guilt from violating the values they were raised with.

Foreign joint ventures have also been the target of such criticism. Some Russians view them as "a convenient front for those trying to make money . . . as fast as possible."[52] Therefore, when working with Russians, foreign firms should avoid presenting an image that could be construed as exploitative of individual Russians or of their society. In addition, foreign firms should respect their Russian colleagues' requests to avoid publicizing their achievements, material possessions, or privileges. They simply don't want to arouse feelings of envy or guilt, since the egalitarian norm of social justice is still strong. However, Western firms should take their cues from their Russian colleagues, because some of them may be more open about their accomplishments and may want recognition and approval.

Third, stress the importance and urgency of taking action

Russian leaders have two components of drive in abundance: energy and tenacity. They are used to hard work, can call upon large reserves of energy when required, and they are capable of persevering in spite of immense obstacles. In the words of Sviatoslav Fedorov, the highly successful surgeon-*cum*-entrepreneur: "The notion that all Russian workers are stupid or lazy is nonsense. But what can you expect if the government takes away property and forces them to live like domestic animals?"[53]

To spur Russian partners to action, then, Westerners should emphasize the importance and urgency of the situation, and stress that the Russians' utmost effort is needed to ensure success. This appeal should also be accompanied by valuable material rewards. The noted Russian economist, Pavel Bunich, commented that Russians who work in Western joint ventures will work hard as long as they are rewarded sufficiently to compensate for the absence of security and benefits they had enjoyed without exerting much effort in state-owned enterprises. Says Bunich, "Who would otherwise want to lose benefits more or less guaranteed by the state?"[54]

Fourth, forge personal relationships

As in any interpersonal interaction, integrity and honesty are crucial for developing a lasting and rewarding relationship with Russian business colleagues. Developing mutual trust and respect with them presents special challenges in light of some Russian practices that violate Western ethical sensibilities. One way to shape ethical behavior is by effectively using the Russian concept of dual ethics. This involves making a genuine and serious effort to forge a strong personal relationship with Russian colleagues, rather than maintaining an arms-length, formal business relationship. An approach of strengthening personal ties is more likely to trigger the ethical behavior, loyalty, and trust that Russians show their closest friends, family members, and colleagues. The tendency, if it existed at all, for Russians to see foreigners as simply impersonal business contacts to be duped and exploited, should be greatly reduced.

Fifth, uphold the highest standards of business practice

Another approach to developing an ethically sound business relationship with your Russian counterparts is to instill respect for business ethics, protocol, and accepted business practices. The market economy is such a new phenomenon in Russia that few people have a complete understanding of its complexities. Furthermore, many otherwise sophisticated Russians are unaware of the official legislation, as well as the unofficial accepted business practices, that keep a potentially destructive free market in check. Westerners should consider it their duty to uphold the highest standards of business practice as a service to Russians who are learning the ways of the world economy. For example, it would be useful to demonstrate how standard Western business procedures eliminate the need to use connections (*blat*) and underhanded methods of doing business.

Sixth, encourage joint problem solving

It is important to have an awareness of the two extremes of self-confidence that Russian colleagues might exhibit. In some cases, low self-confidence may lead them to look to their Western partners to solve problems and provide needed resources. To develop a mutually beneficial long-term relationship, however, it is better for all concerned to take the time to make decisions and resolve issues together. Such an approach, while time consuming, provides a stronger foundation for developing expertise and commitment of both sides.

Seventh, develop a concrete action plan

On some occasions Russians may engage in seemingly impulsive or reckless behavior resulting from over-confidence or bravado. Because of inexperience, they may not fully understand the complexities of a situation, and may overestimate their ability to deal with it successfully, or overlook the steps involved in putting an idea into practice. In such cases it would be helpful to develop a concrete action plan with them to ascertain the feasibility of their ideas.

Endnotes

1. "Moscow Magazine's Top 50," *Moscow Magazine*, December 1991/ January 1992, 52–57.

2. Many Russians believe that there are specific traits characterizing successful women managers. These traits are discussed in S.M. Puffer, "Women Managers in the Former USSR: A Case of 'Too Much Equality'?" in N.J. Adler and D.N. Izraeli, eds., *Competitive Frontiers: Women Managers in a Global Economy* (Cambridge, MA: Blackwell, 1993).

3. S.A. Kirkpatrick and E.A. Locke, "Leadership: Do Traits Matter?" *The Academy of Management Executive*, 5(2), 1991, 48–60. Two cognitive traits identified by these researchers, cognitive ability and knowledge of the business, are not discussed in this article, which focuses on motivational traits.

4. This term is taken from D. Granick, *The Red Executive* (Garden City, NY: Doubleday Anchor, 1962).

5. The discussion of the communist period will focus mostly on senior executives in manufacturing organizations, since the industrial sector was the most emphasized and the most prestigious. Conditions in other sectors such as services and R&D were largely comparable.

6. We will look at executives who are transforming their state-owned enterprises into various forms of private and employee ownership, as well as entrepreneurs who have founded start-up businesses. In 1992, 46,000 enterprises were wholly or partially privatized, bringing the total to six percent of Russian industry (*Economic Newsletter*, Russian Research Center, 16(6), February 20, 1993). Despite this small percentage, privatization efforts are expected to increase dramatically over the next few years. For a comparison of managers in the former Soviet Union with Eastern European managers, see A. Shama, "Management Under Fire: The Transformation of Managers in the Soviet Union and Eastern Europe," *The Academy of Management Executive*, 7(1), 1993, 22–35.

7. M. Mead, *Soviet Attitudes Toward Authority* (New York, NY: William Morrow and Company, 1955); G. Gorer and J. Rickman, *The People of Great Russia: A Psychological Study* (New York, NY: Norton, 1949/1962).

8. N. Vakar, *The Taproot of Soviet Society* (New York, NY: Harper, 1962), 47.

9. Vakar, *ibid.*

10. H. Kuromiya, "*Edinonachalie* and the Soviet Industrial Manager 1928–1937," *Soviet Studies*, 36(2), 1984, 185–204.

11. C.A. Vlachoutsicos, "Key Soviet Management Concepts for the American Reader," in P.R. Lawrence and C.A. Vlachoutsicos, eds., *Behind the Factory Walls: Decision Making in Soviet and U.S. Enterprises* (Boston, MA: Harvard Business School Press, 1990), 76.

12. N.A. Kaniskin, "The Western Executive and the Soviet Executive: A Talk With Nikolai A. Kaniskin," in S.M. Puffer, ed., *The Russian Management Revolution: Preparing Managers for the Market Economy* (Armonk, NY: M.E. Sharpe, 1992), 45–51.

13. D.J. McCarthy, S.M. Puffer, and S.V. Shekshnia, "The Resurgence of an Entrepreneurial Class in Russia," *Journal of Management Inquiry*, 1993, 2(2), 125–137.

14. D.J. McCarthy and S.M. Puffer, "Perestroika at the Plant Level: Managers' Job Attitudes and Views of Decision Making in the Former USSR," *Columbia Journal of World Business*, 1992, 27(1), 86–99.

15. P.R. Gregory, "Soviet Bureaucratic Behavior: *Khozyaistvenniki* and *Apparatchiki*," *Soviet Studies*, October 1989, 511–525.

16. J.B. Shaw, C.D. Fisher, and W.A. Randolph, "From Maternalism to Accountability: The Changing Cultures of Ma Bell and Mother Russia," *The Academy of Management Executive*, 5(1), 1991, 7–20.

17. J. Maynard, *Russia in Flux* (New York, NY: Macmillan, 1948), 30.

18. W.D. Connor, "Equality of Opportunity," in A. Jones, W.D. Connor, and D.E. Powell, eds., *Soviet Social Problems* (Boulder, CO: Westview, 1991), 137–153.

19. A. Sobchak, cited in H. Smith, *The New Russians* (New York, NY: Random House, 1990), 204.

20. N. Shmelev, speech to the Third Congress of People's Deputies, March 12, 1990, reported in *Foreign Broadcast Information Service* (FBIS), March 14, 1990.

21. V.O. Kliuchevskii, *Collected Works*. Vol. 1 (Moscow: Mysl', 1987), 312.

22. Kliuchevskii, *op. cit.*, 315.

23. L.B. Forker, "Quality: American, Japanese, and Soviet Perspectives," *The Academy of Management Executive*, 5(4), 1991, 63–74.

24. P.R. Gregory, "Productivity, Slack, and Time Theft in the Soviet Economy," in J.R. Millar, ed., *Politics, Work, and Daily Life in the USSR: A Survey of Former Soviet Citizens* (Cambridge: Cambridge University Press, 1987), 241–275.

25. S.M. Puffer and V.I. Ozira, *Capital Investment Decisions*, in P.R. Lawrence and C.A. Vlachoutsicos, eds., *op. cit.*, 1990, 183–226.

26. P.R. Lawrence and C.A. Vlachoutsicos, "Managerial Patterns: Differences and Commonalities," in P.R. Lawrence and C.A. Vlachoutsicos, eds., *op. cit.*, 1990, 271–286.

27. J.M. Ivancevich, R.S. DeFrank, and P.R. Gregory, "The Soviet Enterprise Director: An Important Resource Before and After the Coup," *The Academy of Management Executive*, 6(1), 1992, 42–55.

28. S.M. Puffer, Unpublished field notes for *Behind the Factory Walls: Decision Making in Soviet and U.S. Enterprises* (Boston, MA: Harvard Business School Press, 1990). Notes dated 1988.

29. W.L. Tullar, "Cultural Transformation: Democratization and Russian Entrepreneurial Motives." Paper presented at the Academy of Management meetings, Las Vegas, 1992.

30. D.J. McCarthy, S.M. Puffer, and S.V. Shekshnia, *op. cit.*, 1993.

31. F. Barringer, Comment at the conference, Chautauqua at Pitt: The Fifth General Chautauqua Conference on U.S. and Soviet Relations, October 30, 1989. Cited in H. Smith, *The New Russians* (New York: Random House, 1990), 203.

32. N. Shmelev, "New Anxieties," in A. Jones and W. Moskoff, eds., *The Great Market Debate in Soviet Economics* (Armonk, NY: M.E. Sharpe, 1991), 3–35; quote from p. 34.

33. O. Smirnov, cited in H. Smith, *op. cit.*, 1990, 285.

34. W.L. Tullar, *op. cit.*, 1992.

35. H. Sterligov, cited in P. Klebnikov, "A Market Grows in Russia," *Forbes*, June 8, 1992, 79–82; quote from p. 79.

36. P. Hofheinz, "The Pied Piper of Capitalism," *Moscow Magazine*, December 1991/January 1992, 50, 51; R.I. Kirkland, *op. cit.*, 1990.

37. A. Lasov, cited in J. Auerbach, "Coming of Age in Capitalistic Russia," *The Boston Globe*, January 4, 1993, 20, 21.

38. D.J. McCarthy, S.M. Puffer, and S.V. Shekshnia, *op. cit.*, 1993.

39. V.D. Lefebvre, *Algebra of Conscience: A Comparative Analysis of Western and Soviet Ethical Systems* (Boston, MA: D. Reidel Publishing Company, 1982).

40. S.M. Puffer, "Inside a Soviet Management Institute," *California Management Review*, 24(1), 1981, 90–96.

41. R.T. DeGeorge, *Soviet Ethics and Morality* (Ann Arbor, MI: The University of Michigan Press, 1969).

42. D.S. Likhachev, *"Trevogi Sovesti"* ("Pangs of Conscience"), *Literaturnaia Gazeta,* January 1, 1987.

43. D.S. Likhachev, *"Ot Pokaianiia–K Deistviiu"* ("From Repentance–to Action"), *Literaturnaia Gazeta,* September 9, 1987. For a summary in English of these two articles by Likhachev, see V. Krasnov, "Dmitrii Likhachev on Morality, Religion, and Russian Heritage," *Russia Beyond Communism: A Chronicle of National Rebirth* (Boulder, CO: Westview Press, 1991), 81–86.

44. P.C. Roberts and K. LaFollette, *Meltdown: Inside the Soviet Economy* (Washington, DC: Cato Institute, 1990), 97.

45. A. Jones and W. Moskoff, *Ko-ops: The Rebirth of Entrepreneurship in the Soviet Union* (Bloomington, IN: Indiana University Press, 1991), 66–70.

46. V. Volokhov, *"Ubivaiut Vsekh Podriad"* ("People Are Being Murdered One After the Other"), *Novoe Russkoe Slovo,* 13–14 February, 1993, 15.

47. I. Tatelbaum, unpublished interview by Kara Danehy, Northeastern University, Boston, August 1992.

48. A. Kononov, Letter to the editor of *Sobesednik,* 31, August 1990. Translated in J. Riordan and S. Bridger, eds., *Dear Comrade Editor: Readers' Letters to the Soviet Press Under Perestroika* (Bloomington, IN: Indiana University Press, 1992), 230.

49. V.A. Kachenuyk, cited in C.M. Vance and A.V. Zhuplev, "Myths About Doing Business in the Soviet Union: An Interview with Vladimir A. Kachenuyk, Deputy Director, Moscow Personnel Center," *Journal of Management Inquiry,* 1(1), 1992, 66–69.

50. E. Shevardnadze, cited in "The Dark Forces are Growing Stronger," *Time,* October 5, 1992, 64, 65.

51. R. Parker, "Inside the 'Collapsing' Soviet Economy," *The Atlantic Monthly,* June 1990, 68–76.

52. B. Alexseyev, "Joint Ventures: Is the Formula Right?" *Soviet Life,* October 1991, 41.

53. S. Fedorov, cited in R. I. Kirkland, "Curing Communism," *Moscow Magazine,* October 1990, 64–68. Quote from p. 67.

54. P. Bunich, cited in B. Alexseyev, *op. cit.,* October 1991, p. 41.

Part III:

◇

Managing Globally Across Cultures

◆

Section 10: Ethics

Conceptions of ethical business practices vary across cultures on matters concerning the social responsibility of business, bribery and influence peddling, and the like. However, honesty, respect for human dignity, and personal integrity are universal ethical values. The unethical business practices of an American-educated Japanese expatriate manager in **In Los Angeles** are surely not due to a lack of understanding of American culture: he is well aware that the United States is a country in which "survival depends on professionalism." Rather, his behavior violates ethical values held by American business associates as well as his Japanese subordinate, on whom he tries to pin the blame for his wrongdoings.

Los Angeles is also the setting for an incident of unethical behavior by an exploitive and greedy American lawyer in **Payback (Dirty for Dirty)**. After two years of inaction by the lawyer who promised to help him obtain legal immigration status, an angry Mexican construction worker storms the lawyer's office to get back his $1,000 deposit. Yet, "even though he himself felt angry and wronged by the crafty lawyer, a man had to behave according to courtesy." Such is the Mexican concept of honor described in **Thinking of a Plant in Mexico?**

Section 11: Cultures in Contact, Cultures in Change

When people from different cultures come into contact, they often influence and change one another, although not always equally. In

Wanamurraganya: The Story of Jack McPhee, an 84-year-old aborigine recounts his life story of trying to find his place in two cultures in contemporary Australia: "When I was just a native, I was told that if I wanted to get on in the world I had to become a whiteman, but when I tried to do that people would look at me and say, 'Oh you're just a native!' " He advises that "a man should be judged on his own and not as part of a group."

Contact between native peoples and whites is also the subject of **Mister Taylor**. In 1944 Percy Taylor arrives penniless in the Amazon from Boston. By chance he stumbles on the macabre opportunity to export shrunken heads to America at a great profit. In order to keep up with demand and continue to make profits, he and his Indian partners resort to extreme measures, including starting a war with other tribes. "This was progress," yet it couldn't last. "And everyone felt as if they had awakened from a pleasant dream – and when you wake up, you look for it and find emptiness."

India, a country with a long history of relations between native peoples and colonial whites, is featured in **East and West**. British writer, Rudyard Kipling, relates a conversation he had with an Afghan travelling companion who "dressed like an Englishman, and travelled after the English fashion," but who asks, "Why do you try to make us like you?" Equally comfortable criticizing and praising both cultures, the anglocized Afghan is also impressed with Kipling's understanding of him: "God made us all men, and you talk to me as a man to a man." Yet, he asserts that "God has made us different for always."

Section 12: Managerial Insights

Conflict over ethical values is evident in each of the stories included in **Cultures in Contact, Cultures in Change**, and such conflict is also likely to be present in many cross-cultural business relationships. Seven strategies to consider in such situations are offered in **Resolving Cross-Cultural Ethical Conflict: Exploring Alternative Strategies**. The choice of strategy depends on the circumstances, including the degree of influence one has on the situation, intensity of the value, and urgency for resolving the ethical dilemma. For instance, the infiltration strategy is evident in **Mister Taylor**, when Percy Taylor introduces American values of commercialism and consumerism into Amazonian society. The forcing strategy is used in **Payback (Dirty for Dirty)** to get money back from a lawyer. In **East and West**, differences in morality and "notions of honesty and of speaking the truth" could likely be resolved through collaboration and problem solving.

Ethics in the Trenches is an example of how a company doing business in many countries and cultures ensures that its values are upheld. Believing that "a company cannot sustain success unless it develops ways to anticipate and address ethical issues," the Chairman and CEO of Levi Strauss & Co. explains how the company's global sourcing guidelines are enforced with 700 international contractors. While admitting that enforcement of the standards increases costs, Levi's chairman emphasizes their positive impact on long-term interests and profitability. If **Mister Taylor** had such guidelines, his "headhunting" business would never have gotten started, perhaps not even in a fictitious story.

Negotiating With "Romans" provides eight strategies for conducting effective business negotiations with people from other cultures, the objective being "to ensure that both sides perceive that the pattern of interaction makes sense." The conventional wisdom, "When in Rome, do as the Romans do," is not appropriate for every situation. Choice of strategy depends on the degree of familiarity each party has with the other's culture, as well as the opportunities available for coordinating their approaches to negotiation. For instance, the Englishman and Afghan in **East Meets West** are highly familiar with each other's culture, while the American traveller and Amazon Indians in **Mister Taylor** are highly unfamiliar. The article includes specific strategies for Americans negotiating with Japanese that could be useful for the parties in **In Los Angeles**.

Transnational business strategies, the response of leading corporations to the highly competitive and fast-paced global business environment, require transnational managers and human resource strategies. **Managing Globally Competent People** argues that companies can no longer afford to rely on locally-focused expatriate managers working in a single foreign country, but must develop transnationally competent managers with a global business perspective as well as an understanding of numerous cultures. Transnational human resource systems utilize recruitment, development and retention methods such as recruiting people worldwide and using "search and selection procedures that are equally attractive to candidates from each target nationality." Had the Japanese firm in **From Paris** developed a transnational human resource system, the transferred manager might have found the transition easier from France to Tanzania.

A growing number of firms are creating international teams to increase their global competitiveness. Team members are often geographically dispersed in numerous countries and have different professional and cultural backgrounds. Each team is unique, with members selected according to task requirements. **Creating a High Performance International Team** notes that such teams "can bring richer and more appropriate solutions, however, they can also bring increased communication difficulties, interpersonal conflicts and substantially higher costs." Recommendations are offered for creating, managing and participating in geographically dispersed international teams. Issues such as selection of a leader, working languages, methods of balancing participation and managing conflict, and cultural sensitivity are discussed and illustrated.

Section 10: Ethics

◇

10.1 In Los Angeles

◆

Saburō Shiroyama

I

Yukimura thought he had prepared himself for the worst, but the trip to the Los Angeles International Airport proved otherwise. Morito, the new branch manager, just in from Japan, berated Yukimura right there in the terminal. The Yukimura couple were quick to catch sight of the tall Morito stepping out of a customs gate in the JAL lobby and also very fast to duck their heads and bow. Morito, on his part, generously raised a hand and strode up to them. So far so good. But as soon as Morito had staged his formalistic handshake, he glanced all around the lobby and let the couple know of his dissatisfaction.

"Nobody here to meet me?"

"We . . ."

"I'm talking about others."

Because the tone of Morito's voice meant *You two don't count,* the Yukimuras were at a loss for words. They felt insulted, but even more, disheartened to find their new manager so unpleasant.

Most Americans, of course, do not have ceremonious greetings and farewells at airports as the Japanese do. It didn't seem possible that this "legend" who had studied in the United States shortly after World War II and who still spoke in English in his sleep was

Source: Saburō Shiroyama, "In Los Angeles," *Made in Japan and Other Japanese Business Novels,* edited and translated by Tamae K. Prindle, 1989, pp. 91–110. Reprinted by permission of M. E. Sharpe, Inc.

that ignorant about American ways. Besides, he should have known that the Los Angeles branch office of Yukimura's Q-Trading Company had only five staff members, including the local employees. Wasn't it good enough that the deputy manager and his wife had come to pick him up?

"Katō-kun is in Phoenix, and Nakano-kun is in San Diego at the moment," Yukimura spoke apologetically as he looked up at Morito's sparkling glasses.

"And our clients?"

Yukimura caught himself from saying *This isn't Japan, you know* only with some effort.

"Some asked for your arrival time, but I didn't give a definite answer."

"Why? Why didn't you have them come?"

"Because they are Aron Orchards, Halifax Limited, and other nettlesome companies." Yukimura listed the names of the companies that his former manager Ohkubo had tried to avoid and about which the new manager Morito was expected to do something. "They might have given you a hard time right at the first sight of you."

"You don't have to worry about me. I can take care of them. It's not your place to fix things for me," Morito chided unsparingly.

Yukimura's wife, Sayoko, tensed up as she stood next to him.

"I'm not built as delicately as Ohkubo-kun. Nervous breakdowns and ulcers are foreign to me. I'm going to forge ahead without worrying about little things. Please keep that in mind," Morito went on.

Yukimura and Sayoko nodded together in a chain reaction. Actually, they felt that they had to.

This wasn't the end of Morito's carping. When Yukimura drove his Ford Capri from the parking lot to the terminal building exit, Morito looked down at it from where he stood.

"Are you driving it yourself?"

"Yes.

"Don't you have a driver?"

Yukimura's nerves seethed. In the United States, only corporate executives, millionaires, and the like could afford a private chauffeur. Morito should know that by now. What kind of nonsense was he spewing?

"If you don't have a driver, why don't you let your junior staff drive for you?"

This made no more sense than anything else Morito had said. All the Japanese staff were out of town, and no American employees would consider being treated like a chauffeur.

Morito finally settled into the back seat, plopping his gigantic rear onto it.

"You make me feel as if I'm here to depend on you." Morito's abusive talk was another way of scolding, *This isn't the way to receive your business manager. Don't take me for your friend visiting here for a vacation.*

Yukimura started the car wordlessly just as soon as Sayoko slid into the seat next to him. Silently, he retorted, *Coming to the airport with my wife was the best welcome a deputy manager of a small trading company could give to its new manager.*

"It would have worked better if you had brought me a car. I could have driven it back myself," added Morito with annoyance.

This was even more nonsensical. Even assuming that the company would buy a car for the manager, he would have wanted to select it for himself. Renting a car wouldn't have pleased him either.

Having run out of complaints, Morito cut the tip of a cigar and lit it. A powerful smell filled the car. Sayoko usually got a headache from cigar smoke but she was too frightened to roll down the window.

What a nuisance of a manager I've gotten, Yukimura commiserated with himself once again. He had heard of Morito's nickname and reputation, but this was the very first time he had to work directly under him. In a firm the size of his Q-Trading Company, a person with a degree from a top-notch national university and from an American college as well was treasured as the company's "prince" from the beginning of his career. To Yukimura's knowledge, Morito was very demanding at work, yet he would also do a friendly thing like inviting his juniors to a house party. The "prince" used a whip and candy very generously, so to speak. He was thoroughly Draconian in business transactions but had been a big hit in his departments thus far. One could guess that Morito would join the board of directors just as soon as he turned forty if he straightened out the problems of the Los Angeles office during his tenure there. Morito was a big shot and he knew it – or rather, he was a bundle of self-importance. And he made sure that Yukimura felt it under his skin.

Yukimura drove on in silence. Off in the distance, the Santa Monica Bay glistened blue in the twilight. The wind seemed to have blown off the infamous smog. The sky of Los Angeles, with a hue of emerald green, was deep and high.

Suddenly, Morito started showering questions onto Sayoko's back.

"Mrs. Yukimura, how are your children? There's a girl in the sixth grade and a boy in the second grade, isn't there?"

"Yes!" Sayoko nodded in such amazement that her head almost knocked against the windshield.

"I hear that your daughter is good at drawing pictures." Morito had more surprises up his sleeve.

"Oh, no, not at all. . . ." Sayoko blushed like a girl whose hand had been asked for in marriage, and her body stiffened. Earlier, she had been frozen from trepidation; this time she sat in a rapturous trance.

It flashed across Yukimura's mind that this was Morito's trick. He must have checked up on the family situations of his subordinates at the personnel office or somewhere. But did he uncover a detail like his daughter's drawings? This was the art of winning over people's hearts. It was something Yukimura begrudgingly had to take his hat off to.

"Art transcends nationalities. Things are more colorful, and sceneries have a larger scale over here. It will be good to take her for landscape painting and such," Morito continued as he blew out the cigar smoke. Sayoko nodded, drugged by the thick curtain of smoke.

The traffic on the freeway became more congested as Yukimura approached the downtown area. This time, Morito's voice took aim at Yukimura.

"Talking about pictures . . ., isn't Fumihiko-kun, President Hori's son, living with hippies and trying to paint somewhere near here?"

"I think he's taking it seriously these days."

"How hopeless! He has a degree in economics, and is supposed to be continuing his studies here in the United States. The president is very disappointed in him. How is it that a shiftless son like that comes from such an outstanding father?"

Yukimura knew that the question didn't ask for an answer, but he put forth his opinion just the same, "Maybe it's because his father is too outstanding."

"What do you mean?"

"He's compared to his successful father in whatever he does. It's hard for the son. In fact, I've heard Fumihiko-san[1] swear that he would give up his success so that his son wouldn't feel pressured. I think I can understand how he feels."

"Humph." Morito wheezed in a nasal tone. "No matter how you look at it, though, hippies and delinquents are human garbage. He has no right to lecture us as long as he is mixed up with that sort of gang."

"But Fumihiko-san doesn't use drugs; nor does he go for free love. He's just looking to be a free spirit. He just wants to indulge in art."

"If he's that serious, why doesn't he go to Paris or New York?"

"He says he'd be overwhelmed by too many recognized artists in Paris and New York. He feels that there's no spot left for him to sketch."

"Doesn't professionalism mean overcoming that sort of competition?"

Yukimura nodded lightly and continued, "But he's not sure if he really wants to be a professional artist."

"That's precisely where the problem lies. That's why he's a bungler. No wonder the president is disgusted with him."

Yukimura sidestepped Morito's comment and went on. "As you may be aware, the United States is a country of professionals. It's believed that survival depends on professionalism."

"It sure is."

"But more and more laid back young people are choosing to do only what they believe in. You may call them anti-professionals. Success isn't part of their vocabulary."

"The Vietnam war has blighted their minds; that's it."

"Maybe so, but it seems to me that the United States has turned a corner in history. I feel that the whole country is drifing on a lake of lethargy, trying to survive on the borderline between professionalism and amateurism."

"Come on, you softboiled egg! This is why you can't make clear-cut decisions. If you had taken a firmer stance, you could have solved the problems with Aron and Halifax more forcefully."

Yukimura took it in stride. It was possible to insist on Q-Trading Company's way of doing business, but unfortunately the problems weren't the kind that could be solved in a hardheaded business manner. For example, Q-Trading Company was the only Japanese trading company that bought lemons, grapefruit, oranges, and other fruits from Aron Orchards in Riverside City. The original contract called for Q-Trading Company to purchase exclusively all the fruit products of Aron on the condition that Aron discontinue their business with large fruit retailers in the United States. But lately the Japanese market for lemons and grapefruit had become sluggish. And a chronic glut was projected for the future. As a result, Q-Trading Company decided to discontinue purchasing lemons and to begin selectively purchasing grapefruit and oranges. This change was advantageous to the Q-Trading Company only – and there was a ruthless calculation behind it: Aron Orchards wouldn't survive long; the bankruptcy would solve Q's problems.

Aron Orchards was outraged. Intimidated by Aron's violent reaction, Ohkubo, the former manager, stopped going to the Riverside region altogether. There was also a time when armed Aron-affiliated farmers barged in on Q-Trading Company. The branch office found it impossible to force the main office's decision onto the American producers and requested that the main office reconsider the new order.

A similar tension existed with the Halifax Distributor. Two years ago, Q-Trading Company nominated Halifax as a distributor of a Japanese spray system. Halifax Headquarters in Ontario City, some fifty kilometers east of Los Angeles, had a good reputation in the farming communities in southern California and the spray system sold better than expected. Q-Trading Company attributed its success to the high quality of the machinery, while Halifax assumed that it was due to its sales efforts. In either case, commissions bulged significantly along with the sales figures. The Q-Trading Company, now chary of the sales commission, decided to terminate the distributor contract at the time of its renewal. But the contract was supposed to be renewed every two years, unless a breach of confidence intervened. As a pretext, Q-Trading Company accused Halifax of negotiating with an American maker of spray systems. This was another source of headaches at the branch office.

Rather than lose its temper, Halifax went on pleading its case. Because Halifax had entrusted the sales to about twenty salesmen, the contract negotiations directly affected the employment of these people. Naturally, the salesmen came to the Q-office in relays. Some threatened to appeal to the court; others menaced the staff by showing their tattoos and guns. They implied, "If you go about it illegally, we will do the same." Ohkubo requested the contract be renewed once more, but the Tokyo office responded by replacing him with Morito.

Morito suddenly cried out, "Oh, the good old City Hall! It hasn't changed!"

The twenty-eight story, uniquely white City Hall loomed in front of the car.

"You must have lived in the Los Angeles area before." Sayoko turned around to keep Morito company.

"It was over fifteen years ago. I didn't actually live here. I used to live in San Bernardino. I came here from the country now and then. Every time I saw this building I was excited to be in Los Angeles. I felt much closer to Japan."

"It must have been difficult for you."

"Well, there still was a shortage of foreign exchange. I had to make my living at dishwashing, lawn-mowing, orange-picking, and other odd jobs while going to school."

"San Bernardino is the other side of Ontario and Riverside, isn't it?"

"Right."

Isn't this ironic? Yukimura was tempted to remark, *That's near Aron and Halifax!* But he said, "Do you have acquaintances around there?"

"There may still be some, but they were all my enemies. I was pushed into cheap labor everywhere. There was only one old man, the owner of an orchard, who was very nice to me. He was a 'half-breed' with American Indian blood. He told me to marry his granddaughter, get permanent residency, and manage his orchard with her."

"But you didn't."

"Of course not. Who wants to live an empty life at the end of the world? Also, how could I marry an Indian and have kids that holler 'wa wa' all the time?" Morito imitated the voice of American Indians in Western movies and made Sayoko laugh.

Yukimura drew a mental picture of Morito in a Native American village. Somewhere in a corner of that endless orchard, sunburned Morito would be working with his half-breed wife. Vigorous, coppertoned children of mixed blood would be circling around barefoot or on horseback. Not bad at all. Morito fit in the scene neatly. On

the other hand, Morito now looked more like himself. One thing
Yukimura knew for sure was that if Morito had taken the other
path, he could have done without this nincompoop for now.

"The old man passed away last year. It seems that nobody was
there with him. I think I will go to San Bernardino one day and
build a grave for him."[2]

Sayoko nodded approvingly. Yukimura felt as if his wife's gaze
had disparaged him in the light of Morito. He could almost hear
her thinking, *My husband is so different. . . .* Yukimura was only one
year younger than Morito, but there was nothing noteworthy in
his schooling and degrees. A lack of business enthusiasm had already
removed him from the success ladder. He had by now served as
the deputy manager in Los Angeles for three years. If he didn't
watch his step, he might very well be buried alive in this town.

Back in the apartment later that day, Sayoko let out a sigh, "He
notices small things. Morito-san deserves his reputation." She
looked at her husband with a fresh glance and continued, "Come
to think of it, this is a rare opportunity. . . ."

"Opportunity for what?" Yukimura wanted to ask, *An opportunity
to be flattened out?*

"You know, a chance to get on in the world," Sayoko smiled
gently. "He is the future leader of our company. What if you followed him closely?"

"No way!"

"Not just to get ahead, but this may be a way to return to Japan
a bit sooner."

Yukimura didn't bother to answer.

"Living like this, our children go funny. And you and me, too."

Again, Yukimura didn't reply.

"Or else, would you rather live with the Indians somewhere
around San Bernardino, like mud dolls?"

"Why don't you shut up?"

Sayoko became quiet for awhile; she checked Yukimura's face
and repeated loudly, "It's a chance; believe me."

II

The Q-Trading Company was on the third floor of a small building
on Flower Street near the University of Southern California. The

first thing the new manager did was to remodel the small office. He enclosed a corner of the manager's section with a decorative glass partition, put in a new desk, and brought in a new set of waiting room furniture. He also put up an American flag and a Japanese flag beside his desk as some presidents of large American companies do. These modifications added dignity to his office, but they made the rest of the floor space that much smaller. The sad thing was that, after all that renovation, Morito hardly ever stayed in his office.

He took off in his new Cougar XR7, always saying, "A trading company should be in motion." He visited customer companies, stopped by financial organizations, and met with banks and Japanese authorities. In between, he went to play golf for "socialization," as he put it. He was truly energetic. Yet, he left the negotiations with Aron and Halifax – the pending problems – to Yukimura. He didn't pay a single visit to these companies. If somebody from either company came charging in, he made Yukimura deal with them. The partitioned manager's room was a cozy den for Morito. One could even suspect that his frequent outings were a way of avoiding these unwanted visitors. The problem was that Morito, while taking no part himself, commanded Yukimura to bring the two contracts to a complete closure exactly as dictated by the Tokyo office.

"There's nothing to negotiate about. Just spurn their requests. Don't give in to Americans. No, not an inch. Don't even give a hint of giving in," Morito tried to fire up Yukimura.

If Yukimura proposed, "But we need some kind of concession," Morito would raise his voice, "What the heck!" and yell, "We're not one of those large trading companies; we have to be grabby in order to survive; we must earn every penny we can."

"If you're that resolved, would you please talk to them directly?" Yukimura ran out of patience.

"My job is to march forward, to expand our business. This mess you are in is like a postwar cleanup job, a retrenchment, something your staff is entitled to." Morito pounded on the table, and repelled Yukimura with some insults.

Days went by. Yelled at by Morito and beleaguered by Aron and others, Yukimura was lonely. Local employees became standoffish towards him in deference to Morito and Aron. It was more like working in a one-man office rather than a branch office staffed by five. Before, the previous manager had been there to discuss problems and had tried to talk the Tokyo office into reconsidering the contract. But Morito was heartless and couldn't be caught off guard. He had trapped Yukimura behind an iron wall so there was no way out. Yukimura felt crucified. When he was threatened with murder, he felt like casually retorting, *Yeah, go right ahead!* He wasn't all that ready to die, but the apprehension that he might in fact be killed one of these days was always there. Q-Trading Company's business policies were so slipshod that such vengeance almost seemed fitting. But whenever Yukimura threw his life at his opponents, the aggressors backed down. In the end, Q-Trading Company scored a victory, and Morito as its manager got the credit. Yukimura vacantly brooded that the art of using subordinates to personal advantage was another of Morito's talents.

The only salvation for Yukimura was that both Aron and Halifax seemed to understand that their true enemy was not Yukimura but Morito. As their visits became more frequent, they gave up on Yukimura and became proportionately more inquisitive about Morito's whereabouts. The antagonistic clouds hovering over Morito became so thick that his enemies' hostility became palpable.

One day, the president's son Fumihiko showed up, dangling a large necklace of chained nuts and dragging a robe stained by oil paints. Morito abhorred hippies. He wanted to throw a bucket of water over the youngster, but had to politely receive the president's son into his office.

"I should have gone to inquire after you, but because Yukimura-kun told me that your residence changed constantly and it is rather difficult to find you . . . ," began Morito.

"My place isn't something you can call a residence. It's just a den, a temporal inn where a bunch of us sleep, so you'll never find me." After answering Morito, Fumihiko surreptitiously winked to Yukimura.

Actually, Yukimura knew where Fumihiko had his nest. Fumihiko had contacted him at home every time he moved. Not merely because Yukimura had been long in the area, but also because there was something about Yukimura that Fumihiko trusted. Yukimura knew he may have been thought of as easy to win over, but he didn't mind. It would have made him feel good to be depended upon by a young man, even if he weren't the president's son. Because Fumihiko had made it perfectly clear that he didn't want the new manager to know his address, Yukimura had kept it confidential as a token of his sincerity.

"The real purpose of my trip here is to borrow about three thousand dollars," said Fumihiko, brushing his long hair back with his fingers. He explained that his favorite avant-garde artist was holding a private exhibition in New York, he didn't want to miss it, and that, if possible, he wanted to purchase copies of his sketches and other works.

"Do you have your father's permission?"

"Of course not. My father is dead set against my getting into art."

"That's a problem." Morito put a hand on his forehead.

President Hori had a personal savings account with the Bank of America and his bank book was kept in the Los Angeles office. This was an emergency fund to be utilized at the manager's discretion. The exhibition had already started. Fumihiko said urgently, "I may miss the show if I don't get going soon."

Could this be called an emergency case? wondered Morito. If the president was against his son's art fad, drawing on the fund for this purpose would generate his resentment. Morito couldn't make up his mind.

"Would you let me think about it? I'll get back to you. Please leave your address or telephone number."

"That's O.K. . I'll come back tomorrow."

"In that case, how about dinner tomorrow?"

Fumihiko shook his head, "The kind of restaurants you go to don't like sloppy-looking people like me. I don't feel comfortable in those places, either."

Morito didn't reply.

"Do you know that some of us collect scrap cabbage and meat from the trash cans of those restaurants?"

"Like beggars."

"Not really. We do so for another reason. It's an effort to stay out of money-bound society. We don't spend money on luxury; we don't work for money. It's not the easiest thing in the world to do because we are living in a society where a bit of work can quickly earn a meal, as you must know. It takes a good determination to go against the current."

Morito listened to Fumihiko open-mouthed. Fumihiko was talking about a world outside the imagination of a single-minded businessman like himself. The businessman didn't know how to respond other than saying, "It doesn't mean you have to follow their example. . . ."

"I'm not a thoroughbred. I still know the value of money. My visit here proves that."

"That sets my mind at ease a little."

"Also, I'm not about to deny the value of the older generation completely. It's awkward for a son to say this, but I think that my father is a fine man. At least he was good enough to build a company of this size in one generation." As Morito nodded deeply for the first time, Fumihiko added mischievously, "Although his contribution to the financial world may be cancelled out by me."

Having said all he wanted, Fumihiko left, the tail end of his long robe sailing in the air.

"What a scrap of human garbage that is!" Morito spit out. He was truly angry.

Yukimura felt like giving him a bit of a twit. "Isn't that an easy life, though? And, as Fumihiko-san always says, his son will have it made, won't he?"

"He has no qualification to be a father; no qualification even to live."

"But he is harmless."

Perhaps because this sarcasm was a bit too strong, Morito was offended. "What of it?"

Yukimura didn't confront Morito directly. He said, "There wouldn't be wars if the world were inhabited only by his type of people."

Morito lit his cigar and sighed deeply.

"So, what am I going to do about the three thousand dollars?"

Yukimura didn't answer. This truly was none of his business, and it boosted his ego to watch Morito suffer. The easiest solution would be to telephone Tokyo, and ask the president. But the upshot would be at best a presidential scolding, "Can't you make up your mind about a small thing like that?" Morito probably would have to make his own decision and then report the result afterward. It was impossible to guess whether the president would be grateful or resentful for having spent the money. Morito appeared to be tearing his hair out over the problem. It was a very minor affair for the company, but it was a life-or-death problem to him.

Morito's cigar smoke rose higher and higher. In the end, he asked for Yukimura's help, "What do you think?"

"It's up to you."

"I know that, but what would you do in my place?"

"I would help him."

"Why? The president would rather get him out of art, you know."

"I just thought of Fumihiko-san. I didn't think of the president."

"Why not?"

"Well, the money isn't going to be spent for destructive purposes. On the contrary, it may serve as a springboard for Fumihiko-san's growth. Whatever profession he may eventually choose, there's no reason to deprive him of something that enriches his cultural background and spiritual life."

Morito remained silent.

"Furthermore, Fumihiko-san is not the type to ask for something so ardently. He is usually very nihilistic. He sounded unusually enthusiastic today. I could tell how earnest he was about the exhibition."

"Do you mean to say that a hippie may reform?"

"It's not a matter of reforming. I just think that we should give him the thing he truly craves, and beautiful things, too."

"All right, I get it. I'll handle the rest." Morito shut off Yukimura's advice with the whisk of a hand. His expression said that he had suddenly become exasperated at having consulted Yukimura.

"You seem to have lived here long enough to turn yourself into a hippie supporter. Just watch out for yourself so that you can still be useful in Japan," Morito snarled. "Are you ready to prove your worth with the Aron and Halifax cases? Go at it and teach them a lesson!"

In the end, Manager Morito handed Fumihiko the three thousand dollars. This pleased Fumihiko, but his father's response was different. When Morito reported to the Tokyo office with some fear and trepidation, the executive secretary conveyed the president's message that he was outraged by the manager's "putting his hand on uncalled-for business." Since the president was planning a trip to the United States in the near future, he would inquire about the details of the matter when he stopped in Los Angeles, so "Morito had better be prepared for the worst." The message was unexpectedly harsh.

Morito was out of sorts. He wreaked his frustration on Yukimura. "It wasn't my idea to give him the money. It's you who made the decision."

"But you said to leave the rest up to you."

"I just got here, and didn't know anything. That's why I respected your opinion."

"Even then . . ."

"I had nothing to base my judgment on. As a matter of fact, that was the first time I met Fumihiko-kun. How could a stranger to a place make the right decision? All I could do was to be guided by your information and suggestion." Morito got heated up by his own argument as he talked. "The original sin was that you let that hippie have the run of our office just because he's the president's son. You and Ohkubo-kun spoiled him. No, the general easy-handed way you go about managing welcomes this sort of disaster." Morito had completely forgotten how civilly he had welcomed Fumihiko into the manager's office. "Listen, this problem was handled by you, not by me. Let's make it clear that you took the responsibility; you made the decision. It's your job to vindicate everything to the president. Don't drag me into it because I have no idea what's going on." After this bout of excited proclamation, Morito swung his gaze behind his shiny glasses in another direction.

Yukimura couldn't believe it. He was dumbfounded. Not only was he irritated by Morito, but he had also become disgusted with the shallowness of his wife, who was infatuated by this man's personality. What did she know about big shots and great chances? Following this man would only make one rotten to the core.

How could a deputy manager venture to explain his position to the president? All Yukimura could do was to own up to the truth, to describe the situation plainly. After that, he would just have to sit through a flurry of presidential abuses and wait for the verdict, which would probably be a demotion.

"Enough. You may go back to your work." Morito was all authoritarian.

Yukimura was glad to leave; not seeing Morito was as much his wish as Morito's. He was beginning to fear that if he stayed there much longer he might throw Morito out the window.

III

Morito built a grave for the orchard owner who took care of him during his student days. He replaced the simple wooden marker, which had been put up by those who were not related to the orchard owner by blood, with an ostentatious black marble tombstone. The graveyard was in the suburbs of San Bernardino.

It was decided that the branch office staff would attend the renovation ceremony. Morito drove his Cougar XR7, and Yukimura and his junior staff member Nakano were instructed to follow in the Ford Capri. Morito assumed the role of an authoritarian leader, making them go in two separate cars when one would have done the job just as well.

Morito's tombstone renovation plan was picked up by a local paper, the *San Bernardino Times,* which didn't overlook even the smallest local event. Neighboring small-town newspapers like *The Ontario Chronicle* and *The Riverside Evening* joined the chorus and printed flashy illustrated articles about the "beautiful Japanese spirit."

It was the "beautiful Japanese spirit" all right. Morito's feeling for the half-Indian orchard owner was genuine, the gravestone was of fine quality, and it was built with great care. Yukimura could appreciate this generosity. But Morito was embarrassed to have Yukimura and others see things in that light.

"I'm doing this out of sheer self-interest. No growing bud comes out of everyday business transactions. But this sort of publicity expands our business network. You people should quit digging small holes for yourselves and start looking for new ways," he said.

The newspaper articles struck some people quite differently. Many threatening letters and protesting telephone calls flew in from the Aron-related people around Riverside, and from Halifax salesmen based in Ontario. They threatened, "Don't try to make yourselves look noble at our cost," "Remember you're going to pay for this when you come this way," and many more maledictions. The "beautiful spirit" grated on them. Their abuse was not in their words alone; a true threat of violence resonated between the lines. Any mention of this, however, only made Morito bellow with laughter.

"It's just the American way of doing things. The United States prides itself on toughness. Haven't you learned that yet?" After saying this, Morito suddenly frowned and added, "Businessmen in trading companies are no different from the foot soliders on the battlefront. Nobody says so, but we all came prepared to find a watery grave, and death in an open field. We don't get anywhere if we let these screwballs get on our nerves."

The sky was clear and there was no wind on the day of the renovation ceremony. This meant that a thin gray smog hung in the Los Angeles sky.

Morito, Yukimura, and Nakano left work early. The two cars, one following the other, sped straight east on Interstate 10. Up until halfway through the two-hour drive, the scenery was like an extension of Los Angeles, sprinkled with factories and clusters of houses. After that, farmlands and orchards sprawled over the vista. Farmhouses played hide and seek every so often from behind avenues of palm trees and forests of eucalyptus. There were people driving tractors and spraying chemicals.

This part of the scenery was something Yukimura couldn't watch so innocently. The spray equipment might have been sold by the Halifax salesmen, and some of the orchard workers might be members of Aron-affiliated farms. He feared that his car as well as Morito's might be identified by these people and ambushed. Maybe Morito shared the same anxiety. When they passed through the suburbs of Ontario City, where the Halifax headquarters was located, Yukimura sensed that Morito's car speeded up.

Before long, the San Bernardino National Forest and the Box Springs Mountains started to loom in the mist to the north and south of the highway respectively. San Bernardino was situated in the middle of a basin.

Morito had said that the orchard at which he previously worked was sold and the old man's house was torn down after his death. He had shown no interest in visiting the remainder of the orchard, but headed directly to the graveyard on a small hill slightly east of the town. It was surrounded by an ocean of orchards. In the orange orchard just before the graveyard, Mexican immigrants silently trimmed the lower branches. They wore rags and squirmed like mud dolls. Everyone had the gloomy face of a serf. Yukimura felt that calling them serfs was not too wide of the mark. Mexicans surge into the United States to escape poverty, but the immigration regulations are strict. The situation helps create a number of illegal immigrants who will put up with any adverse working condition. Their "bosses," who use their influence to find employment for them, exploit them and may go so far as to cut their lives short. Only recently, for example, a "boss" who had murdered nearly ten Mexicans was arrested at an orchard in a border region.

Below their feet, ever so many oranges formed a carpet of golden yellow. Nature shakes off the bad oranges at an early stage; only the ripened, good quality fruit is harvested in the end. As the result of this highly expensive procedure, the oranges harvested in the end had the richness and luxury of having absorbed the life force of countless premature relatives.

Mulling these things over in his mind, Yukimura was suddenly awakened from his drifting thoughts. His Q-Trading Company had promised to buy all of these oranges but had suddenly switched to selective purchasing. They had reneged on the original contract and chosen a way that was much more costly to the producers. The angry oranges and the orange workers assaulted him in lifelike vividness.

The gigantic sun gradually reclined westward. A breeze had started to pick up. At the graveyard, the priest gave a short prayer. Three men and women chosen from the church choir sang several hymns. Finally, Morito offered a bouquet of flowers and knelt in front of the tombstone. As directed, Nakano took some snapshots from different angles.

Morito remained motionless long after many pictures were taken. He would not get up. His large body froze into a statue, and a larger shadow drawn by the setting sun stretched along the ground. *Apricot flowers?* Petals of cherry-blossom-like flowers alighted on his shoulders. Morito's glasses glistened in the twilight. Facing the sun, Yukimura couldn't tell for certain, but it seemed that Morito's tears made his glasses shine. The graveyard fell into total silence. The only sound was the movement of the Mexicans some distance away drifting up like waves. Morito did not raise his head. It looked as if he would stay there for many more hours.

The priest cleared his throat. Morito's large sunbeam-laden shoulders finally rose. Dark clay clung to his pants knees. Morito briefly thanked the priest and the choir, and took care of the business matters by himself, hardly looking at Yukimura or Nakano. He only said, "All right, let's go," and got into his Cougar XR7.

Yukimura and Nakano rushed to their Ford Capri and chased after him.

"The manager is acting strange today," said Nakano, who had joined the company only three years ago.

"He may have been crying."

"The old man must have taken really good care of him."

"I guess."

Their cars raced by the Mexican laborers. In the evening sun, the workers looked worn out. They turned vacant and apathetic eyes towards the cars.

"The manager must have been made to work like them."

"I doubt it." Yukimura answered dryly, but remembered that there were some places around there called "Chino," which was Spanish for "Chinese." There was a time when Chinese and Japanese were dirt-crawling laborers. It wouldn't be surprising if Morito had been included in the penurious labor force of Chinese and Japanese students during the postwar period. The shame and regret of having fallen slave to the pitiless drudgery . . . The difference in treatment must have made the old orchard owner seem like a saint. Was it an outburst of dammed up sentiment that had made Morito a praying clay statue?

Come to think of it, Morito had shown no interest in visiting the places of his memorable past other than this graveyard, after coming this close to them. Could it be that all the other places would only open old wounds with painful freshness? He had once said, "They all mistreated me." Stretching his imagination one step farther, Yukimura recalled that Morito had two false front teeth. Morito had casually explained that he fell and broke them while he was in the United States, but did they have a hidden connection with the hard labor? Yukimura also wondered if Morito's avoidance of Aron and Halifax might not have been rooted in his resentment of the white people of the region, and not a matter of business strategy.

The basin opened up toward the west as if beckoning to the open pasture. A huge red sun was about to set on the horizon. The Cougar XR7 sprinted past the vast scenery, like a white leopard, aiming at Los Angeles. Morito's silhouette looked much smaller than life-size. And every now and then, the gold of the setting sun bleached out the white Cougar and Morito's silhouette. They looked lonely and neglected.

"That car has been following us for a long time," said Nakano when they approached Ontario.

Yukimura looked in the rearview mirror. Two old cars were trailing behind them. Lanes were open on their right and left. The two cars had plenty of time and space to pass, but they stayed very close behind. Each had three or four passengers. Strange! Should he honk at Morito and let him know? What would Morito do about it? It was a straight highway in the middle of empty land. There was no service area; exits and junctions were some distance away. Oncoming cars floated up and down into their vision on the other side of the highway, but the lanes on this side had nothing other than the taillights that had just disappeared in the horizon. The highway was already darkened by the violet dusk.

"It's weird. What shall we do?" asked Nakano.

At that moment, the two cars suddenly sped up and pulled into the passing lane. They passed Yukimura's car. One of them raced its engine and flew in front of the Cougar. The other stayed right next to the Cougar to cage it in. The Cougar, now sandwiched between the two, reduced speed and stopped in the breakdown lane. Yukimura's Ford passed them before it came to an abrupt halt. Many shadows rolled out of the black cars and ran toward the Cougar. Then came the ring of swearing voices. The blasting of a bullet cut through the wind. With their doors open, Yukimura and Nakano hung back. Another bullet. The Cougar honked. It kept on honking. Morito's torso seemed to have fallen across the steering wheel. The men floored their accelerators, and the two cars that had swallowed those shadows sped off.

Yukimura and Nakano ran up to the Cougar. A front tire was shot out, tilting the car body. Morito's bloodless face hung over the steering wheel. It rose slowly and the honking stopped. Blood soaked his left thigh. Apparently the men didn't intend to kill him. But Morito's body was stuck to the steering wheel. When the two men tried to lift him, a horrible stench stung their noses.

"Oh, I . . ." Morito tried to say something with unfocused eyes.

Yukimura and Nakano looked at each other. They detected the cause of the stench. Morito had excreted in terror. It wasn't anything to laugh about; it was pathetic.

IV

President Hori arrived in Los Angeles. Because Morito was hospitalized, Yukimura had to explain the three thousand dollar incident. The thought that he was saving Morito's skin rather than being incriminated by the manager made it easier to surrender himself to whatever fate awaited him. He prepared himself for the severest scolding, but the president started talking before Yukimura had finished, with a friendly smile on his face, "Fumihiko wrote to me from New York. He said that he gave up the idea of becoming an artist. He realized that he wasn't gifted enough. The show must have had some true masterpieces. He was crushed. He even hinted at coming back to Japan. He said that he couldn't keep on goofing off with the assumption that we are always there to wait on him."[3] The president then broke into a genuine smile and changed the subject, "I'm going to ask you to manage this office from now on. I don't mean temporarily; I mean officially."

"But Morito-san is . . ."

"I'll send him back to Japan as soon as he comes out of the hospital. I'll have him take it easy in our research division or somewhere. I misunderstood him. I used to think that his type made good businessmen, but I think perhaps not any more."

"His type?"

"You know what I mean. Those who have worked under him can explain better than I."

Does "his type" mean a practical and bluffing kind? Yukimura wanted to ask. Had the president seen Morito praying stone-still on a hill aglow with the setting sun? And what did the president know about Yukimura himself? Did he know that Yukimura wanted to go back to Japan? Rather than taking the managerial post, he wanted to go back now, even if he had to miss a promotion, and maybe catch another chance sometime later.

The president took Yukimura's silence as his expression of gratitude and carried on, "It's about time you made it to a manager's post. Besides, we need someone like you from now on who is familiar with the local circumstances. We are stepping into a world where many more conflicts, graver than those of Aron and Halifax, are likely to turn up."

The exhausted faces of the Mexican workers flashed in Yukimura's mind, and so did the golden carpet of oranges lying around their feet. He felt an unexplained load fall on his shoulders. Looking up with his inner eyes, he saw the white tower of the City Hall rise in the navy-blue sky of southern California, like an insensitive giant.

10.2 Payback (Dirty for Dirty)

◆

Patricio F. Vargas

Wilshire Boulevard was bustling with people glad to be out during the lunch hour after a week of unusually heavy rain in Los Angeles. The wide, fancy street was crowded with people, mostly women, animated by the marvelous, pleasant change in weather: bees streaming out of dark, humid hives, into brilliant sunshine, coming alive.

Women seductively, attractively dressed, glad to expose their femininity in revealing clothing. Sexy shoes and alluring dresses with lively, inviting faces, their eyes darting, looking, addressing, flirting – just great to be out walking, letting men look at them. The two men, pretending nonchalance, using their peripheral vision, swiveling from side to side of the street, checking out all the possibilities for a flirtation or just an eyeful of female.

The blue pickup glided slowly down Wilshire towards the tallest of the buildings, on the 3400 block.

"You know what the son of a whore has done for me? For $1,000 I've gotten a receipt and a letter! ¡Hijo de su pinche, puta, perra madre! He made me so many promises. And to think I trusted that fucking lawyer!" the squat Mexican troglodyte said animatedly to the driver, another Mexican, who sat with an intense, preoccupied air as he drove and enjoyed the women on the busy boulevard.

Source: Patricio F. Vargas, "Payback (Dirty for Dirty)," *Best New Chicano Literature,* edited by Julian Palley, 1989, pp. 100–104. Reprinted by permission of The Bilingual Press.

"He said he could get all my family documented for only $2,300, and all I got in two years was a receipt!"

The driver, nodding in understanding and faint boredom at hearing the complaining repetition . . . rehearsing in his mind what his strategy was going to be once he sized up the lawyer. The simple peasant's litany and pleas for help were beginning to weary him.

They parked at the rear of the tall, ritzy, imposing building and headed for the 25th floor.

"You should have seen how well he treated me, had the two kiss-ass secretaries translate for me every minute . . . and once I handed him the $1,000 I never heard from him again!" The beefy man, grossly overweight at 5 feet 5 inches and 250 pounds, kept up his running commentary. An ambulatory washing machine of a man, his thick arms and thicker body thrashing through the air, trying to keep up with his rescuer; bull-like neck, powerful shoulders and trapezius bulging, years of plastering made visible in his bunched-up muscles as he trundled along.

Taking the elevator, they continued to speak in Spanish, disconcerting the other passengers, who outwardly pretended not to hear, but who inwardly strained their ears to catch the meaning of the alien sounds, recoiling slightly at the foreign look and sound of the two chattering Mexicans in the small space.

"Wanna see a guy named Phil, works here," said the younger man to the caged-in receptionist, and they were both admitted into the winding recesses of the plush law offices of twelve lawyers who had their full names inscribed in the tall wall of the wide, lush lobby, crowding each other out of the huge brass plate.

Philip Rombly III (as his business card read) was taller than the taller Mexican and wore a black suit. His thick, curly, dark hair surrounded a soft, unformed, tanned face that had a little swarthy radish for a nose; small, blue, darting eyes that stood still and widened for emphasis completed his face.

"Manny Rodríguez! Glad to see you! What's up?" asked the lawyer in a silly, inappropriate way, of the peasant who stood in the doorway, unsure as to the strange etiquette of these white men who smiled and shook your hand warmly while you tried to look angry and offended.

"Came to get Manuel's $1,000," said the younger Mexican without preamble to the surprised lawyer.

"Now I told him that I needed a letter of employment from his employer before I could start the citizenship procedure. Tell him that."

The Mexican walked to the large easy chair opposite the lawyer's desk and sat down without invitation. Manuel followed suit.

"It's been two years and you never moved on the case. Now he wants his money back and we'll leave," he said, ignoring the lawyer's request.

"I can't move without that letter, you tell him that. It's all his doing. I've done a lotta work on his case. I've put in a lot of time." Putting his hand on the phone as he talked, he put on his professional voice and asked his secretary to bring in the "Rodríguez file."

They both ignored Manuel . . . he wasn't there. Manuel, the aggrieved party, sat silently, only half understanding the goings-on . . . a spectator in his own fight. He understood bricks, mortar and wood; they were honest, with straightforward natures, as long as you followed basic rules of nature and geometry.

Building materials had a noble simplicity; they were not out to trick or deceive you. Although some were easier to work with than others, you could always trust them to behave in a thoroughly predictable manner. Materials were so strong yet so vulnerable if only you knew their secrets. It was a matter of contradictions and opposite natures: his hands, though horny, were soft compared to wood, yet he could bend steel and order it around; concrete, in its liquid state, was a hapless gruel manipulated into any shape or container, but once hardened it became as immutable as any thousand-year-old rock. Wood and tile became plastic in his hands, yielding beauty and utility.

Soft hands enslaving hard wood and metal. Some materials were more slavish than others, but all surrendered their strength and might to the seductive cunning of manually applied physics, persuading, convincing them.

Materials he could understand, but men, who knew them? How could you tell? What was so right for one was nearly death to another. It was not possible to understand men.

His rescuer was a learned man, cultured; he could even speak English and write. And yet he seemed almost a hoodlum as he addressed the lawyer, so disrespectful! Even though he himself felt angry and wronged by the crafty lawyer, a man had to behave according to courtesy, even in anger, not like this, like a commoner!

If only he could speak English, if only he could fight for himself, if only he knew what to do.

The secretary politely knocked, entered, and handed her boss the file.

"See, look here," he said, pointing to the bulging file the secretary brought in. "It's all there."

"We want the $1,000, not talk. I've already blown two hours on you; I can't wait anymore. We're going to lean on you if you don't deliver." The Mexican slouched, quietly menacing.

"I don't want trouble, but look at the work I've done. Can't we compromise, say $500? Tell him."

"Phil, you made a few calls, wrote a few notes maybe, that's about all. This guy's a working slob; he lives from hand to mouth, after busting his balls on any construction job he can find. He does real work; you're a lawyer." The Mexican took off his dark glasses with deliberate, slow movements as he sat up in the large chair, coming from his recumbent, leisurely slouch.

"This guy uses his body like a cheap tool every day. Parts of his body are older than the rest from overuse. He's 54 and all he has is a twenty-year-old truck and second-rate tools and you want to take him. He travels back and forth from Mexico without papers, doesn't speak English, and because you treated him nice after he put in doors for you, he thought he could trust you. I'm going to give you a hundred bucks for your work. Give him back $900 and we're even," said the Mexican, never looking at the apprehensive lawyer, speaking quietly into his lap.

The lawyers's mind raced, weighing the pros and cons; caught between his not wanting to "lose" $900 and the unknown fear that was overcoming his sense of economy.

He felt guilty and threatened. The work he had done on the case was minimal and he had never been so bluntly confronted. The Mexican's cold, indifferent manner had penetrated his social shell of self-confidence. It was eerie. The stocky, English-speaking Mexican reminded him of the mean neighborhood greaseballs he had grown up with in Pomona. That quiet, indirect, cold aggression that would suddenly explode in mindless fury. They didn't seem to care. If you were friends, they would slash their bellies open for you. But if you messed with their sisters, they would look up your entire family.

On the other hand, they were so dumb and fearful of authority. They would respectfully retreat before any show of authority or official sanction. They always seemed apologetic and smiley, especially the older ones. It was the younger ones that seemed to have a vague grasp of their rights. Still, you never knew. He might be able to talk sense into the spick, but he seemed so remote. These guys were primitive.

"Look, maybe we can talk about this," he said to the reclining menace. "I don't have any money right now."

"How much you got in your wallet? Take it out!"

Mechanically, realizing the Mexican was implacable, he took the wallet out and held out for all to see the $40.00 he had.

"See, I have no money!" he said, realizing his hopes for negotiations were evaporating.

"What about those rings? Take them off. How much are your teeth worth?"

The lawyer felt his composure fall from him; he was being robbed in his own office and he could not stop himself from cooperating. He felt ten years old again, being shaken down by neighborhood spicks. Oh, God.

"I can't take them off. I never do," he said, nearly whining, extending his large, soft hands, palms down, towards the Mexican, and then brandishing them like shields, waggling his large wooly head for emphasis, his eyes widening.

School had let out an hour ago and his mother would be searching the route to school. I got to get home.

"All right. Make out a check for $900."

"I haven't got it," squeaked out Phil, against the wall, his heart thundering.

"You don't seem to appreciate the gravity of your situation, Phil. I don't want to hassle with you; I now know what you look like, you know what I look like, and you'll never see me again. I don't ever want to see you again," the Mexican said, his droopy moustache making his face appear melancholy with his slow, soft, menacing voice contradicting his looks.

Phil scrambled in his mind for the checkbook, but in reality his ego moved slowly and calmly and wrote out the check in his large, tidy handwriting.

The Mexicans took the check and left.

The lawyer took the rest of the day off.

◇

11.1 Wanamurraganya: The Story of Jack McPhee

◆

Sally Morgan and Jack McPhee

I've had a think, and before I say anything, I want to say this. The way I see things is based on the way I've had to live, please remember that.

I want to talk about stations. They were built on black labor. On sour bread, damper, roo meat and whippings. The squatter had it hard too, because life in those days was hard, but they made money out of it. Two generations on their families are all right, ours aren't. Many of them are now wealthy men with land and businesses and respect, we have nothing.

I can only explain it like this. Two friends of mine were working on a station. The manager, who was an okay fella, went away and put a new bloke in charge. There was a good garden there, my friend looked after it while his wife worked in the house. Now the new boss loved watermelon and my friend had some in the garden.

Source: Sally Morgan and Jack McPhee, "Wanamurraganya: The Story of Jack McPhee," excerpted from *Australian Literature: An Anthology from the Land Down Under*, edited by Phyllis Edeson, 1993, pp. 101–104. Reprinted by permission of Fremantle Arts Centre Press.

He was told he wasn't allowed to have any of those melons, even though my friend had grown them himself. Instead, when the boss had eaten the good part, he would throw him the leftovers. For years the whiteman's been getting the sweet part of the melon and the blackman, if he's lucky, has had to be content with leftovers.

I can honestly say that I have tried very hard in my life to live quietly and to better myself and my family. When I was just a native I was told that if I wanted to get on in the world I had to become a whiteman, but when I tried to do that people would look at me and say, 'Oh you're just a native!'

Some people think all Aborigines are the same, yet we have different tribal groups, different languages, different customs. Our color isn't even the same, some of us are black, some are brown, some are only light. Some of us can speak language and some know only English; some can read and write and some can't. Some of us are no-hopers and alcoholics, and others are working men who know right from wrong. People see a few rotten apples and write us off. I've known whitemen who were bastards and I've known whitemen who were the best mates a man could have. I'm sick of people thinking we all look and think the same. A man should be judged on his own and not as part of a group.

Now, about Mulba things, I think it's very sad that some of our people feel ashamed of the old culture, especially our languages and dancing. I speak five Aboriginal languages and I can sing in seven. I know many Mulbas who can speak their language but won't. Sometimes when I'm sitting in the South Hedland shopping center, I wait until I see some of my countrymen coming and then I call out to them in language. They get very embarrassed. I tell them I'm not ashamed of my language and they shouldn't be either. I'll speak my language anywhere.

You see, their idea is this. They think if they talk language the white people might think they're running them down. Over the years I've seen the same thing happen at corroboree time. White people are very interested in corroborees, but my people get worried about singing in language in case someone says, 'Oh speak bloody English will ya?!'

For many years there was ill feeling in the North between black and white. No one wanted us to go up in the world, we were classed next to a dog. I'm happy to say that's changing. However, I don't agree with some of the black people who won't speak to white people. They're getting silly themselves now. They blame the white people for everything, especially the past, but I think there are some things happening now that they're responsible for. Young people drinking and stealing, old people gambling everything, mothers and fathers not wanting to work or look after their kids. We had none of that in my day.

It's hard because Mulbas see things differently. We'd rather lend twenty dollars to someone than pay the rent. If people owe us money and won't pay we just walk away. We've got to be in a group all the time, we won't spread out and make an independent living for ourselves. The grandmothers won't say no to anything. They keep taking in all the children the young people don't want instead of making them care for those kids themselves.

Also, if things are all right now like people say, then why are all these boys dying in jail? I just can't understand that and it really worries me. I am very worried about the young Aboriginal boys and girls and what's going to become of them if they keep on the way they are. I know there are some good ones who try their best, that's why I'm going to make a scholarship, to help the ones that are trying to help themselves. I want to do that, and I want to be remembered as someone who made mistakes like everyone else, but who came through in the end and did something good for his people.

I'm roughly eighty-four now and I've been through a lot in my life. I have to tell you that it's only as you get to the end of your life that you start to realize what things are really important to you. I've been through the Exemption Certificate and Citizenship and I've struggled to live up to the whiteman's standard, but here I am, old, and good for nothing, and what keeps coming back to me? Dances, singing, stories the old people used to tell. Every night I lie in bed and sing myself to sleep with all my old corroboree songs. I go over and over them and I remember that part of my life. They're the things I love, they're the things I miss.

My friend Peter Coppin, I think of him as a young bloke, but he must be in his sixties by now, you should hear him talk about me. He points to me in front of real young fellas and says, 'You see that fella there, he looks like a whiteman now, but I remember him all dressed up in cockatoo feathers, paint and pearlshell, singing and dancing, doing all the things blackfellas do. He's the only old one left who remembers how it used to be, he's the only one who's number one fella to me.'

$\diamondsuit$

11.2 Mister Taylor

$\blacklozenge$

Augusto Monterroso

"Somewhat less strange, although surely more exemplary," the other man said then, "is the story of Mr. Percy Taylor, a headhunter in the Amazon jungle.

"In 1937 he is known to have left Boston, Massachusetts, where he had refined his spirit to the point at which he did not have a cent. In 1944 he appears for the first time in South America, in the region of the Amazon, living with the Indians of a tribe whose name there is no need to recall.

"Because of the shadows under his eyes and his famished appearance, he soon became known as 'the poor gringo,' and the school children even pointed at him and threw stones when he walked by, his beard shining in the golden tropical sun. But this caused no distress to Mr. Taylor's humble nature, for he had read in the first volume of William C. Knight's *Complete Works* that poverty is no disgrace if one does not envy the wealthy.

"In a few weeks the natives grew accustomed to him and his eccentric clothing. Besides, since he had blue eyes and a vague foreign accent, even the president and the minister of foreign affairs treated him with singular respect, fearful of provoking international incidents.

"He was so wretchedly poor that one day he went into the jungle to search for plants to eat. He had walked several meters without

Source: Augusto Monterroso, "Mister Taylor," *And We Sold the Rain*, edited by Rosario Santos, translated by Edith Grossman, 1988, pp. 183–190. Reprinted by permission of Four Walls and Eight Windows.

daring to turn his head when, by sheerest accident, he saw a pair of Indian eyes observing him intently from the undergrowth. A long shudder traveled down Mr. Taylor's sensitive spine. But Mr. Taylor intrepidly defied all danger and continued on his way, whistling as if he had not seen anything.

"With a leap, which there is no need to call feline, the native landed in front of him and cried: 'Buy head? Money, money.'

"Although the Indian's English could not have been worse, Mr. Taylor, feeling somewhat ill, realized the Indian was offering to sell him an oddly shrunken human head that he was carrying in his hand.

"It is unnecessary to say that Mr. Taylor was in no position to buy it, but since he pretended not to understand, the Indian felt horribly embarrassed for not speaking good English and gave the head to him as a gift, begging his pardon.

"Mr. Taylor's joy was great as he returned to his hut. That night, lying on his back on the precariously balanced palm mat that was his bed, and interrupted only by the buzzing of the passionate flies that flew around him as they made love obscenely, Mr. Taylor spent a long time contemplating his curious acquisition with delight. He derived the greatest aesthetic pleasure from counting the hairs of the beard and moustache one by one and looking straight into the two half-ironic eyes that seemed to smile at him in gratitude for his deferential behavior.

"A man of immense culture, Mr. Taylor was contemplative by nature, but on this occasion he soon became bored with his philosophical reflections and decided to give the head to his uncle, Mr. Rolston, who lived in New York and who, from earliest childhood, had shown a strong interest in the cultural manifestations of Latin American peoples.

"A few days later, Mr. Taylor's uncle wrote to ask him (not before inquiring after the state of his precious health) to please favor him with five more. Mr. Taylor willingly satisfied Mr. Rolston's desire and – no one knows how – by return mail he 'was very happy to honor your request.' Extremely grateful, Mr. Rolston asked for another ten. Mr. Taylor was 'delighted to be of service.' But when in a month he was asked to send twenty more, Mr. Taylor, simple and bearded but with a refined artistic sensibility, had the presentiment that his mother's brother was making a profit off of the heads.

"And, if you want to know, that's how it was. With complete frankness Mr. Rolston told him about it in an inspired letter whose strictly businesslike terms made the strings of Mr. Taylor's sensitive spirit vibrate as never before.

"They immediately formed a corporation: Mr. Taylor agreed to obtain and ship shrunken heads on a massive scale while Mr. Rolston would sell them as best he could in his country.

"In the early days there were some annoying difficulties with certain local types. But Mr. Taylor, who in Boston had received the highest grades for his essay on Joseph Henry Silliman, proved to be a politician and obtained from the authorities not only the necessary export permit but also an exclusive concession for ninety-nine years. It was not difficult for him to convince the chief executive warrior and the legislative witch doctors that such a patriotic move would shortly enrich the community, and that very soon all the thirsty aborigines would be able to have (whenever they wanted a refreshing pause in the collection of heads) an ice cold soft drink whose magic formula he himself would supply.

"When the members of the cabinet, after a brief but luminous exercise of intellect, became aware of these advantages, their love of country bubbled over, and in three days they issued a decree demanding that the people accelerate the production of shrunken heads.

"A few months later, in Mr. Taylor's country, the heads had gained the popularity we all remember. At first they were the privilege of the wealthiest families, but democracy is democracy, and as no one can deny, in a matter of weeks even schoolteachers could buy them.

"A home without its own shrunken head was thought of as a home that had failed. Soon the collectors appeared, and with them, certain contradictions: owning seventeen heads was considered bad taste, but it was distinguished to have eleven. Heads became so popular that the really elegant people began to lose interest and would only acquire one if it had some peculiarity that saved it from vulgarity. A very rare one with Prussian whiskers, that in life had belonged to a highly decorated general, was presented to the Danfeller Institute, which, in turn, immediately donated three and a half million dollars to further the development of this exciting cultural manifestation of Latin American peoples.

"Meanwhile, the tribe had made so much progress that it now had its own path around the Legislative Palace. On Sundays and Independence Day the members of Congress would ride the bicycles the company had given them along that happy path, clearing their throats, displaying their feathers, laughing very seriously.

"But what did you expect? Not all times are good times. Without warning the first shortage of heads occurred.

"Then the best part began.

"Mere natural deaths were no longer sufficient. The minister of public health, feeling sincere one dark night when the lights were out and he had caressed his wife's breast for a little while just out of courtesy, confessed to her that he thought he was incapable of raising mortality rates to the level that would satisfy the interests of the company. To that she replied he should not worry, that he would see how everything would turn out all right, and that the best thing would be for them to go to sleep.

"To compensate for this administrative deficiency it was indispensable that they take strong measures, and a harsh death penalty was imposed.

"The jurists consulted with one another and raised even the smallest shortcoming to the category of a crime punishable by hanging or the firing squad, depending on the seriousness of the infraction.

"Even simple mistakes became criminal acts. For example: if in ordinary conversation someone carelessly said 'It's very hot,' and later it could be proven, thermometer in hand, that it really was not so hot, that person was charged a small tax and executed on the spot, his head sent on to the company, and, it must be said in all fairness, his trunk and limbs passed on to the bereaved.

"The legislation dealing with disease had wide repercussions and was frequently commented on by the diplomatic corps and the ministries of foreign affairs of friendly powers.

"According to this memorable legislation, the gravely ill were given twenty-four hours to put their papers in order and die, but if in this time they were lucky enough to infect their families, they received as many month-long stays as relatives they had infected. The victims of minor illnesses, and those who simply did not feel well, earned the scorn of the fatherland, and anyone on the street was entitled to spit in their faces. For the first time in history the importance of doctors who cured no one was recognized (there were several candidates for the Nobel Prize among them). Dying became an example of the most exalted patriotism, not only on the national level but on that even more glorious one, the continental.

"With the growth achieved by subsidiary industries (coffin manufacture in particular flourished with the technical assistance of the company) the country entered, as the saying goes, a period of great economic prosperity. This progress was particularly evident in a new little flower-bordered path on which, enveloped in the melancholy of the golden autumnal afternoons, the deputies' wives would stroll, their pretty little heads nodding yes, yes, everything was fine, when some solicitous journalist on the other side of the path would greet them with a smile, tipping his hat.

"I remember in passing that one of these journalists, who on a certain occasion emitted a downpour of a sneeze that he could not explain, was accused of extremism and put against the wall facing the firing squad. Only after his unselfish end did the intellectual establishment recognize that the journalist had one of the fattest heads in the country, but once it was shrunken it looked so good that one could not even notice the difference.

"And Mr. Taylor? By this time he had been designated as special adviser to the constitutional president. Now, and as an example of what private initiative can accomplish, he was counting his thousands by the thousands; but this made him lose no sleep, for he had read in the last volume of the *Complete Works* of William C. Knight that being a millionaire is no dishonor if one does not scorn the poor.

"I believe that this is the second time that I will say that not all times are good times.

"Given the prosperity of the business, the time came when the only people left in the area were the authorities and their wives and the journalists and their wives. Without much effort Mr. Taylor concluded that the only possible solution was to start a war with the neighboring tribes. Why not? This was progress.

"With the help of a few small cannons, the first tribe was neatly beheaded in just under three months. Mr. Taylor tasted the glory of expanding his domain. Then came the second tribe, then the third, the fourth and the fifth. Progress spread so rapidly that the moment came when, regardless of the efforts of the technicians, it was impossible to find neighboring tribes to make war on.

"It was the beginning of the end.

"The little paths began to languish. Only occasionally could one see a lady taking a stroll or some poet laureate with his book under his arm. The weeds once again overran the two paths, making the way difficult and thorny for the delicate feet of the ladies. Along with the heads the bicycles had thinned out, and the happy optimistic greetings had almost completely disappeared.

"The coffin manufacturer was sadder and more funereal than ever. And everyone felt as if they had awakened from a pleasant dream – one of those wonderful dreams when you find a purse full of gold coins, and you put it under your pillow and go back to sleep, and very early the next day, when you wake up, you look for it and find emptiness.

"Nevertheless, business, painfully, went on as usual. But people were having trouble going to sleep for fear they would wake up exported.

"In Mr. Taylor's country, of course, the demand continued to increase. New substitutes appeared daily, but nobody really believed in them, and everyone demanded the little heads from Latin America.

"It happened during the last crisis. A desperate Mr. Rolston was continually demanding more heads. Although the company's stocks suffered a sharp decline, Mr. Rolston was convinced that his nephew would do something to save the situation.

"The once daily shipments decreased to one a month, and they were sending anything: children's heads, ladies' heads, deputies' heads.

"Suddenly they stopped completely.

"One harsh, gray Friday, home from the stock exchange and still dazed by the shouting of his friends and their lamentable show of panic, Mr. Rolston decided to jump out the window (rather than use a gun – the noise would have terrified him). He had opened a package that had come in the mail and found the shrunken head of Mr. Taylor smiling at him from the distant wild Amazon, with a child's false smile that seemed to say 'I'm sorry, I won't do it again.' "

11.3 East and West

◆

Rudyard Kipling

O nce upon a time, when the Himalayas were but callow crestlings, the Aravalis formed a chain of islands running north and south across the ocean that then buried India. "And where the city roars hath been/The stillness of the central sea." Up to this point my record of an unsentimental journey from Ajmir to elsewhere had progressed beautifully; but my friend Sinbad the traveller entered, and with him a mountain of luggage. He was not exactly a blood relation, or even connected by race; being a Peshwari Yusufzai, and a *Kazi* to boot. Still he came from the Punjab, and was therefore welcome. "It is hot" said Sinbad removing the dust-coat that fettered his massive torso: – "Bring me soda-water, O peon!" The peon was a Panjabi Mahommedan, and had forgotten the soda-water. "Pig!" quoth my friend Sinbad, and slapped him on the head twice. "Very good" said the peon, and walked away. My friend Sinbad and I fell atalking.

But here let me describe him – this Afghan who dressed like an Englishman, and travelled after the English fashion, and used soap and shoe-horns and corkscrews and nail-scissors, an English of the finest water. They lie who say that the Afghans are not the Tribes that went astray. My friend Sinbad had the head of a Rabbi, such as men put in paintings – brown, olive color, marked like the face of a cliff set in black hair firm as wire. It was a grand head on its

---

Source: Rudyard Kipling, "East and West," *The Complete Works of Rudyard Kipling*, AMS Press, 1993, pp. 256–261.

bull neck, and our tongue suited it not; God having made it for Pushto; or a more gutteral speech if such a one exist.

"He is a pig" said my friend Sinbad. "All native servants are pigs. Is this not so?" The head was the head of Essau indeed, but the sentiments seemed foreign to it. "They are all pigs" said I; and my friend Sinbad settled himself cross-legged on the seat and was silent – sunk in impenetrable reserve. There is but one Interpretress who speaks all the tongues of the East, and appeals to all hearts; and her name is Tobacco. My friend smoked. Further, he smoked from my cigar-case. The East and the West confronted each other on opposite sides of a first class carriage. The East yawned.

(Under the shadow of the Edwardes' Gate in Peshawar, lives an old shop-keeper. It was he who told me many many lies, but one truth. "All *Kazees* will talk if you let them alone. Most Afghans not." I let my friend Sinbad alone, and smiled. My friend Sinbad talked.)

We had acquaintances in common. It was the first stepping stone. We knew many officials. This was the second. We had met each other before. Careful cross-verification of dates showed this to be true. This was the third.

Sinbad fenced in his speech. Was preposterously virtuous; unnaturally advanced; inordinately civilized. I was no servant of the Government. Held no post of authority or responsibility; and loose views on many things. Sinbad fenced no longer. We descended from generalities into particulars and affairs political.

"Who will be our next Lieutenant-Governor?" asked Sinbad. "God knows!" said I. "We shall see." "It may be Mr. Cordery or Sir Lepel Griffin" quoth he. "They are high in favor with the Viceroy. And what do you think?" said I. "They are strong men" said Sinbad; and he rubbed his knees softly. "Either will be good." "And our present Lieutenant-Governor" said I "What do you think of him?" My friend blew the smoke through his nostrils and replied. "He is a hard man to natives. He will not listen to them when they come to talk. You know this also, do you not?" "I have never gone to talk to him. It may be as you say, I have heard so." My friend looked distressed. It was possible that I had lied. I hastened to reassure him. He smoked more easily. "And what do you think of Sir Alfred Lyall?" asked I. "Have you had dealings with him?" My friend Sinbad slapped his thigh: – "Yes! Ah! He is a jewel of a man. He will hear you always." "Tell me something I want to know" said I. "With you people, is it not true that you prefer a man who will listen, when you come to *mulaqat Karo* him, even though he gives you no redress, to a man who will not hear you, even though he *does* do something for you?" "Say it again" said my friend. I repeated the clumsy sentence, and Sinbad thought. A *chinkara* grazing among the tussocks without in the sunshine bounded away from the train, and had nearly reached the horizon before he answered. "By Jove!" said he, "I believe you are right. We are a queer people!" It is strange to hear an Afghan say "By Jove!" and "queer," but my friend Sinbad was very English. He had annexed Britannia – shield, trident and lion – as he had another side to him – the reverse of the coin stamped with the Queen's Head. So English was he, that I could discuss many things without – visibly at least – wounding his feelings. "But you also are a queer people" said he. "Why do you try to make us like you." It was the reverse of the Queen's Head – the protest against the soap and the nail scissors; the trowsers that chafed, and the coatsleeves that cut. "We are all mad, we English, from our birth up," said I. "It is our custom." My friend Sinbad laughed and the windows rattled: – "That is a joke; but there is much truth in it. But I tell you that you are doing a little good. Not much, you understand, but still a little." "As how?" said I. "I will explain. When I was a child, I began to study the English language. That was in Peshawar thirty years ago. All my friends and relations said that I should become an infidel, a *kafir*, and were very angry. Nowadays one hears nothing of that sort of prejudice. One can be a good Mahommedan and speak English tolerably well at one and the same time. You have done this much good anyhow." "And in other ways is the English Government of any use?" I was prepared for what would follow. My friend Sinbad spoke at great length on the peace and the law and the order of the land, and stopped short. "And then?" "Well, I will tell you the truth. In many ways you are a good Government, but in many ways you are great – you are, yes, you are awful fools." (He took a fresh cheroot and began again). "You have two fools of parties in your country. Is it not so. Every five years one party does one thing, and the next five years the other party comes and undoes it. How can you make *pukka bundabusts* with the Ameer, with Russia or with anybody else? Who is to believe you? It is not the country's fault, of course! It is the fault of a party – your great fools of parties. I tell you that you are just as bad as the Hindus and Mahommedans at Mohurrum time; only with you it is always Mohurrum. You are one country; why do you not be sensible and have one party?" I was not prepared to explain the whole British Constitution with all its sacred rules and ordinances off hand. I took refuge in blue clouds of smoke and bowed my head. My friend Sinbad then returned to the charge. "When you have only one party" (Shades of Chamberlain and Churchill and the holy two millions of electors!) "and that party lasts for ever, there will be no Government on earth like yours. As it is, you are in many ways great fools." Perhaps my friend Sinbad's deep bass voice added force to the statement which was old enough in all conscience, but novel from the odd twist he gave it.

His eye caught by the flutter of a lady's dress on the platform. "Who is that?" asked Sinbad. "An Englishwoman travelling alone from one end of India to the other." "Yes! Yes! I know that but – Ah! I see what you mean. You mean that we cannot do that. No; it is true enough. By Jove! I tell you that a native lady would cry like a baby all the way from Calcutta to Peshawar. She would not know what 'ticket' meant. You could not leave her alone without help for a minute. She would die of fright!" "And do you consider that an advantage?" said I. "Most certainly not. You are entirely in the right there. Quite so. That is where we make our mistake. One of these days it will be set right, but not now or a hundred years hence." (My friend Sinbad slapped his thigh more vigorously than ever.) "And how will it be set right?" "One of these days both Hindus and Mahommedans will see that it is safer to let out their women than to keep them in *purdah*. Outside there are hundreds of thousands of eyes, and a woman cannot go wrong if she would. Inside the *purdah* (My friend Sinbad checked himself and played with his watch chain) things are sometimes different." "It is a great pity" he continued reflectively "that we never educate our wives." (I thought he was playing for the gallery; and sucked the end of my cheroot in silence. But he was not): "I tell you that a married woman who is intelligent is a great help. She can talk to a man about his work and his ambitions after he is out of office, and that is a great help. I have met men – of this country you know – who have married English wives, and they have told me so. Our women are great fools. They are pretty, of course; but that is all. It would be pleasant to find one that can talk." My friend Sinbad looked pensive; his mind wandering along some well worn *pugdandi* of thought.

Presently his eye brightened, and he shook himself: – "By Jove! I was a great devil in my youth. A great devil, by Jove!" He threw back his head and laughed aloud – not with the laughter of civilization, but the laughter that betrayed his origin – mirth, savage and boisterous that had nothing in common with gold watch-guard, English clothes, patent trunks or first-class tickets. I confess I liked him the better for it. He was of his own people again. Thereafter spoke and laughed hugely over queer tales of crooked intrigue, in which midnight assassination on housetops, stealthy prowls through narrow blind gullies, feud, lust, and blood were picturesquely intermingled. And the lamps that they put into the roof near Jaipur, for it was growing dusk, jangled and rattled as he laughed. Yes, my friend Sinbad was better in this fashion. I forgave him the shoehorns, and the trunks, and the corkscrews, and button hooks with which he had encrusted himself. "Come!" he concluded. "You are the first Englishman I have spoken to like this. God made us all men, and you talk to me as a man to a man. By Jove, you shall eat with me! It is a poor meal but we will eat together after the fashion of my country." And after the fashion of his country did my friend Sinbad and I eat. He rose and washed his hands from the wrist. I followed suit; and watched while he got the meal ready on the seat of the carriage. "Look you, I can eat with knives and forks like you can, but when I am alone I eat like my people. One can be as English as the English and yet remain very much a native. Is it not so?" And with one or two of his stories still ringing in my brain I answered that indeed it was very much indeed so. Sinbad was wrong in saying that his was a poor meal. It was the richest that I have ever eaten – a compound of mutton, cabbage, potatoes, butter and condiment.

Whether the novelty of the meal predisposed me in its favor, or whether I was genuinely hungry I cannot tell, but it seemed a most excellent dish. Terribly unwholesome and indigestible, but savory and appetizing. My friend Sinbad helped me to the daintiest bits on a piece of bread, but my clumsy western fingers made an unmitigated failure of the business. Whereupon he placed a *chapatti*, plate-wise, at my disposal and the meal went merrily forward. At its conclusion we rose and washed our hands, and paid mutual compliments of the most constrained kind; forgetting that just before we had been talking as "a man to a man." Presently, however, over the after-dinner smoke, conversation drifted into free and unfettered channels. We spoke of travelling allowances, and the yearly growing stinginess of the Government. "It is a rich Government" quoth my friend Sinbad "Rich as a *bunnia*, and twice as mean." He quoted instances of reduced expenditure to prove this, and branched off on to a discourse on the comparative morality of nations. "What I say is this; and this I do not say to all Englishmen. God made us different – you and I, and your fathers and my fathers. For one thing we have not the same notions of honesty and of speaking the truth. That is not our fault, because we are made so; and in a land where most men are liars, it is the same just as if most men were truth tellers. And look now what you do? You come and judge us by your own standard of morality – that morality which is the outcome of your climate and your education and your traditions. You are, of course, too hard on us. And again I tell you that you are great fools in this matter. Who are we to have your morals, or you to have ours? You know that in three generations a pure-bred Englishman dies out in this country. I have seen that as well as read it in books. And yet you think that we are to be judged by your morals. It is a mistake." My friend Sinbad quoted the case of a native official who, not so long ago, had been judged by our standard of morality and found sadly wanting as an instance in point. "You say he was a blackguard, is it not so?" asked my friend Sinbad. "It is said that he was a blackguard" I replied suavely. "Well by Jove! he was a blackguard from your own point of view. A big blackguard. But he was what you call a "strong" man, and he did much good work for our Government." (My friend Sinbad was English once more, and had reannexed Britain), "Much good work; and work that no one but a strong man could have done. If we had let him alone, he would have done much more. Not with clean hands perhaps, but still better than anyone else." The Gospel of Expediency always delighted me, and moreover I had a sneaking affection for that "big blackguard" – a respect born of his magnificent vitality: his astuteness and most British coolness under trying circumstances. My friend Sinbad and I agreed cordially on this point. God made us – East and West – widely different. We could not adopt each other's clothes or customs. Why insist upon uniformity in morals? My friend came out with a quotation from a French author to clinch the matter – accent and delivery both faultless. Not only had he annexed Britain then – this extraordinary jumble of conflicting nationalities, – but the Republic as well. There were French novels in his portmanteaux. Thereafter we spoke French for a season; till the kaleidoscopic *Kazee* took refuge in Persian and Arabic, and we returned together to the safe intelligibility of English. An hour passed in the discussion of domestic trivialities – light converse on horses, the women of all India, the wines of all Europe, and the depravity of native servants. Lastly we touched on the why and the wherefore of a recent judicial appointment in the Punjab. "It was not wise" quoth my friend Sinbad "neither Hindus nor Mahommedans were pleased; and the Commission were very angry. One of the *burra Sahibs* in the Punjab told me that he did not think the appointment should be in the gift of a Provincial Government. I think so too. The Supreme Government should nominate. I tell you it was not a good thing." The train rattled into that Zag-a-Zig in the desert – Bandakui – and our roads were divided.

"You change here?" said my friend Sinbad. "I am sorry. You have talked with me and smoked with me and eaten with me like a man. Shall I say as a compliment that you are almost worthy to be an Afghan?" "And you Sinbad to be an Englishman but" – "Ah, yes, my friend. It is true. But God has made us different for always. Is it not so?" And as I dug up the sleepy *Khansamah* for a cup of abominations called tea, me thought that Sinbad had stumbled upon a great truth.

Literally and metaphorically we were standing upon different platforms; and parallel straight lines, as every one does not know, are lines in the same plane which being continued to all eternity will never meet.

Section 12: Managerial Insights

◇

12.1 Resolving Cross-Cultural Ethical Conflict: Exploring Alternative Strategies

◆

John Kohls and Paul Buller

Introduction

As the global economy becomes increasingly interdependent, cultural conflict becomes ever more prevalent. At the same time societal concern for ethical corporate behavior is on the rise. These two forces intersect to highlight a particular problem of multinational businesses and any company involved in international trade or business. This is the problem of making ethical decisions when different cultures have contradictory or inconsistent ethical perspectives. Alternative ways of responding to these kinds of ethical conflicts are discussed in this paper. Even though some tentative answers are proposed, the paper is meant to be exploratory, looking at territory which has not had very much attention.

Alternatives for responding to cross-cultural ethical conflict form a continuum from complete adaptation to the host culture's ethical standards to complete insistence on the application of home country

Source: John Kohls and Paul Buller, "Resolving Cross-Cultural Ethical Conflict: Exploring Alternative Strategies," excerpted from *Journal of Business Ethics*, 1994, pp. 31–38, Vol. 13.

standards. Adaptation has strong roots in a large body of literature which encourages managers to become more familiar with a host culture, to avoid offending native sensibilities, and to build effective working relationships based on respect for the way they do things. Adaptation is also supported by the ethical stance of cultural relativism which claims that the standards of each culture determine what is right in that culture. Another factor underlying the adaptation approach is the strong support for tolerance in much of the West, and unwillingness to judge the values and standards of others. All these promote a view summarized in the adage "When in Rome, do as the Romans do."

On the other hand, most of those who seriously study ethical issues are dissatisfied with any kind of relativism. They maintain that ethical standards are universal, and that cultural behavior which does not meet those standards should be identified as unethical. Thus, support of governments which oppress their people, ways of doing business which do not respect human life, and those which depend on deception, are all unacceptable no matter what the culture. Cultures may make ethical mistakes just like individuals, and those which condone slavery or torture for example, need to be enlightened, not tolerated.

The position of this paper is that neither of these responses is satisfactory by itself. Rather, as managers face ethical conflicts, the appropriate strategies for dealing with them will depend on the nature of the specific ethical situation. We propose that the appropriate response depends on the centrality of values at stake, the degree of social consensus regarding the ethical issue, the decision-maker's ability to influence the outcome, and the level of urgency surrounding the situation. First, we will describe alternative approaches for dealing with ethical conflict. Then we will propose a model for selecting the appropriate response.

Strategies for resolving ethical conflict

First, it is important to recognize the different strategies available to managers. The following list of seven approaches was taken from Buller *et al.* (1991) and is based loosely on Ruble and Thomas' (1976) conflict resolution model. The approaches described are not intended to be exhaustive or mutually exclusive, but provide a range of possible responses to cross-cultural ethical conflict.

Avoiding.   Described as the low involvement approach, a party simply chooses to ignore or not deal with the conflict. The conflict may dissipate, but usually smolders and flares up at a later time. Strong parties can ignore the conflict when they are pleased with the status quo. For them, it may be a form of forcing. Avoiding is a frequent choice when the costs of pursuing a conflict are high. For example, one may decide not to sue someone who has wrongfully damaged her business, because the legal costs could bankrupt the company, or one does not mount a defense against a lawsuit to avoid prolonged publicity.

Forcing.   In this approach, one party forces its will upon the other. Forcing is often used when one party is stronger than the other. Host country officials sometimes use their power to demand payoffs for initiating or continuing a business operation. Similarly, multinational companies sometimes demand practices that are inconsistent with the indigenous cultures of the host countries in which they operate.

Education – persuasion.   This mechanism attempts to convert others to one's position through providing information, reasoning, or appeals to emotion. For example, multinationals often extol the virtues of free enterprise. As U.S. MNC's conduct business in host countries, they also have the opportunity to communicate the importance of due process for employees, and protecting employee health and safety.

Infiltration.   By introducing your values to another society, an appealing idea may be spread. This may be done deliberately, or it may be unintentional. The values associated with freedom and consumerism are examples.

Negotiation – compromise.   In this strategy, both parties give up something to negotiate a settlement. The resulting compromise usually leads one party or the other (or both) to feel dissatisfied with the outcome and that the basic conflict has not been resolved. The recent negotiations on unfair trade practices between Japan and the U.S. are a good example.

Accommodation.   In this approach, one party merely adapts to the ethic of the other. A foreign company may meet U.S. expectations for legally precise agreements in order to do business in the U.S. market, and an American businessman might learn to drink saki to do business in Japan.

Collaboration – problem solving.   In this strategy, both parties work together to achieve a mutually satisfying solution, a win-win outcome in which both their needs are met. This approach is most likely to address the sources of the conflict. An example might be in the discussions leading to an agreement between a multinational company and host country in which both desire an agreement satisfying to the other as well as themselves, to help insure an effective, long-term relationship.

It is our position that the appropriate conflict strategy will depend upon the issue involved and the circumstances surrounding that issue. There are appropriate occasions for each of the seven strategies. In order to develop a model to guide these choices, it is necessary to describe a classification system for ethical conflicts.

Types of ethical conflict

Not all ethical conflicts are of the same importance or the same significance. Giving gifts to those with whom one does business, which is accepted practice in many cultures, is greatly restricted in other countries and perceived as setting up a potential conflict of interest. In one case the receiver of the gift takes it as an appropriate sign of respect, and an expected way of building a relationship; in the other case the receiver may be offended by the gift and suspicious of the gift-giver and his motives. Here the conflict may be interpreted as minor, since the intention and the interpretation of the gift is not as a direct means to influence the business partner's decisions. On the other hand, a gift designed to sway the decision maker toward making a judgment in your favor is definitely a bribe. This second conflict involves more basic values. It has to do with our perception of what is fair play in the business world. Both cases conflict with the Western view of what is appropriate, what is 'right,' and what is ethical. However, it may be that the first conflict, when fully understood, is more one of business etiquette; and the second conflict, when fully understood deals with more fundamental standards of fairness.

These examples suggest a continuum of values at stake in the ethical conflict. In order to describe these values or standards we examine two factors regarding the particular standards at issue, centrality and social consensus. To more fully categorize ethical conflict situations, we also address two contextual factors, ability to influence the situation (power) and the need for immediate action (urgency). These four factors are far from exhaustive, but provide a beginning point in our effort to distinguish types of conflict.

Centrality recognizes a continuum of values. At one end are those values central to a culture, or central to the manager's understanding of what is really important in life; at the other end are values which are important, but much less so because they are less central. An example of such a continuum of values from core to periphery might look like Figure 12.1.1.

Many ethical dilemmas faced by managers require that some values be sacrificed to preserve others. In making a decision which is ethical, one must be careful that core values are not sacrificed to preserve more peripheral values. In the same way, when values conflict across cultures, it is important that core values, like respect for others, are not sacrificed for more peripheral values, like consistency. For the sake of exploration, two levels of centrality are proposed: (1) core values, and (2) peripheral values.

Donaldson (1989) proposes ten natural human rights. Among these are the right to freedom from torture, the right to nondiscrimi-

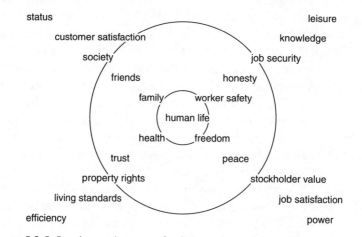

Figure 12.1.1   A continuum of values

natory treatment, the right to freedom of speech and association, and the right to political participation. These proposed rights may be debated, but if they are natural rights they would qualify as core values. They could not then be sacrificed or compromised unless to preserve other equally core values, even if they are not recognized in some nations and cultures.

A second classification of values is based on home culture consensus. If a value at stake is not widely shared in the home culture, it may be considered less important and therefore more easily sacrificed by a manager. Providing flex-time or maternity leave to respond to family needs of employees may be important to some in Western culture, but since it is not universally practiced, there is home-culture precedent for not providing it in another country where it would be unrealistic. Again, two levels can be suggested (1) universally valued in the culture and (2) rarely valued in the culture. The combination of centrality and consensus we refer to as intensity (see Jones, 1991).

It would seem reasonable that the higher the intensity of the values at stake, the more one should strive to maintain those values and standards; the lower the intensity, the greater should be the willingness to compromise or adapt. Figure 12.1.2 presents a model of how each of the conflict strategies might apply to different categories of issues.

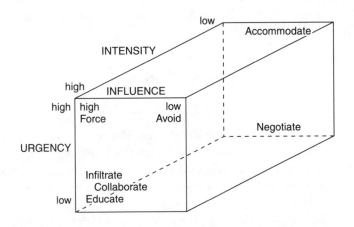

Figure 12.1.2 A contingency model of cross-cultural ethical conflict
strategies

A third factor to consider is the influence one has over the situation. Again there is a continuum from no ability to change the situation to complete control over the situation. In situations where you have no influence you have little choice but to accommodate and adapt to the host environment, or if core values are involved one may avoid the conflict by removing onself or not entering the situation in the first place. In situations of complete control there will be a temptation to force one's own views on others. But this will not be appropriate except for core or near core values. The primary impact of this fact is to limit the strategy options available. Where a number of options are given in the model for dealing with core value conflicts, a low degree of influence may make only one of the suggested strategies feasible.

The final factor is urgency. The choice of conflict strategy will also depend on how quickly or how slowly something must or can be done in the situation. As with the influence factor, degree of urgency limits the strategy options available rather than pointing to more desirable options. In situations of great urgency, strategies of avoidance, forcing or accommodation can work. Strategies of infiltration, education, negotiation or collaboration take too much time.

Much of the discussion so far has been highly conceptual. Real world applications of the model will illustrate how it can assist managers in selecting conflict strategies. In order to illustrate how different strategies may be applied, examples of ethical conflict will be discussed.

Case applications

Case A

In a case prepared by Arthur Kelly (Beauchamp and Bowie, 1989) an American manager is confronted with the Italian style of submitting tax returns. This involves understanding taxes, hiring a *commercialista* to meet with a tax authority, and negotiating a tax for the company. The amount of tax agreed upon depends in part on the size of a *bustarella* (bribe) given to the tax authority. The American manager is disturbed both by lying on the tax return and by the apparent bribery of the tax official. He submits his tax return "American-style" and refuses to hire a commercialista. He is eventually forced to meet with tax officials and his bank is made to pay taxes approximately three times the tax on the original return.

Case B

As reported in Swinyard *et al.* (1990), software piracy costs American industry hundreds of millions of dollars of lost revenues. Asia is often regarded as particularly troublesome. In the West, copying and selling software or any intellectual property is simple thievery. Typically, Asian cultures emphasize the obligation of the developers of intellectual property to share their developments with society. Asian nations "traditionally believe that copyright is a Western concept created to maintain a monopoly over the distribution and production of knowledge and knowledge-based products" (Altback, 1988, as quoted in Swinyard, 1990, p. 656). Despite U.S. pressure, software still does not have legal copyright protection in Indonesia, Malaysia, Thailand, and China as of 1988. Even where software piracy is illegal, protective legislation "goes firmly against the grain of Asian culture." (p. 662)

Case C

A Western businessman is considering opening a small business in India producing a product he believes is particularly suited to the needs of Indian people. He inquires into the procedure for doing so and finds that he must make numerous payoffs, not directly to government officials, but to numerous unofficial middlemen. He has to use stamp paper sold by the government for recording all legal transactions. Inexpensive stamp paper on which most of his work will be done is only available from unauthorized agents who have cornered the market, and he must pay a premium over the denomination amount to get the paper from the agent, but it is a small amount. He must then obtain a business license. In order to do so, he must contact an unofficial agent who knows the procedures and the people to contact, and for a fee he will get things done quickly. The substantial fee is shared with a government official who also shares it with those above and below him in the bureaucracy who have anything to do with processing the application. Without the personal contacts he must wait a long time to get his license. The same procedure is required to get a permit from the Department of Industries, and then to get a tax return account from the local governing body. Here he must be extra generous or he may find he is assessed a large amount in taxes.

These cases can be useful illustrations of the application of this model in that they exhibit serious cross-cultural ethical conflicts but also differ from each other in the intensity of the ethical issues and the degree of influence the involved parties can exercise over the situation.

Analysis – case A

In the Italian tax practices case, both honesty and the corruption of government officials seems to be core or near core values. But a fuller understanding of the situation is required. It is apparent that in Italy, submitting a false and favorable tax return is not deceptive. The tax authorities expect returns to show taxes owing at between 30 percent and 70 percent of actual. In fact, it is an accurate return which is deceptive, suggesting to tax authorities much higher than the actual corporate profits. Although submitting accurate tax returns, even though deceptive, may have some value, the value is not nearly as central as avoiding deception. It is certainly reasonable for the American to accommodate to the Italian-style of handling tax matters based on the analysis so far.

The issue of bribery is not handled so easily. It is understandable why the American would be uncomfortable with the payment of a bustarella. Although it is probably not a core value like life or liberty, paying your fair share, fair treatment by authorities (meaning equal treatment based on law), and avoiding corruption in government are certainly moderately core issues. In addition, these values are at least broadly held in American society. If this is the case, accommodation to the system is not acceptable. What strategies are available? Forcing a different approach and collaboration are not feasible given the low degree of influence. Avoidance might be required if these were high intensity values, but the model suggests negotiation and compromise may be more appropriate for moderate intensive values.

A compromise strategy might involve understating taxes but refusing to pay the bustarella. The company will probably pay more than its fair share of taxes, but will avoid the extreme taxes paid by the American bank in this case. Another compromise would be to pay the bustarella, but attempt to estimate what is required to get fair and reasonable treatment from the tax authority. Paying only this amount avoids getting special favorable treatment, and thus paying less than the taxes fairly owed. These actions preserve the manager's (and home country) values of fairness of results, even though he will still be uneasy with the process. This compromise also involves the manager in implicitly supporting a tax system he believes to be corrupt. The use of 'compromise' in this discussion is obviously not a compromise reached with another person with whom you are negotiating. It is instead a compromise between the demands of different principles, expectations, and a partial accommodation with the Italian approach. Over a longer period of time the model also points to other possibilities. In particular, it may be possible to fight the tax system from outside it, perhaps through education, supporting anticorruption campaigns in the media, and through political activity. This may not be the only solution, but application of the model does insure recognition of the difficulty and complexity of this cross-cultural ethical conflict, and provides a solution which aims at being both realistic and ethical.

Analysis – case B

In this case, American software companies are facing a situation which involves moderately central, broadly held values in the protection of intellectual property rights. The Swinyard et al. article (10) suggests that the value and expectation of sharing intellectual property is also moderately central and broadly held in Asian countries. American software companies have at least some influence and possibly substantial influence through technical protection strategies and through efforts of the U.S. government. Based on the model, appropriate strategies could be negotiation, education, and collaboration. Since these are not central values, forcing does not seem appropriate. Another difficulty with forcing is inadequate influence. Enforcement depends on governments whose cultures do not support this approach. Education efforts may have a very long-term effect, but will be ineffective in changing cultural attitudes in the short run. Negotiation is a possibility. Perhaps reducing the strictness of protections would make it more palatable in these cultures. Collaboration is even more promising. If the governments, or the foreign companies involved, have something to gain by providing protection against software piracy, they will have a vested interest in enforcing the policy. Giving the government a share in the sales of bona fide products, or licensing local companies at favorable terms, would give them both a stake in effective protection. This is probably not a truly win-win strategy since the Western value is being preserved at the expense of the Eastern value. But the development of the software in the West depends on its protection. Without protection in the West, Asian countries would not have the software to copy. Sacrificing the protection value would be self-defeating. Collaboration in this case is really only trying to find a way to make protection work in a culture which does not hold this value.

Analysis – case C

In the third case, the Western businessman is also facing bribery issues as in the first case, a moderate intensity issue. But there is a difference. Except for the tax situation, he would be making payments to get officials to do what they are supposed to do anyway. Government workers are paid very low wages in India, and these payments are considered by many to be an acceptable way to add to their income. Of course, those government officials in important posts and having a great deal of power are also very wealthy due to widespread bribery. Since the major problem with bribery is the potential for favoritism and corruption, and since this would not be the case except in the tax situation, the facilitating payments are probably a somewhat peripheral issue. There is also some recognition of this practice in the West where we tip waitresses, hotel workers, and others whose wages are known to be low. The use of agents who know the ropes is also common. They are usually lawyers who know how to move through bureaucratic and legal obstacles, and they are paid very well. Based on this analysis, these problems would be given a moderately low intensity ranking suggesting an accommodating strategy.

The payments to tax authorities are more than facilitating payments, and additionally these practices are part of a much larger set of practices which involve true corruption and bribery of government officials. These are moderate intensity values in the West. Although these practices are widespread and apparently unavoidable, they do not have the support of the public. When corruption is made public, it is a scandal. People do not approve of it, but feel helpless to change it. So many people with power depend on the current system that changing it would be enormously difficult. What should the strategy be when the common practice is inconsistent with common values in host country? Even though he has no influence on the practice, the intensity of the issue demands a strategy other than accommodation. Some negotiation may be possible, but the obvious option is avoidance by not setting up business in India. Only if other values (economic values to the natives, a uniquely helpful product like a vaccine or solar energy panel, or some other benefits), are more important than those that would be sacrificed, would the manager from the West be justified in establishing his business in India.

In each of the above cases, our interpretation of how the model might be applied is given. This interpretation is open to debate. Our primary aim is to show the richness of analysis the model promotes, and its ability to guide the choice of conflict resolution strategy in these cases.

References

Altback, P.: 1988, 'Economic Progress Brings Copyright to Asia,' *Far Eastern Economic Review* **139**(9), 62–63.

Beauchamp, T.: 1989, *Case Studies in Business, Society, and Ethics* (Prentice Hall, Englewood Cliffs, NJ).

Buller, P., J. Kohls and K. Anderson: 1991, 'The Challenge of Global Ethics,' *Journal of Business Ethics* **10**, 767–775.

Donaldson, T.: 1989, *The Ethics of International Business* (Oxford University Press, New York).

Jones, T. J.: 1991, 'Ethical Decision Making by Individuals in Organizations: an Issue-contingent Model,' *Academy of Management Review* **16**(2), 366–395.

Ruble, T. and K. Thomas: 1976, 'Support for a Two-dimensional Model of Conflict Behavior,' *Organizational Behavior and Human Performance* **16**, 145.

Swinyard, W. R., H. Rinne and A. K. Kau: 1990, 'The Morality of Software Piracy: A Cross-cultural Analysis,' *Journal of Business Ethics*, 655–664.

◇

12.2 Ethics in the Trenches

◆

Robert D. Haas

A quick scan of today's headlines shows that ethical dilemmas are everywhere. Prudential-Bache Properties Inc. is sued by its investors, who allege it sold limited partnerships misleadingly; corruption and mismanagement cause the fortunes of Gitano Group Inc. to collapse; and executives of the American subsidiary of Honda Motor Co. Ltd. are charged by federal prosecutors with accepting bribes from dealers in exchange for franchises and hot-selling models.

What's going on? Have our ethical standards deteriorated, or are these headlines just a result of intensive media scrutiny? Can companies afford to be ethical in today's fiercely competitive environment, or are ethics a costly and convenient luxury?

I believe – and our company's experience demonstrates – that a company cannot *sustain* success unless it develops ways to anticipate and address ethical issues as they arise.

Drawing multinational lines

At Levi Strauss & Co., we're integrating ethics and other corporate values (such as empowerment and diversity) into every aspect of our business – from our human-resources programs to our vendor relationships. Let me illustrate our approach to linking ethics and

Source: Robert D. Haas, "Ethics in the Trenches," *Across the Board*, 1994, pp. 12–13. Reprinted by permission of Across the Board.

business conduct with an area of increasing importance to many multinational corporations – the sourcing of products in the developing world.

Levi Strauss operates in many countries and diverse cultures. We must take special care in selecting our contractors and those countries where our goods are produced in order to ensure that our products are being made in a manner that is consistent with our values and reputation. In early 1992, we developed and adopted a set of global-sourcing guidelines that established standards our contractors must meet to ensure that their practices are compatible with our values. For instance, our guidelines ban the use of child and prison labor. They stipulate certain environmental requirements. Working hours can't exceed 60 hours a week, with at least one day off in seven. Workers must be present voluntarily, have the right of free association, and not be exploited. At a minimum, wages must comply with the law and match prevailing local practice.

We also recognize that there are issues beyond the control of our contractors in some countries, so we developed a list of country-selection criteria. We will not source in countries where conditions, such as the human-rights climate, would run counter to our values and have an adverse effect on our global brand image. Our decision to undertake a phased withdrawal from China, for example, was due largely to human-rights concerns. We remain hopeful that the human-rights climate will improve so we can reverse our decision.

Similarly, we will not source in countries where circumstances expose our traveling employees to unreasonable risk; where the legal environment makes it difficult or jeopardizes our trademarks; and where political or social turmoil threatens our commercial interests. In mid-1992 we suspended sourcing in Peru due to concerns regarding employee safety. Recently, we were able to lift the suspension because conditions in Peru have improved, although we still have not placed any business in that country.

To develop our guidelines, we formed a working group made up of 15 employees from a broad cross-section of the company. The working group spent nine months at the task, during which time its members researched the views of key stakeholder groups – sewing-machine operators, vendors, contractors, plant managers, merchandisers, contract productions staff, shareholders, and others. The working group then used an ethical-decision-making model to guide its deliberations. The model is a process for making decisions by taking into consideration all stakeholders' issues.

Once our guidelines were in place, training sessions were held for 100 in-country managers who would have to enforce them with our 700 contractors worldwide. Training included case studies and exercises in decision-making. The managers then made presentations on the guidelines to our contractors, conducted on-site audits, and worked with them to make those improvements identified as necessary.

Vexing dilemmas

Drafting these guidelines was difficult. Applying them has forced us to find creative or unconventional solutions to vexing ethical dilemmas.

For example, we discovered that two of our manufacturing contractors in Bangladesh and one in Turkey employed underage workers. This was a clear violation of our guidelines, which prohibit the use of child labor. At the outset, it appeared that we had two options:

- instruct our contractors to fire these children, knowing that many are the sole wage earners for their families and if they lost their jobs, their families would face extreme hardship; or
- continue to employ the underage children, ignoring our company's stance against the use of child labor.

Other companies facing this issue might have simply instructed contractors to fire underage workers on the spot. For Levi Strauss, this was undesirable. But we couldn't ignore our corporate values either. Looking beyond the obvious options, we came up with a different approach that led to positive benefits all around.

The contractors agreed to pay the underage workers their salaries and benefits while they go to school. (They do not work during this time.) Levi Strauss pays for books, tuition, and uniforms. When the children are of working age, they will be offered full-time jobs in the plant, which they are not required to take. Today, 14 children are attending school in Bangladesh, while another six are in school in Turkey.

And how did Levi Strauss benefit? We were able to retain three quality contractors who play an important role in our worldwide sourcing strategy. At the same time, our value and brand image were protected.

At times, adhering to these standards has added costs. To continue working for us, some contractors had to add emergency exits and staircases, improve ventilation or bathroom facilities, reduce crowding, and invest in water-treatment systems. The costs of these requirements were passed on to us in the form of higher unit prices. In other cases, we have forgone cheaper sources of production due to unsatisfactory working conditions or concerns about the country of origin.

Conventional wisdom holds that these added costs place us at a competitive disadvantage. Certainly, they limit our options and squeeze profit margins. But over the years, we have found that decisions that emphasize cost to the exclusion of all other factors do not best serve a company's – or its shareholders' – long-term interests. Our five straight years of record sales and earnings, and a doubling of the size of our business in as many years, support our conclusion.

Moreover, as a company that invests hundreds of millions of advertising dollars each year to create consumer preference for our products, we have a huge stake in protecting that investment. In today's world, an exposé on working conditions on *60 Minutes* can undo years of effort to build brand loyalty. Why squander an investment when, with foresight and commitment, reputational problems can be prevented?

But don't take our word for it. There is a growing body of research evidence from respected groups that shows a positive correlation between good corporate citizenship and financial performance. These studies underscore that companies driven by values and a sense of purpose that extends beyond just making money outperform those that focus only on short-term profits. The former have higher sales, sustain higher profits, and have stocks that outperform the market.

These findings mirror our experience. Our values-driven approach has helped us:

- identify contractors who really want to work for Levi Strauss;
- gain customer and consumer loyalty because they feel good about having us as a business partner or about purchasing our products;
- attract and retain the best employees;

- improve the morale and trust of employees because the company's values more closely mirror their own personal values;
- initiate business in established and emerging markets because government and community leaders have a better sense of what we stand for and what to expect from us; and
- maintain credibility during times of unplanned events or crisis.

The conclusion is clear: There are important commercial benefits to be gained from managing your business in a responsible way that best serves the enterprise's long-term interests. The opposite is equally clear: There are dangers of not doing so.

◇

12.3 Negotiating with "Romans"

◆

Stephen E. Weiss

"Smith," an American, arrived at the French attorney's Paris office for their first meeting. Their phone conversations had been in French, and Smith, whose experience with the language included ten years of education in the United States, a year of residence in France with a French family, and annual trips to Paris for the previous seven years, expected to use French at this meeting. "Dupont," the Frenchman, introduced himself in French. His demeanor was poised and dignified; his language, deliberate and precise. Smith followed Dupont's lead, and they went on to talk about a mutual acquaintance. After ten minutes, Dupont shifted the topic by inquiring about Smith's previous work in international negotiations. One of Dupont's words – "opérations" – surprised Smith, and he hesitated to respond. In a split second, Dupont, in fluent English, asked: "Would you like to speak in English?"[1]

Smith used the approach to cross-cultural interaction most widely advocated in the West, with a history dating back to St. Augustine: "When in Rome, do as the Romans do." It had seemed to be a reasonable way to convey cooperativeness, sensitivity to French culture, and respect for Dupont as an individual. But Smith

---

Source: Stephen E. Weiss, "Negotiating with Romans," *Sloan Management Review*, Spring 1994, pp. 52–61. Reprinted by permission of Sloan Management Review.

overlooked important considerations, as have many other people who continue to recommend or follow this approach.[2]

The need for guidance for cross-cultural negotiators is clear. Every negotiator belongs to a group or society with its own system of knowledge about social interaction – its own "script" for behavior.[3] Whether the boundaries of the group are ethnic, organizational, ideological, or national, its culture influences members' negotiations – through their conceptualizations of the process, the ends they target, the means they use, and the expectations they hold of counterparts' behavior. There is ample evidence that such negotiation rules and practices vary across cultures.[4] Thus cross-cultural negotiators bring into contact unfamiliar and potentially conflicting sets of categories, rules, plans, and behaviors.

Doing as "Romans" do has not usually resolved this conflict effectively. (Throughout this article, the terms "Romans" and "non-Romans" are used as shorthand for "other-culture negotiators" and "own-culture negotiators," respectively.) "Fitting in" requires capabilities that relatively few non-Romans possess; most cultures involve much more than greeting protocols.[5] The approach takes for granted that Romans accept a non-Roman's behaving like a Roman when, actually, many Romans believe in at least some limits for outsiders.[6] Also, the approach presumes, misleadingly, that a Roman will always act Roman with a non-Roman in Rome.

Today's challenges should motivate a cross-cultural negotiator to search for additional approaches or strategies. An American negotiator may meet on Tuesday with a group of Japanese who speak through an interpreter and meet on Thursday one-on-one with a Japanese who is fluent in English and a long-time personal friend. In addition, geographical referents are blurring: just off of Paris's Boulevard St. Germain, an American can go to a Japanese restaurant in search of Japanese food and customs, yet find there Chinese waiters who speak Chinese to each other and French to their customers. Indeed, Americans negotiate with Japanese not only in Tokyo and Los Angeles but at third sites such as London. They may forgo face-to-face meetings to communicate by fax, E-mail, telephone, or video conference. Some of these negotiators have one day to finalize a sale; others have fourteen months to formulate a joint venture agreement. This variety of people and circumstances calls for more than one strategic approach.

What are the options for conducting negotiations in culturally sensitive ways? What should non-Roman negotiators do, especially when they lack the time and skills available to long-time expatriates?[7] How should the non-Roman businessperson prepare to use a culturally responsive strategy for negotiation with a particular Roman individual or group in a particular set of circumstances?

This article presents a range of eight culturally responsive strategies for Americans and other groups involved in cross-cultural negotiations at home and abroad. The corresponding framework takes into account the varying capabilities of different negotiators across different circumstances and thus provides options for *every* cross-cultural negotiator. Among other benefits, it enables a negotiator to move beyond the popular, one-size-fits-all lists of "dos and don'ts" for negotiating in a particular culture to see that what is appropriate really depends on the negotiating strategy. In short, this article offers the manager a broadened, realistic view of strategies for effective cross-cultural negotiation.

Eight culturally responsive strategies

Stories of cross-cultural conflict – faux pas and "blunders" – abound.[8] They highlight feelings of anxiety, disorientation, misunderstanding, and frustration, and they tempt negotiators to try to minimize apparent behavioral differences by "matching" or "imitating" their counterparts' ways. But there are more fundamental goals for a cross-cultural negotiator.

> *Consider what often happens when Americans negotiate with Japanese. Viewing negotiation as a process of exchange involving several proposal-counterproposal iterations, Americans inflate their demands in initial proposals and expect later to give and receive concessions. Their Japanese counterparts often do not promptly reciprocate with a counterproposal. Thus the Americans offer concessions, hoping that they will kick the exchange model – "the negotiations" – into gear. The Japanese, however, ask many questions. By the end of the talks, the Americans feel frustrated with the extent of their concessions and conclude that Japanese do not negotiate. Although the Americans may believe that the Japanese are shrewdly trying to determine how much their American counterparts will concede, it is quite likely that these Japanese are operating from a different model of negotiation: negotiation as a process of gathering*

information, which, when consistent and complete, will reveal a "correct, proper, and reasonable" solution.[9]

Research on communication suggests that the minimal, fundamental goal for non-Romans is to ensure that both sides perceive that the pattern of interaction makes sense.[10] For negotiation to occur, non-Romans must at least recognize those ideas and behaviors that Romans intentionally put forward as part of the negotiation process (and Romans must do the same for non-Romans). Parties must also be able to interpret these behaviors well enough to distinguish common from conflicting positions, to detect movement from positions, and to respond in ways that maintain communication. Yet a non-Roman's own script for negotiation rarely entails the knowledge or skills to make such interpretations and responses.

Figure 12.3.1 shows the range of negotiation characteristics that may vary across cultures. The basic concept of the process, for instance, may be one of distributive bargaining, joint problem solving, debate, contingency bargaining, or nondirective discussion. Groups and organizations may select their negotiators for their knowledge, experience, personal attributes, or status. Protocol may range from informal to formal; the desired outcome may range from a contract to an implicit understanding.

A culturally responsive strategy, therefore, should be designed to align the parties' negotiating scripts or otherwise bring about a mutually coherent form of negotiator interaction. This definition does *not* assume that the course of action is entirely premeditated; it can emerge over time. But a culturally responsive strategy does involve a clear goal and does consist of means by which to attain it. Effectively implemented, such a strategy enables the negotiators to convey their respective concerns and to respond to each other's concerns as they attempt to reach agreement.

By contrast, strategies that do not consider cultural factors are naive or misconceived. They may sometimes be successful for non-Romans, but they are hardly a reliable course of action. One such strategy is to deliberately ignore ethnic or other group-based differences and operate as if "business is business anywhere in the world." A "business is business" approach does not avoid culture; it actually represents a culture, one usually associated with U.S. businesspeople or a cosmopolitan elite. Negotiators cannot blithely assume the predominance of this particular business culture represented in their negotiations.

General Model

1. Basic Concept of Process

   Distributive bargaining / Joint problem-solving / Debate / Contingency bargaining / Nondirective discussion

2. Most Significant Type of Issue

   Substantive / Relationship-based / Procedural / Personal-internal

Role of the Individual

3. Selection of Negotiators

   Knowledge / Negotiating experience / Personal attributes / Status

4. Individuals' Aspirations

   Individual ◄————————————► Community

5. Decision Making in Groups

   Authoritative ◄————————————► Consensual

Interaction: Dispositions

6. Orientation toward Time

   Monochronic ◄————————————► Polychronic

7. Risk-Taking Propensity

   High ◄————————————► Low

8. Bases of Trust

   External sanctions / Other's reputation / Intuition / Shared experiences

Interaction: Process

9. Concern with Protocol

   Informal ◄————————————► Formal

10. Communication Complexity

    Low ◄————————————► High

11. Nature of Persuasion

    Direct experience / Logic / Tradition / Dogma / Emotion / Intuition

Outcome

12. Form of Agreement

    Contractual ◄————————————► Implicit

Figure 12.3.1 Cultural Characteristics of Negotiation

Source: Adapted from S. E. Weiss with W. Stripp, *Negotiating with Foreign Business Persons* (New York: New York University Graduate School of Business Administration, Working Paper #85–6, 1985), p. 10.

The framework shown in Figure 12.3.2 organizes eight culturally responsive strategies according to the negotiator's level of familiarity with the counterpart's culture; the counterpart's familiarity with the negotiator's culture; and the possibility for explicit coordination of approaches.[11] For the sake of clarity, it focuses on negotiations between two parties, each belonging to one predominant culture.

"Familiarity" is a gauge of a party's current knowledge of a culture (in particular, its negotiation scripts) *and* ability to use that knowledge competently in social interactions.[12] Operationally, high familiarity denotes fluency in a predominant Roman language, extensive prior exposure to the culture, and a good track record in previous social interactions with Romans (which includes making correct attributions of their behavior).[13] This is no mean accomplishment; it takes some twenty-four to thirty-six months of gradual adaptation and learning for expatriates to "master" how to behave appropriately.[14] Note that negotiators can consider using the strate-

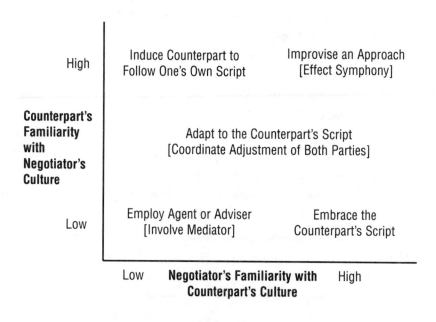

Brackets indicate a joint strategy, which requires deliberate consultation with counterpart.
At each level of familiarity, a negotiator can consider feasible the strategies designated at
that level and any lower level.

Figure 12.3.2 Culturally Responsive Strategies and Their Feasibility

gies feasible at their level of familiarity and *any* strategies correspond-ing to lower levels of familiarity.

The strategies in brackets in the figure are those that require coordination between parties. Although all negotiators must ulti-mately coordinate their approaches with counterparts during the talks, if only tacitly, sometimes parties can explicitly address coordi-nation and coherence issues.

Low familiarity with counterpart's culture

The negotiator who has had little experience with a counterpart's culture has a choice of two culturally responsive strategies and, depending on the counterpart's familiarity with the negotiator's culture, a possible third. If the counterpart's familiarity level is low, neither party is well equipped cross-culturally; their interaction can be facilitated by changing the people involved.[15] That is, the negotia-tor can employ an agent or adviser or involve a mediator. If the counterpart's familiarity level is high, a third strategy becomes feasi-ble: inducing the Roman to follow the negotiating script of one's own cultural group.

• **Employ Agent or Adviser.** To augment his or her own capabili-ties, a business negotiator can employ cultural experts, translators, outside attorneys, financial advisers, or technical experts who have at least moderate and preferably high familiarity with both the coun-terpart's and the negotiator's cultures. These experts serve two dis-tinguishable roles, as "agents" who replace the negotiator at the negotiating table or as "advisers" who provide information and recommend courses of action to the negotiator.

> *In 1986, a U.S. chemical company that had bartered chemicals for tobacco from Zimbabwe hired an American commodities trader in London to negotiate the sale of the tobacco and some chemicals to Egyptian officials and executives. The Egyptians were offering payment in com-modities; the U.S. company sought $20 million cash. As an agent, the American trader engaged in lengthy meetings, rounds of thick coffee, and late-night talks with the Egyptians and succeeded in arranging cash sales of the Egyptian commodities to the United Kingdom, Bangla-desh, and other countries.[16]*

The value of this strategy depends on the agent's attributes. Skilled, reputable agents can interact very effectively with a negotiator's counterpart. However, their employment may give rise to issues of increased structural complexity, trust, and ownership of the process, not to mention possible cultural tensions between principal and agent.[17] Clearly decipherable by a counterpart, this strategy works well when the counterpart accepts it and the particular agent involved.

Employing an adviser involves other actions and effects.

Between 1983 and 1986, IBM prepared proposals for a personal computer plant for approval by Mexico's National Commission on Foreign Investment. The company hired Mexican attorneys, consulted local experts such as the American Chamber of Commerce and U.S. embassy staff, and met with high-level Mexican government officials. These advisers provided information about political and social cultures and the foreign investment review process, access to influential individuals, and assessments of the leanings of key decision makers on the commission.[18]

A negotiator can select this strategy unilaterally and completely control its implementation. Of all eight strategies, this one is the least decipherable, sometimes even undetectable, by the counterpart. It is also uniquely incomplete in that it does not directly provide a script for negotiating. The negotiator must go on to select, with or without the adviser's assistance, a complementary strategy.

• **Involve a Mediator.** The use of go-betweens, middlemen, brokers, and other intermediaries is a common practice within many cultures and represents a potentially effective approach to cross-cultural negotiation as well. It is a joint strategy; both negotiator and counterpart rely on a mutually acceptable third party to facilitate their interaction. In its most obvious form, the strategy involves contacting a mediator prior to negotiations and deliberately bringing him or her into the talks. A mediator may also emerge, as happens when the "introducer" (*shokaisha* in Japanese[19]) who first brought the negotiator to the counterpart continues to play a role or, in team-on-team negotiations, when an individual involved in the talks who does not initially have authority as a mediator, such as an interpreter, becomes a de facto mediator in the course of the negotiation. Such cross-cultural mediators should be at least moderately and preferably highly familiar with the cultures of both parties.

In the 1950s, an American truck manufacturer negotiated a deal to sell trucks to a Saudi contractor because of the intermediation of Adnan Khashoggi. Khashoggi, the son of the personal physician of the founder of Saudi Arabia, had met the manufacturer while in college in the United States and learned about the contractor's needs upon returning to Saudi Arabia. This was his first "deal," long before his involvement with Lockheed and Northrop. By the 1970s, each of his private jets reportedly contained two wardrobes: "one of three-piece suits, shirts, and ties; . . . the other of white cotton robes [and] headdresses, . . . the full traditional Arabian regalia."[20]

With this strategy, a negotiator faces some uncertainty about the negotiation process: Will the mediator use one side's negotiation script at the expense of the other's? If the mediator is from a third culture, will he or she use that culture's ways – or introduce something else?[21] In relying on a mediator, the negotiator relinquishes some control of the negotiation. Then again, the mediator can educate the negotiator about the counterpart's culture and bring out ideas and behavior from each side that make the interaction coherent. It is important to find an individual who is not only appropriately skilled but who will also maintain the respect and trust of both parties.[22]

- **Induce the Counterpart to Follow One's Own Script.** Deliberately inducing the counterpart to negotiate according to the model common in one's own culture is feasible when the counterpart is highly familiar with one's culture. Possibilities for inducement range from verbal persuasion to simply acting as if the counterpart will "come along" – as happens when Americans speak English to non-American counterparts known to speak English as a second language.

When U.S.-based ITT and CGE of France conducted merger talks in the mid-1980s, negotiators used "an American business – American M&A [merger and acquisition]" approach, according to French participants. The French went along with it (despite their unfavorable impressions that it consisted of a "vague" general concept of the deal, emphasis on speed, and formulation of long contracts), because only U.S. law and investment firms had the capacity to carry out this highly complex negotiation. Although their motivations are not exactly known, ITT lawyers have stated that their chief negotiator followed their own methodical style, one developed within ITT.[23]

The pros and cons of this strategy hinge on the counterpart's perception of the negotiator's motivations for pursuing it. The counterpart may conclude that the negotiator is naive or deliberately ignorant of cultural differences; arrogant; culturally proud but not antagonistic; or merely using an expedient strategy.[24] It is reported that IBM's Thomas Watson, Sr., once said: "It's easier to teach IBM to a Netherlander than to teach Holland to an American."[25] Using one's own ways could also be the result of mistakenly concluding that the two parties share one culture (e.g., Americans and English-speaking Canadians).

For this strategy to work most effectively, the negotiator should convey that it is not based on a lack of respect for the counterpart or for the counterpart's culture. It is the counterpart, after all, who is being called on to make an extra effort; even with a high level of familiarity with the negotiator's culture, a counterpart usually feels more skilled and at ease with his or her own ways. (Were the counterpart to *offer* to follow the negotiator's script, we would be talking about an embrace strategy by the counterpart, which is described below.)

Moderate familiarity with counterpart's culture

The negotiator who already has had some successful experience with a counterpart's culture gains two more strategic options, provided that the counterpart is at least moderately familiar with the negotiator's culture. The unilateral strategy is to adapt one's usual approach to the counterpart's. The joint version is to coordinate adjustment between the two cultures.

• **Adapt to the Counterpart's Script.** Negotiators often modify their customary behavior by not expressing it to its usual degree, omitting some actions altogether, and following some of the counterpart's ways. The adapt strategy refers to more than this behavior, however; it refers to a broad course of action usually prompted by a deliberate decision to make these modifications.[26]

In the early 1980s, American negotiators in the Toyota-Ford and GM-Toyota talks over car assembly joint ventures prepared by reading books such as James Clavell's Shogun *and Edwin Reischauer's* The Japanese, *watching classic Japanese films (e.g., "Kagemusha"), and frequenting Japanese restaurants. Then they modified their usual negotiating behavior by: (1) paying extra attention to comportment and protocol, (2) reducing their expectations about substantive progress in the first few meetings, (3) providing Japanese counterparts with extensive, upfront information about their company and the U.S. business environment, and (4) trying "not to change positions too much once they had been voiced."*[27]

A major challenge for the negotiator considering this strategy is to decide which aspects of his or her customary negotiating script to alter or set aside. The aspects most seriously in conflict with the counterpart's may not be easily changed or even readily apparent, and those most obviously in conflict or easily changed may not, once changed, markedly enhance the interaction. Marketing specialists have distinguished between customs to which non-Romans must conform, those to which non-Romans may but need not conform, and those from which non-Romans are excluded.[28] Although a marketing specialist has a fixed, one-sided target in seeking entry into the counterpart's arena, these distinctions may also guide some of the cross-cultural negotiator's deliberations.

A counterpart usually notices at least some evidence of a negotiator's use of the adapt strategy. Deciphering all of the modifications is difficult. It may also be difficult for a counterpart to distinguish an adapt strategy from a badly implemented embrace strategy (described below). Further, if both the negotiator and the counterpart pursue this strategy on their own initiative, their modifications may confuse rather than smooth the interaction. Still, a negotiator can independently make the choice to adapt and usually finds at least some areas within his or her capacity to do so.

• **Coordinate Adjustment of Both Parties.** The parties may develop, subtly or overtly, a joint approach for their discussions; they may negotiate the process of negotiation. The jointly developed script is usually a blend of elements from the two parties' cultures; it is not totally distinct from them yet not wholly of one or the other. It may take various forms.

> *At the outset of a 1988 meeting to discuss the telecommunications policies of France's Ministry of Industry and Tourism, the minister's chief of staff and his American visitor each voiced concern about speaking in the other's native language. They expressed confidence in their listening capabilities and lacked immediate access to an interpreter, so they agreed to proceed by each speaking in his own language. Their discussion went on for an hour that way, the American speaking in English to the Frenchman, and the Frenchman speaking in French to the American.*

In a special case of this strategy, the parties "bypass" their respective home cultures' practices to follow the negotiating script of an already existing, third culture with which both have at least moderate familiarity. The parties know enough about the other's culture to recognize the limits of their capabilities in it and the desirability of additional guidance for their interaction.

> *Negotiations over MCA's acquisition by Matsushita Electric Industrial Company in 1990 were conducted largely via interpreters. At one dinner, MCA's senior American investment banker and Matsushita's Japanese head of international affairs were stymied in their effort to communicate with each other until they discovered their fluency in the same second language. They conversed in French for the rest of the evening.*[29]

Professional societies, trade groups, educational programs and institutions, and various other associations can similarly provide members with third scripts for conduct. This phenomenon is dramatically illustrated, within and between teams, when people who do not share a language play volleyball or soccer socially. The sport provides a script for behavior.

Overall, this strategy has the benefits of the adapt strategy while minimizing the likelihood of incompatible "adjustments." For some Roman counterparts (e.g., Arabs and Chinese), verbally explicit implementation of this strategy for interaction will be awkward – even unacceptable.[30] Other groups' members will appreciate its decipherability and the shared burden of effort that it implies. Since both parties must go along with it, the negotiator's opportunity to "veto" also preserves some control over its implementation.

High familiarity with counterpart's culture

Finally, the negotiator highly familiar with a counterpart's culture can realistically contemplate, not only the five aforementioned strategies, but at least one and possibly two more. If the counterpart is not familiar with the negotiator's culture, the negotiator can unilaterally embrace the other's negotiating script (i.e., "do as the Romans do"). If both parties are highly familiar with each other's cultures, they can jointly or unilaterally search for or formulate a negotiating script that focuses more on the individuals and circumstances involved than on the broader cultures. Such strategies may radically change the process.

- **Embrace the Counterpart's Script.** The embrace strategy calls for the negotiator to use the negotiation approach typical of the counterpart's culture.

> *In the 1970s, Coca-Cola undertook negotiations with a state-run, foreign trade organization in the People's Republic of China in order to produce and sell cola drinks there. The company sent one of its research chemists, a China-born man with no business background, to Cambridge University to study Chinese language and culture studies for a full year. Later acclaimed to be highly knowledgeable about China, this chemist was the most active negotiator for Coca-Cola in what became a ten-year endeavor.*[31]

Relatively few individuals should attempt this strategy. It demands a great deal of the negotiator, especially when the cultures involved differ greatly. In general, it requires bilingual, bicultural individuals – those who have generally enjoyed long-term overseas residence.

When implemented well, especially when very different cultures are involved, this strategy is clearly decipherable by a counterpart. (When it is not, a counterpart may confuse it with an adapt strategy.) Furthermore, the embrace strategy can make the interaction relatively easy and comfortable for the counterpart. The strategy requires considerable effort by the negotiator, and its implementation remains largely – but not completely – within the negotiator's control.

- **Improvise an Approach.** To improvise is to create a negotiation script as one negotiates, focusing foremost on the counterpart's particular attributes and capabilities and on the circumstances. Although all negotiators should pay some attention to the Roman counterpart as an individual, not all can or should improvise. The term is used here as it is used in music, not in the colloquial sense of "winging it" or of anyone being able to do it. Musical improvisation requires some preconception or point of departure and a model (e.g., a melody, basic chord structure) that sets the scope for performance. Similarly, the negotiator who improvises knows the parties' home cultures and is fully prepared for their influence but can put them in the background or highlight them as negotiation proceeds.

> *In the early 1990s, Northern Telecom, a Canadian-owned telecommunications equipment supplier with many Americans in its executive ranks and headquarters in both Mississauga, Ontario, and McLean, Virginia, maintained a "dual identity." Its personnel dealt with each other on*

either an American or a Canadian basis. On the outside, the company played up its Canadian identity with some governments (those unenthusiastic about big American firms, or perhaps not highly familiar with American ways), and played up its American identity with others.[32]

This strategy is feasible only when both parties are highly familiar with the other's culture. Without that level of familiarity, the negotiator would not know what the counterpart is accustomed to or how he or she is affected, and would not be able to invoke or create ways to relate to the counterpart effectively; nor would the counterpart recognize or respond to these efforts appropriately. At the same time, since the counterpart is highly skilled in at least two cultures and may introduce practices from both or either one of them, it is extremely important to consider the counterpart as an individual, not just as a member of a culture. High familiarity enables the negotiator to do just that, because he or she does not need to devote as much effort to learning about the counterpart's culture as other negotiators do.

During the Camp David "peace" talks between Egypt, Israel, and the United States in the late 1970s, then President Jimmy Carter set up a one-on-one meeting with Prime Minister Menachem Begin to try to break an impasse. Carter took along photos of Begin's eight grandchildren, on the backs of which he had handwritten their names. Showing these photos to Begin led the two leaders into talking about their families and personal expectations and revitalized the intergovernmental negotiations.[33]

This strategy is often used at high levels, especially at critical junctures, but it need not be limited to that. It can counteract the treatment of a counterpart as an abstraction (e.g., stereotype) and can facilitate the development of empathy. It also seems particularly efficacious with counterparts from cultures that emphasize affective, relationship factors over task accomplishment and creativity or presence over convention.

On the down side, the cultural responsiveness of the improvise strategy is not always decipherable by the counterpart. When a top-level negotiator is involved, the counterpart may assume that the negotiator's strategy is to appeal to status or authority rather than to recognize cultural issues. If the strategy overly "personalizes" negotiation, its implementation can lead to the kinds of problems once pointed out in former U.S. Secretary of State Henry Kissinger's "personal diplomacy": becoming too emotionally involved, failing to delegate, undercutting the status of other possible representatives, and ignoring those one does not meet or know.[34] The strategy may not be appropriate for all cultures and may be difficult to orchestrate by a team of negotiators. It also offers fewer concrete prescriptions for action and greater uncertainty than the four other unilateral strategies. Nevertheless, its malleability should continue to be regarded as a major attribute.

• **Effect Symphony.** This strategy represents an effort by the negotiator to get both parties to transcend exclusive use of either home culture by exploiting their high familiarity capabilities. They may improvise an approach, create and use a new script, or follow some other approach not typical of their home cultures. One form of coordination feasible at this level of familiarity draws on both home cultures.

For their negotiations over construction of the tunnel under the English Channel, British and French representatives agreed to partition talks and alternate the site between Paris and London. At each site, the negotiators were to use established, local ways, including the language. The two approaches were thus clearly punctuated by time and space. Although each side was able to use its customary approach some of the time, it used the script of the other culture the rest of the time.[35]

Effecting symphony differs from coordinating adjustment, which implies some modification of a culture's script, in that both cultures' scripts may be used in their entirety. It is also one resolution of a situation where both parties start out independently pursuing induce or embrace strategies. Perhaps the most common form of effecting symphony is using a third culture, such as a negotiator subculture.

Many United Nations ambassadors, who tend to be multilingual and world-traveled, interact more comfortably with each other than with their compatriots.[36] Similarly, a distinct culture can be observed in the café and recreation area at INSEAD, the European Institute of Business Administration, which attracts students from thirty countries for ten intensive months.

Overall, the effect symphony strategy allows parties to draw on special capabilities that may be accessible only by going outside the full-time use of their home cultures' conventions. Venturing into these uncharted areas introduces some risk. Furthermore, this strategy, like other joint strategies, requires the counterpart's cooperation; it cannot be unilaterally effected. But then, as former U.S.

Ambassador to Japan Edwin Reischauer suggested about diplomatic protocol, a jointly established culture – the "score" of a symphony – makes behavior predictable.[37] It can also make it comprehensible and coherent.

Implications

A cross-cultural negotiator is thus not limited to doing as the Romans do or even doing it "our way" or "their way." There are eight culturally responsive strategies. They differ in their degree of reliance on existing scripts and conventions, in the amount of extra effort required of each party, and in their decipherability by the counterpart. As a range of options, these strategies offer the negotiator flexibility and a greater opportunity to act effectively.

Because the strategies entail difference scripts and approaches, they also allow the negotiator to move beyond the simplistic lists of behavioral tips favored to date in American writings. For example, an American working with Japanese counterparts is usually advised to behave in a reserved manner, learn some Japanese words, and exercise patience.[38] Such behavior applies primarily to an adapt strategy, however, and different strategies call for different concepts and behaviors. Table 12.3.1 gives some examples of how an American might behave with Japanese counterparts, depending on the unilateral strategy employed.

Similarly, for his meeting with Dupont in Paris, Smith could have considered strategies other than "embrace" and its associated script. An adapt strategy may not have necessitated speaking exclusively in French. Table 12.3.2 suggests some ways he might have behaved, given each unilateral strategy. Smith might also have contemplated using strategies in combination (e.g., "adapt," then "embrace"), especially if meetings had been scheduled to take place over a number of months.

At the same time, only the negotiator highly familiar with the counterpart's culture can realistically consider using all eight strategies. The value of high familiarity, as a current capability or as an aspiration to achieve, should be clear. The value of the cultural focus should also be clear, notwithstanding the importance of also focusing on the individual counterpart (Part 2 of this article will expand on this point). Culture provides a broad context for under-

Table 12.3.1   Recommended Behavior for Americans Negotiating with the Japanese*
(by type of culturally responsive strategy)

Employ
- Use "introducer" for initial contacts (e.g., general trading company).
- Employ an agent the counterpart knows and respects.
- Ensure that the agent/adviser speaks fluent Japanese.

Induce
- Be open to social interaction and communicate directly.
- Make an extreme initial proposal, expecting to make concessions later.
- Work efficiently to "get the job done."

Adapt
- Follow some Japanese protocol (reserved behavior, name cards, gifts).
- Provide a lot of information (by American standards) up front to influence the counterpart's decision making early.
- Slow down your usual timetable.
- Make informed interpretations (e.g., the meaning of "it is difficult").
- Present positions later in the process, more firmly and more consistently.

Embrace
- Proceed according to an information-gathering, *nemawashi* (not exchange) model.
- "Know your stuff" cold.
- Assemble a team (group) for formal negotiations.
- Speak in Japanese.
- Develop personal relationships; respond to obligations within them.

Improvise
- Do homework on the individual counterpart(s) and circumstances.
- Be attentive and nimble (improvising entails different behaviors for different Japanese).
- Invite the counterpart to participate in mutually enjoyed activities or interests (e.g., golf).

*These are examples, not a complete listing, of attitudes and behaviors implied by a negotiator's use of each strategy.

standing the ideas and behavior of new counterparts as well as established acquaintances. It also enables the negotiator to notice commonalities in the expectations and behavior of individual members of a team of counterparts, to appreciate how the team works as a whole, and to anticipate what representatives and constituents will do when they meet away from the cross-cultural negotiation. As long as the negotiator intends to go on negotiating with other Romans, it behooves him or her to pay attention to commonalities

Table 12.3.2   Recommended Behavior for Americans Negotiating with the French*
(by type of culturally responsive strategy)

Employ
- Employ an agent well-connected in business and government circles.
- Ensure that the agent/adviser speaks fluent French.

Induce
- Be open to social interaction and communicate directly.
- Make an extreme initial proposal, expecting to make concessions later.
- Work efficiently to "get the job done."

Adapt
- Follow some French protocol (greetings and leave-takings, formal speech).
- Demonstrate an awareness of French culture and business environment.
- Be consistent between actual and stated goals and between attitudes and behavior.
- Defend views vigorously.

Embrace
- Approach negotiation as a debate involving reasoned argument.
- Know the subject of negotiation *and* broad environmental issues (economic, political, social).
- Make intellectually elegant, persuasive yet creative presentations (logically sound, verbally precise).
- Speak in French.
- Show interest in the counterpart as an individual but remain aware of the strictures of social and organizational hierarchies.

Improvise
- Do homework on the individual counterpart(s) and circumstances.
- Be attentive and nimble (improvising entails different behaviors for different French individuals).
- Invite counterpart to participate in mutually enjoyed activities or interests (e.g., dining out, tennis).

*These are examples, not a complete listing, of attitudes and behaviors implied by a negotiator's use of each strategy.

---

across negotiation experiences with individual Romans – to focus on cultural aspects – in order to draw lessons that enhance effectiveness in future negotiations.

As presented here, the eight culturally responsive negotiation strategies reflect one perspective: feasibility in light of the negotiator's and counterpart's familiarity with each other's cultures. That is a major basis for selecting a strategy, but it is not sufficient. This framework maps what is doable; it should not be interpreted as recommending that the best strategies for every negotiation are those at the highest levels of familiarity – that improvising is always better than employing advisers. The best strategy depends on additional factors. In its own right, the framework represents a marked shift from prevailing wisdom and a good point of departure for today's cross-cultural negotiators.

References

1. All examples that are not referenced come from personal communication or the author's experiences.

2. Contemporary academic advocates of this approach for negotiators include:
   S. T. Cavusgil and P. N. Ghauri, *Doing Business in Developing Countries* (London: Routledge, 1990), pp. 123–124;
   J. L. Graham and R. A. Herberger, Jr., "Negotiators Abroad – Don't Shoot from the Hip," *Harvard Business Review,* July-August 1983, p. 166; and
   F. Posses, *The Art of International Negotiation* (London: Business Books, 1978), p. 27.

3. The concept of a script has been applied by:
   W. B. Gudykunst and S. Ting-Toomey, *Culture and Interpersonal Communication* (Newbury Park, California: Sage, 1988), p. 30.

4. See, for example, N. C. G. Campbell et al., "Marketing Negotiations in France, Germany, the United Kingdom, and the United States," *Journal of Marketing* 52 (1988): 49–62; and
   J. L. Graham et al., "Buyer-Seller Negotiations around the Pacific Rim: Differences in Fundamental Exchange Processes," *Journal of Consumer Research* 15 (1988): 48–54.
   For evidence from diplomacy, see:
   R. Cohen, *Negotiating across Cultures* (Washington, D.C.: U.S. Institute of Peace Press, 1991); and
   G. Fisher, *International Negotiation: A Cross-Cultural Perspective* (Yarmouth, Maine: Intercultural Press, 1980).

5. See J. L. Graham and N. J. Adler, "Cross-Cultural Interaction: The International Comparison Fallacy," *Journal of International Business Studies* 20 (1989): 515–537. The authors conclude that their subjects adapted to some extent, but a lack of adaptability could also be convincingly argued from their data.

6. For an experimental study showing that moderate adaptation by Asians in the United States was more effective than substantial adaptation, see:
   J. N. P. Francis, "When in Rome? The Effects of Cultural Adaptation on Intercultural Business Negotiations," *Journal of International Business Studies* 22 (1991): 403–428.

7. The majority of leaders of North American firms still lack any expatriate experience and foreign language ability, according to:
   N. J. Adler and S. Bartholomew, "Managing Globally Competent People," *The Executive* 6 (1992): 58.

8. See, for example, D. Ricks and V. Mahajan, "Blunders in International Marketing: Fact or Fiction?" *Long Range Planning* 17 (1984): 78–83. Note that the impact of faux pas may vary in magnitude across cultures. In some cultures, inappropriate behavior constitutes an unforgivable transgression, not a "slip-up."

9. M. Blaker, *Japanese International Negotiating Style* (New York: Columbia University Press, 1977), p. 50.

10. See V. E. Cronen and R. Shuter, "Forming Intercultural Bonds," *Intercultural Communication Theory: Current Perspectives,* ed. W. B. Gudykunst (Beverly Hills, California: Sage, 1983), p. 99. Their concept of "coherence" neither presumes that the interactants make the same sense of the interaction nor depends always on mutual understanding.

11. Although similar in form, this plot differs in theme from the "model of conflict-handling responses" developed by:
    K. W. Thomas and R. H. Kilmann, *Thomas-Kilmann Conflict Mode Instrument* (Tuxedo, New York: Xicom, Inc., 1974).
    It also differs in key variables from the "Dual Concerns" model of:
    D. G. Pruitt and J. Z. Rubin, *Social Conflict: Escalation, Stalemate, and Settlement* (New York: Random House, 1986), p. 35ff.
    Moreover, neither of these models appears to have yet been applied cross-culturally.

12. This notion of familiarity draws on Dell Hymes's concept of communicative competence. See:
    R. E. Cooley and D. A. Roach, "A Conceptual Framework," *Competence in Communication,* ed. R. N. Bostrom (Beverly Hills, California: Sage, 1984), pp. 11–32.

13. See, for example, R. W. Brislin et al., *Intercultural Interactions* (Beverly Hills, California: Sage, 1986);

A. T. Church, "Sojourner Adjustment," *Psychological Bulletin* 91 (1982): 545–549;

P. C. Earley, "Intercultural Training for Managers," *Academy of Management Review* 30 (1987): 685–698; and

J. S. Black and M. Mendenhall, "Cross-cultural Training Effectiveness: A Review and Theoretical Framework for Future Research," *Academy of Management Review* 15 (1990): 113–136.

14. J. S. Black and M. Mendenhall, "The U-Curve Adjustment Hypothesis Revisited: A Review and Theoretical Framework," *Journal of International Business Studies* 22 (1991): 225–247.

15. Changing the parties involved is commonly mentioned in dispute resolution literature. See, for example:
R. Fisher and W. Ury, *Getting to Yes* (Boston: Houghton Mifflin, 1981), pp. 71–72.

16. S. Lohr, "Barter Is His Stock in Trade," *New York Times Business World,* 25 September 1988, pp. 32–36.

17. For empirical research on negotiating representatives and their boundary role, constituents, and accountability within a culture, see:
D. G. Pruitt, *Negotiation Behavior* (New York: Academic Press, 1981), pp. 41–44, 195–197.
With respect to agents, see:
J. Z. Rubin and F. E. A. Sander, "When Should We Use Agents? Direct vs. Representative Negotiation," *Negotiation Journal,* October 1988, pp. 395–401.

18. S. E. Weiss, "The Long Path to the IBM-Mexico Agreement: An Analysis of the Microcomputer Investment Negotiations, 1983–1986," *Journal of International Business Studies* 21 (1990): 565–596.

19. J. L. Graham and Y. Sano, *Smart Bargaining: Doing Business with the Japanese* (New York: Ballinger, 1989), p. 30.

20. R. Lacey, *The Kingdom: Arabia and the House of Sa'ud* (New York: Avon Books, 1981), pp. 464–466. See also:
P. E. Tyler, "Double Exposure: Saudi Arabia's Middleman in Washington," *The New York Times Magazine,* 7 June 1992, pp. 34ff.

21. For additional ideas about what a mediator may do, see:
P. J. D. Carnevale, "Strategic Choice in Mediation," *Negotiation Journal* 2 (1986): 41–56.

22. See J. Z. Rubin, "Introduction," *Dynamics of Third Party Intervention,* ed. J. Z. Rubin (New York: Praeger, 1981), pp. 3–43; and S. Touval and I. W. Zartman, "Mediation in International Conflicts"

Mediation Research, eds. K. Kressel and D. G. Pruitt (San Francisco: Jossey-Bass, 1989), pp. 115–137.

23. S. E. Weiss, "Negotiating the CGE-ITT Telecommunications Merger, 1985–1986: A Framework-then-Details Process," paper presented at the Academy of International Business annual meeting, November 1991.

24. Such positions have been associated with people in nations with long-established cultures, such as China, France, and India. For instance, some Mexican high officials who speak English fluently have insisted on speaking Spanish in their meetings with Americans. While this position could be influenced by the history antipathy in the U.S.-Mexico relationship and the officials' concern for the status of their office, it also evinces cultural pride.

25. "IBM World Trade Corporation," Harvard Business School, reprinted in S. M. Davis, *Managing and Organizing Multinational Corporations* (New York: Pergamon Press, 1979), p. 53.

26. Adapting has been widely discussed in the literature. See, for example: S. Bochner, "The Social Psychology of Cross-Cultural Relations," *Cultures in Contact,* ed. S. Bochner (Oxford: Pergamon, 1982), pp. 5–44.

27. S. E. Weiss, "Creating the GM-Toyota Joint Venture: A Case in Complex Negotiation," *Columbia Journal of World Business,* Summer 1987, pp. 23–37; and
S. E. Weiss, "One Impasse, One Agreement: Explaining the Outcomes of Toyota's Negotiations with Ford and GM," paper presented at the Academy of International Business annual meeting, 1988.

28. P. R. Cateora and J. M. Hess, *International Marketing* (Homewood, Illinois: Irwin, 1971), p. 407.

29. C. Bruck, "Leap of Faith," *The New Yorker,* 9 September 1991, pp. 38–74.

30. See C. Thubron, *Behind the Wall* (London: Penguin, 1987), pp. 158, 186–187.

31. L. Sloane, "Lee, Coke's Man in China," *The New York Times,* 5 February 1979, p. D2.

32. W. C. Symonds et al., "High-Tech Star," *Business Week,* 27 July 1992, pp. 55–56.

33. Found among the exhibits at the Carter Center Library and Museum, Atlanta, Georgia.

34. R. Fisher, "Playing the Wrong Game?" *Dynamics of Third Party Intervention*, ed. J. Z. Rubin (New York: Praeger, 1981), pp. 98–99, 105–106.
   On the additional problem of losing touch with constituencies, see the 1989–1991 Bush-Gorbachev talks described in:
   M. R. Beschloss and S. Talbott, *At the Highest Levels* (Boston: Little, Brown, 1993).

35. See C. Dupont, "The Channel Tunnel Negotiations, 1984–1986: Some Aspects of the Process and Its Outcome," *Negotiation Journal* 6 (1990): 71–80.

36. See, for example, C. F. Alger, "United Nations Participation as a Learning Experience," *Public Opinion Quarterly*, Summer 1983, pp. 411–426.

37. E. O. Reischauer, *My Life between Japan and America* (New York: Harper and Row, 1986), p. 183.

38. N. B. Thayer and S. E. Weiss, "Japan: The Changing Logic of a Former Minor Power," *National Negotiating Styles*, ed. H. Binnendijk (Washington, D. C.: Foreign Service Institute, U.S. Department of State, 1987), pp. 69–72.

◇

12.4 Managing Globally Competent People

◆

Nancy J. Adler and Susan Bartholomew

Top-level managers in many of today's leading corporations are losing control of their companies. The problem is not that they have mis-judged the demands created by an increasingly complex environment and an accelerating rate of environmental change, nor even that they have failed to develop strategies appropriate to the new challenges. The problem is that their companies are incapable of carrying out the sophisticated strategies they have developed. Over the past 20 years, strategic thinking has far outdistanced organizational capabilities.[1]

Today, people create national competitiveness, not, as suggested by classical economic theory, mere access to advantageous fac-tors of production.[2] Yet, human systems are also one of the major constraints in implementing global strategies. Not surprisingly therefore, human resource management has become "an important focus of top management attention, particularly in multinational enterprises."[3]

The clear issue is that strategy (the *what*) is internationalizing faster than implementation (the *how*) and much faster than individual managers and executives themselves (the *who*). "The challenges [therefore] are not the 'whats' of what-to-do, which are typically

---

Source: Nancy J. Adler and Susan Bartholomew, "Managing Globally Competent People," excerpted from *Academy of Management Executive*, August 1992, pp. 52–65. Reprinted by permission of The Academy of Management.

well-known. They are the 'hows' of managing human resources in a global firm."[4]

How prepared are executives to manage transnational companies? How capable are firms' human resource systems of recruiting, developing, retaining, and using globally competent managers and executives? A recent survey of major U.S. corporations found only six percent reporting foreign assignments to be essential for senior executive careers, with forty-nine percent believing foreign assignments to be completely immaterial.[5]

Which firms are leading in developing globally competent managers and executives, and which remain in the majority and lag behind? That majority, according to a recent survey of 1500 CEOs, will result in a lack of sufficient senior American managers prepared to run transnational businesses, forcing U.S. firms to confront the highest executive turn-over in history.[6]

This article recommends changes in global human resources management at two levels: individual and systemic. First, from an individual perspective, it recommends skills required by individual managers to be globally competent, highlighting those which transcend the historic competencies required of international and expatriate managers. Second, from a systems perspective, it recommends a framework for assessing globally competent human resource systems. It then shows that the majority of North American firms have much room for improvement in developing both globally competent managers and globally effective human resource systems.

By contrast, it describes the approaches of some of the world's leading firms that distinguish them from the majority. There is no question that world business is going global; the question raised in this article is how to create human systems capable of implementing transnational business strategies. Based on their research, the authors support the conclusion of the recent *21st Century Report* that "executives who perceive their international operations as shelves for second-rate managers are unsuited for the CEO job in the year 2000, or indeed any managerial job today."[7]

Transnationally competent managers

Not all business strategies are equally global, nor need they be. As will be described, a firm's business strategy can be primarily domestic, international, multinational, or transnational. However, to be effective, the firm's human resource strategy should be integrated with its business strategy. Transnational firms need a transnational business strategy. While superficially appearing to be a truism, transnational firms also need a transnational human resource system and transnationally competent managers.

As summarized in Table 12.4.1, transnationally competent managers require a broader range of skills and traditional international managers. First, transnational managers must understand the world-

Table 12.4.1 Transnationally competent managers

Transnational Skills	Transnationally Competent Managers	Traditional International Managers
Global Perspective	Understand worldwide business environment from a global perspective	Focus on a single foreign country and on managing relationships between headquarters and that country
Local Responsiveness	Learn about many cultures	Become an expert on one culture
Synergistic Learning	Work with and learn from people from many cultures simultaneously	Work with and coach people in each foreign culture separately or sequentially
	Create a culturally synergistic organizational environment	Integrate foreigners into the headquarters' national organizational culture
Transition and Adaptation	Adapt to living in many foreign cultures	Adapt to living in a foreign culture
Cross-cultural Interaction	Use cross-cultural interaction skills on a daily basis throughout one's career	Use cross-cultural interaction skills primarily on foreign assignments
Collaboration	Interact with foreign colleagues as equals	Interact within clearly defined hierarchies of structural and cultural dominance
Foreign Experience	Transpatriation for career and organization development	Expatriation or inpatriation primarily to get the job done

wide business environment from a global perspective. Unlike expatriates of the past, transnational managers are not focused on a single country nor limited to managing relationships between headquarters and a single foreign subsidiary. Second, transnational managers must learn about many foreign cultures' perspectives, tastes, trends, technologies, and approaches to conducting business. Unlike their predecessors, they do not focus on becoming an expert on one particular culture. Third, transnational managers must be skillful at working with people from many cultures simultaneously. They no longer have the luxury of dealing with each country's issues on a separate, and therefore sequential, basis. Fourth, similar to prior expatriates, transnational managers must be able to adapt to living in other cultures. Yet, unlike their predecessors, transnational managers need cross-cultural skills on a daily basis, throughout their career, not just during foreign assignments, but also on regular multicountry business trips and in daily interaction with foreign colleagues and clients worldwide. Fifth, transnational managers interact with foreign colleagues as equals, rather than from within clearly defined hierarchies of structural or cultural dominance and subordination. Thus, not only do the variety and frequency of cross-cultural interaction increase with globalization, but also the very nature of cross-cultural interaction changes.

The development of transnationally competent managers depends on firms' organizational capability to design and manage transnational human resource systems. Such systems, in turn, allow firms to implement transnational business strategies. Before investigating firms' capability to implement transnational business strategies, let us briefly review a range of global business strategies along with each strategy's requisite managerial skills.

The globalization of business: strategy, structure and managerial skills

Since World War II, industry after industry has progressed from dominantly domestic operations toward more global strategies. Historically, many firms progressed through four distinct phases: domestic, international, multinational, and transnational.[8] As firms progress towards global strategies, the portfolio of skills required of managers undergoes a parallel shift.

Domestic.   Historically, most corporations began as domestic firms. They developed new products or services at home for the domestic market. During this initial domestic phase, foreign markets, and hence international managerial skills, were largely irrelevant.

International.   As new firms entered, competition increased and each company was forced to search for new markets or resign itself to losing market share. A common response was to expand internationally, initially by exporting to foreign markets and later by developing foreign assembly and production facilities designed to serve the largest of those markets. To manage those foreign operations, firms often restructured to form a separate international division. Within the new international division, each country was managed separately, thus creating a multidomestic nature. Because the foreign operations were frequently seen as an extension – and therefore a replication – of domestic operations, they generally were not viewed as state of the art.

During this international phase, a hierarchical structure exists between the firm's headquarters and its various foreign subsidiaries. Power and influence are concentrated at corporate headquarters, which is primarily staffed by members of the headquarters' national culture. It is during this phase that firms often send their first home country managers abroad as expatriates. Cross-cultural interaction between expatriate managers and local subsidiary staff thus takes place within a clearly defined hierarchy in which headquarters has both structural and cultural dominance.

During this phase, international management is synonymous with expatriation. To be effective, expatriate managers must be competent at transferring technology to the local culture, managing local staff, and adapting business practices to suit local conditions. Specifically, international expatriate managers require cultural adaptation skills – as does their spouse and family – to adjust to living in a new environment and working with the local people. They must also acquire specific knowledge about the particular culture's perspectives, tastes, trends, technologies, and ways of doing business. Learning is thus single country focused – and culturally specific – during the international phase.

Multinational.   As competition continues to heighten, firms increasingly emphasize producing least-cost products and services.

To benefit from potential economies of scale and geographic scope, firms produce more standardized products and services. Because the prior phase's multidomestic structure can no longer support success, firms restructure to integrate domestic and foreign operations into worldwide lines of business, with sourcing, producing, assembling, and marketing distributed across many countries, and major decisions – which continue to be made at headquarters – strongly influenced by least-cost outcomes.

During the multinational phase, the hierarchical relationship remains between headquarters and foreign subsidiaries. In addition, with the increased importance of foreign operations to the core business, headquarters more tightly controls major decisions worldwide. However, headquarters' decisions are now made by people from a wider range of cultures than previously, many of whom are local managers from foreign subsidiaries posted on temporary "inpatriate" assignments at corporate headquarters. These "inpatriates" are not encouraged to express the diversity of national perspectives and cultural experience they represent. Rather, they are asked to adapt as the firm implicitly and explicitly integrates them into the organizational culture which is still dominated by the values of the headquarters' national culture. While multinational representation increases at headquarters, cultural dominance of the headquarters' national culture continues, remaining loosely coupled with structure.

For the first time, senior managers, those leading the worldwide lines of business, need to understand the world business environment. Similarly for the first time, senior managers must work daily with clients and employees from around the world to be effective. International and cross-cultural skills become needed for managers throughout the firm, not just for those few imminently leaving for foreign postings. Expatriates and "inpatriates" still require cultural adaptation skills and specific local knowledge, but these are not the dominant international skills required by most managers in a multinational firm. For the majority, learning needs grow beyond local context to encompass a need to understand the world business environment. In addition, multinational managers need to be skilled at working with clients and employees from many nations (rather than merely from a single foreign country), as well as at standardizing operations and integrating people from around the world into a common organizational culture.

Transnational. As competition continues to increase and produce lifecycles shorten dramatically, firms find it necessary to compete globally, based simultaneously on state-of-the-art, top quality products and services and least-cost production. Unlike the prior phase's emphasis on identical products that can be distributed worldwide, transnational products are increasingly mass-customized – tailored to each individual client's needs. Research and development demands increase as does the firm's need for worldwide marketing scope.

These dynamics lead to transnational networks of firms and divisions within firms, including an increasingly complex web of strategic alliances. Internationally, these firms distribute their multiple headquarters across a number of nations. As a result, transnational firms become less hierarchically structured than firms operating in the previous phases. As such, power is no longer centered in a single headquarters that is coincident with or dominated by any one national culture. As a consequence, both structural and cultural dominance are minimized, with cross-cultural interaction no longer following any pre-defined "passport hierarchy." It is for these firms that transnational human resource strategies are now being developed that emphasize organizational learning along with individual managerial skills.

To be effective, transnational managers need both the culturally specific knowledge and adaptation skills required in international firms, and the ability to acquire a worldwide perspective and to integrate worldwide diversity required in multinational firms. As a consequence, one of the transnational manager's primary skills is to exercise discretion in choosing when to be locally responsive and when to emphasize global integration.

Moreover, the integration required in transnational firms is based on cultural synergy – on combining the many cultures into a unique organizational culture – rather than on simply integrating foreigners into the dominant culture of the headquarters' nationality (as was the norm in prior phases). Transnational managers require additional new skills to be effective in their less hierarchical, networked firms: first, the ability to work with people of other cultures as equals; second, the ability to learn in order to continually enhance organizational capability. Transnational managers must learn how to collaborate with partners worldwide, gaining as much knowledge as possible from each interaction, and, transmitting that knowledge quickly and effectively throughout the worldwide network of operations. This requires managers who both want to learn and have the skills to quickly and continuously learn from people of other cultures.[9]

Transnational human resource systems

The development of such "transnationally competent managers," as discussed previously, depends upon firms' capability to design and manage transnational human resource systems. The function of human resource systems, in general, is to recruit, develop, and retain competent managers and executives. Beyond these core functions, we add utilization: human resource systems facilitate the effective "utilization" of those managers who have been recruited, developed, and retained. Therefore, a transnational human resource system is one that recruits, develops, retains and utilizes managers and executives who are competent transnationally.[10]

Three dimensions of a transnational human resource system

For a transnational human resource system to be effective, it must exhibit three characteristics: transnational scope, transnational representation, and transnational process. We will describe each briefly, and then discuss their implications for recruiting, developing, retaining, and using human resources.

Transnational Scope.   Transnational scope is the geographical context within which all major decisions are made. As Bartlett and Ghoshal have stated, global management is a "frame of mind," not a particular organizational structure.[11] Thus, to achieve global scope, executives and managers must frame major decisions and evaluate options relative to worldwide business dynamics. Moreover, they must benchmark their own and their firm's performance against worldclass standards. They can neither discuss nor resolve major issues within a narrower national or regional context. An example is Unilever's "Best Proven Practices." This British-Dutch consumer products firm identifies superior practices and innovations in its subsidiaries worldwide and then diffuses the outstanding approaches throughout the worldwide organization.[12]

Transnational representation. Transnational representation refers to the multinational composition of the firm's managers and executives. To achieve transnational representation, the firm's portfolio of key executives and managers should be as multinational as its worldwide distribution of production, finance, sales, and profits. Symbolically, firms achieve transnational representation through the well balanced portfolio of passports held by senior management. Philips, for example, maintains transnational representation by having "the corporate pool." This pool consists of mobile individuals representing more than fifty nationalities, each having at least five years of experience and ranked in the top twenty percent on performance, and all financed on a corporate budget.[13]

Transnational process. Transnational process reflects the firm's ability to effectively include representatives and ideas from many cultures in its planning and decision-making processes. Firms create transnational process when they consistently recognize, value, and effectively use cultural diversity within the organization; that is, when there is "no unintended leakage of culture specific systems and approaches."[14] Transnational process, however, is not the mere inclusion of people and ideas of many cultures; rather, it goes beyond inclusion to encompass cultural synergy – the combination of culturally diverse perspectives and approaches into a new transnational organizational culture. Cultural synergy requires "a genuine belief . . . that more creative and effective ways of managing people could be developed as a result of cross-cultural learning."[15] To create transnational process, executives and managers must be as skilled at working with and learning from people from outside their own culture as with same culture nationals.

Today's firms: how transnational?

A survey was conducted of fifty firms headquartered in the United States and Canada from a wide variety of industries to determine the extent to which their overall business strategy matched their current human resource system, as well as identifying the extent of globalization of their human resource strategies. The results paint a picture of extensive global business involvement. Unfortunately, however, similar involvement in recruiting, developing, retaining, and using globally competent managers is lacking.

Global strategic integration

The fifty firms made almost half of their sales abroad, and earned nearly forty percent of their revenues and profits outside of their headquarters' country (the United States or Canada). Similarly, almost two fifths of the fifty firms' employees worked outside the headquarters' country. Yet, when these firms reviewed their human resource systems as a whole, and their senior leadership in particular, they could not reveal nearly as global a portrait.

For example, in comparing themselves with their competitors, the fifty firms found themselves to be more global on overall business strategy, financial systems, production operations, and marketing. However, they found their human resource systems to be the least global functional area within their own organization. Moreover, unlike their assessement in other functional areas, they did not evaluate their human resource systems as being more global than those of their competitors.

Similarly, the senior leadership of the surveyed firms was less global on all three global indicators – scope, representation, and process – than each firm's overall business performance. For example, an average of only eight countries were represented among the most senior one hundred executives in each firm. Half of the companies reported fewer than four nationalities among the top one hundred executives. Firms therefore have less than a quarter of the international representation in their senior leadership (eight percent) as they have in their global business performance (ie., sales, revenues, and profits: forty percent). Similarly, of the same top one hundred executives in each firm, only fifteen percent were from outside of North America. This represents less than half the internationalization of the senior executive cadre (fifteen percent) as of business performance (forty percent). Moreover, using experience, rather than representation, yields similar results. Of the same one hundred leaders, almost three quarters lacked expatriate experience, with only a third reporting any international experience at all. Not surprisingly, less than one in five spoke a foreign language. On no measure of international experience is the senior leadership of these North American firms as international as the business itself.

Transnational human resource integration

Firms' organizational capability to implement transnational business strategies is supported by transnational human resource management systems. As discussed, such systems should exhibit all three dimensions – transnational scope, transnational representation, and transnational process. These three global dimensions are clearly important for each of the four primary components of human resource systems – recruiting, developing, retaining, and utilizing globally competent people. Each will therefore be discussed separately. Unfortunately, the results of this study indicate that firms' human resources management systems have not become global either as rapidly or as extensively as have their business strategies and structures.

Recruiting.   For recruiting decisions, transnational scope requires that firms consider their business needs and the availability of candidates worldwide. Similar to the firm's strategic business decisions, some recruiting decisions must enhance worldwide integration and coordination, others local responsiveness, and others the firm's ability to learn.[16] Local responsiveness requires that firms recruit people with a sophisticated understanding of each of the countries in which they operate; this includes recruiting host nationals. Worldwide integration requires that recruiting be guided by worldclass standards in selecting the most competent people from anywhere in the world for senior management positions. Individual and organizational learning requires that people be selected who are capable of simultaneously working with and learning from colleagues from many nations: people who are capable of creating cultural synergy.

Transnational representation in recruiting requires that firms select managers from throughout the world for potential positions anywhere in the world. In a literal sense, it requires that talent flows to opportunity worldwide, without regard to national passport.

Transnational process in recruiting requires that firms use search and selection procedures that are equally attractive to candidates from each target nationality. Selection criteria, including the methods used to judge competence, must not be biased to favor any one culture.

Similarly, incentives to join the firm must appeal to a broad range of cultures. The antithesis of transnational process was exhibited by one U.S. firm when it offered new college recruits from the Netherlands one of the same incentives it offers its American recruits: free graduate education. The Dutch candidates found this "benefit" amusing given that graduate education in the Netherlands – unlike in the United States – is already paid for by the government and thus free to all students.

Rather than encouraging high potential candidates, this particular incentive made Dutch students hesitate to join a firm that demonstrated such parochialism in its initial contact with them.

The fifty surveyed firms reported that their recruitment and selection activities were less than global in terms of scope, representation, and process.

Development. In managerial development, transnational scope means that managers' experiences both on-the-job and in formal training situations prepare them to work anywhere in the world with people from all parts of the world; that is, it prepares them to conduct the firm's business in a global environment. Transnational firms search worldwide for the best training and development options and select specific approaches and programs based on worldclass standards.

To achieve transnational representation, training and development programs must be planned and delivered by multinational teams as well as offered to multinational participants. To be transnational, programs cannot be planned by one culture (generally representatives of the headquarters' nationality) and simply exported for local delivery abroad. By contrast, using a transnational approach, American Express created a multinational design team at headquarters to develop training approaches and programs which were subsequently localized for delivery around the world. At no time did American cultural values dominate either the process or the programs.

Transnational process in development requires that the approaches taken effectively include all participating cultures. Thus, the process cannot encourage greater participation by one nationality to the exclusion of other nationalities. Ericsson and Olivetti provide examples of a transnational development approach. Each company created a management development center in which both the staff and executive participants come from all regions of the

world. To minimize the possibility of headquarters' cultural dominance, neither company located its managment development center
in the headquarters' country – Sweden or Italy – but rather both
chose another more culturally neutral country.[17]

For transnational firms, foreign assignments become a core component of the organizational and career development process.
"Transpatriates" from all parts of the world are sent to all other
parts of the world to develop their worldwide perspective and cross-
cultural skills, as well as developing the organization's cadre of
globally sophisticated managers. Foreign assignments in transnational firms are no longer used primarily to get a job done in a foreign
country (expatriation) or to socialize foreign country nationals into
the home country headquarters' culture ("inpatriation"), but rather
to enhance individual and organizational learning in all parts of
the system ("transpatriation"). Using a "transpatriation" approach,
Royal Dutch Shell, for example, uses multifunctional and multinational experience to provide corporate wide, transnational skills.
Shell's "aim is that every member of an operating company management team should have had international experience and that each
such team should include one expatriate . . . [Similarly, at IBM],
international experience is [considered] indispensable to senior positions."[18]

In the survey, the fifty firms reported that their training and
development opportunities were less than global on all three dimensions of human resource strategy: transnational scope, transnational
representation, and transnational process. . . . Similar to recruitment, training and development approaches currently are not nearly
as global as are overall business strategies. To reduce the gap between
the relative globalization of firms' strategies and their less-than-
global human resource systems, firms must learn how to recognize,
value, and use globally competent managers. As one surveyed executive summarized, closing the gaps begins by having "the key organizational development activity . . . focused on allowing people of
different nationalities to meet and to get to know each other, and,
through these linkages, to meet the needs of the company."

Retaining. Transnational scope in retaining managers means that
decisions about career paths must consider the firm's needs and
operations worldwide.

Performance incentives, rewards, and career opportunities must meet worldclass standards such that the firm does not lose its most competent people. Firms must benchmark excellence in their human resource systems against their most significant global competitors in the same ways that they assess the relative competitiveness of their research and development, production, marketing, and financial systems.

Transnational representation requires that organizational incentives and career path opportunities be equally accessible and appealing to managers from all nationalities. Firms with transnational human resource systems do not create a glass ceiling beyond which only members of the headquarters' nationality can be promoted.

Transnational process requires that the performance review and promotion systems include approaches which are equally appropriate to a broad range of nationalities. The process by which promotion and career path decisions are made should not be innately biased towards any one culture, nor should it exclude particular cultures. The underlying dynamic in transnational process is not to institute identical systems worldwide, but rather to use approaches which are culturally equivalent. Shell for example, ensures this transnational orientation by having managers' "career home" be in "a business function rather than a geographical place."[19] As one surveyed senior executive summarized, firms considered to be outstanding in transnational human resource management are "flexible enough in systems and practices to attract and retain the best people regardless of nationality."

Utilizing.   Transnational scope in utilization means that managers' problem solving skills are focused on the firm's worldwide operations and competitive environment, not just on the regional, national, or local situation. To assess the competitive environment in transnational human resource management, the fifty surveyed firms identified leading North American, European, and Asian companies. The top North American firm was perceived to be IBM, followed by General Electric, and Citicorp. The surveyed firms identified Royal Dutch Shell as the leading European firm, followed by Nestle and Philips, along with British Petroleum and Unilever. Sony was selected as the leading Asian firm, followed by Honda, Toyota, and Mitsubishi. Yet, in reviewing the pattern of responses, a significant proportion of the surveyed firms do not appear to be benchmarking excellence in global human resource management at all, and an even greater number appear to be geographically limiting their perspective to a fairly narrow, parochial scope. For instance, almost a fifth of the surveyed firms (all of which are North American) could not name a single leading North American firm. Even more disconcerting, more than a third could not identify a single excellent European firm, and half could not name a single excellent Asian firm.[20]

Beyond scope, transnational representation in utilization means that managers and executives of many nationalities are included in the firm's critical operating and strategic planning teams. Managers from outside of headquarters are not "out of sight and out of mind"; rather they are integrated into the worldwide network of knowledge exchange, continual learning, and action. For example, as Unilever's director of management development explains:

> "In recent years, I have had several product group directors . . . [want] an expatriate on the board of the local company. Not just because they haven't got a national, not just because it would be good for the expatriate, but because it would be good for the company to have a bit of challenge to the one-best-way of doing things."[21]

Transnational process in human resource utilization means that the organization culture does not inherently bias contributions from or towards any particular cultural group. The human resource system recognizes the firm's cultural diversity and uses it either to build culturally synergistic processes that include all cultures involved or to select the particular process that is the most appropriate for the given situation.

Illusions and recommendations

From the prior discussion, it is clear that transnational human resource systems are both fundamentally important for future business success and qualitatively different from prior approaches to human resource management. Equally evident is the fact that North American firms' human resource systems are not nearly as global as their business operations on any of the three fundamental human resource dimensions: transnational scope, transnational representation, and transnational process. Competitive demands appear to have "outrun the slow pace of organizational change and adjustment . . . [with] top management beginning to feel that the organization itself is the biggest barrier to competitive and strategic development."[22] It is telling that in most cases the respondents found the survey itself to be important and yet very difficult to complete, primarily because their firms did not systematically collect or keep data on any aspect of global human resource management.

The remaining question is why. There appears to be a series of illusions – of mind traps – that are preventing firms from acting in a global manner, including recognizing the mental gap between their current human resource approaches and those necessary to succeed in a highly competitive transnational business environment. Many of the surveyed executives recognized that their firms simply "lack global thinking" and "lack global business strategies," largely due to the "massive U.S. imprint on human resource practices." According to many of the American executives, firms must "stop thinking that the world begins and ends at U.S. borders," "stop having a U.S. expatriate mentality," and begin to "realize that the world does not revolve around us." This pattern of responses suggests the following seven illusions.

Illusion one: if business has gone well, it will continue to go well

No, today is not like yesterday, nor will tomorrow be a projection of today. Business has fundamentally changed, and human resource systems must undergo similar transformational changes to stay relevant, let alone effective. As Kenichi Ohmae has pointed out, "Today and in the twenty-first century, management's ability to transform the organization and its people into a global company is a prerequisite for survival because both its customers and competitors have become cosmopolitan."[23]

Illusion two: we have always played on a level playing field and won

No. The North American economies (and therefore North American firms) have had an advantage: they were the only developed economies left intact following World War II and were thus "the only game in town." Today, Asia, Europe, and the Americas each have highly competitive firms and economies, none of which will continue to prosper without being excellent at including people and business worldwide. As Ohmae has observed, "The key to a nation's future is its human resources. It used to be its natural resources, but not any more. The quality and number of its educated people now determines a country's likely prosperity or decline"; so too with global firms.[24]

Illusion three: if we manage expatriates better, we will have an effective global human resource system

No. Doing better at what was necessary in the past (expatriate management) is not equivalent to creating systems capable of sustaining global competitiveness today. Whereas the temptation is to attempt to do better at that which is known (in this case, the simple expatriation of managers), the real challenge is to excel at that which is new. Transnational firms need transnational human resource systems to succeed. Better managed expatriate transfers will only improve one small aspect of existing human resource management, not create an overall transnational system.

Illusion four: if we're doing something, we must be doing enough

No. Focusing on only one of the three transnational dimensions – scope, representation, or process – is not enough to transform domestic, international, or multinational human resource approaches into truly transnational systems. Bringing a "foreigner" onto the board of directors, for example, gives the illusion of globalization, but is insufficient to underpin its substance.

Illusion five: if "foreigners" are fitting in at headquarters, we must be managing our cultural diversity well

No. This is a multinational paradigm trap. In multinationals, foreigners must adapt to the headquarters' culture, including learning its native language. Multinationals typically see cultural differences "as a nuisance, a constraint, an obstacle to be surmounted."[25] In transnational firms, all managers make transitions, all managers adapt, and all managers help to create a synergistic organizational culture which transcends any one national culture.

Illusion six: as national wealth increases, everyone will become more like us

No. To the extent that the world is converging in its values, attitudes, and styles of doing business, it is not converging on a single country's national pattern, even that of the world's wealthiest nation. "The appealing 'one-best-way' assumption about management, the belief that different cultures are converging at different paces on the same concept of organization, is dying a slow death."[26] Moreover, transnational firms need to create transnational cultures that are inclusive of all their members, not wait for the world to converge on a reality that looks like any particular firm's national culture, even one that looks "just like us."

Illusion seven: if we provide managers with cross-cultural training, we will increase organizational capability

No. Increased cognitive understanding does not guarantee increased behavioral effectiveness, nor is enhanced individual learning sufficient for improved organizational effectiveness. Simply increasing the number of cross-cultural training programs offered to individual managers does not ensure that they will actually use the skills on a regular basis, nor that the firm as a whole will benefit from the potentially improved cross-cultural interaction. To benefit, the individual must want to learn that which is not-invented-here and the organization must want to learn from the individual. To enhance organizational capability, managers must continually work with and learn from people worldwide and disperse that knowledge throughout the firm's worldwide operations.

Despite the seemingly insurmountable challenges, firms are beginning to address and solve the dilemmas posed by going global. To date, no firm believes it has "the answer," the solution to creating a truly transnational human resource system. However, a number of firms are currently inventing pieces of the solution which may cohere into just such a system. For example, as John Reed, CEO of Citicorp, describes:

> "There are few companies in the world that are truly global. . . . Our most important advantage is our globality. Our global human capital may be as important a resource, if not more important, than our financial capital. Look at the Policy Committee, the top thirty or so

officers in the bank. Almost seventy-five percent have worked outside the United States; more than twenty-five percent have worked in three or more countries. Half speak two or more languages other than English. Seven were born outside the United States."[27]

Perhaps, then, a primary role of transnational human resource executives today is to remain open to fundamental change and to continue to encourage the openness and experimentation needed to create truly global systems.

The authors would like to thank the Ontario Centre for International Business for generously funding this research. See "Globalization and Human Resource Management," (Nancy J. Adler and Susan Bartholomew) in *Research in Global Strategic Management: Corporate Responses to Global Change*, Alan M. Rugman and Alain Verbeke (eds.), Vol. 3, (Greenwich, Conn.: JAI Press, 1992) for further details of the research design and results of the study.

Endnotes

1. Christopher A. Bartlett and Sumantra Ghoshal, "Matrix Management: Not a Structure, a Frame of Mind" *Harvard Business Review*, July-August 1990, 138.

2. See Michael E. Porter, *The Competitive Advantage of Nations* (New York: The Free Press, 1990).

3. Paul A. Evans, Yves Doz, and Andre Laurent, *Human Resource Management in International Firms* (London: Macmillan Press, 1989), xi-1.

4. Ibid.; also see Gunnar Hedlund "Who Manages the Global Corporation? Changes in the Nationality of Presidents of Foreign Subsidiaries of Swedish MNCs During the 1980s," Working Paper, (Institute of International Business and the Stockholm School of Economics, May 1990).

5. See Donald C. Hambrick, Lester B. Korn, James W. Frederickson, and Richard M. Ferry, *21st Century Report: Reinventing the CEO* (New York: Korn/Ferry and Columbia University's Graduate School of Business, 1989), 1–94.

6. Ibid.

7. Ibid., 57.

8. See Nancy J. Adler and Fariborz Ghadar "International Strategy from the Perspective of People and Culture: The North American Context," in Alan M. Rugman (ed.), *Research in Global Strategic Management: International Business Research for the Twenty-First Century; Canada's New Research Agenda*, Vol. 1, (Greenwich, Conn.: JAI Press, 1990) 179–205; and "Strategic Human Resource Management: A Global Perspective," in Rudiger Pieper (ed.), *Human Resource Management in International Comparison* (Berlin, de Gruyter, 1990), 235–260.

9. See Gary Hamel, Yves Doz, and C. K. Prahalad "Collaborate With Your Competitors and Win," *Harvard Business Review* 89(1), 1989, 133–139.

10. For a review of international human resource management, see Nancy J. Adler, *International Dimensions of Organizational Behaviour*, 2nd ed. (Boston: PWS Kent 1991); Peter J. Dowling "Hot Issues Overseas," *Personnel Administrator*, 34(1), 1989, 66–72; Peter J. Dowling & R. Schuler, *International Dimensions of Human Resource Management* (Boston: PWS Kent, 1990), Peter J. Dowling & Denise E. Welch, "International Human Resource Management: An Australian Perspective," *Asia Pacific Journal of Management*, 6(1), 1988, 39–65; Yves Doz & C. K. Prahalad "Controlled Variety: A Challenge for Human Resource Management in the MNC," *Human Resource Management*, 25(1), 1986, 55–71; A. Edstrom & J. R. Galbraith "Transfer of Managers as a Coordination and Control Strategy in Multinational Firms," *Administrative Science Quarterly*, 22, 1977, 248–263; Evans, Doz, & Laurent, (1989) op. cit.; Andre Laurent "The Cross-Cultural Puzzle of International Human Resource Management," *Human Resource Management*, 25(1), 1986, 91–101; E. L. Miller, S. Beechler, B. Bhatt, & R. Nath, "The Relationship Between the Global Strategic Planning Process and the Human Resource Management Function," *Human Resource Planning*, 9(1), 1986, 9–23; John Milliman, Mary Ann Von Glinow, & Maria Nathan, "Organizational Life Cycles and Strategic International Human Resource Management in Multinational Companies: Implications for Congruence Theory," *Academy of Management Review*, 16(2), 1991, 318–339; Dan A. Ondrack, "International Human Resources Management in European and North American Firms," *Human Resource Management*, 25(1), 1985, 121–132; Dan A. Ondrack, "International Transfers of Managers in North American and European MNEs," *Journal of International Business Studies*, 16(3), 1985, 1–19; Vladimir Pucik, "The International Management of Human Resources," in C. J. Fombrun, N. M. Tichy, & M. A. Devanna (eds.), *Strategic Human Resource Management* (New York: Wiley, 1984);

Vladimir Pucik & Jan Hack Katz, "Information, Control and Human Resource Management in Multinational Firms," *Human Resource Management*, 25(1), 1986, 121–132; and, Rosalie Tung, *The New Expatriates: Managing Human Resources Abroad* (New York: Harper & Row 1988), and "Strategic Management of Human Resources in Multinational Enterprises," *Human Resource Management*, 23(2), 1984, 129–143; among others.

11. Op. cit., 1990.

12. Unilever's "Best Proven Practice" technique was cited by Philip M. Rosenzweig and Jitendra Singh, "Organizational Environments and the Multinational Enterprise," *Academy of Management Review*, 16(2), 1991, 354, based on an interview that Rosenzweig conducted with Unilever.

13. See Paul Evans, Elizabeth Lank, and Alison Farquhar, "Managing Human Resources in the International Firm: Lessons from Practice," in Paul Evans, Yves Doz, and Andre Laurent, 1989, op. cit., 138.

14. Kenichi Ohmae, *The Borderless World: Power and Strategy in the Interlinked Economy* (New York: Harper Business, 1990), 112.

15. Andre Laurent, op. cit., 1986, 100.

16. See C. K. Prahalad and Yves Doz, *The Multinational Mission: Balancing Local Demands and Global Vision*, (New York: Free Press, 1987); also, for a discussion of global integration versus local responsiveness from a business strategy perspective, see Michael E. Porter, "Changing Patterns of International Competition," *California Management Review*, 28(2), 1986, 9–40; and Christopher A. Bartlett, "Building and Managing the Transnational: The New Organizational Challenge," in M. E. Porter (ed.) *Competition in Global Industries* (Boston: Harvard Business School Press, 1986), 367–401, who explicitly developed the concepts, along with initial work and elaboration by: Christopher A. Bartlett & Sumantra Ghoshal, *Managing Across Borders: The Transnational Solution* (Boston: Harvard Business School Press 1989); Yves Doz, "Strategic Management in Multinational Companies," *Sloan Management Review*, 21(2), 1980, 27–46; Yves Doz, Christopher A. Bartlett, & C. K. Prahalad, "Global Competitive Pressures and Host Country Demands: Managing Tensions in MNCs," *California Management Review*, 23(3), 1981, 63–73; and Yves Doz & C. K. Prahalad, "Patterns of Strategic Control Within Multinational Corporations," *Journal of International Business Studies*, 15(2), 1984, 55–72.

17. See Evans, Lank and Farquhar, op. cit., 1989, 119.

18. Ibid., 130–131; 139.

19. Ibid., 141.

20. An even more disconcerting display of ignorance was that four surveyed firms listed 3M, Citicorp, Ford, and General Motors as European firms, and in another four responses, Dupont, Eastman Kodak, Coca-Cola, and Wang were identified as leading Asian firms.

21. Evans, Lank, and Farquhar, op. cit., 122.

22. Paul Evans and Yves Doz, "The Dualistic Organization," in Evans, Doz, & Laurent, op. cit., 1989, 223: based on the earlier work of Doz, "Managing Manufacturing Rationalization Within Multinational Companies," *Columbia Journal of World Business*, 13(3), 1978, 82–94; and Prahalad and Doz, op. cit., 1987.

23. *Beyond National Borders* (Homewood, Illinois: Dow Jones-Irwin, 1987), 93.

24. Ibid., 1.

25. Evans, Lank & Farquhar, op. cit., 115.

26. Ibid., 115.

27. Noel Tichy and Ram Charan, "Citicorp Faces the World: An Interview with John Reed," *Harvard Business Review*, November-December, 1990, 137.

$\diamond$

12.5 Creating a High Performance International Team

$\blacklozenge$

Sue Canney Davison

Establishing the context of the growing number of international teams

The number of international teams is growing rapidly as companies reorganize to compete in the global marketplace. The influence of the different cultures makes the interpersonal interaction in the team more complicated than within teams of one nationality. It affects the way the team works together, especially if the team is spread out across different countries. Each team is unique. High performance cannot be captured in a ready-made formula for how to create synthesis between imaginary French, Japanese, Taiwanese and Russian team members. High performance is created through channelling the forces at play.

In companies such as ABB, Unilever, the Hong Kong Shanghai Banking Corporation, GEC Alsthom, Alcatel, Royal Dutch/Shell group and IBM, a matrix of international teams is already in place. In other companies such as Daimler Benz, Fiat, The Kone Corporation, Westpac and The Broken Hill Proprietary Company, international teams are being used to shift the dominance of the headquarter national cultures.

Source: Sue Canney Davison, "Creating a High Performance International Team," excerpted from *Journal of Management Development,* 1994, pp. 81–90, Vol. 13, No. 2. Reprinted by permission of MCB University Press.

Mixed nationalities in a team can bring richer and more appropriate solutions. They can broaden a manager's interpersonal skills and contribute towards creating a company-wide network. However they can also bring increased communication difficulties, interpersonal conflicts and substantially higher costs. When do the costs outweigh the benefits? Do some mixes of nationalities work together bettter than others? In reality, the exact mix of nationalities is seldom chosen, it emerges as a by-product of the task. Most people are chosen because they have the necessary country knowledge, responsibilities or technical expertise to complete the task. The extra expense is a constraint the team has to work within. Some teams are having difficulties, other teams are very successful; what is the difference? Companies need to know and learn.

There are lessons for the managers who create the teams; there are considerations about working at geographical distances and there are lessons for the team members and leaders.

Creating and managing an international team

Choosing the right mix of people

As with any team, the first task is to choose a group of people who incorporate, as a group, the skills necessary to complete the task. In an international team, there is also a need for a common working language and sufficient shared goals. There are the added dangers of vested national interests and historical regional competitiveness.

Removing the constraints

The next most important and difficult tasks are to "bust the bureaucracy" and to find an adequate budget. International teams benefit the company as a whole and tend to threaten individual fiefdoms. If country managers need to be persuaded to second one of their best people for a few years, help from higher up the organization may need to be called in. There are also "part-time" teams which meet every month or so. They often run in addition to and parallel with, the work that the individuals are paid, evaluated and promoted for. Extra finances need to be found to support the extra costs that the geographical distances will create. When a manager starts looking for appropriate people, a common retort from other country manag-

ers is "So long as I do not have to pay the airfares and it doesn't
interfere with the work they are already doing here, yes, they can
join your team; in fact they may learn something."

Assessing the costs of the geographical distances

A geographically dispersed team needs to develop a realistic balance
between joint team meetings and the work done in between. At
the beginning it is important for the team to meet each other in
order to agree what they are doing and to meet later in the project to
argue and review decisions. Sharing information and implementing
action can be done at a distance. One manager who was put in
charge of a team that had never met, but "dialogued" over fax,
phone and e-mail, had a nervous breakdown. It does not work.
Effective group techniques can shorten team meetings and e-mail
and computer networks can improve and lighten communication
between meetings. Both involve the company in making an initial
investment.

Sharing the rationale with the team

After setting the overall objectives, giving a time frame and direction,
the overall manager must be available to the team to give advice
and remove unforeseen obstacles. Initially this means explaining
how and why the team is being set up and its role within the rest
of the company. The manager should also make the team aware of
possible imbalances and encourage them to work around them.

Appreciating the influence of nationality

Nationality, as represented by what passport you carry, is not a
variable that is important in international teams. The importance
of national culture is that it can have a moderating influence on a
number of other factors, e.g. attitudes, values, behaviors, expectations, background and common language fluency. If the team members are representing different countries they can also be affected
by the status of the organization within that market, by the size of
the market share, by belonging to the acquired company as opposed
to the acquirer or by historical difficulties between one market or
function and another.

A European marketing strategy team may be made up of peer marketing managers each from a different European country operation. The team is balanced in nationalities. However if the headquarters are in the UK, is there a subtle weighting that the UK marketing manager will have more influence than the others? Is there a subtle hierarchy based on the size of operations in each country? If there is a subgroup of people from the headquarters, will they dominate the others? Innovative ideas often start away from the vested interests and bureaucracy of the center.

Choosing the right leader for the task

The interpersonal dynamics and communication patterns will be more complicated in an international team than in a nationally uniform team. The team leader will need sensitive group management skills and an understanding of the cultural differences at play. Should these "group" skills override technical skills as the criteria for selecting the leader? Both cultural influences and the nature of the task will play a role.

A charismatic multilingual French manager was asked to bring a number of long established independent European bakery firms under one brand name. He used his many languages and interpersonal skills to cajole, negotiate, persuade, and create ultimatums to bring the team together. His technical baking skills were not called for.

Teams with a co-ordinating task need a leader with good administrative skills. The leader of a transatlantic R&D team will need a high level of technical research skills as well as administrative and interpersonal skills. Team leaders may also be chosen because they have the highest level of influence to sell the outcomes to the rest of the organization. However in some instances, the cultural norms may influence the choice. In Germany and Japan a very high premium is usually put on the leaders' technical skills. That is how they earn the respect of the team. In Italy or Chile the premium can be on the status and influence that the manager holds within the organization.

In choosing a team leader, it is important to remember that the leader must act as a role model. In two existing international top teams, both CEO's dominate the interaction. Both are appreciated for their executive abilities and for turning their respective companies around from negative positions. The Finnish CEO managing a Finnish/UK merger stresses team spirit, common language, consensus through debate. He encourages managers to participate in the debates outside their areas of responsibility and to tell him when he is wrong. The Italian CEO managing an Italian/US merger tends to work one-to-one with a small number of Italian colleagues; the large top team meeting is a place to share these decisions. The few US managers expected decisions to be made through debate and are disappointed. English is the agreed common language, however, when the argument becomes lively, it tends to happen in Italian, not English and the Americans feel left out.

Taking the implementation of the task into account

Managers creating the teams must also consider the implementation of the teams' findings. In a large international drinks company a taskforce has been set up to cut costs within an 18-month time frame. As it was likely that most of the production cuts would be made in Italy, it was a sensible move to appoint an Italian finance expert to the team; the best person to sell the bad news.

Lessons for the managers setting up the teams

- Choose the people with the best skills and knowledge to both plan and implement the task.
- Assess the costs, double them and find the money from within the organization.
- Remove the bureaucratic barriers and if necessary seek higher support in the organization.
- Involve the team members' managers in the process. Persuade them to include the team outcomes in the members' performance evaluation.
- Share the reasons why people have been chosen and the possible imbalances that they should be aware of and work around them.
- Offer training and support in group skills if necessary.
- Explain the influences of national cultures. Offer training and support in using intercultural differences to create value to themselves and the outcome.
- Match the leader to the task and make all the team members accountable for the outcomes.

- Give clear terms of reference, time scales and direction and be available if the team needs you.

Managing the geographical distances

In the Finnish case above, although the headquarters are based in Finland, only the CEO and the financial controller are based there. The other three top vice-presidents were free to choose any European headquarters as their operating base. It works because there is a high level of trust and a very disciplined communication pattern. Every month they have a board meeting at one of the regional headquarters or company offices somewhere in the world. Between meetings they have a telephone conference every Monday to share information and conduct a very organized set of telephone conferences for the company results every month. The benefit of being geographically dispersed is that the top team is always out in the company, encouraging networking and cross-fertilization and bringing a first-hand knowledge of events to the board meetings.

Only full-time special purpose teams tend to be located together. Otherwise managers operate as a team from their different bases and meet at regular intervals. The administrative, travelling and communication costs are likely to have been underestimated. If the company does provide the increased budget, they will expect a special return and very high performance. What is the best use of the teams' time?

Establishing the team before working apart

The team will need to come together to establish a common orientation and to agree common objectives and goals. In this initial stage they also need to create a common language and to "get a feel for where each one is coming from," to discover the strengths and weaknesses of the team and to explore the different expectations around the style and depth of team interaction.

Having established some degree of interpersonal comfort and agreed their goals, the team can then work at a distance to collect information, share information, clarify tasks and implement the decisions agreed. In some cultures, nothing is taken seriously unless it is written down. In others, people do not feel they have communicated until they have spoken to the person directly, even if they have written to them. Teams may need to agree to do both.

Using the technology available

E-mail networks help. At the moment, few transnational teams outside computer companies have effective computer networks. Using an e-mail network speeds up communication and makes it much easier to share, edit and review large amounts of information. This is especially true if the team needs to share complex three-dimensional computer models developed with computer-aided design programs. Whole models seen from many angles can be sent back and forth for refinement and comment. Eventually virtual reality will allow people to work at a distance simultaneously on a model design.

If the team needs to review their overall objectives, change their orientation, question values or principles or renew their strategy then they will need to meet together again. The risk of misunderstanding across faxes, e-mail and video conferencing on these value-related issues is very high.

In summary

- *In time together:* Establish objectives, goals and interim targets, build relationships, resolve differences, make decisions, evaluate and review progress and if necessary change values, policies and principles.
- *In time apart:* Establish a disciplined and regular system of communication, find and share information; clarify goals, implement agreed actions and update others on progress. Prepare for joint meetings in advance, send all background reading and information in advance and anticipate your colleagues' questions and needs.

Working within the team

Implementing the "team basics"

An international team needs high performance goals, mutual accountability and an interdependent task as does any national team. The team basics of clarifying and agreeing a working method and performance goals, surfacing assumptions and differences, actively listening and participating are the same. In international teams, applying the basics before rushing to complete the task is all the more important. The differences in expectations and approach are likely to be far higher.

As in any team, the task, the method chosen to complete the task, the personalities, the leadership role and style, the team roles, behavior, emotional links and the timing will all have an impact on the effectiveness of the team. We know from research and experience that culture will have a moderating effect on the decision-making process, the learning styles, the behavior, the attitudes towards status, formality, business relationships and the task or people orientation of each individual.

Establishing "cultural" or personal feedback

People often ask, "Are they like that because of their culture or personality?" Within any one culture you would expect a wide spread of individual preferences on the factors outlined above. Research suggests that the effect of culture is to create a statistically measurable national norm on each one. Culture moderates but does not override personality. Experience of different cultures can change the effect of the original cultural influence.

The extent to which someone's behavior and expectations are due to the influence of their national culture or a natural outcome of their personality, is an ongoing lengthy debate. As yet no line has been drawn. The important point is that in many cultures, feedback, both positive and negative, is very difficult. In international teams, it is much easier to legitimately discuss cultural differences than it is to give feedback on personal differences. Talking about cultural differences can be established as neutral territory. We have all been influenced; there are no rights or wrongs; good or bad. There are combinations of similarities and differences which work easily; there are others that have to be surfaced and worked through.

Talking about national culture may not cover all the behaviors that need to be reviewed. One US/UK team chose a "managerial grid" as a feedback tool. A mixed Asian and European team chose three learning orientations. When one Hong Kong Chinese man got into difficulties, the team was able to suggest that he could act a little less "red" (action oriented) and become more "green" (people oriented). He listened without taking offense or losing face.

Choosing the working languages

Most British and Americans do not seem motivated to learn other languages whereas Dutch, Belgian, Hong Kong Chinese and other cultures learn two, three, four or more. Often, because of the lack of choice, the common business language chosen is English. This can allow the English and Americans to dominate, often by speaking incomprehensible colloquial English instead of the second-language business English that has developed in the business world.

It can work the other way also. Subgroups can use side discussions in other languages to build up alliances. Second-language English speakers are sometimes accused of using language as an excuse to not participate. Leaders can work around this by asking each person to share their view. Other team members can be encouraged to translate for them; in extreme cases outside translation facilities can be offered. There seem to be different sensitivities around speaking a foreign language. Finnish, Japanese and German tend not to speak unless they know exactly what they are talking about and can express it perfectly. The French are stereotyped as not appreciating or listening to anything but perfect French.

Demanding that only one language is spoken can also exclude people. Many words have no exact translation or can mean various things across different languages. Where the language differences are extreme, such as between Chinese and English, teams have sometimes agreed to allow side discussions in subgroups in their own languages in order to check their mutual understanding. They have then paraphrased their discussion and shared it with the whole team in a common language.

Obviously the more common languages there are among the team, the easier it is to explain details and check understanding. When the top executive team of an Italian subsidiary based in France presented and discussed their company in German to the German company they were buying out, it made up for months of trust building. When teams have built up trust, they often begin to enjoy the multiplicity of languages and meanings and have fun with them.

The team and team leaders must work to encourage tolerance and interest around the language differences. It is important to legitimize asking for clarification and repetition and encourage people to explain the same thing two or three different ways from the beginning. The leader needs to give time, especially at the beginning, for everyone to express themselves and be disciplined about regularly summarizing and checking understanding to keep a balance of participation. This builds up the group cohesion that allows the team to pick up speed without losing people.

Balancing the participation

Do team members feel free to interrupt each other or not? Culture can strongly modify a person's tendency to talk (or gesture) along with someone for support (an Italian trait), to interrupt and talk over someone (an American and increasingly British trait), or to wait for a space to speak or to be asked for an opinion (an East and South East Asian trait and usual for a non-fluent common language speaker). In English the subject, verb, and object is usually at the beginning of the sentence and the rest is secondary information. This allows impatient English speakers to interrupt each other freely without losing too much of the overall meaning. On the other hand in German, Hindi and Chinese however, the verb (and tense) is at the end of the sentence. In Japanese the custom is cut to build up to the main point rather than put it at the beginning. A Japanese expressed having "learned to put the point at the front, otherwise they do not hear me." People who feel free to interrupt can dominate those who do not.

Turning intercultural conflict into creativity

Cultures also have very different ways of resolving conflicts. These range across "shoot first, make up later," argue it out on the facts, use a neutral third party arbitrator, listen to the elders, or a mediator whose job it is to negotiate, cajole and persuade the two sides to work together. The team needs to find out what works for that particular mix of people. Different tools and methods can be tried. In cultures that avoid open conflict, the idea that contentious debate can also be creative and not personal may need to be explored. Noticeably Honda has introduced *wayagaya* creative debate groups in order to find better solutions to a wide range of problems on the shop floor. Those used to dramatic gestures and raising their voices may need to adapt their styles.

It is unlikely that a team which avoids conflict will reach a high performance level. Surfacing and working through conflicting differences is not the same as accommodating each other. In one joint consortium the two managing directors, one a charismatic autocratic Frenchman and the other a democratic participative German sat back to back in the same office. They learned to accommodate each other, but did not surface and resolve their differences. The consortium has not survived, pulled apart by different interests and skills.

The team can also anticipate key moments within the task when cultural differences are likely to come into play. In strategic planning for instance there is likely to be little difficulty in individuals sourcing and collecting the necessary information and coming together again to share it. The conflict is likely to arise at the point where the group has to decide how to develop the information into an argued plan. It is also the point where the team needs all the creative ideas they can find. At this point the team can take time out to brainstorm using group techniques such as Metaplan, Hexagons and Groupware. As the debate was getting heated, one high-level team chose this time in the planning process to brainstorm at high volume in the squash courts. As a result, they channelled their conflict creatively.

Making sure none of the team members is left out

Some team members often become excluded. Suggestions are ignored; a team member is left out when the group splits into smaller groups; people are not given time to explain what they mean in a foreign language. Subtle and unsubtle prejudices about the levels of education and expertise between international and regional officers, between people from "developed" and "developing" countries, between men and women distort the balance of the team.

Individuals or subgroups can also be left out of the decision-making process. A team may have opted for decisions based on consensus. When the very different positions of the members become apparent, a workable solution can seem impossible. At this point a team needs to find, or create, some common thread to build on. Instead, what often happens is that the team will persist in arguing about their differences. In frustration, individuals will start building alliances with the people who seem at least partially similar. Gradually more and more members join the alliance out of frustration and the remaining few outsiders give up in despair. No synthesis of differences has been found and some of the team are left resentful. The decision-making process has to be conscious and agreed on by everybody.

It takes discipline, courage and sensitivity to confront the often unconscious forces that exclude some people from the process. It can be a high risk. High performing international teams have consciously taken those risks or have just been incredibly lucky.

Lessons for those participating in and leading international teams

- Start slowly and end faster; start fast and maybe not end at all.
- Use outside help if necessary to establish group and intercultural skills at the beginning. Create a common language for giving feedback, surfacing cultural differences and talking about the groups interaction. Learn group brainstorming skills such as Metaplan and hexagons if they are relevant.
- Someone, the leader or a team member needs to encourage meaningful participation from all members, keep a visual record of what is being said, regularly summarize and check consensus and understanding and to keep track of time.
- The leader or facilitator must also be prepared to use their intuition and insight to surface and confront the underlying differences and prejudices that are causing tension or excluding a team member.
- Develop a decision-making process that avoids unconscious alliances and allows everyone to participate.
- Build in time for discussing and reviewing the overall group process. This increased awareness is an essential ingredient of high performance.

Differences in attitudes, values, behavior, experience, background, expectations, language and location create far more complex dynamics in international teams than most national ones. These teams have become an integral part of the survival and growth of most international companies. They are challenging, frustrating, costly opportunities for participants to learn and grow. There are no universal formulae for success. The task is to use the similarities and differences and the dynamics that these can set up and to turn them to the group advantage. If the team members have reached a high level of emotional security, can laugh, joke, question and play devil's advocate with each other while completing the task, then it has done well.

A high performance international team will have also accessed all its resources. It will have continuously reviewed and questioned how effectively the team interaction has been molded to fit the task. Digging into the differences is a high risk. It can also yield new and unthought of solutions to the task at hand and move the company one step nearer to being an effective global network.

Note

Examples come from doctoral research at London Business School and research conducted with D. Hambrick, C. Snow and S. Snell for the international consortium of executive development and research.